W0017865

Taggert of the Marines

By David Ekardt

Copyrighted February 2001

"Thank God for the Marines. At least they still turn out men. Crazy and wild to be sure. Mad as March hares, each and every one of them, but true men for all of that…and dashing to boot!"

Quote from Sammy Amalu Columnist
Honolulu Morning Star 1971

Copyright 2003 by David Ekardt
ISBN 978-1-54398-323-4

First Printing by Rosedog Books 2003

Second Publishing Book Baby 2019

Prologue

*"What a Brilliant Prospect does the Event
Present to every Lad of Spirit who is
          Inclined to try his Fortune in this
highly renowned Corps.*

*Thousands are at this moment endeavoring to get on
Board Privateers where they will serve without pay
or reward of any kind whatsoever, so certain does
their chance appear of enriching themselves by
PRIZE MONEY! What an enviable Station then must
the CONTINENTAL MARINE hold--- who with far
superior advantages to these, has the additional
benefit of liberal Pay, and plenty of the best
Provisions, with a good and well appointed Ship
under him, the Pride and Glory of the Continental
Navy; surely every Man of Spirit must blush to
remain at Home in Inactivity and Indolence when his
Country needs his Assistance.*

***Where then can he have such a fair opportunity,
reaping Glory and Riches in the Continental
Marines, a Corps daily acquiring new Honors****, and
here, once embarked in American Fleet, he finds
himself in the midst of Honor and Glory, surrounded
by a set of fine fellows,* **Strangers to Fear, and who
strike Terror through the Hearts of their Enemies
wherever they go!"***

From the first Marine Recruiting Poster, January 1776

Some of that sounds like what a Marine recruiter said to me in June of 1969 when I enlisted! The above quote from the first Marine Recruiting poster reflects the spirit and sense of adventure that has been part of the Marine mystique since those first days back in 1775 when the Corps was born. It has remained alive throughout the history of the Corps, and is still alive today.

Come on board for a great sea tale of those first Marines during the American Revolution. Theirs was a time of honor, and great personal sacrifice of those who fought to establish this great nation. If you are a fan of C.S. Forester's, *Hornblower* series, or of Alexander Kent's, *Bolitho* series, you will enjoy this novel. This is the first in what is sure to be a great collection of tales of the Marine Corps. They will follow the involvement of the Taggerts as they answer the call to arms as Marines throughout the history of our nation. Researched from the journals of Marines of the times, this proves to be an exciting tale of both land and sea action during the American Revolution. So join in, and like Sergeant Angus Lanigan said, *"Aye, that's the beauty of being a Marine Lad! You'll be aboard a ship! No mud! We stay on board; we fight on board, no mucking about in the mud. The only time we go ashore is to visit some exotic port and get to know the pretty lassies!"*

Contents

Taggert of the Marines by David Ekardt

1
An Incident at Sea

Boom!

The sound of the cannon reverberated across the open water as the ball sent a geyser of water skyward a hundred feet in front of the bow. "Turn her into the wind if you please, helmsman!" ordered William Taggert, the ship's owner and captain.

"Aye, aye, sir." replied the helmsman as he grappled with the big wheel.

"Those damned British naval ships are a thorn in my side!" he swore.

"Why are they stopping us Father?" asked his son Sean, who acted as third in command after his older brother Thomas.

"They are probably looking for deserters again, that or just to harass us colonials. With the rebellious stirrings in Boston and the other cities, they are putting pressure on everyone to assert their authority." he replied in his thick Scottish brogue.

"They've lowered a boat. Look the marines are loading into it! Do you think they mean to seize us?" asked Thomas, as he trotted back to the wheel where his father and brother were. At twenty-five he was not much bigger than his brother, who was two years his junior.

"You boys stop gawking and get the lads aloft to trim sails while we await our guests. Be off with you now!" he bellowed. The brothers sent the hands aloft to bring in the sails while they watched the progress of the longboat full of red-coated marines and one naval officer. The sailors pulling on the oars had a tough go at it, as the wind had picked up speed and kicked up the waves.

Sean looked across the waves at the two-decker. Only one gun port was open, that of one of the bow-chasers, so they did not expect any trouble. The ship was a magnificent sight, all trimmed out, freshly painted and gilded. He recognized it as the *Huntress*, a twenty-four gun, two-deck frigate. Sean had seen it before since its arrival from Portsmouth a year ago to help keep the colonies in check.

He climbed back down the ratlines as the boat pulled alongside. First up the side was the marine lieutenant, who saluted in the direction of his father. He was followed by ten of his men, all bearing muskets with bayonets fixed. Last on board was the naval lieutenant, a pale weasel-looking man, not a pleasant fellow to be sure. He did not render a salute at all, but instead, looked around at the crewmen, sneering at each one.

"State your business, so that we might be on our way!" demanded his father.

"Don't presume to give me orders, old man! This scow might be your ship, but I am Lieutenant Jennings of His Majesty's Navy! You colonials must be reminded that you have a king, and his wishes must be obeyed even over here. You keep a civil tongue in your mouth, or I'll have you keel-hauled!" He spat the words out.

"I will not be berated by a lowly officer such as you! Now state your damn business, before I throw you off my ship meself!"

"You Scots are all pig-headed. We are to inspect this ship, its cargo and its crew. We are looking for contraband weapons and deserters. If any are found to be on this vessel, if you can call it that, we will confiscate it and the vessel to be sold for the government. Lieutenant Hawkins, you will detail some of your men below to inspect the cargo, while I look over these 'seamen', pitiful looking lot that they are!"

"Roight, you heard the man, sergeant, take two men below with you and look things over. Be sure not to damage anything." ordered the marine officer, showing his dislike for the naval officer.

"Aye, aye, sir!" snapped the sergeant, as he pointed to two men and headed below. The others stood in a line with their muskets held at their sides.

"You men, get aft and stand by your captain, so that we can keep an eye on you!" barked Lieutenant Jennings.

The crewmen slowly started moving to the rear after they saw their captain nod to them. Thomas stood next to his father and whispered, "Father, don't push this one, he does not seem to be right in the head."

"Don't worry about me, laddie, just keep out of this. You ca' not let tyrants such as him get the better of you," he counseled his son.

They watched as the lieutenant pulled a belaying pin from the rail and strutted in front of the men, starring each one in the eyes.

9

"You, roll up your sleeves. You have the looks of a navy man, and I'll wager that you'll have the tattoos to prove it." The seaman, Michael Innes, glanced at his captain and rolled up his sleeves, exposing the tattoo of crossed cannon barrels on his right forearm.

"I was gunner's mate on the old *Pelican,* sir. I was paid off when she went into ordinary five years ago. Came to America on one of the Hudson's Bay Company ships."

"Silence, you impudent dog!" Jennings shouted at the man after striking him across the face. "You'll be coming with us until we can verify your story."

The lieutenant eyed the next few men sneering at each one. "You come forward!" he said pointing the belaying pin at Hugh MacPherson in the second row.

Hugh eased his way forward and glared down at the officer, a full head shorter than he.

"What's your story? You look like a navy man also."

"Sorry sir, but you are mistaken. I grew up in the Colony of Pennsylvania, and have worked for the Taggerts for five years now."

"No matter, I do not believe you. Where is this ship bound?"

"We are headed for New York with our cargo, some of which belongs to the army," Old man Taggert called out.

Jennings paced back and forth in front of the men, watching for their reactions. One of the newest men, who just signed on a year ago, suddenly turned his face from the glare of the man.

"Turn and look at me, you scum!" he barked at the seaman, as he used the belaying pin to turn the man's head. "I knew it! I do not ever forget a face! You jumped ship in New York while you were on a watering party!" He grabbed the crewman and threw him on the deck.

"You leave him alone! No one gets beaten on my ship!"

"Silence, old man, or I'll silence you myself!"

"Easy Father, watch your temper," Thomas whispered.

"You traitorous whelp! It was you in New York!" Jennings screamed at the huddled figure in front of him.

"Please sir, I had to get back to my child!" Johnson cried out, as Jennings raised the belaying pin over his head and brought it down on him, "You'll wish you had never lived by the time I get done with you!" He nearly screamed the words as he started to beat the man as hard as he could.

"Damn your eyes, I told you that no man gets beaten upon my ship!" bellowed William Taggert as he rushed forward and grabbed the lieutenant's hand in mid swing. The two men's eyes locked, determination glaring from Taggert, hatred from the lieutenant.

"Marines, stand to attack!" barked the marine officer as his other men came from below. "Marines, you will stand at the ready and make no move!" he clarified his order as all eyes watched the conflict before them.

"All clear below, sir!" reported the sergeant.

Behind the men, standing facing the marines, Sean took the slow match that his father used to light his pipes, from its protective container and lifted one of the swivel guns from its mount.

"Unhand me, you Scottish swine! I'll see you hang for this!"

"I warned ye to not be beating on my crew, and now as promised, I'll be throwing you off my ship!" smiled William as he lifted the officer and bodily dumped him overboard, to the cheers of his men.

Sean pushed in front of the crew, swivel gun cradled in his left arm, and slow match in his right hand. "Now, if you gentlemen would be so kind as to lay down your weapons and leave this ship!"

The marine officer stepped forward. "We'll not be laying down our weapons however, we will leave your ship," he said with amusement in his tone.

"Sergeant, get the men over the side. We'll be returning to the ship. Oh yes, and kindly fish Lieutenant Jennings out of the water." He stood looking Sean directly in the eyes.

"Roight, you heard the man, off with you lads, quickly now!" he ordered.

Everyone stood watching the marines disembark, as the marine officer stood his ground. As soon as his men were over the side, he broke out into a grin and said, "He deserved to be thrown over the side sir and I salute you for your actions. Now, as soon as he gets back to the ship, he'll be demanding for the captain to hunt you down, so you had better set sail as soon as I get off your ship. I'll be sure to take our time rowing back so that you can get under way. Head for shallow water fast. We have just replenished our stores, so we are riding low in the water and won't be able to follow."

He saluted and turned to go. He stopped at the side, looked at Sean and said," You know, lad, I fired a swivel gun like that once. It kicked me hard in the stomach and knocked me back into the mast. I couldn't stand up straight for a week. I would not recommend it. Also, the next time that you try that bluff again, you could at least take the plug out of the barrel to give your opponent the illusion of it being loaded. I like your spunk there, laddie. If you ever want some adventure, you can join my marines any day." He smiled as he stepped over the side.

The crew all laughed at his advice to Sean, who turned meekly and shrugged his shoulders in response. His father made everyone jump when he bellowed, "You heard the man, get aloft with you, lads, and set sail! We need to be running before they get back to their ship!"

The men all jumped to the ratlines and headed aloft. True to his word, the marines took their time fishing the officer from the cold water. He could barely talk as he broke out into uncontrollable shivers.

"Lads, who will give the use of their coats to warm this poor man?" Hawkins asked, fighting a smile. All his men and the sailors sitting at the oars took pleasure in the lieutenant's discomfort. Every one of them had at one point been the object of his unwarranted punishments.

"Come now, lads, even I will shed my coat to warm him." Hawkins took his coat off and put it around the shivering officer. Reluctantly, three of his men followed suit. "There now. Are ye comfortable, Lieutenant Jennings?"

"Get me back to the ship!" Jennings managed to make himself heard, as he shivered uncontrollably, "Hurry they are getting away!"

"Well now, that they are, aren't they? You just sit tight. It is more important to see that you are warmed up fast before you succumb to the cold." Hawkins smiled at the other man's discomfort. He glanced around and saw the *Osprey's* crew had set the sails and the little ship leapt forward in the water.

"All right now lads, let's be getting back to the ship now, but don't strain yourselves at the oars; I wouldn't want you splashing more cold water on this poor man now." Jennings was bundled up in the bow of the boat and could not see the grins on the faces of his men.

Hawkins glanced back at the *Osprey* to see if they were under way. He was pleased to see the canvas spread out on the yardarms filling with the wind. The oarsmen watched him to see if they were to start rowing in earnest, but he shook his head at them, so they kept at their slow pace.

The *Osprey* was a full mile distant by the time the longboat reached the *Huntress*.

"Look, they are just sending their men aloft now!" Sean called over to his father from his perch on the ratlines. His father strode to the transom and peered aft to watch the two-decker set sail.

He watched as the men in the longboat climbed up the side of the frigate. He could just imagine the conversation on the deck as the soggy officer reported to his captain. He admired the precision of the ship's crew as the longboat was hoisted on board at the same time that the sails were filling out.

Old man Taggert watched the scene on the deck of the frigate through his glass. There was a blue-coated figure waving arms in the air in front of the other officers on deck. He smiled at the thought of the embarrassment that the junior officer must be dealing with. Taggert watched as the frail figure of the officer ran to the bow of the frigate to the bow chaser. Just then a burst of smoke emanated from the bow-chaser poked through its port. Suddenly, the transom blew apart as a cannon ball smashed through it, sending splinters everywhere. Sean and his brother ran to their father's side as he lay, writhing in pain, his left chest impaled by a foot-long jagged splinter.

"Thomas get the ship into the shallows! Sean, get me below and get this damned stick out of me now!" the old man ordered as he passed out.

The brothers jumped to their duties. Sean grasped the splinter and slowly pulled it out. He looked at the jagged edges of the splinter, knowing that there had to be pieces still in his father's chest. He pulled his scarf from around his neck and plugged the hole in his father's chest. "Jones, Becket, Miller, come give me a hand!" he called out.

Together the men gently lifted the old man, as Sean guided them below. They made their way to the aft cabin, carefully putting the old man in his bunk. "Fetch me the sail maker. He'll have to sew up this wound before Father bleeds to death." Sean looked at Miller, who ran off to get the sail maker. He did not go far, as Black had anticipated his skills as soon as he heard what had happened.

"Let me through there, boys, Sean how bad is it?" asked Black, as he pulled thread and needle from his jacket pocket.

"'Tis bad, the worst I've seen. He's bleeding in his lung. See how he is spitting blood? I'm not sure the stitches will do."

"Lord, that is an almighty hole. Lad, we need to cauterize it to seal it up inside," Black said, as he pushed his cap back on his head.

"That's my thought too. Miller, get the cook's poker red hot and bring it to me fast." Sean turned as he gave the order. "I've done this once before for a spear wound. Last year when I was out in Pennsylvania at my uncle's, I assisted the doctor doing that for one of the militia men who got run through with a Seneca spear. This is different though, for I fear that there are bits of wood down in there. I'll probe a bit to see what I can get out."

Cautiously Sean sunk his fingers into the wound, feeling through the blood welling up in the hole. He managed to get his fingers on two small bits of wood and pull them out.

"Make sure that there are no more in there, laddie. If we close him up with splinters in there, the wound will get infected and he may die," Black advised.

Sean nodded assent and dug some more. He brought up one more piece, but could feel no more. He wiped his bloody hand on a rag Jones handed him.

The men watched their patient as they waited for the hot iron. Miller came back, holding it, wrapped in rags to keep his hand from being burned.

"All right now boys, hold him tight. Even though he's unconscious, he'll jump. Everyone ready?" he asked, as he looked them all in the eyes. The men nodded as they gripped the old man's legs and arms. Sean laid across his father to keep his movements to a minimum, and then inserted the hot iron into the hole in his chest. The smell of burning flesh and blood sickened the men, as they held tight. Old man

Taggert's body jerked in spasms from the pain, but then fell motionless.

"Sew him up now, Black. Then I'll bandage him. Thanks for your help, men. Tell the cook to give you a round of grog now, and then see if you're needed topside. I can tell by the movement of the ship, we've made it to shallow water."

"Aye sir, and we all hopes he makes it all right sir. He's a good captain, tough but he's always done right by us. He don't deserve to be taken low like this." Miller replied.

"Thanks," was all Sean said as he turned his attention to Black's sewing. He watched the grizzled seaman's nimble fingers stitch the flesh as if it were sailcloth. When he finished, Sean bandaged him while Black held the old man up in bed.

"Stay here with him William, while I check on our escape." Sean said as he ducked out of the cabin.

There waited Plato Jones, his father's steward. Plato was a freeman. He and his brother Julius had joined the crew in Havana, where the Taggert crew had rescued them from slavers. Their master had set them free when he died from a shipwreck off the Cuban coast. The Taggerts had known them and their master for years, and were surprised to learn of their misfortune.

The Taggerts had come across the brothers in Havana when they stopped there for fresh water and food. The crew of a slaver had tried to kidnap the Jones to replace some of their cargo that had died in the crossing, and old man Taggert would not stand by and let them be taken. It had been quite a scene on the Havana docks, the crews of two ships fighting each other.

The men of the *Osprey* gave better than they got and drove the slavers away. In the melee a Chinaman, Xing Xao, had assisted them. He had been stranded in Havana by his crewmates. He, too, became part of the crew of the *Osprey*.

"Is master Taggert gonna be alright, suh?" Plato asked.

"Yes, I think so, Plato. You can go in and sit by him. He'll be needing your services when he wakes up. Remember, Plato, he does not want you calling him 'master'. On board this ship you call him Captain, or Mister Taggert. We have no masters on board." Sean smiled.

"Yes suh, Mister Taggert. I'll take good care of him, you go take care of the ship," Plato beamed.

Sean climbed the steps back to the deck. He was hit with a blast of cold air and buttoned his coat. He looked up at the set of the sails, once satisfied, he turned towards the wheel.

Thomas was at the helm himself, intensely watching what lay ahead. Sean looked back and could see the British ship far behind them paralleling the reef that it could not cross.

The sound of three cannons came across the water as three water spouts raised up in the sea fifty feet aft of the *Osprey*. "They don't want us going in there," Sean said as his brother smiled.

"This string of islands will shelter us from their prying eyes. They expect we are going to New York, and that's the direction I'm letting them see us go, but we'll change course before long when we're out of their sight. I'll wager they'll sail on ahead of us to try to catch us outside New York Harbor," Thomas said to the men around him.

"Father is resting, he's lost a lot of blood. He should be all right as long as the bleeding has stopped. None the less, let's get him home fast so we can get him to a doctor," Sean said to his brother.

"I heard you handled that wound like a physician yourself little brother."

"Well, I did get practice while out there at Uncle James' place. I had to pull militia duty when the Senecas were acting up; I did patch up a few wounded men. Some with wounds worse than Father's. I'll never forget the terrible things those savages did to some of the settlers out there... just barbaric. Excellent fighters to be sure, but just downright cruel."

"Boys, get aloft and get the topgallants and royals off her, it will make it harder for the British t' see what we're about after we round the island here. The tall pines there will hide our masts," Thomas called out as the ship came to the first island. The men scrambled up the rigging to take in the sails.

"While you were out farming and fighting Indians with Uncle James, Father showed me several tricks of the trade, Little Brother. These barrier islands come in handy for getting away from pirates or British." Thomas said as he passed control of the wheel back to the helmsman. "Just keep her steady. With just the mains and jib on her we'll have enough to keep steerage way and a little speed on her behind the islands."

The two brothers stood by the side rail as they watched the carpenter and his assistants working to repair the transom. The three men worked steadily, with the job halfway done in just the hour since the attack.

"There's trouble brewing for sure, Thomas. The people of the colonies are fed up with the British. The folks out west have been hoarding weapons, powder and shot for the past year. They are training the militias not just for protection from the Indians, but from the British as well. Every port we put into, it's the same story. People want to separate the colonies from King George and Parliament."

"Aye, Sean, and now with what has happened to Father, you know he'll be laid up for a couple of months. He'll be wantin' to get back to sea, and I've a mind to keep the *Osprey* in port for the winter to keep from having to deal with the navy harassing us. I really have mixed emotions about this. We've always been loyal to the Crown, but they've gone too damned far this tine!" He slammed his hand on the rail as he spat the words out.

"We can no' let them keep us in port, Thomas. If we stay in, then they ha' got the better of us. We must keep the business going. We both ha' had enough time at sea to keep our customers' goods flowing and make good trades down in the islands. Hell, we can even beat the pirates when they attack. The men will stay with us if we set sail again; they've been loyal to Father and us for years. We can do this, Thomas."

"I know, Sean, we should, but let us wait until we get home, with Father being cared for before we decide what to do. We may even find ourselves in the middle of a bloody war by then! Now you look after things up here. I'm going below to warm up and sit with Father."

"Sir, whatever you decide, you should know the crew will be behind you, no matter what," said Wilson, the helmsman. "I couldn't help overhearing what you were talking about. If you decide to stay in port, continue the trade, or join the war, we will be there with you. Your father has always treated us well, better than the navy, and better than most captains. He knew Johnson was a deserter when he signed on, but when he saw the scars on his back from the cat-o-nine-tails, he would not turn him away. He told Johnson to keep quiet about his desertion, but every night he would break out crying about his poor wife and child. Damn those press gangs in England!" he spat as he cursed.

"The poor lad told us of what happened. 'Twas late at night when the frigate put into harbor and sent the press gangs into the streets of his town to take men to fill the needs of the ship. When they broke down the door of his home, Johnson tried to put up a fight. He was bashed over the head. When he came to, his pregnant wife lay dead on the floor next to 'im. She had taken a swing with a broom at the officer in charge. He backhanded her, which sent her flying into the wall, breaking her neck. They didn't even let him stay to take care of his infant daughter and bury his wife. They dragged 'im off, after getting a neighbor woman to get the child. I 'ear that your father 'as 'ad onc of your relatives to find the child, and 'as arranged for it to be brought 'ere to Johnson. 'Tis a fine thing 'e 'as done there, your father!"

"Aye, he does have a soft spot in him. Just don't ever say that loud enough for him to hear you, or he'll have us both standing watch from the top of the main mast!" Sean smiled as he responded.

It was reassuring that *Osprey's* crew of forty-five souls were of such stalwart nature. Most were from the old country. Whether they came from Scotland,

Ireland or England herself, they were all able men. Some had run away from the law, angry fathers of their pregnant girlfriends; some had left the navy because of harsh treatment. Of the fifteen men that had at one time been in His Majesty's Navy, every one of them bore the marks of the cat on their backs. Sadistic officers sometimes overdid the harshness of Navy discipline. Not one of these men had ever shown disrespect or laziness in their work.

For some, this ship was the only home and family that they had. The Jones brothers, Plato and Julius, once slaves, then freemen working on board their master's ship, had the benefit of having some education. Plato served as steward and assisted the ship's clerk. Julius was more the warrior and preferred the duties of able-bodied seamen. Then there was Xing Xao, the Chinaman; Anthony Monacelli, the Italian; Ivan Petrov, the Russian; Herman Baum, the Prussian; Peter Svenson, the Swede, who very much resembled his Viking ancestors; Peter Jarmolowski, the Pole; and Jose Martin Rodrigues, the Spaniard.

The crew very much resembled the usual mix of characters to be found in any port around the world. In any port almost every nationality could be found. Many were cast-offs, run-aways, or men just looking for new adventures.

As mixed a lot as the crew was, they all worked in harmony. As with most sailors, they knew once the ship left port, she and their very survival depended on each man doing his job, and each man being able to rely on each other. There was no room for discord on so small a vessel.

The *Osprey* lazily made its way on the lee side of the islands, with very little wind to push her along. She was a good ship, an armed merchantman, some ten years old. The *Osprey* was ninety feet long stem to stern, and twenty-four feet wide at the beam. She mounted four four-pound carriage guns and six swivel guns. Small armament to most, but large enough to deal with the likes of the pirates that they sometimes encountered.

The family had been a seafaring family for generations. They had moved to the colonies forty years earlier. The family had been prosperous, trading in the islands for rum, spices and a myriad of items. They also shipped indigo and cotton from the southern colonies to Boston and Philadelphia for shipment to England.

Sean looked up at the masthead pendant, noticing that the wind was still from offshore, what little was not blocked by the tall pines and low hills of the islands. "Johnson!" Sean called to the sailor that had suffered the beating, "How are you feeling?"

"I'm all right, sir. I got a hard head, he didn't even break the skin." replied the sailor sheepishly.

"Good! Do you feel like a climb?"

"Yes sir, I'm right as rain."

"Take my glass, and go up the main mast and see if you can spot our adversaries."

"Roight, sir, I'll do my best." The seaman took the proffered spyglass and scurried up the shrouds. Sean stood and watched him climb to the dizzying top of the main mast. Johnson managed the climb faster than he could. Sean regularly climbed the riggings; however he had never let on about his general dislike of being that high off the deck.

The seaman reached the top, and after placing himself in as comfortable a position as he could, stretched out the glass and scanned the horizon between the trees. With only the lower sails in use, and they being shielded by the island, the *Osprey* was almost invisible to the lookouts of the British ship. The *Huntress* had her full spread of canvas set, and Johnson could easily see her through the trees.

"She's turned about, sir! She's headed back out to sea!" he yelled as loud as he could. The men below heard him and let out a cheer! They had outmaneuvered and outsmarted a British frigate.

"Sir, we had better be thinkin' of turnin' the ship around, we're about to run out past this last island," Wilson advised.

"Thank you, Thomas, I hope to do just that. All hands aft!" Sean called out. The men all hurried to join him by the helmsman. They chattered good-naturedly while they waited for the slower members of the crew.

"All right now, lads, we'll be needing to turn around to head for Philadelphia now, and we don't have the wind in our favor. See ahead? We have enough room to turn her around, but this will take quick action on everyone's part. What little wind that reaches us here has shifted round. Here's what we'll do. I want the anchor party to stand by to drop the starboard anchor, and when it catches, get it hove tight. You top men, get up there and start taking in the remaining sails as fast as you can, then stay put. As soon as the current pushes the ship around the anchor, you boys here who will be standing by at the capstan will haul in the anchor as soon as we've turned, and you top men will set the sails as soon as they start hauling in the anchor."

"That's a mighty tricky maneuver thar, sir!" Miller pointed out.

"Yes it is, but we don't want to overshoot the last island and be seen by the British turning around in open water. If we do that, they'll know for sure that we are not going to New York."

"But Johnson has seen them turn out to sea," another voice called out.

"Aye, that they have, but I'll wager that was just to draw us out; that's what I would do! Now everyone get to your stations! Be prepared to move as soon as I give the orders!" The men all sped off as soon as he gave the word.

Sean watched as the men stood by the anchor and capstan, while the others crawled out along the yardarms. "Ease off to starboard just a bit more. That will give us more room to swing around. Easy does it, ready men?" he called out.

"Aye, sir! they all replied.

"Steady now on course; anchor party, drop anchor! Take in sail! Quickly now!" Sean watched the activity on the yardarms intently, as he glanced at the waters around the small ship. He could feel the anchor as it bit hard on the rocky bottom. The current was starting to swing the ship gently to port.

"Helmsman, keep the rudder amidships, quartermaster, get your men on the capstan now, and get the anchor hove tight. Don't give her anymore slack or we'll swing too wide and end up on the beach," he called out to the men at the capstan. They jumped at their task, quickly taking in the slack on the anchor. They held tight, straining against the capstan bars, as the current pushed the ship further around.

Sean glanced at the masthead pennant to see that they would have the wind behind them by the time the turn was complete. All eyes were on the shifting shoreline of the mainland and the island, as the stern of the ship swung toward the beach of the mainland.

"If the anchor don't hold, sir, you'll have hell to pay from your father!" the helmsman pointed out to Sean.

"You are right about that!" he replied as he watched the progress of the turn. The ship was almost in position. Sean waited for just a few seconds more, as the current did the work for them. His hands were sweating, and he controlled his nervousness by clasping them behind him so the men could not see.

"Now, set sail! Heave to on the capstan, and get that anchor up!" The men let out a collective grunt as they threw themselves against the capstan bars. Sean ran over and threw his weight into the effort. He looked up to see the sails come fluttering down from the yardarms and burst out as the wind caught them.

"Hooray!" The men broke out in a cheer as they felt the anchor give way, and they moved around the capstan more freely. As soon as the anchor was up, the anchor party lashed it to the cathead to make it secure. The ship jumped forward, as a fresh gust of wind came up the channel.

"Now that was one slick piece of sailing, Little Brother! When I heard the splash of the anchor, I wasn't quite sure what you were about. But as soon as I felt the ship give way to the current, I thought for sure you had gone mad! Father had come to, so I couldn't leave him, but it appears that you have done well in my absence!"

"Thank you, Thomas, but let's just not tell Father about this until he's back on his feet! The British turned out to sea. However, I figured they were doing that to draw us out, at least that is what I would have done in their place."

"Deck below, the *Huntress* has turned towards New York!" called Johnson from his perch.

"Looks as though you thought right, Sean. Now we can get to Philadelphia, and have father cared for." He turned to the men on the deck. "Hands aloft! Get all the sails back on her so we can get home as fast as this old gal will get us there!"

The men took to the rigging, and within minutes the *Osprey* was under full sail, as fast as was possible. The ship took on a life of her own as the sails boomed, as soon as the wind filled them.

"Aye, Brother, feel her now! This is when the old girl is the most fun, when she has her sails full and flies through the waves! Just listen to her sounds of life. The bustle of the canvas, the creaking of the yardarms, blocks and tackle! Feel her respond to the wind as she dances across the waves! Her timbers arcn't groaning, they're singing the song of the sea!" Thomas exclaimed.

"This is when I like sailing the most. She is like a spirited horse when she is running with the wind. Thomas, I really missed this when I was out West. The feel of the deck as she rides the troughs, the salt spray in the face reaching all the way back here when it breaks across the bow as she plunges into another trough. We are lucky indeed to have such a spirited ship. Listen to the wind singing through the rigging!" Sean replied.

The two stood watching the sea race beneath them as the ship plowed through the waves. The crew made themselves busy, checking the rigging and trimming the sails. The thought of the British ship erased from their minds for the time being as they attended to the needs of their ship.

"Look at them, Sean. We have men from nations all around the world who live and work together on this ship. We are a world unto ourselves, and here they have all been able to put their differences aside to become as one. If these ruffian types are able to do this, the nation that the rebels are trying to form may just survive. The colonies are full of people from all over Europe, where they were enemies, or run out of their own countries for their beliefs. Yet here in this new world ,they are able to find peace and harmony with their neighbors."

"I agree with you. I saw this on my travels out to Uncle James'. The people on the frontier are the same way. Many find it hard to communicate with each other, still speaking their native tongues, yet they pull together to help each other carve out farms and towns from the wilderness. If the King and his cronies would just treat us as they should, we would not have the threat of war hanging over our heads," Sean responded.

"The people in Boston are having a hard time of it, with the British troops occupying the city. The militia has kept them bottled up within the city. I ca' not imagine the Lobsterbacks will stay put for very long. I fear come spring there may be some hard fighting coming. From what we saw in Jamaica and the

Bahamas, it appears the crown is sending more supplies and troops to put an end to the unpleasantries. Since the shooting started at Lexington back in April, they've been sending more of everything to support their troops in Boston and New York. They won't stay in those cities sitting on their arses for long."

"What about us? I mean we 'ave always been loyal to the crown, but with this happening to Father, I don't see how we can stay out of it. It's possible that they will come hunting us for this incident. We may have to choose sides," said Sean.

"Well, Little Brother, we'll cross that bridge when we get there. Right now we just have to concentrate on getting Father home."

The two stood watching the shipboard activities and the weather as the day wore on. They took turns sitting with their father, who drifted in and out of consciousness. Late in the day, Sean unwrapped the wound when his father was awake, and drained fluid from it. The wound looked and smelled free of infection, and his father appeared to be handling the pain.

Plato helped Sean and stayed with the old man. When he was awake, Plato got him to drink and eat a few morsels of fresh meat. He read to him from his Bible, as the old man liked to hear his deep voice as he had done so many times before.

As the sun set, Sean took over the watch with Quartermaster James Cameron, and Boatswain Isaac Buchanan. "Looks like a squall coming in sir," commented Cameron when Sean came back on deck.

"I agree. Call the men out to shorten sail while there is a little light left. We'll run a little further out from shore if you please, Mister Munro. We wouldn't want to be blown ashore in the dark tonight." He smiled as the relief helmsman acknowledged the order and turned the big wheel enough to point the bowsprit out to sea.

"Hands aloft!" called out Buchanan as he rang the ship's bell. Within minutes the rigging came alive with the men of the watch racing out along the yardarms as they fought the unruly canvas. They were practiced at the art, which showed as they had reefed the sails within a matter of minutes.

"Isaac, if you would be so good as to inform Mister Donlon and Mister Kelly to be sure to secure the galley fires as soon as the men have all been fed. We are in for a blow tonight, so they need to douse the fires until this weather passes," Sean ordered his quartermaster.

"Aye, sir, would ya be wantin' a mug o' tea before it gets cold?" he asked.

"Yes, have Donlon bring up a kettle and mugs for us. We'll need all the help we can get tonight. This wind is already going right through my coat," he responded as he turned up his collar and shoved his hands into his pockets.

The squall was bearing down on them and would reach them in another half-hour. When Cameron and Donlon appeared back on deck, Sean and the others welcomed the hot mugs of tea. Tea had become scarce back home with the protests. They had picked up just enough for their voyage home. The hot brew warmed the men temporarily.

The men put their weather gear on just before the squall hit. The sea turned angry, and the tiny ship was tossed about like a cork. The *Osprey* ran before the wind, but even with the reduced sails, she heeled over at a sickening angle as she rose and fell on the huge waves. The tossing about would do his father no good, yet Sean was powerless to prevent the motion.

The storm lasted most of the night, and twice Sean had to send the crew to the top to tend to the sails. Both times he regretted having to risk their lives, however he knew, as well as they that if they refused to do their tasks, the ship could be lost.

The crew remained below decks with the exception of Sean, Cameron, Buchanan, Munro and the lookout, John Randolph. As was general practice, safety ropes had been lashed around their positions before the weather had gotten too rough. The storm was exhilarating, with the *Osprey* wildly rising to the crests of the waves and then plunging seemingly out of control down into the depths of the troughs. More than once, Sean could see the bowsprit disappear in the waves as they came crashing over the bow and racing down the decks, straight for the men clustered around the wheel.

As the night wore on, the storm kept up its relentless pounding of the ship. Sean and the others had been relieved at midnight, exhausted from their exertions on deck fighting the big wheel. They retired below decks, too exhausted to get out of their wet clothing before falling asleep.

Before Sean turned in, he checked on his father. Plato and George Pratt, the clerk, were there half asleep in chairs in the small cabin. "He's had a rough go of it so far. If this storm doesn't break soon, it may not go well for him," Plato told Sean, echoing what Thomas had told him when he came on deck to relieve him.

"I don't want to disturb him now, so I'll wait till morning to look at the wound again. The skin around it is not warm and he doesn't appear to have a fever, so he may pull out of this yet," Sean observed.

"You go on and get some sleep, Mister Taggert, you been through enough for one night I'll take care of him."

"Thank you, Plato, I do na' think I'll argue that point with you," Sean said. He took one more look at his father and left the cabin. His cabin was right outside, to the left of the door. His cabin was more like a closet, with a bunk which was high enough for his sea chest to be put underneath it, and a small writing stand at the end of the cabin at the foot of his bunk.

Sean pulled off his wet clothes, hung them over his chair, and then collapsed on the bed. He managed to pull the covers over him before falling asleep. He was so used to the wild pitching of the ship that it did not even bother him as he slept, nor did he notice the lessening of the wild motion when the storm passed about three in the morning.

"Sir, 'tis time to get up." Sean heard the voice of Cameron, who stood over him, candle in hand. "The storm has passed, and we are beating back towards the mainland."

"Thank you, James. Has the watch been rousted out yet?" Sean asked, half asleep.

"Aye, sir, the cook is getting them fed. I figured that you'd be wantin' to check in on the captain, so's I brought you some food and tea, and put it there on your desk."

"Good man, I will indeed check him over. If you

have eaten, go topside and tell my brother that I'll be there shortly."

Cameron knuckled his forehead in salute and closed the door to the cabin as he backed out. Sean sat up and ran his fingers through his hair. He reached over for the mug of tea and took a few healthy swigs. He bit off a chunk of beef and set about to get dressed. Sean pulled his sea chest out from under his bunk and took out fresh clothes. His wet things had been removed from his cabin and were being attended to by Plato or the clerk. They both fussed over his father, brother and himself.

He sloshed some water in the basin and shaved quickly as he ate. When he was finished eating and dressing, he ducked out of his cabin and into his father's. The old man looked rather gray in the candlelight. He was awake, and smiled at Sean.

"Come in, Son. How are you this morning?"

"Good, but more importantly, how are you feeling?" Sean asked.

"I ha' been better laddie, no argument about that!"

"All right, let's set you up, so I can take a look at that," Sean said as he helped his father sit upright. He and Plato removed his shirt and bandages. Sean noticed a faint odor from the wound, which was not good. As looked at the wound, he noticed another small piece of wood had worked its way to the surface, so he gently pulled it out. After he drained the fluid from the wound, he poured some whiskey into it, causing his father to wince.

"That sure stings worse than that damned piece of wood that you pulled out o' me!" his father snorted.

"You old warhorse, you've been hurt worse and never uttered so much as a peep. Are you going to try to make me believe this whiskey really hurts?" Sean chided his father.

"If you want to use that, you could at least let me drink some first," he smiled back. "That way I could at least enjoy it!"

"You'll be fine. Complaining like that is a good sign. Now, I have to go relieve Thomas. We should be close to rounding Cape May and will be in Delaware Bay in an hour or so, if we did not get blown out to sea too far. Now you just lie back and get some sleep; I know you had a rough night of it."

Sean left the cabin and climbed the steps to the deck. The sun was just breaking over the horizon. The wind was brisk, and the sky was clear of the clouds of the storm that had assailed them through the night. No land was in sight.

Thomas was at the rail taking a bearing with his sextant. Sinclair was at his side jotting down the reading. Together they stretched out the chart and plotted the position of the *Osprey*.

Sean walked the length of the deck, pausing to inspect the set of the sails and the tautness of the rigging. The deck was still wet, and he walked carefully to avoid slipping. He leaned over the rail at the bow to inspect the anchors, which both appeared to be secure after last night's beating. He watched as four dolphins played in the bow wave, racing just ahead of the ship's bow. He never ceased marveling about the creatures' speed and gracefulness.

Sean walked back on the opposite side of the deck to relieve his brother, stopping to check the lashing on the cannons and checking the rigging from the opposite side. "Good morning, Thomas. It appears we weathered the storm well last night."

"Yes, we did. I just checked our position, and we did not get blown too far off course, although it will take us longer to pass Point May than I had hoped." he replied pointing to the map. "We should get there in about three or four hours. Once the storm abated last night, I tried to bring her in closer to shore, but the wind was not at all helpful. How is Father this morning?"

"He is full of complaints, so he is feeling better in spite of being tossed about last night. The wound is not looking as well as I had hoped, but it is not showing signs of infection yet."

"Aye, that is good. Now we may want to anchor up in the bay for the night, and not go too far up the river in the dark. That was quite a blow last night and the river is bound to be high and full of debris. I wou' no want to risk running aground or being run through by some tree floating downstream."

"I agree, no sense in risking that. That should put us in Philadelphia by noon tomorrow. Now get some food and some sleep."

"That I will. Wake me if there are any problems." Thomas and his shift retired below decks, while Sean's shift came on deck stretching and stomping their feet to keep warm. The men turned to holystoning and swabbing the decks as they had so many times before.

Sean directed the quartermaster to detail men aloft to check for frayed lines above, always a danger after a rough blow as they had been through. The morning was taken up with such mundane tasks, the routine of which was not broken until the lookout's cry, "Land on the starboard quarter!"

The men stopped from their tasks to stand at the rail and gaze out at the distant shoreline. Sean joined a group at the rail. "'Tis always good to see after a long voyage, sir!" exclaimed Richard Sharp.

"Aye, that it is. I guess that baby of yours will be walking by the time we get home now, eh Richard?"

"I certainly think so. He was trying hard to before we left. Did you see the boat that I carved for him sir?" Sharp asked.

"Indeed I did. That is a fine looking longboat that you ha' carved. That is an art that I ha' never mastered, carving that is."

"It just takes a lot of practice and time. Many of my early creations went directly into the fire to be sure. I'll carve ye one next time out."

"Thank you, Sharp, that would be most kind. I have a small collection of ships at home, and a longboat would be a proud addition to it."

Sean and the men returned to their work. He watched the weather pennant at the main mast, wary of any changes as they approached land. True to Thomas's reckoning, they were approaching Cape May, the entry point to Delaware Bay, just as he figured.

Sean took his glass and climbed out onto and halfway up the shrouds of the mainmast to see what was ahead. The Delaware River must be running high and mad from the storm, as the change in water color even this far out was noticeable. There was some debris floating ahead of them, but it was very scattered, and nothing of any threat to the ship.

Towards noon, the *Osprey* rounded the Cape and entered the mouth of the bay. Sean had to have the sails trimmed as they approached, and as soon as they were in the bay proper, he had them shortened to slow their speed.

The wind had backed around in their favor, and the ship made good time against the river's flow. Not wanting to be going too fast in the event of large driftwood, it was necessary to slow the ship down. The tide was high and starting to recede slowly.

It was good to have land nearby again. There were few houses and signs of life as they crawled up the wide mouth of the bay. Not as wide or long as the Chesapeake Bay, still the Delaware was quite imposing. As the receding tide increased in speed, Sean once again sent the men aloft, this time to set more sail to offset the rushing water.

He had posted two men in the bows to alert the helmsman to the approach of large driftwood. Twice within the last hour, the helmsman had to alter course to avoid hitting uprooted trees floating downstream.

"It was a hell of a storm for us out on the ocean, but it appears to ha' been worse on land. It is unusual to have a large storm this late in the year," Sean commented to Cameron.

"Aye, Sir that it was. The worst I think that I weathered was at sea, when we were tossed around by that hurricane off Jamaica two years ago. Waves as high as the mainmast, and me having to be on the wheel! After four hours of that, my hands were nothing more than raw meat. Took three weeks to heal, they did."

"I remember Thomas and Father talking about that one. Sorry I missed that one, but there will always be more, eh? We'll try to maintain our speed till just before dark. There are plenty of coves along the river to anchor in for the night. I'll have the men ready the kedge anchor, for I think we better anchor fore and aft tonight." Sean said as he went forward to find the boatswain.

He found Isaac Buchanan below deck, overseeing a work party that was securing the lashings on the cargo in the hold. "The cook found that some of the cargo had gotten loose in the storm, so I had the boys go through the hold to secure everything again. It don't look like we ha' any damage."

"Fine Isaac. When you are through here, have the men prepare the kedge, with plenty of rope and the long boat to place it when we drop anchor tonight. I don't want to wake up in the morning to find our arse on the river bank!"

"That wou'na' do at all sir. I'll get them on it straight away," Buchanan responded.

The rest of the day passed as so many did on board ship, just another day full of routine work. As night approached, Sean saw a cove that was large enough for the *Osprey* and had the men go aloft to shorten sail.

The anchor party was ready, while the longboat with the kedge anchor was swung out and lowered. As the ship came to a halt in the shelter of the cove, the port anchor was dropped. The crew of the longboat pulled around the aft of the ship and caught the rope lowered to them. They pulled away from the ship, and after securing the kedge to the rope, dropped it overboard. The men on board the ship pulled in unison, until the anchor bit into the river bottom. They secured their end, and the *Osprey* was tied tight for the night, out of the current full of debris.

The whole crew came on deck at sunset to relax and enjoy the scenery around them. The leaves had all turned to their fall colors weeks ago, and what was still on the trees made for a colorful setting. The air was clear and crisp with the temperature dropping as the sun set.

They stood in groups, excited in the knowledge that they would be home the next day. Home to their wives, their children, or their sweethearts. They chattered about the things they would do while home. The chill in the November night did not deter their stay on deck. The men stomped their feet and sipped their grog to keep warm. Ben Morrison broke out his fiddle, and Matthew Ross brought out his flute. Together the two livened up the gathering with all the favorite tunes of the crew. Some even joined arms, in mock dance as the effect of the grog took hold.

Since the voyage was nearly over, and the night was so cold, Thomas had allowed the men an extra mug each, knowing that it was not much warmer below decks. "Look at them, Sean," he mused. "With all they go through each voyage, they still manage to sing and dance. They are a hardy lot!"

"Aye, Brother that they are." Sean replied. He thought about the sailor's lot in life. The life of a sailor was a hard life. It was full of hardship and danger. The food, once the fresh stores were exhausted, consisted of casks of salted pork or beef. There were times when a new cask was broken open and found to be rancid and of no use, cutting into the daily ration. Fresh water was sometimes a problem, if bilge water managed to seep into the casks in the hold. Worms and other creatures were found to grow in the sealed casks.

The dangers of going aloft to tend to the sails at the height of the storms; the possibility of being swept overboard often meant instant death in the chill waters, as too often, the ship could not navigate back against the wind to search for the unfortunate soul, the disease they found themselves exposed to in foreign ports; the cramped living conditions, being called on at any time of day or night to race up and down the shrouds; aye, it was a hardy lot indeed that could do these things day in and day out and still come back for another voyage.

Sean strolled to the side of the deck and looked out across the water to the shore. The light from the captain's quarters cast a warm glow across the river below. He could smell the wood smoke from two distant cabins whose light glimmered through the trees.

"Still thinking about that tavern wench in Havana, I bet!" Thomas said as he approached his pensive brother at the side. "She was quite a playful little nymph, now, wasn't she?"

"You better not say that around Father, or he'll have my hide! Besides, as I recall, you were dallying with one of the girls in that tavern also, so be careful!"

"Your secret is safe with me!" he responded playfully. "We'll get an early start tomorrow, so get some sleep. I want to get under sail at sunrise."

"Right, be sure to have the last watch hoist the longboat out in the morning so that we can warp her out into the main channel with the morning shift." Sean reminded him. "I'm going to check on Father, then turn in for the night. See you tomorrow."

Sean took one more look at the masts and the scene on the deck before going down the steps to the deck below. He entered his father's cabin to see him sitting upright, playing a game of chess with his clerk, George Pratt.

"Just in time, Son. He has beaten me again," the elder Taggert announced.

"You must be feeling better; just don't push yourself, Father," Sean chastised him. He sat on the edge of the bunk, and unraveled the bandages. He was immediately struck by a faint odor that he knew should not be there. He reached over for the candle on the table and held it close to the wound. The skin around it had turned pale red, the sure sign of infection.

"Sit still now Father, I want to probe the wound again," he said as he wiped off the liquid that seeped out. He inserted the probe and managed to work out another small sliver of wood.

"What's the matter, Sean? I can tell by the look on your face that all is not well," his father asked.

"Your wound is looking a bit angry, but I have pulled out another piece that has worked its way through the skin. I don't feel any more in there, so let's hope that that was what was causing the redness." He cleaned the wound again with the whiskey and gently wrapped it in clean bandages.

"You get to sleep now, so you're rested for seeing Mother tomorrow. A few days of her cooking should put you back on your feet again. Plato, you and George make sure that he gets some sleep. Make sure the two of you get some sleep too; it looks like you both need it. Good night, all."

"Good night, sir, and we will make sure he does as you say," Plato replied. "Now Captain sir, you heard him, that's enough chess for tonight, you get to sleep so's we can too."

"All right, Plato, the two of you turn in also. I'll be fine."

"We'll be staying up in shifts sir, so that one of us will be at hand if'n you be needin' us," replied Pratt.

In his cabin, Sean threw his coats and hat into the chair by his bed. He took only enough time to take his shoes off before rolling under the blanket. The wound was infected, slightly, but it may get worse. He could have done nothing more than he had done. There was just no way of knowing how many small slivers there might be in the lung and meat of his chest. Only time would tell whether or not all was well.

He had heard tell that the worst wounds in sea battles were not the wounds of cannon fire, musket fire, or swords, but that of splinters. The battering that a ship took from cannon fire would send showers of splinters of all sizes flying through the air. More men would be killed or laid low by them, and most would die of the infections caused by the small pieces left deep within the wounds.

He could not get to sleep, knowing that his father may not survive the wound from the shot fired into their ship by the navy ship. The navy ship of their own government! The thought of it still riled him. It was no wonder that the colonists wanted to be shed of the crown!

He awoke the next morning to the creaking of the hoist as the men on deck hoisted the longboat over the side. It was still dark as he splashed some water on his face, dressed and went on deck.

As he came on deck, the cold air of the morning struck him. He had not been prepared for it and immediately started to shiver. "Good morning, Boatswain Stark. I see that you have gotten everything in readiness?" he asked as the boatswain came over to him.

"Aye, sir that we have. The boys have gotten the longboat hoisted out, and the cable has been put in place. You're on deck early, sir. Your brother just went down for some hot tea."

"I'm headed there myself, just wanted to come up and stretch my legs. As soon as the next watch comes up, have your men sent below and fed."

"Aye, sir. They'll not be grumblin' too much about their meal as long as it's plenty hot. "Tis a cold one this morning."

Sean turned and went below. He got a mug of hot tea, and a pitcher of hot water so that he could shave. Back in his cabin, he finished shaving and donning a clean uniform. It would not do showing up in homeport in his dirty uniform coat.

The men of his watch had just mustered on deck as Sean appeared again. They chattered excitedly, partly from the cold and partly from being so close to home. "Have the longboat crew disembark, and take up the kedge. As soon as they have freed that, they can take up the cable and warp us out as we weigh anchor. The starboard watch will be right back up to set all sails except for the mains. That ought to give us enough sail to get upstream and still see what is in front of us. Once we get under way, I'll want two men on the foretop to keep a close watch on river traffic, debris and snags. I also want a couple of men in the bowsprit nettings with marlinspikes to push away any wayward logs coming our way."

As soon as the men were detailed off to their assignments, Sean stood next to the helmsman as the work details started their tasks. As soon as the longboat crew had pulled up the kedge, they hauled it back on board. The *Osprey* swayed gently on the anchor cable, still holding it in place.

The longboat crew worked its way to the bow of the ship, accepted the towing cable, and took up position in front of the ship.

"Weigh anchor!" Sean called out. The boatswain and the capstan crew acknowledged, and the men took to the bars, pushing for all they were worth to pull the ship to the anchor. As they did, the starboard watch came back on deck after having eaten a quick breakfast, and took to the shrouds.

Thomas came up beside his brother. "It appears that you have things under control. I knew that we could make an officer of you yet!" he chided his brother.

"Thanks for your confidence. Did you check in on Father? I did not want to wake him."

"Yes I did, he was sleeping well. I'm glad we're getting home to where we can get the doctor and some medication for him."

"I'm worried that an infection has started. It showed signs of it last night. The anchor has come up. Now it's up to the crew in the longboat," Sean said, as he felt the deck roll slightly. They stood and watched as the anchor party lashed the big anchor into place after it broke free of the water. The longboat crew dug their sweeps into the brown river water, and the tow cable became taut. Ever so slowly, the *Osprey* started forward, nosing into the river current. As it nosed past the entrance of the cove, they felt the morning breeze coming straight up from the south. The boatswain called out the order to set sail, and instantly the sails were let loose to catch the wind.

The ship nudged forward a little faster, until it was under its own power. The longboat paused in the river, until the ship came alongside. Once they hooked onto the chains, the men scrambled up the side.

"Have the boat secured aft, Mr. Buchanan. It needs to be wet down so the planks swell back to proper shape. They were getting a bit dry," Sean ordered.

"Aye, Sir, you men 'eard 'im, get the boat secured aft!" Buchanan barked, sending the boat crew jumping to get the boat secured. It would save them the trouble of hoisting it back on board.

Slowly at first, then as it got further out into the expanse of the ever-narrowing bay, the *Osprey* started to gather speed. With luck, they would be in Philadelphia after the noon meal. The last leg of the trip was uneventful, yet it required the crew to be on constant lookout. The traffic on the river increased the further up river that they got. All manner of craft came into view, the occupants waving as they passed. Canoes, flatboats, gondolas with their broad sweeps, ocean-going transports, all were present on the river.

The current had slowed from the maddening pace that it flowed the day before, making their progress easier. The further up stream they went, the narrower the bay grew. The shoreline was lined with trees, with an occasional clearing with cabins and fields. Several creeks and streams broke the monotony of the shoreline.

Soon, Delaware was no longer on the western bank, as their home colony of Pennsylvania was passing by. On the eastern bank was the colony of New Jersey. This was a beautiful passage during the summer when all the trees were full. Now with most of the leaves off the trees, it had a dark, foreboding look.

The number of houses along the banks and the number of vessels on the river were steadily increasing, marking the nearness of their final destination, Philadelphia.

Sean and Thomas were walking the deck and were near the bow when the smoke of many chimneys rose above the trees in the distance. The first rooftops and steeples came into view.

"Little Brother, we have made it home. This is the most beautiful city of all the ones we visit in our voyages, and not just because it is home," remarked Thomas as he stood by the rail.

"I agree, Thomas. Ever since Dr. Franklin pushed to have the city streets paved in cobblestones and lamps erected on all the streets to light up the night, it is by far the most modern of cities. The brick houses and buildings are a sight for sore eyes, to be sure," Sean replied.

"Is the boat crew ready for docking?" asked Thomas.

"Yes, Stark will take charge when it's time. I'll have the sails reefed in a few minutes to slow us down. It wouldn't do for us to go plowing into the boat traffic in the harbor now would it?" Sean chuckled.

"You won't ever let me live that incident down, will you?" Thomas laughed as he made the accusation remembering his first time that Father had let him bring the *Osprey* into the harbor. He had neglected to take in sails and nearly run down three small lighters in the harbor.

"Not as long as it still gets your goat! I can still see Father standing there all stony-faced, about to burst, trying to let you figure out your mistakes," Sean fired back laughing.

"Aye, it does, but with each passing year, I can laugh at it more. As soon as we tie up at the wharf, we'll send Johnson on ahead to get Dr. Heinrich to the house. James should have the carriage at the warehouse, so we should be able to transport him to the house directly," Thomas replied.

"Yes, the quartermasters and boatswains can oversee the unloading of the cargo while we see to Father. Well, we should look to the task of getting docked. We are close enough to take in sail," Sean observed.

The two strolled back to the helm, passing out orders as they went. Sean sent the men to the shrouds to reef the sails, while the boat crew climbed down into the longboat that had been pulled alongside. The men bailed out several inches of water as they waited for the ship to slow down.

Sean was pleased with the speed and skill of the men as they reefed the sails. The forward motion of the *Osprey* slowed rapidly as the river current pushed against it. The boat crew pulled in front of the ship and secured the tow cable passed to them. Pulling for all they were worth, to the singing of one of their sea shanties, they inched the ship closer to the wharf.

As soon as they were close enough, Stark ordered two men to the wharf. As soon as they climbed up, the cable was passed to them, and they secured it to one of the pilings. Quickly they ran to the end, in time to catch a line that came snaking through the air to them. Once they had the line secured, they watched as the men on board the ship pulled the lines and brought the *Osprey* to the wharf, until it gently bumped the posts.

The dockside came alive with activity as James Taggert and his men came out of the family warehouse and raised the gangway to the side of the ship. Casual onlookers shouted to them as they stood by, watching as the ship was secured for its stay in port. Johnson was the first down the gangway as he scurried off to find the doctor. Several wives and children of the crew started showing up, as their approach had been announced by word of mouth as soon as it had been sighted a few miles down river.

Sean always marveled at how fast word could travel along the riverfront. He waved to James, who was barking orders out to the warehouse men as they prepared the dock and hoists to off-load the cargo.

"James, bring the carriage around quickly!" Thomas shouted to his brother. James looked quizzically but waved acknowledgement. He turned and walked around the back of the warehouse and led the horse and carriage to the dock.

Sean had gone below deck to see to moving his father. His clerk had packed all his clothing and belongings that would be taken to the house. Plato and his brother Julius were ready to carry the elder Taggert up to the deck. "Careful now, Father, you let them take you out; you do not need to be straining yourself," Sean ordered as his father started to grumble about being treated like a child.

Sean was worried about the wound. When he checked on him earlier, he felt the skin around the wound was hot to the touch, and the redness had deepened. He stood back as the two Jones brothers lifted him and carried him up the narrow steps to the deck. The crew moved out of the way as they carried him to the gangway and down to the waiting carriage.

"James, Father had been hit by a splinter when the navy fired on us. We'll explain more later, but now we must get him home and have Dr. Heinrich treat him. You get the work started on unloading and then come up to the house, Thomas and I are going to go up there with him now."

"All right Sean, I had already sent a runner to alert Mother that you were back when we got word that you were down river. Make sure that she gets some extra help with him," James said to his brother as he went over to the carriage to see their father.

"James, get that worried look off your face, I'll be fine in no time. How's things around here?" old man Taggert asked before James could speak.

"Everything is fine, but don't you get going about the business, you need to get well before you burden yourself with that."

He just nodded in response. The ordeal of being moved had caused him pain. His clerk, Pratt, loaded his belongings into the carriage and sat beside him.

"Plato, you and Julius come to the house with us. After you help us there, you can have a hot meal. Do you have anywhere to stay in town?"

"No, suh, we figured to sleep on the ship."

"Well, there is extra room in the servants' quarters at the house, if you want to sleep in a real bed for a while. I know that Father would appreciate having you read to him," Sean offered.

The four men walked behind the carriage all the way to the house. As they walked, friends and business associates greeted them along the way. Finally they came up the drive to their house. The two-story brick house was one of several along the tree-shaded street. They had paved the drive with cobblestones to match the street. A high wrought iron fence surrounded the property that the house was on. The windows were bordered with shutters, and high Greek columns held the roof of the porch.

There was a carriage at the front of the house, and on the porch they could see Johnson, the doctor and their mother standing there waiting. In a flurry of skirts, their mother raced out to meet them. She went directly to their father to check on him. "What ha' ye gone and done now, William Taggert?" she scolded as she walked along with the carriage, holding his hand.

"Ah, 'tis good to see you too, my dear. Now don't you start frettin' o'er me, the boys ha' been doin' that for the past few days!"

She turned and greeted her sons. As soon as the entourage reached the house, she took over and started barking orders to all around.

"Molly, you show these two to the bedroom, and turn the bed down for Mister Taggert. Sean, you and Thomas take his baggage upstairs. Mr. Stark, you stand by to get anything that Dr. Heinrich needs."

With that, the Jones brothers once again lifted their captain and followed Molly up the wide stairs.

Mrs. Taggert and the doctor followed them, with Sean and Thomas bringing up the rear. Sean gave the doctor a running account of how he treated the wound.

"It sounds as if you have done all that can be done, Sean. Now I'll see what I can do," Assured Heinrich.

They entered the room as the Jones brothers laid the old man on the bed and arranged the pillows for him so that he could sit up. The exertions and movement had taken a toll on him. Sean noticed how pale he looked.

They all stayed back as the doctor unwrapped the wound and inspected it. He probed the wound, and spread a poultice on it before wrapping it with fresh bandages.

"You lay back and relax, William. The next day should tell the story. I'll tell you straight out, you know I would not hold back from you. The wound is festering; you may be in danger yet. You're a tough old bird, and I give you a better than fair chance of surviving. Most men with a wound like this would have passed on by now."

"Thank you, Henry. Why don't you stay for a while and pass the time?" asked William Taggert.

"I'll be back later this evening, William. I have to check in on a couple of other patients. Besides I think it better that you spend time with your wife."

"I'll see you to the door, sir." Offered Sean.

"Sean, what you did was a good piece of work. I have rarely seen a man with such a bad splinter wound survive though. It is a testament to your medical knowledge that he has survived. I do not hold out much hope for him though. The infection has spread. Just make him comfortable for the next few days, and his passing should be peaceful. He's a strong one, but I fear not strong enough to beat this foe."

"Thank you, doctor. We'll do what we can." Sean replied as he walked the doctor to his carriage.

As they stood on the portico, the doctor stopped and said to Sean, "You had better keep the ship in port for a while, the tensions have been increasing here between the Government and the Colonials. The navy will try to hunt you down to avenge the insult to one of its officers. There have been incidents all over, and I fear we will be at war before long. Now with General Washington having the British Army under siege in Boston, I'm afraid things will only get worse."

"Aye, that they will, from what we ha' been hearing in all the ports we stopped at. We will probably stay in port for a while. We did have cargo for New York, but since we turned from there because of the navy, we'll send it on another ship instead. We even had some supplies for the British Army there," Sean replied.

"Well, good day to you. I have some more patients to see. I'll be back later this evening."

Sean watched him drive off; he then turned to go back inside. He went to the kitchen to get a bite to eat and found the Jones brothers there, being served heaping plates of food. James and Thomas came in to join them, Thomas recounting the incident to his younger brother as they entered the kitchen.

"Things ha' been heating up since you ha' been gone. The Continental Congress just a few weeks ago ha' voted to create a navy and a few days ago to form two battalions of marines. They came all along the docks trying to purchase ships from any who would sell. They even asked about the *Osprey*."

"I tell you, it has been much on my mind since this happened that we ca' no' stay out of this much longer. I know Father had wanted to stay clear of having to choose sides, but after what they did to him, his own government, I do no' see how we ca' no' take up arms against the King!" Thomas declared.

"Father will not be pleased if you do this," James commented.

"Father may not live out the week because of what they did!" Sean interjected. "It has been welling up inside me since he was wounded, yet until this moment, I ha' been trying to keep it in check, but I want to avenge our Father! That officer is a marked man in my eyes!"

"Aye, mine too, Little Brother, but we must keep our wits about us. Revenge is a double-edged sword that can cut its own master, as well as the enemy." Thomas warned.

The three sat at the table with the Jones brothers and helped themselves to some fresh pie. They spent the rest of the afternoon talking and visiting with the friends and relatives that stopped by to see if they could help, once the word got out as to what had happened to their father.

The next two days William Taggert's condition grew worse. He lapsed in and out of fevers. His wife stayed by his side. On the second day, when he was lucid, he called for his three oldest sons. They came in and sat in chairs pulled up alongside the big bed.

"Lads, I know I ha' very little time left, so I want to pass on some advice before I go over to the other side. I can tell by the looks on your faces that you have hatred building inside you for what has happened to me. I ca' no' stop that from happening. However I can give you guidance. We ha' been loyal subjects to the Crown all of our lives, and God-fearing seamen. If I was whole again, I do no' think that I could stay out of the fray that is coming. The Crown has gone too far in its treatment of we colonials, and I say that not just because o' what has happened to me." He paused to catch his breath, each word taking an effort to continue.

"I hereby give my blessing to you to follow your own conscience on this matter. Do not go out seeking revenge! That will only get you killed. Go out for a higher purpose, that of freedom and equal treatment under the law. That is worth fighting for, not revenge! If you go out seeking revenge, dig a grave for yourself first, as revenge kills your spirit and will get yourself killed too. Now as to the *Osprey*, a ship can only have one master, and that should be Thomas. You are the better sailor and as the oldest, the ship would go to you. Sean, you ha' always been the adventurous one, be second in command, or take over the fighting aspect of running a warship, you have the talent for it. I saw this in our encounters with the pirates."

"James, you ha' always been the business-minded one of the lot of you, and it will be up to you to keep the business running the best you can. We have enough money to buy another ship, maybe smaller to keep the business afloat. We will no' go broke for a year or two."

He broke out into a coughing spasm that wracked his whole body. He spit blood into a kerchief that he had in his hand. "One more thing. I ha' taught you boys many things, the most important is how you deal with others. Remember what I ha' taught you. When you ha' others under you who look to you for leadership, give them that. You ca' no' get loyalty and good work from men when you beat them. Men must be lead not driven. In charge, you must inspire your men by setting the example, being fair, and teaching them what they must know. If you do these things, you will always have a good crew and be successful." Once more he broke out in a coughing spasm that left him even weaker.

"Now you lads give me your word that you'll do as I ha' said, so that I can be assured that you will be safe."

The three brothers gave the elder Taggert their word, and after each gave him a long embrace, they left the room. Their mother stepped outside the door and said, "I had told him of the conversations that you have been having with the others that have been stopping by. He had overheard one of your talks also. The old fox is not always asleep when you're sitting in there with him. Now I expect that you take his wishes to heart," she admonished them.

"Mother, I speak for all of us, we will abide by his wishes," Thomas assured her.

"Good, now go get out of the house for a while. I want to spend some time alone with him while he is awake."

The three left the house and rode in the carriage down to the docks. The *Osprey* had been unloaded and rode high in the water. The recipients of the cargo destined for Philadelphia had picked up their shipments. That which was bound for New York sat in the warehouse. They walked the deck of the ship, inspecting it as they went. A few deck hands were replacing worn cordage and making minor repairs.

The three brothers spent an hour in this manner, talking of what they should do. They would walk a few steps, pause and talk, then move on.

As they reached the stern, Sean looked up at the Union Jack on the staff. He spat over the side, stepped up to the staff, and brought the flag down. The men working on deck stopped their work to watch. "This flag will never fly o'er this ship again!" he exclaimed, and threw it down.

He did not look back or acknowledge the cheers of the men, but left the ship. He was torn inside-torn between his devotion to his family and to the crown. In that one action, he determined the course he would take.

2
Peg Mullan's
Tun Tavern

"Sean, Thomas, hello!" a voice called out as Sean walked down the gangplank to the dock. Climbing off a big bay horse was Sam Nicholas, an old friend of the family.

"Hello, Sam, how are you, old friend?" responded Sean as he walked over to the man and shook his hand. Nicholas helped run the family tavern, The Conestogoe Wagon on Market Street. He was also a member as were the Taggerts, of the gentlemen's fishing club known as the Schuykill Fishing Company, and of the Gloucester Fox Hunting Club. Many persons of prominence in the community belonged to one or both of the clubs, such as John Cadwalader, Thomas and James Warton, Robert and Samuel Morris, John Nixon, Clement Biddle, and Thomas Willing, all of whom were now embroiled in the events at hand.

"It is good to see you, old friends," he said enthusiastically as Thomas and James came down the plank. "I was just up to the house to visit, and just missed you. I did get to speak with your father for a moment; you gentlemen have my deepest sympathy. I hope that I did not interrupt anything here. Sean, you appear to be vexed."

"You did no' interrupt anything, Sam, we were just talking business. What say we go over to your tavern for dinner and we can catch up on what you ha' been up to?" Sean asked.

"Aye, we should, but if we go there, I'll get caught up with all my customers. What say we go over to Peg Mullen's instead?" he responded.

"Yes, Tun Tavern, that is a good choice, we ha' no' eaten there in quite a while." Thomas added.

"Good, it is settled. I'll tie my horse on the back of your carriage and we'll ride together," he said as he walked his horse around to the rear of the carriage. "You lads have been out of touch for a while, and much has transpired since last we spoke. That was the week before you left on this last voyage. We did catch some nice fish that day, didn't we?"

"That was a nice spot, and if my reel ha' no' broke, I would ha' out-fished you as always," Thomas added.

"Aye, that you may have! We may be able to get one more foxhunt in before the snows come. However with all the members being so caught up in preparations for war, we may not get much of a turnout." Nicholas offered.

The four talked of fishing and fox hunting on the short drive to the tavern at the corner of King Street and Tun Alley. When they got to the tavern, all four of them were quite chilled from the bitter cold November night.

"I'm going to head back home, I'm not much up for dinner," James said as they stood outside the tavern.

"Go ahead and take my horse, I'll come back to the house with your brothers and fetch him back." Nicholas offered. James climbed on the horse and waved as he kicked him into motion.

"What's this?" Sean asked as he read a notice posted on the menu board next to the door. He tried to read it in the flickering light of the street lamp.

"That's the resolution passed by Congress two weeks ago, Friday, November tenth, to form two battalions of Marines. The Naval Committee led by John Adams of Massachusetts held its meetings upstairs here. Since they voted last month to form a Continental Navy, they got around to voting on the formation of the Continental Marines this month," Sam pointed out.

"Read it out loud, Sean, your eyes are better than mine," Thomas directed his brother.

"All right. '*10 November 1775, Congress passed the following resolution: Resolved that two battalions of Marines be raised consisting of one colonel, two lieutenant colonels, two majors and officers as usual in other regiments. That they consist of an equal number of privates with other battalions. That particular care be taken that no person be appointed to office or enlisted into said battalions but such are good seamen, or so acquainted with maritime affairs as to be able to serve to advantage by sea when required. That they be enlisted and commissioned for and during the present war between Great Britain and the Colonies, unless dismissed by order of Congress. That they be distinguished by the names of the First and Second Battalions of American Marines, and that they be considered a part of the number, which the Continental Army before Boston is ordered to consist of.*' Sounds impressive. Can we go inside now, it is cold out here?" Sean asserted.

"I agree, let's continue this inside by the hearth," Nicholas replied. The three men went inside. The warmth of the tavern, and the aroma of the beefsteak dinners that the tavern was so well known for, greeted them. The tavern was half full and they made their way to a table by the hearth.

"Good evening, gentlemen!" came the greeting from Peg Mullen as she came over to greet them. "Sam Nicholas, you are getting to be a regular around here these days. Sean, Thomas, it is good to see you both safe. We heard about your father, such a shame. He is too good a man to be struck down that way."

"Thank you, Mrs. Mullan. How's Robert, I don't see him?" Thomas asked.

"Oh, he was not feeling too good tonight so he went home early. What do you men want? Are you eating or just drinking?"

"A wee bit, of both my dear woman. How about three mugs of hot buttered rum, and three platters of your wonderful beefsteak dinners?" Sam responded.

"We'll have you' lads warmed up in no time," she said as she hurried off to the kitchen.

"Now, lads, let me continue our discussion we were having. As you saw posted outside, Congress wants to raise two battalions of Marines. They have already started assembling a small fleet. You remember the old *Black Prince*? She is now being refitted as the flagship *Alfred*. Three others are being converted into the *Columbus*, *Cabot* and *Andrew Doria*. They have authorized four more but haven't gotten them yet." He paused as Peg came back with three large steaming mugs of rum.

"Now I am not going to sit idly by and not get involved. As a matter of fact, I have put in for a commission in the Marines, and expect to receive it any day now. I have had some experience at sea, and with connections, should be able to get commissioned. How about joining in with me? Sean, with your militia training, you would be a perfect officer."

"I don't know, Sam," Sean said after taking a drink of the hot brew. "I ha' no' made up my mind yet as to just what to do. We were discussing it earlier when you came along at the wharf. What do you think, Thomas?" he asked his brother.

"Father has given his blessing on whatever we decide. I don't feel comfortable though in making a move until we see if he is going to recover or go under. I should know where I stand in a few more days," Thomas offered.

"Just think, Thomas, you a Naval Captain in command of the *Osprey*, ship of war, with your brother Sean as your Lieutenant of Marines by your side! The British will run from the seas when you two are unleashed on them!" Sam joked.

"Aye, that they will, we would get this business over within the year!" boasted Sean. They all laughed at their antics as Peg's helper came out and put three platters of food, all piled high, in front of them.

The three joked all through dinner. Sean observed their friend. He was older than both of them, thirty-one by his own admission. Quaker by birth, his father had been a successful blacksmith and had helped his wife to open a tavern when her child rearing was done. Sam was well educated, as were they. He had spent a few years at sea, and had always been an adventurer. He had come back to town to help his mother run their prosperous tavern, where he had made many influential friends. Nicholas was well known to the gentry of the area, as he had extended his influence into the fishing and fox hunting clubs that they belonged to. As the evening wore on, Sean thought that he would end up signing on with him.

"Excuse me, gentlemen," an older man in his forties interrupted them from the next table. He was with his wife, a young woman and small child. "I could not help but overhear you talking about the formation of Marines, and I would like to offer my services. I am Sergeant Major Angus Lanigan, late of His Majesty's Marines."

"Well, Sergeant Major, won't you join us for a bit?" offered Sam. "We'll have another round of rum here," he called to Peg. The four men made their introductions as the older man sat at their table. It was obvious that he was used to being in command as he addressed them, ramrod straight back, and very proper manners.

"I was in His Majesty's Marines, nigh onto twenty-eight years when I resigned. See that little boy at our table? That is my grandson, my only son's child. I left the service after he had been killed by a press gang that had burst into his house. Late one night, they came into our town while I was out to sea. My son was pummeled by the press gang when they broke his door down, and right before the eyes of his wife and child, you see her sitting there with my wife, struck him severely about the head, and killed him. With not so much as a 'by your leave,' they roughed her up and left. When I got home the following month, I resigned, packed up the three of them and came to this new land. Been doing carpentry work ever since the last two years. I will no' support a government that does such things to its own people," the older man offered his story.

"I'm sorry for your loss. These two lads have a similar story with what happened to their father," Sam stated.

"Aye, I heard of Captain Taggert's attack. I have done some work for him these past two years, and know him to be a good man. You lads have my sympathies. My offer stands. I ha' talked it over with my wife, and she agrees. It is time to put an end to the abuse. So when you get your commission and start recruiting, count me in."

The four men talked well into the night, talking politics and telling sea stories. By the time Peg and her helpers were ready to close the tavern for the night, they had become fast friends.

Two days later, William Taggert passed on during the night. The family and friends gathered at the house early in the day, then went to their Presbyterian church for a final service. The church was packed with family, friends and the crew of the *Osprey* with their families. Along the walls of the church hung the portraits of other ship captains who had died. Taggert's now hung among them, with a black shroud draped across the frame. The picture had just been finished the previous year, and had hung in the great hallway of their house.

After the service, the crowd moved out and across the street to the small cemetery, where the coffin was lowered into the freshly dug grave. Sean, Thomas, James and their two younger brothers and one sister crowded around their mother as the coffin was lowered.

As the minister said a few last words, Sean noticed a group of four men standing at the entranceway of the graveyard. They all wore dark overcoats to ward off the bitter, cold wind; however, they appeared to be military from their bearing. The mourners all filed past the family, dropping in handfuls of dirt, paying their respects. Sean nodded to Thomas to look at the strangers.

"Do you know them?" Thomas asked.

"They're too far to see for sure, but there is something familiar about them," Sean responded as he saw their one quartermaster, James Cameron, walk over and address them. Sean saw a glimpse of red as the man in front brought his arm from beneath his greatcoat to doff his hat. It appeared that Cameron was having a terse discussion with the man.

Cameron glanced over and saw Sean looking over at him. He beckoned him and walked towards the crowd where Sean was standing. Sean broke loose from the line of mourners and met up with Cameron halfway to the gate.

"What's afoot James?" he asked.

"Mr. Taggert, sir, them's the Lobsterback Marines from the ship what killed your father! They came to pay their respects and to talk to you," he replied angrily.

"They have a lot of nerve coming here on this day!" Sean said. Before he could take a step, someone grabbed his arm; it was his brother Thomas.

"Easy Sean, this is not the time nor place for a disturbance. Remember it was the Marine Lieutenant that helped us get away. Let's calm down and go talk to him." Thomas urged his brother.

"You are right, he did that. I'm all right, you can let go of my arm," Sean said, regaining his composure. The two walked over to the waiting group, followed by Sam Nicholas and the men of the *Osprey*, who one by one got wind of who the strangers were. They left their families and gathered behind the Taggert brothers as they met up with the four over coated strangers.

"What do you want here, haven't your kind done enough to us?" Sean said as calmly as he could. He glanced over his shoulder and saw that most of the crew were now behind him. He gazed across the faces of the four men in front of them, all of whom apparently were not fazed at facing such a large gathering.

"Gentlemen, on behalf of myself and the crew of the *Huntress,* let me express our deep feelings of regret for your loss. We were dispatched to come here after we arrived in New York to find that you had turned south to your homeport," Lieutenant Hawkins offered.

"I accept your statement out of having been brought up with good manners, yet I strongly recommend to you to turn away from here and leave as fast as you can. There arc a lot of people in this town that would not appreciate your gesture of kindness. You gave us a chance to escape that day, and I am giving you that same chance in return. Leave here and do not return," Thomas advised. There was a murmur of assent from the crewmen, many of who would just as soon pummel the four men senseless.

"I accept your response and advice. We will be taking leave of you. Not everyone on board our ship is as hateful as Lieutenant Jennings. I am in no way going to speak on his behalf, nor defense. He was wrong in what he did. If it is of any consolation, when we got into New York, our captain had him removed from the ship and turned over to the admiral's staff. The captain wanted you to know this. My orders from the admiral, however, were to arrest your father for his assault on a King's officer so that protocol was protected. However, in light of his death, there is no further reason for us to be here," Hawkins explained.

"Tell me, if you had found that he was not dead, would you have carried out your orders?" Sean asked.

Hawkins stepped closer to Sean. "Funny thing is that I could swear that I saw your ship setting sail out of the harbor when I got here. I hand picked these men knowing that they would see the same thing as I did."

"Thank you for that. So what is to become of that bastard that killed our father?" Sean asked.

"I would like to tell you that he was drummed out of the Navy. As it is, he is from a very influential family to whom the admiral owes some debt. No, instead of getting punished, he was given command of the twelve-gun brigantine, the *Charon*. Aptly named for one such as he. He has been given the task of searching out privateers and smugglers, so be on the watch for him," Hawkins informed them.

"Thank you for your kindness. Now it would go better for you if you leave now before you are spotted in those red uniforms," Thomas urged.

"That we will. I say, is that not Angus Lanigan coming through the crowd there? We served together several years. Sergeant Major Lanigan, it is so good to see you after all these years!" Hawkins exclaimed, holding out his hand as the older man passed through the men gathered there.

"Aye, I thought it was you, young Lieutenant Hawkins! It is a pleasure to see you again also. It has been what-about three years now? I can remember when you were just a fresh faced, no-shaving ensign. You appear to have done well and heeded all my advice." Lanigan responded.

"I heard that you had come to America with your family. It was a damned shame about your son, Angus; I understand why you resigned after that. So what are ye doing with yourself these days?"

"I have been doing carpentry work, and helping the wife raise our grandchild. I'm afraid that the next time we meet, though, that we will be on opposite sides of the argument. I am going to be adding my experience to the folks seeking freedom from the Crown. How about it, ye have more good in ye to keep in the King's service. Why don't you lads stay and join in with us?" Angus asked his old friend.

"No, Angus, I cannot do that. My family would disown me were I to do that. I am torn between duty to the King and to what should be the right thing to do some times. You know that though, from our conversations that we used to have. I wish that I could stay and catch up on old times with you, Angus, but it appears we have drawn too much attention to us. We must take leave of you. Gentlemen, good evening to you all. We will take advantage of the darkness coming on to get out of town." With that said, Hawkins saluted the men and spun on his heel. His men fell in behind him, and together they walked down the street to where their closed carriage awaited them.

"Not a bad sort for a bloody Bullock!" one of *Osprey's* crewmen said.

"Sirs, the crew wanted me to talk to you now that your father has passed on. We know that you are not going to try to stay out of the coming fight, and well sir, we are all in with you, every man-jack of us!" Cameron stated to Sean and Thomas.

"Thank you, James, thank all of you men. I know Father respected you men and looked at you as being part of his family, each and every one of you. Yes, Sean and I have been talking about what to do. It is impossible for us not to take sides in this conflict, and it is no secret anymore that we will not side with the Crown. We intend to enlist the services of the *Osprey* in the Continental Navy. Sean is pondering whether he wants to go as second in command, or as being an officer in the Marines. We will all meet tomorrow at the warehouse to discuss this further. Now it is getting too cold out here to continue this discussion, so take your families home, and meet with us after the noon meal tomorrow. Good night to you all," Thomas spoke to the crew.

The men wandered off into the darkening evening, as the Taggerts gathered up the family and headed back to their home. Once there, the elder Taggerts sat in the parlor with their mother, while the other members of the household prepared dinner.

"Mother, we know what a bad time this is for this, but we need to address this now. We spoke with Father a few days back, and he gave his blessing on what choices we were to make. Time has come for us to take up arms in this conflict. We have talked it over in great length and have decided to take the *Osprey* and join the Continental Navy. We have spoken to the crew today and will firm things up with them tomorrow. We wanted to tell you of this now before your heard it from someone else," Thomas apprised the matriarch of the family.

"My sons, I knew that you would be doing this before you did. I ca' no' say I am happy with this, but I know it is in the Taggert blood. Nothing could stop your father from going off and fighting in the last war with the French, and I am wise enough to know that nothing I can say to you would stop you from joining in this war." She paused while Sean and Thomas looked down at their feet.

"I trust that you lads will look out for each other and use good judgment. I know that your father taught you enough to expect that of you. Now come give me a hug, and let's go in and join the others. We should all be together this night, as there will be precious few other nights that we will be." She stood up when she finished talking. All three of her sons embraced her. They all went into the dinning room where the rest of the family had gathered.

The Taggerts and their relatives spent the evening reminiscing about the past and musing about the future. It was near midnight when they all left to go home. Scan went to his room to go to bed. He placed his candle on the table next to his bed, and stirred up the fire in the fireplace. It had grown cold outside, and the windows were frosting up. He expected that it would snow tonight, judging by the clouds that hovered over the town.

After undressing, he pulled back the covers and climbed into bed. It was always good to be home and sleep in a real bed, not just a pallet in his cramped cabin on board the *Osprey*. He did miss the motion of the ship though, and always found it a little difficult to get to sleep the first few nights ashore.

He watched as the flickering fire cast strange shapes of light across the ceiling as he lay there. So much had happened the past few weeks. He had prepared himself for the possibility of his father dying from the moment that he had first bandaged him up. Even so, he could not have imagined the great feeling of loss that he now felt.

He tried to block it out as he thought of what he must do in the next few days. They would have to see to loading victuals on board the *Osprey* for her upcoming voyage. Until they signed her on, they would not know what lie ahead of them. He had decided to talk to Sam again about being a Marine. It was a natural choice, as he was accomplished in the art of being a soldier as well as being a sailor. There was so much to consider, so many decisions to be made. It was well into the night before he finally drifted off to sleep.

The next day after breakfast, he and his brothers went to their warehouse to check on any deliveries. They found none, and quickly went inside out of the cold wind coming off the river. Inside, James built a fire in the pot-bellied stove, another of Dr. Franklin's inventions. It radiated heat all through the office. They busied themselves with the amount of freight that they still had in the warehouse unclaimed. It was time to try and auction some of it off so that they could get good currency for it while there was still plenty to be had.

"We have so much here. Look at all this-cloth, harnesses, plows; it is amazing how fast this accumulates, and such a variety of things. Oh, and let's not forget about this shipment of cannons and shot for the British in New York. I say we give it back to them one cannonball at a time," Sean stated as he looked at the powerful-looking twelve-pounders that they had taken on as a shipment from Jamaica for the army in New York.

"I agree. We will not waste our time trying to find another ship to take this shipment to New York for us. As of now, I declare them unclaimed freight. As a matter of fact, I was thinking last night, we should add them to *Osprey*, to give her more bite," Thomas added.

"I don't know about that, brother. She only has four-pounders now, do you think her timbers are strong enough to support them?" Sean asked.

"I'll have the carpenters look things over, but I think she'll be able to handle them. Also I think we should close in the railing from the bow to the entry port. It is closed in from there back, and I think that we should do that, to give added protection to the crew in any fighting that we do, plus it will also give us the opportunity to place an extra gun or two forward," Thomas said as he pointed out the window at the *Osprey*.

The morning slipped away as they worked. The crewmen started to show up individually, or in small groups. They all pitched in on the tasks necessary to prepare the ship for sea. They were not to have their meeting until after the noon meal, so a little before noon, Sean left to get something to eat, as his brothers were not hungry.

He rode his horse up the street and made his way to Market Street to find his friend Sam at his tavern.

He tied the horse off at the front, and entered the raucous Conestogoe Wagon Tavern. As he entered, he gazed around the room, trying to locate Sam. In the corner surrounded by several men drinking ale, he saw him, talking boisterously to his companions.

"Sean, Sean, come over here, look what I have!" he called out to Sean as his eyes were finally accustomed to the light in the place.

"Make way, lads, let young Mister Taggert through here. Sean, I have it. I have my commission as Captain of Marines, signed here by John Hancock himself this very morning!" Sam beamed at his friend.

"That's wonderful! Let me be one of your first enlistees!" Sean responded.

He made his way to Sam and took the paper from his hand. He read the commission order and remarked about the size of John Hancock's signature.

The two sat and talked for a few minutes before Sean's platter of food was put in front of him.

"I'll want to take a couple of dinners along for my brothers. I know that by the time I get back, they'll be hungry. Now, Sam, I was not jesting, I do want to join you. Thomas is having a meeting with the Naval Committee and will offer the services of the *Osprey*."

"Sean, I accept your offer, but I will want you as a lieutenant, not as an enlisted man. You have too much knowledge of military affairs and training to waste as anything but an officer. I have a few others ready to sign up also. I have been trying to talk Robert Mullan into joining, and he is interested, but right now he has some health problems, and needs to take care of family business before he is ready too. Maybe by spring he will be ready. Now I want to pair you up with Lanigan as your sergeant. The two of you will be very useful in training the men." Nicholas paused long enough to wave to some more people who had just come in the door.

"Sean, we will start recruiting tomorrow. I have a couple of young lads who can play the drum and fife, to go through the city with us to round up some likely lads. How many of your crew will be wanting to be marines instead of sailors?"

"There will be a few, I'm sure. Some of the lads have had some training already. What about muskets, powder shot and uniforms?" Sean asked.

"Pitifully few and far between. We have some weapons promised, powder is woefully in short supply, and uniforms--whatever they have on their backs. We had discussed making them green and buff, cut along the lines of the Continental Army; however, material is in short supply."

"Maybe not. We have several thousand yards of cloth at the warehouse, and if I remember correctly, there was some green and brown among the lot. I'll make sure when I get back. We have several muskets, pistols, and cutlasses on board the ship, maybe enough for twenty men," Sean offered.

"Good, at least we can arm and dress the men for your ship. Listen, before you go, I want you to sign the muster roll here, and I'll draw up your commission papers. Sean, as of this moment, you are Lieutenant Taggert of the Continental Marines!" Sam clapped him on the back, causing him to choke on his food.

The two talked for a while longer, giving each other ideas for forming the two battalions that were called for. At this moment, Nicholas was to be in charge. When Sean was finished eating, he took his leave of the gathering, and with his brothers' food, returned to the warehouse. Most of the crew was present and busy on board the ship.

"I brought you and Thomas some lunch. Where is he?" he asked James.

"Right after you left he went down to meet with the Naval Committee. He expected to be back any time now," James relayed as he opened the package of food and drew in a deep whiff of the aroma of the beefsteak dinner. He took it to his desk, sat down and started to devour it.

"I thought that you were not hungry?" Sean chided him.

"I wasn't, at least not until I smelled this as you came in the door," James said in between bites.

Just then, Thomas came through the doorway, shivering from the cold. "Well, I have done it. I talked with the Naval Committee, and the *Osprey* is now officially part of the Continental Navy, and I am now a Captain in that Navy!" he beamed with pride.

"Congratulations Captain, I am now Lieutenant in the Continental Marines!" Sean shot back. "I signed up at lunch with Sam Nicholas. He is to be in charge of putting together the two battalions. From what I gather, there is a special purpose for the Marines as soon as he gets them formed, but he will not say what it is."

"I won't know what is in store for the ship yet. They want to come over and inspect it. From what they told me, the *Osprey* is more ready for sea than any of the other vessels they have so far, so we might get sent right out on patrol. I expect them to be here later this afternoon," Thomas reported as he tore into the dinner that Sean had brought him.

"I suppose that as soon as you two get done eating, we better bring the men in and break the news to them," Sean suggested.

The door opened and Joseph Sinclair, one of the quartermasters, came into the office. "Pardon, sirs," he said as he knuckled his forehead in salute, "but you wanted me to let you know when all the men had shown up. The last two just came up now."

"Thanks, Joseph, why don't you have them muster in the warehouse where we'll all be out of the wind; we have a lot to talk about. Plato has been warming up the rum, so there should be plenty to take the chill off," Thomas instructed.

"Aye, sir, the lads sure will appreciate that!" he said with a smile, and scurried out the door. The crewmen started filing through the door into the warehouse, as Thomas finished his meal. They lined up to get their steaming mugs of hot buttered rum and found crates, barrels or packages to sit on as they waited for the three Taggerts to come out.

As soon as they saw that the men were situated, Thomas glanced over to Sean, and said, "Well Lieutenant, let's go recruit some sailors and marines!"

"Aye, aye, Captain!" Sean replied with a smirk and saluted his brother. The two walked out and gladly accepted hot mugs from Plato. They took a few sips, then Thomas raised his mug high and said, "Men of the *Osprey*, let us drink a toast to Freedom!"

He could not have chosen his words better. Each man came to his feet, raised his mug, and cheered. "'Ere's to the *Osprey*!" came a shout from the back of the group, followed by many voices chiming in to that toast.

"Down with King George!" came another toast. That was followed by a chorus of cheers, hoots and hollers. Thomas let the men settle back down before speaking.

"Many of you have expressed your feelings on the subject of the Rebellion. Many of you have very good reasons to want to join in the fray. Many of you have known the hardships imposed by an aristocracy which has gotten out of control with its greed and contempt for its subjects. Many of you are ready to be a part of the change that is coming. My brothers and I have talked in great length, not just because of our father's death, but what the government has been doing to we colonials. They have ignored their own laws long enough. They have overtaxed us long enough. They have abused us on the seas long enough. They have tried to force the products and goods of England on us by the use of force, long enough." He paused while he looked around at the rough-hewn, weather-beaten faces of his men.

"For these reasons, we have decided to join the colonial forces in opposition to the Crown! This very day, I have enlisted my services, and the services of the *Osprey,* in the Continental Navy. Sean has enlisted in the Continental Marines as an officer. Together we will help throw the Lobsterbacks from our shores. None of you men are obligated to join us, and no one will cast disparaging looks on anyone who does not want to join in," He paused to let his words sink in.

"There is a new kind of nation that will be born out of this turmoil, one where everyone can have his own opinion and not be afraid of being jailed or driven away because of it. Any of you men that want to join us, let us know. Some of you may want to continue to serve as sailors; some of you may want to serve as marines. Whatever you decide, we will appreciate your service for the cause of Freedom."

Sean stepped forward and addressed the men, "All of you men, whether you have been with us for years, or for a few months, have all served us well, and we know you to be of good character. There is no one among you that we would not want to serve with us. Take your time now, and think this over. This is a serious choice to make. If you join us, you will become enemies to the Crown--that carries a heavy consequence. Think this through for your own sake, for the sakes of your families. Give us your answer by tomorrow morning, as we will have to get all that join us signed up." Sean stopped as the door to the warehouse opened, and a blue-uniformed officer stepped in out of the cold.

"Good day, gentlemen, Thomas. For those of you who do not know me, I am Captain Josiah Wilkins of the Continental Navy, here to inspect your ship. From what I have seen walking by her, she seems fit enough. I also must admit, I was listening to you gentlemen outside, and I say bravo to you. Bravo to all you men who take up the cause. We have the opportunity to forge a new nation here by our actions. This is something that does not happen often in history; so do not take this lightly, gentlemen. This is a momentous time in the history of the world. Colonial men have already shocked the Lobsterbacks by the way they have stood and fought them. This should have shown the King that we mean business and will not be trampled on!" he beamed as the men applauded him.

"You lads take your time now and talk things over between yourselves while I take the captain on board and show him the ship." Thomas instructed them. "Come now, Captain Wilkins, let's go inspect the *Osprey*. I know that you know my brother Sean?"

"Aye, that I do, we got acquainted at your father's funeral, God rest his soul," he said as he shook Sean's hand. Together the three walked out the door and over to the gangplank.

"She's a trim looking craft," Wilkins said as he stepped onto the deck. "How's the rigging?"

"The cordage is in good shape. The lads replaced the last of the frayed lines yesterday. After that storm we ran through, we had some that wore awfully thin," Sean replied.

They followed Wilkins as he walked first to the bow, and then to the stern, stopping to examine everything along the way, lashing here, ringbolt there. He gazed up at the set of the yardarms and tugged on a line, looking at every knot and coil of rope.

"How's the hull? Got much weed growing on her bottom? A couple of the ships we have procured have up to ten feet of the stuff. That's enough to slow a good ship down to a crawl in a good wind," Wilkins queried.

"We had it cleaned last year. It is no more than a foot or so long. I had a work party using pole scrapers working on the sides below the water line. Since the hold is near empty, she is riding high enough in the water to clean off quite a bit. Tomorrow we'll warp her out and turn her around so that we can get to the other side," Thomas answered.

"Four-pounders, eh? Not much bite to her," Wilkins observed.

"Ah, that is about to be remedied," Sean interrupted. "We took on a shipment in Jamaica for the Lobsterbacks in New York, six twelve-pounders. We have inspected the timbers, and it is the opinion of the carpenter that they are strong enough to bear up under them. We are going to replace the four-pounders with them, and move them forward. The carpenter is completing plans to close in the railings for more protection."

"That should work. These timbers look strong enough for those guns. Also I will trade out these four-pounders for four nine-pounders. We have a sloop that these four–pounders would be good for. I'll have them brought over tomorrow. How are you set for powder and shot?" asked Wilkins.

"We have plenty of shot; however, we are a little short of powder. We used a bit too much last trip out fighting off some pirates off of Jamaica. We have almost enough small arms to arm the crew," Sean added.

"Well, powder is a bit of a problem, everyone is short of it, which brings me to what we have in mind for you now that I have seen your vessel. It is by far in the best shape of all of ours so far, and I want you to get under way as soon as is practical to seek out and take whatever British shipping that you can. It will be a couple of months before we can assemble the fleet in good enough shape to venture out, so any intelligence and supplies that you can provide will be put to good use. And this is all hush-hush," advised the fleet captain.

"It should take us a couple of weeks to get prepared. Sean is going to be recruiting marines, and I'll have to replace any of the crew that want to join him."

"I'll talk to Nicholas to try to get Sean his share of recruits as fast as possible, so that you can take them with you. It will do the lads good to get some experience right away."

They walked back into the main cabin where the older man sat down at the captain's desk. Thomas and Sean sat in the high-back padded chairs. "Lads, there is not much in the way of supplies that I can promise you. We are short of everything. I see that you have your men in uniforms; I know your father was a stickler about that, so that takes care of that. I can authorize you as much victuals as you need. Canvas and cordage, try to get what you can. I'll try to get you vouchers for that," Wilkins offered.

The three conversed for two hours, and when they returned to the warehouse, quartermaster Sinclair addressed them. "Sir, we has all decided, we are with you. The lads are willing to go anywhere you two say to go. Some of the lads do want to be marines. They'll be getting' with you, sir." He said to Sean.

"Thank you, men, one and all! When you finish this cask of rum, you can go home for the day. Be back here in the morning at sunrise. Those of you who are going to sign up with Sean, see him on your way out," Thomas announced to the men.

"Good show, men! Now I'll have a drink with you before I go," Wilkins exclaimed as he took up an empty mug, filled it and drank down a healthy amount. When he was done, he took his leave of the group. Thomas and Sean joined with the men as they chattered excitedly about what they had decided on.

'Sirs, there is one other matter at hand that we want to discuss with you. It's Johnson sir. We took a vote and we want him to stay in port. You see, sirs, me and a few of the others were orphans, and we'd hate to see his little one grow up without parents. Now that 'is sister and little one 'as arrived, thanks to your father, 'e should stay ashore and raise the child. 'E's a good man and we all like 'im, so we want to see 'im and his baby safe and sound," Sinclair pleaded.

"Thomas, I think our crew is getting soft!" Sean laughed. "You men have done a very kind thing here for your messmate. I ca' no' see why we should no' take your advice. 'Tis settled, Mr. Johnson, you are now part of our shore staff. You can help James run the business here."

"Thank ye, sirs, oh thank ye so much. I, I … " He could say no more, as he broke down in tears and sobbed.

"Sean patted him on the back and announced, "All right, you men that want to be marines, stay for a few minutes, and the rest of you can go home."

One by one and in small groups they tapered off for the evening. They could be heard joking and singing as they walked down the wharf towards their homes or taverns. Sean looked at the group that had gathered before him.

"Plato, if you would be so kind as to list the men as I call them off." Sean looked to Plato who came out of the office with fresh paper quill and ink. He set them down on a crate just the right height to write on.

"Joseph Sinclair, David Beckett, Edward George. Edward, as a Delaware, you do not have to fight in this," Sean said

"I have come to see the sea. You brought me here so that I could see what the sea was and what lay beyond. What you do in this fight, I understand. It is a good thing. I will help you do this," came the reply. Several of the men complimented him and clapped him on the back.

"Excellent! Let's see who's next. Julius Caesar Jones, Anthony Monacelli, Jose Martin Rodrigues, Herman Baum, Peter Svenson, and Peter Jarmolowski. You men have chosen to be marines, and I thank you. I will be recruiting some more. We decided on about twenty-five altogether. Joseph and David, since you two have had experience in leading men you will be corporals. We will have the benefit of having Sergeant Lanigan, formerly of the Royal Marines, with us. He will aid in training and giving us the benefit of his experience."

"Will we be having uniforms, sir?" asked Beckett.

"There are none yet; however, we have all that cloth over there to make some. Those with wives, ask them if they can get together to make us some. I'll have Mother get the ladies at church to lend a hand. We'll have them made to resemble the army uniforms, only in green. If there are no more questions, we'll meet here in the morning. Good night to you, Marines."

The men took their leave and left the warehouse. It had grown cold inside after the men left, so Sean, Thomas, Plato and James retreated into the warmer office. "I'll work on reorganizing the crew and filling the gaps tomorrow," Thomas said.

"It should not be difficult to replace the officers. We have good men who can take over the vacant positions. I'll get my men busy first thing tomorrow, as soon as they arrive, removing the cannons and placing the new ones. I'll leave Sinclair in charge of that while I go with Sam and do some recruiting," Sean replied.

"We have a lot to get accomplished in the next week or so. I want to replace as much of the canvas as we can find replacements for. There is enough for at least half the sails here, and I'll try to find enough for the rest. I'll have Pratt work on getting the food stores replenished and brought on board. That should take the rest of the week at least, what with the militia and army hoarding as much as they can get." Thomas said.

"Yes, they have. I will have to try and see if Sam will be able to get us proper muskets and bayonets for my men. The muskets we have on board, I would rather not have to use them if we can get newer ones," Sean replied.

The two spent the next few hours discussing which crewmen should be promoted and what supplies they should need to procure. It was well after dark when they were finished. The brothers climbed into their carriage and headed home. Over dinner they discussed the day's events with their mother. She agreed to get the ladies of the church to make uniforms for Sean's men.

"You get a uniform from your friend that you want us to copy, and we should be able to turn them out in a few days. We can do the work right here in the house. All we'll need from you is to let us get the measurements of the men, and have the cloth brought up here," she instructed.

"Thank you, Mother. It will be good for you to have something to keep you occupied with, and have your friends around for a few days. The men will appreciate having the uniforms," Sean assured his mother.

The next morning, after Sean had gotten his men working on removing the small cannons, he headed over to Sam's tavern. There he found his friend dressed out in a handsome green and buff uniform.

"Do you like it, Sean?" he asked.

"Aye, it is good. You make a very dashing figure in that uniform. I have arranged to have some made for my men. Here's a list of the men who I recruited from the crew," he said as he handed the paper that he pulled from his pocket. Sam took it from him, looked it over and handed it to his assistant, who promptly listed the names on it onto another muster list.

"That is a good start. We'll go around today and try to enlist some more stout fellows for you. The Naval Committee has informed me that they want you fully manned and ready for sea within two weeks. Sergeant Lanigan will be here shortly; he already went out for a bit right before you got here. We'll get you a uniform for your folks to copy for your men. Now if you would, take this bundle and go upstairs. This is a spare that I had made. You can use it until yours are ready. You see, as soon as I applied for a commission, I had my tailor make me a couple of uniforms. I knew that I would be commissioned, and wanted to be ready as soon as that happened," he smiled at Sean.

Sean took the proffered bundle wrapped in paper and tied with twine upstairs and found an empty room. He shed his clothes and dressed in the buff-colored trousers, white shirt, and vest. He then donned the green frock. There was a mirror on the wall, and he stood before it, to straighten the neck cloth. The figure in the mirror was impressive. He immediately liked the green more than the army blue.

Sean gathered his clothes and bundled them up into the paper wrapping. Back downstairs, he was applauded by Sam and some of the others lounging in the tavern.

"Now that is one sharp-looking lad!" exclaimed a waitress. Sean blushed at the attention that he got from the people in the room.

"Now, Sean, let's get down to business. As we decided, you should have at least twenty-five men with you. That will be a bit much for the size vessel that you have, However, I want you to get these men trained and experienced so that if we have to dole them out to other ships, they will at least know their jobs. I suggest that you do as in the Royal Navy; your men can be in charge of the mizzenmast. That will be their shipboard duty above their duties as marines. Lanigan can help you train them. Get them plenty of target practice; many of them will not know how to fire a weapon. You can do this while under way. While ashore, get them used to drilling. You know how to drill them after your time in the militia. I want you to produce a top-notch detachment, is that understood?"

"Aye, that it is." He recognized the seriousness in

his friend's tone. It was a side of him that he had not known until now. He was grateful that Sam knew how to take command. The two discussed many particulars before Lanigan got back. He came through the door with a small lad that had a drum strapped over his shoulder, and another carrying a fife. Behind him came three men.

"Good morning, sirs!" he said as he stopped at the table and saluted his officers. He was bundled up in his old ship's coat, uniform trousers and boots.

"Good morning, Sergeant, I see that you have brought in some lost sheep with you." Sam replied as he returned the salute.

"Aye, that I did, sir, and good stout lads they are at that too. I gathered them up coming out of the brothel right down the street a bit. Do you know that once I told them that King George was going to tax their favorite establishment, they just naturally wanted to sign right up!" beamed the older man.

"Sergeant, I'm not sure that is one of the things that is to be taxed," whispered Sean.

"Not that it has been announced yet, sir, but I know it will probably get around to that." He winked as he responded. "Now let me introduce to you our new recruits. This young man is Ben Tyree, a seaman. Next we have Ethan Thomas, and Obadiah Potts, both also late of the sea."

Sean and Sam looked the men over. All were in their early twenties, about five-feet-six, and by their weather-beaten faces, it was plain that they were sailors. Their hands were rough and calloused from fighting canvas in wind and rain. They all had an air of confidence about them.

"Welcome to the Marines, gentlemen! I am Captain Nicholas and this is Lieutenant Taggert of the *Osprey*. The lieutenant will be your commanding officer. Now, what experience do you men have?"

"We all ha' been at sea for five-six years, sir. All in merchant ships, never any navy ships. We all have had run-ins with pirates, so's we all know how to fight. Me and Ethan have worked the cannons too," replied Potts.

"Good, good, now you men get yourselves a good meal, then get on over to the Taggert wharf and help prepare the ship for sea. We will be over later in the day, as soon as we gather up some more men," Nicholas ordered.

The three sat at a bench close to the hearth to warm up. They were served a good breakfast which they eagerly devoured. Once they were finished, they left to get their gear from their lodgings and report to the *Osprey*.

"Now, gentlemen, let us brave the cold and go get some more lads like those to enlist," Sam announced as he stood up.

The three men, along with the drummer and fifer, went out into the street and paraded along the streets that sported most of the public houses and taverns. The two lads kept up a spirited string of tunes as they went along. Several people stopped them along the way to ask which army, militia, or ship that they were recruiting for, as this had become a common thing in Philadelphia of late.

One such person to stop them was the notable Dr. Benjamin Franklin. "Good morning to you, gentlemen. How are you doing this cold day?" he asked.

"Dr. Franklin, let me introduce my companions here," Sam replied. "This is my lieutenant, Sean Taggert, and his sergeant, Angus Lanigan, retired from His Majesty's Marines. As you know, we are attempting to raise two battalions of them."

"Yes, I heard of your appointment, Captain Nicholas. It is good to see you in uniform. I have always imagined you to be the adventurous sort from our conversations. Now if you are trying to stay within your mandate of enlisting only men with a seafaring background, you may come up very short on your muster rolls. Since the Naval Committee purchased ships, the town has been getting drained of all men of that sort. You may want to try to enlist those who are, shall we say, not so experienced in seafaring matters. Your best bet may be over in Germantown. It seems there are plenty of stout fellows over there. I must say I like the painting on that drum; it matches that flag I have seen so many of. The coiled rattlesnake, and 'Don't Tread On Me.' That is very appropriate. Well, good luck to you, gentlemen, our cause is just," Franklin said as he turned and walked on.

"He is an odd sort." Sean said as he watched the older man walk away. "I've heard so much about him but have never met him before. He has an incredible mind with all the useful inventions and ideas he comes up with. As busy as he is, it's a wonder that he has any time at all to think things up."

"He is that, but he is also right about trying to latch onto sailor men to fill our ranks. Let's head on over to Germantown and see how we can do," Nicholas commented.

The little procession continued on its way. As they approached the tavern called the Hoffbrau Haus, the door flung open, and a man came tumbling out into the street in front of them. Without saying a word, he jumped to his feet and charged back into the tavern, dragged out another man who was clearly twice his size, hauled back and drove his fist into the man's belly, then gave him an uppercut as he doubled over. The big man collapsed in front of his antagonist.

"I think we have found just the sort of fellows that we are looking for!" smiled Lanigan as he approached the two.

The big man got to his feet unsteadily as he looked down at his friend and mumbled something to him. The little man looked up and said, "Never say anything like that to her again!"

"Good morning, gentlemen," Lanigan addressed them. "I see that you two like a little action, do you now? We are in search of men like you who can fight, and like action; would that be you now?"

"Dat depends, who are you and vat do you vant?" The little man asked as he brushed dirt off his clothes from his earlier tumble.

"I am Sergeant Lanigan, and these are Captain Nicholas and Lieutenant Taggert of the American Marines, and we are recruiting men to fill the ranks with good men as yourselves," he said as he shook their hands.

"I am Johannes Heinrich, and dis is mein friend Rudolph Hauser. So you are looking for marines, neither of us have any experience on boats." He said as all the men shook hands all around.

"Ah, laddie, let me tell you, there is no need for any seafaring background. We'll teach you everything you need to know. Oh, and do be careful about calling them boats, the sailors get a little upset at that. Call them ships or you may be in for a fight."

"We have been thinking of enlisting for some excitement. I'm not much for getting all muddy marching around in circles."

"That's the beauty of being a marine! You'll be on board ship, no mud! We stay on board, and we fight on board. The only time we go ashore is to visit some exotic port and get to know the pretty, brown-skinned lassies there!" Lanigan continued, turning his head long enough to wink at his companions.

"No mud? Do ve get uniforms like dey have?" he said as he pointed at Sam and Sean.

"That's roight, no mud, and you will be fitted out with uniforms just like them. Tell me, just what do you two do?"

"I'm a jeweler, I verk in mien fadder's store. Rudolph here is a baker. Ve both are bored midt our lives and vant someding different for a while," he replied as his friend nodded in agreement.

"Well, laddies, come inside with us, and we'll buy you a beer or two," Lanigan said as he put his arms around their shoulders and guided them inside.

"The old man sure is a silver-tongued devil. I wouldn't be surprised if he gets everyone in that tavern signed up!" Sean said as he and Sam looked at each other and went inside. Once inside, Lanigan was in his prime, telling sea tales of his service on the sea. The beer kept flowing as he talked to the men. Three hours and several large pitchers of beer later, the marines staggered out of the tavern, with the two recruits and four others. Together they marched back to the Conestogoe Wagon Tavern, where they signed up the men.

"You men get your affairs in order, bring your gear and be down at the Taggert wharf first thing in the morning," Sean told them as they finished their meal. Once they acknowledged their instructions, the new men left the tavern.

"Remind me never to do this in the morning again! It is way too early in the day to drink that much beer! Too bad fighting the war isn't like recruiting, it would be so much more fun and civilized!" Sam mused as he drank down some hot chicory tea. "I sure hope we can get things settled and start getting regular tea again. This is not bad, but it just is not like the good old tea we used to get."

"That is all the more reason to get into the fray and bring it to a quick end. With lads as the ones we have gathered up, we should do all right," Sean observed. He, too, was feeling the effects of the German beer that they had swilled in the name of Freedom earlier.

"Sergeant Lanigan, I have to say that you if you fight half as good as you tell stories, this war will be over before we know it," Nicholas said to his sergeant.

"Ah, sir, you get the knack of knowing what to say to the lads after you observe them a moment or two. Those first two lads had too much time on their hands and were bored. Give them a challenge and they will see it to the end. The others, each had a weakness that I worked on. 'Tis much better than using the press gang methods."

"Aye, that it is. Now why don't we go out one more time this afternoon, and this time we will rally them over by Tun Tavern. Robert was keeping an eye out for likely subjects for me."

The men spent the rest of the afternoon recruiting and signing the new men up at Tun Tavern, and by sundown had signed on fourteen new men. As they were leaving the tavern with the recruits, they saw a young man running towards them.

"Slow down there, my good man, you near run us down! Now what's afoot that you are running as if the devil 'imself is after you?" Lanigan barked at him as he caught him by the shoulders.

"The devil is after me, and 'e's carrying a scatter gun. He caught me with 'is daughter, and 'e's out to shoot me dead, that one is!" the winded youth exclaimed.

"Roight, now we'll see what we can do about this. Get behind the men. You men stand in closer together so that 'e can't be seen. Roight, good, that's it!" he instructed. Lanigan and Sean took up a discussion with the men as a portly, older gentleman carrying a shotgun came around the street corner a block away. As he approached the group, Sean stopped him.

"What is going on there, sir, you look as if you are about to burst?"

"Did you gentlemen see a lad run by here a few moments ago?" he asked in between trying to catch his breath, having put the butt of his shotgun to the ground and leaned heavily on it.

"Why, that we surely did. He ran past 'ere as if he had the wings of Mercury on 'is feet. What did the lad do, steal something?"

"No. The damnable lay-about of a lad was about to mount me daughter in our carriage house! I warned 'im to stay away from my girls, but 'e keeps showing up. This time I caught 'im just before 'e soiled my daughter!" The man spat on the ground. "I aim to shoot him to put an end to 'is dallying!"

"I see then. Well, good hunting. "E went down that way, and darted down the next alley. As heavily as 'e was breathing, 'e will be slowing down to take a rest before long, so you should be able to catch up to 'im. Good day to you then sir." Sean saluted him as the man took off.

As soon as the elder man rounded the corner into the alley, Lanigan spoke up, cutting short the suppressed laughter of the men. "Come out 'ere, laddie; the devil has gone for now. Let me look at you. You are what, eighteen or nineteen?"

"Twenty sir," Tte lad responded.

"Aye, now how did you get in this predicament then, and what is your name?"

I'm Michael Calhoun. I have been dallying with 'is older daughter Patricia who is twenty. She gets around you know, she must 'ave 'ad 'alf of Philadelphia by now."

"Is that Patricia Parker? The lad's right, me and my mate 'ad a go at 'er, and a fine ride that little filly gives, if ye know what I mean." Offered Robert Hadley.

"So you got caught doing the town trollop, eh?" Lanigan asked.

"Oh no, sir, it was 'er sister who's seventeen. She put Patty up to asking me to, well, you know, break 'er in, so to speak," Came the reply. This brought on a rousing bout of laughter even Sean could not help joining in on.

"Well, laddie, 'tis a fortunate thing indeed that you ran into us. You see, we'll be leaving town in a bit and we'd love to 'ave you join us for a little sea voyage. Now how does that sound to ye? I bet that once the old man finds out that you have had at both 'is daughters, you will be skinned alive!"

"You are right about that. Sure, I'll go with you, me folks are both dead and there's nothing keeping me 'ere," the lad replied.

"Excellent!" Sean exclaimed. You 'ave just become our last recruit." He reached out and shook his hand. "Welcome to the Marines. You are a regular Lothario at that, so let's see how well you can fight!"

With that they all resumed their walk back towards the docks. They would all start their training the next day on the wharf under the tutelage of Sergeant Lanigan.

3

The American Marines

The wind came off the river, sending chills throughout his body. Sean stood with Captain Nicholas and Sergeant Lanigan, as they watched the new recruits fall in line on the cobblestone street of the wharf. The men chattered excitedly, stomped their feet to keep warm, some with gloves, some with their hands jammed into pockets or in their armpits.

Beckett and Sinclair, both appointed corporals, herded them into two lines facing the officers. "Now, sirs, after you have your talk with them, it is best that you leave them in the hands of me and the corporals for the first couple of days. It is not proper for gentlemen to be doing what needs to be done to get these gallows-dancers into shape. After we work them for a couple of days, they will be ready for you," Lanigan counseled the two.

"Sergeant, I have the utmost confidence in you and your abilities. The lieutenant and I have to look into supply matters and getting a few new officers trained. After you have your way with the men, the lieutenant will take over to assist you in drill and musketry. The other new officers have little or no experience in these matters, so I need Sean to teach them. We have a few old timers who had been part of the American Marines companies that the British put together during the war with the French, and they will be quite an asset for the other officers in training the other men as we get more recruits," Nicholas instructed.

"Sergeant, I hope to have the new officers instructed in two days, so I should be able to join you then. We will teach them the finer arts of drill, musketry, sword fighting and tactics then, so be gentle with them." They all chuckled after Sean had said that.

The three men walked over and faced the two ranks. Sinclair and Beckett stood in front of the two rows and saluted the officers as they approached. "All men have arrived and are accounted for, sirs, be that as they are." Sinclair's report drew a few snickers and comments from the men.

Nicholas ignored that and addressed the men. "Good morning to you, men, and congratulations, you are the first Marines to join in the fight in conjunction with the Continental Navy! Some of the individual colonies have their own navies and collections of privateers, both of which have their own form of marines. You men here, however, are a national force of marines, or Continental Marines, separate from any one colony, yet for the benefit of all." He paused to look each man in the eyes.

"You have the distinction to be the first such force for the new nation that we are trying to form from the colonies of the Crown. We will be the first of many to come. You men will be attached to the *Osprey* for now, and will be leaving as soon as the ship is ready for sea. Now I will turn you over to your commanding officer whom you all have met, Lieutenant Taggert."

"Thank you, Captain, and thank you, men, for coming out here this morning. Yes, you are a new force on the continent, and you will be a force to be reckoned with under the tutelage of Sergeant Lanigan and myself. In the next two weeks we will train you in everything that you will need to know to be good marines and to stay alive. For those of you who have not been to sea before, Corporals Sinclair and Beckett will teach you all that you will need to know as we get under way. Now we have some women coming here this morning to take measurements for your uniforms. You will show them the utmost respect, as they are all good women, not tavern trollops." He let them have a laugh at that.

"The sail maker and his mates will be busy making hammocks for you men, so for the next few nights until they are finished, you may all retire to your homes for the night, or if you prefer, you can bed down in the warehouse during training. We have enough blankets for you and should be able to find enough mess gear for all of you. Before you leave here today, you will be given a list of things that you will need to supply for yourself. If any of you need money to purchase these things, see my brother James before you go." Sean stood by to see if there were any questions.

"Men, you will be in tight quarters on board ship, and this time of year, most everyone stays below decks unless needed for duty, so if you have any problems with each other, get them worked out before we sail. If you cannot and problems arise, they will be dealt with under the articles of war. While on land, you are governed by the laws of the army. Either way, it will not go easy for troublemakers." He let his words sink in for effect.

"Now that that is over with, let's move on to better things. A few of you have your own weapons, and that is fine, but they will be locked up with the rest of the weapons. We will be trying to get new muskets and gear for each of you; however the Army and militias have first choice. I will do my best to get what we can to supplement what we have on board. If anyone knows of a supply of powder, let Sergeant Lanigan know, because everyone is in short supply of that."

"Now if there are no questions, I will turn you over to Sergeant Lanigan and the corporals for your initial training. You may have some hot rum with lunch, but other than that there is plenty of hot chicory tea for all. Once again, it is a good thing that you men have done by joining us. Do a good job for us and we will do the same for you. Now I have to train some other officers, so I place you in the hands of the sergeant," Sean concluded.

"Company attention!" Lanigan barked. "Hand salute!" he ordered as he saluted Sean. He cringed as he saw from the corner of his eye that some men saluted with their right hands and others their left.

He watched as the two officers walked off, then turned to face his recruits. "Roight, now as you heard, I will be training you the next couple of days while the officers try to get you all that you will need and train others themselves. If you learn well, and learn how to do as you are told as soon as you are told, you will stay alive in battle! If you do not, or if you hesitate, or try to discuss your orders before acting on them, you will find yourselves either cut in two by a cannonball, or riddled full of holes by a well-aimed volley from the enemy." Lanigan talked as he walked up and down the two ranks.

"Ah just bring them on, there's nothing to be afraid about," a voice came from the back rank.

"Who said that? Who said that?" Lanigan nearly screamed as he whirled on his heel to face the men. "Which one of you boil-brained idiots said that?"

"I said that, Michael Calhoun," came the answer.

Lanigan shouldered his way through the front rank and drew up in front of the culprit, who stood there smiling. "So we have us a bloody 'ero, 'ere do we now? Tell me, Mister Calhoun, just how many men have you killed in battle? How many battles have you been in? Come on now, tell all of us of your bloody 'eroics!" He was nose-to-nose with the man, nearly screaming in his face. He heard a few muffled chuckles from down the line, but ignored them.

"I ain't been in any battles, but it can't be that bad," he smirked.

"Just what have you been doing with your life there, Mister Calhoun?" he drilled his antagonist.

"I'm a wheelwright, and carriage builder by trade."

"A bloody wheelwright? Now there's an occupation that sees a lot of dying." He paused while the men laughed.

"Now let me tell you there, laddie, I seen cocky ones like you who think they know it all, and yet when the cannonballs and musket balls are flying, are the first ones to piss their trousers! I'll be watching you when we get into battle, so I can see just how long you can stand it before you piss yourself! Boyo, there is nothing short of hell itself that is any more terrible than battle.   "When the man next to you has 'is head taken off by a cannonball, and you get splattered by 'is brains and blood, you'll understand,

and you'll want to turn and run. You'll want to find a deep, dark hole to crawl into in the 'opes that the terror will pass you by. When you slip and fall into a pile of muck, that just minutes before was a friend's innards, you'll understand just 'ow foolish you were here this day. I'll be watching you!" He spun on his heel and took his place before the two ranks.

"Now we will try to warm you lads up, now doesn't that sound like a grand idea?" They all answered in the affirmative.

"Good, then we all can agree on something. Now it will become one of your duties as a marine to take your position on the fighting tops. If you turn around and look up at the masts, the fighting tops are the platforms 'alfway up. Now it is important that you be able to climb up there in a hurry, and when it is time for battle, you will be climbing up there carrying your weapons, a satchel full of grenades and possibly even a swivel gun. So to warm you lads up, you will practice climbing to the crosstrees that are way above the fighting tops. You will climb up the foremast, down the other side, up the mainmast, down again, and up and down the mizzenmast. After you have done this a few times, you should be plenty warm and ready for some drill."

"You can't be serious? All the way to the top?" a voice called out.

"Roight, I said all the way to the top, you never know when you might have to be a lookout, and have to go all the way up there. Now if you laddies are ready, we will see what you are made of. Attention! Roight turn!" He waited to see them make their turn, seeing them break out in confusion as many turned the wrong way.

"Jaysus, Mary and Joseph!" he swore. "Do ya not know your left from your right?" he screamed. "How many here do not know your left from your right?" He looked at them as he watched several hands rise up. He put his hands on his hips, looked at them, hung his head down and just stood there shaking his head for a minute.

"The former sailors among you, do you know your port from your starboard?" He watched as several of them nodded their heads. "Good! Now your left is your port, and your roight is your starboard. Does that clear things up a bit? Now see the direction that the ship is facing? Turn and look in the same direction." He waited until they had all gotten to face the correct direction.

"Now as you look to the front of the ship, the port, or left side is that way, and your starboard side, or roight side is that way!" He pointed the directions out to them.

"Now starting off on your left foot, march forward, turn and go up the gangplank when I say to. You will follow Corporal Sinclair, and he will get you started on your climb at the foremast. Now forward march!" He shook his head as several of them started on the wrong foot. "It's going to be a long war with beef-witted scuts like you. Now get along with you!"

The men dutifully marched up the gangplank and headed to the foremast. Sinclair spaced them out so that they could climb without stepping on each other or knocking each other off. Lanigan watched and then called out to Beckett. "Start the second group up the mainmast so that they get this over with faster. When you get to the fighting tops, do not go onto them through the hole; climb out and over the futtock shrouds like the sailors do. You don't want sailors showing you up, do you?" he barked at the first men who were about to reach the fighting tops. They struggled to climb up the sides of them, yet they made it.

Lanigan stood back and watched their progress. Once the two groups had successfully climbed all three masts once, they stopped to catch their breath. "Now that wasn't so bad now, was it?" he called to them.

"Not for you it wasn't. How come you don't do this too? Can't you climb up them masts, Sergeant?" called out a winded voice.

"So you think that I can't climb them with the best of you?" Whichever of you pox-ridden barnacles said that care to test your ability against mine, step forward!" he said as he unbuttoned his boat cloak and laid it across the rail.

"Come on now, step forward, I accept your challenge!" he bellowed.

Calhoun stepped forward, still breathing hard. "I said it, and I challenge you."

"Ah, Mister Calhoun again is it? Boyo, I'll be making you eat those words. Are ye a bettin' man now? If you, are then I'll bet your rum ration for the day that I'll outdo you. What say, up and down the mainmast and mizzen and whoever gets done first gets the other's rum ration. What say, laddie, are you up for it?" Lanigan challenged him.

"An old man like yew?" he turned towards the others as several chuckled and jeered the two. "All right, the main and the mizzen. I just don't like being given orders by someone who can't do what e's tellin' me to be doin'" Calhoun replied.

"Are ye sure about this, laddie? If you are, let's go right now!" he yelled as he swung out up onto the ratlines and started climbing. He was climbing out over the fighting top, as Calhoun was halfway there. Without slowing down, Lanigan reached the crosstree and looked down as he stood up on it to cross over to the other side for his descent.

"Come on, laddie, you're slowing down!" he called down to Calhoun who was struggling to get over the side of the fighting top. He started down the other side to the cheering of the men below. Even the sailors had stopped their work to watch the contest.

Sean came back down to the wharf to retrieve some notes that he had left behind and saw the spectacle. He was amazed at the dexterity that the elder Lanigan showed as he leapt down to the deck ran over to the mizzen and started to climb. Calhoun was just getting down to the deck as Lanigan reached the crosstree of the mizzen.

The men did not notice his approach as he walked up the gangplank. He stood watching the men as they cheered the two. Lanigan waited at the top as Calhoun started his ascent. He took his time coming down the other side and reached the deck as Calhoun started his descent.

When he reached the deck, he came over to the group winded and somewhat humiliated.

"There now, laddie, are ye satisfied that your sergeant will not be giving you any orders that he himself cannot do?" Lanigan challenged him.

"Aye, Sergeant, that I am, but what of the officers?" he managed to get out between breaths.

"You are a hard one to convince!" Sean's voice broke through the crowd. "Now if any you think that I ca'no' climb those masts, raise your hands!" He waited to see that none of them did so.

"Good, then all ye others follow me!" he shouted as he jumped up and started his climb to the main fighting top. The others joined suit and by the time he reached the crosstree, he could see his whole command rapidly catching up to him. He went down the other side, and upon reaching the deck, Lanigan pointed to the mizzen, and he started up the rigging of that one, the men following close behind.

He reached the deck after completing the climb and waited for the others to finish and form up in their lines.

"Now, let there be no mistake. Neither the sergeant nor I will be asking ye to do anything that we ourselves would not be willing to do! Does this sit well with ye then?" he barked at the men.

"Yes, sir!" came the chorus of replies.

"Good! Carry on then, Sergeant," he said as he gave Lanigan a wink of a co-conspirator. He went below to retrieve his papers. When he came back on deck, the sergeant had the men grouped forward, explaining different parts of the ship and having them repeat the nomenclature as they went. He was an amazing, man the sergeant, Sean thought to himself.

Sean returned to Sam at the Conestogoe Wagon Tavern where they met with a few of the new officers. Captain Joseph Shoemaker, and Lieutenant Isaac Craig, Captain John Welsh, Lieutenants Fitzpatrick, Cummings, Williams, Dayton, Parke and Miller were all ready to start training and recruiting.

The first day after the social portion of the gathering was out of the way, Nicholas let Sean take over and teach the officers the fine art of drill. Only a few of the men had had any experience, and they would be paired off with sergeants that had experience. The new officers each took turns drilling the others until they had the basic commands and movements down pat.

The second day they were coached in basic military tactics, fighting on board ships, and general marine duties on board warships. The third day, they all went down to the wharf to observe Sergeant Lanigan handling the recruits. They stood back and watched him teach them drill and proper marching.

"They look far better today than they did just the other day," commented Nicholas. "Sergeant Lanigan certainly has a way with them, and with the more colorful use of the King's English!" He smiled as they heard Lanigan unleash a tirade of curses at his hapless victim who still had trouble determining which was left or right. The other officers chuckled, but were impressed with the way the men before them, raw recruits of just three days were performing under the watchful yet loud sergeant.

"I certainly hope the sergeants that we have joining us this afternoon are just as good as he is," Captain Shoemaker commented.

"Oh, I think that you will be pleased with them. The British trained them all during the war with the French, and every one of them appears to be cut from the same cloth as Lanigan," Nicholas replied.

The rest of the morning, Sean and Nicholas worked with the officers in the warehouse in the use of swords. Only a couple of them had any training in swordplay, but the others picked up on it quickly, and with a little more practice, would be able to hold their own. That afternoon, the officers met with the sergeants and got acquainted. They then set out how they would split the city up for their recruiting forays the next day,

Half of them would work out of the Conestogoe Wagon Tavern and the others would work out of Tun Tavern. While the marines trained outside, they were joined by onlookers eager to watch the men train. Some of them cheered them on while a few hecklers made fun of them.

"Now, laddies, don't ye be paying them any mind. I want your full attention. Think of them flap-mouthed toads as part of your discipline training. They can take the place of the noise and confusion of battle. And if any of ye breaks rank to chase them, you'll be answering to me!" Lanigan warned them.

As it was getting dark, the onlookers faded off into the night. "Now, laddies, I will tell you this, you are doing much better. I might just make proper marines out of the likes of you yet!" he smiled. "Now be off with ye, it's getting too damned cold out here without the sun!" he ordered. The men cheered and left for their homes.

Sean came out with the officers as they all broke up for the night. He walked over to Lanigan with two hot mugs of rum and stood by a small fire on the wharf for warmth. "Sergeant Lanigan, here's to your health," he said as he raised his mug.

"Here's to yours, sir, and to our lads, they are turning out to be a good lot. I have trained many a marine in my day sir, and I'd match these boys with the best of them. Don't you fret, sir, when we get into a fight, they will prove themselves, I have no doubt," Lanigan observed.

"They are a spirited group that is certain. And I know that they have come to respect you and what you are trying to do for them," Sean replied.

"All in a day's work, sir, all in a day's work. Have ye heard about when the uniforms will be ready? The sooner we get them looking like marines, the sooner they will become marines. And what about the weapons?" Lanigan asked.

"We may have the uniforms by tomorrow. I'll know for sure tonight. Once we get them looking good, we can try for the weapons. We were discussing that today. The Congress has little to spare, and we are on the bottom of the list. Captain Nicholas has the paperwork for weapons, however, he has had some problems with the supply people. Some of these men are real cutthroats and expect bribes for the supply orders to be filled! Can you imagine that?" Sean said with indignation in his voice.

"Laddie, it is the same in every war, and in every country. I could tell you horror stories about trying to get good food, weapons and clothing for the fighting men of the Royal Navy and Marines. The Royal Army units had it no better. The men who have the Parliament in their hip pocket also stand to make a profit on the war effort. It is no different here in that respect."

"I suppose that you are right. Tomorrow I will be training with you, and if Nicholas gets me the proper paperwork, we will take the men and procure our allotted supplies. We may have to be persuasive though."

"Ah, laddie, don't you be worrying. Let's get our men into their uniforms, and you'd be surprised at how persuasive they will be!" Lanigan smiled.

The two stood by the fire until it sputtered out. James, who had closed up the warehouse and brought the carriage around front, joined them. The other two climbed aboard and they drove off. After they dropped Lanigan at his house, Sean and James continued to their home.

As they came up the drive, the last of a string of carriages was leaving. They were the ladies of the church and wives of the marines who had been busy sewing the uniforms. The brothers walked in the front door after the servant took the carriage from them. There were uniforms, piles and scraps of cloth in every room of the first floor.

"Welcome home, boys." their mother said as she greeted them. Thomas came out of the drawing room, stepping over a pile of completed uniform coats. "Dinner will be ready in a few moments. Sean, we finished up the last of the coats this evening. The trousers, waistcoats, and neck cloths are also all ready. Your men can be in full uniform tomorrow," she beamed.

"Thank you, Mother," he said as he bent over to give her a kiss on the cheek. "I see that you had more than enough cloth for the lot."

"Oh yes, and more. We made two uniforms for each man, head to foot. Yours are up on your bed. Some of the wives took their husbands' uniforms home with them tonight, so some of your men will show up in the morning looking like marines. I'll have the servants load these into the wagon in the morning so that you can take them down with you.

The ladies and I will be there by nine to make any adjustments they may need," she said.

After dinner, Sean went upstairs and tried his uniforms on. His mother inspected him to be sure that he was properly fitted. When they finished, it was late, so they retired for the night. As Sean drifted off to sleep, he pondered the events of the week. The lads were shaping up nicely under the watchful, yet at times profane, instruction of Lanigan. He had worked wonders with the men, and they respected him.

The next level of training would be weapons and maneuvers. Some of the men had never fired a weapon before, which would make things interesting. He had arranged with a local farmer to use a portion of his farm for target practice. The carpenter and a work party would go out tomorrow and set up logs to be used as targets as soon as the men received their muskets and pistols.

Morning seemed to have come too fast as the servant shook Sean awake. After washing and dressing in his new uniform, he went downstairs to the kitchen for breakfast. It was still dark out, and he could see the servants hustling outside with their lanterns as they loaded the wagon.

He wolfed down the eggs and hot porridge, not bothering to sit down. He stood by the hearth to get the last full warmth that he would have the rest of the day. It was hard on the men to be out in the near-freezing weather all day training. The only respite that they had from it was when they stood around the small fires lit on the wharf, or when they had their lunch inside the warehouse. It had been so cold the past two days that even the onlookers did not stay to watch them. He wondered to himself as he gazed at the crowd each day, which of them were in the employ of the British, reporting any information about them for a few pieces of gold or silver.

He put the thought from his head filled his pouch with some hot biscuits and a small slab of cooked bacon to supplement his lunch. At least while they remained in port they would eat plenty of fresh food.

When Thomas and James finished their breakfast, the three left the house. Sean rode on the wagon with the servant while his brothers took the carriage. True to form when they arrived at the warehouse, Lanigan was already there, stoking up one of the fires to keep him and his chicory tea warm.

"Sergeant Lanigan, do you ever sleep?" Thomas asked him as he stepped out of the carriage and walked straight to the fire.

"Ah, good morning to you, gentlemen. 'Tis the fate of the sergeants of the world to be ever vigilant!" he beamed in reply, sipping his tea.

Sean joined him after giving instructions to the servant and the warehouse crew who had showed up where to put the bundles of clothing. "I see that your wife took your uniforms home with her last night, Sergeant. I must say you look ever so much the professional sergeant in that green frock. The color was a good choice; different from the enemy and also from the naval colors," Sean observed.

"Aye, thank you, Sir. I must admit, after wearing the King's red for all those years, I do admire the change. It does set us apart from all the others," Lanigan replied.

Streaks of light started appearing in the sky, and the features of the dock and ships started to be recognizable. Slowly the men started arriving for the day's training, some in their new outfits, some in their own clothes. As they arrived, Sean shooed them into the warehouse to find the bundles with their names on them.

They started changing immediately, putting their spare uniform and clothing in their sea chests that were still being held in the warehouse. As the sun broke over the horizon, burning off the frost that had settled everywhere, the men were finally all in uniform.

"All right, lads, fall out into formation outside, and let's have a look at ye in the daylight." Lanigan commanded happily. He watched them file out the door, nodding in approval of their looks. They would do, these lads in green, he thought to himself.

"Fall in!" shouted Sinclair. The men formed up in their two ranks, corporals Beckett and Sinclair at the head of their squads, Lanigan in front.

Lanigan stood there, hands clasped behind his back, rocking back and forth on his heels. "Well, it is a fine sight for my sore eyes this morning to see you lads all finally looking alike. The uniforms suit you nicely, that they surely do. You men look as sharp as any Royal Marines that I had the pleasure of being associated with in all my years as a British Marine." He smiled as he said this to his men, and then called them to attention as he sensed Sean coming out of the warehouse behind him. He swiveled around to attention, saluted his commanding officer and said, "*Osprey* Marines ready for inspection, sir!" He put special emphasis on the word, 'Marines.'

"Thank you Sergeant! Today I think we can truly call you Marines. I do believe that you are all standing a little taller and straighter this morning.

Congratulations, Marines, I know that you will do us proud! Sergeant, shall we inspect the company?" Sean asked.

"Aye, sir, that we should." Together, Lanigan in the lead, they walked the two ranks, stopping to talk to each man in turn. With the exception of different shoes on each man, they all appeared to be the same, even to the black round hats they wore.

Just as they finished up, Captain Nicholas showed up on horseback. He dismounted and tied his horse to the hitching post. He stood there for a moment admiring the assembled company before him as Sean and Lanigan took their places in front of the ranks.

"Sir, the *Osprey* Marines are formed and ready, sir." Sean announced.

Nicholas returned the salute and said, " Good morning, Marines. I am duly impressed with your looks this morning. You are a fine looking company! You have progressed very well in your training, and at this point lack only one thing: weapons. I have here the authorization for your arms; however, there may not be enough on hand to arm you. Lieutenant Taggert will march you over to the supply depot this morning and attempt to get you armed. Get what you can, for I'm afraid that we are on the bottom of the list of importance. The other companies are not as far along as you, and will be relegated to guarding the ships of the Navy until they are ready to sail with us. Since you and this ship are just a few days from being ready for sea, you will be leaving as soon as all stores are aboard for patrol duty. You will be expected to attack any enemy shipping that you can, and gather as much intelligence as is possible, so you see it is important to get as much as you are able to today."

"Thank you, sir, we will endeavor to get the supplies relinquished to us," Sean said as he took the proffered letters of procurement from Nicholas.

"Good luck, Sean. Get them armed and trained with the weapons. I understand that the *Osprey* will be ready in three more days. Is that correct?" Sam asked him in a lowered voice.

"Aye, sir that she will be. Don't worry, we'll get what we need, and as soon as we do, I'll be taking them outside of town for target practice," Sean assured him.

"I don't care what you do to get what you need, just use your best judgment. Try not to get into trouble," Sam cautioned his friend.

"Don't you fret, we'll have everything under control." Sean stepped back and saluted. Nicholas returned the salute and mounted his horse.

"Good luck, Marines." He called out as he kicked his horse into motion. Sean watched as he rode off.

"Sergeant Lanigan, we do have enough cutlasses on board to arm all the men. Have your corporals take them on board and arm them. We want to make a good impression at the supply depot this morning. Bring one for me also." He grinned.

"Aye, aye, sir. Well, you heard him, lads, Corporals Sinclair and Beckett, take the men on board and get them armed. No playing around with the cutlasses, boys. I don't want you to get blood all over your nice new clothes." He smiled as the men laughed.

Within minutes, the men had reformed, each with a cutlass strapped to his side. Sean adjusted the belt and scabbard of the heavy cutlass at his side. He had trained the men for a few hours one afternoon with them, so they all handled them like they had been used to it for years.

"Sergeant, let's take the lads on a little stroll. The wagon will follow us. Let's move out." He turned and headed up the wharf. Behind him he listened as Lanigan barked his commands and heard the footsteps of the company on the cobblestones behind him. He watched his breath precede him in clouds. It was still near freezing, yet the cold did not seem to bother him. He felt a surge of pride as he thought of how the men looked as they fell in this morning, and now as he heard them all marching in step. They had come a long way in a short time. They had become Marines.

They had marched the two miles to the supply depot, and were challenged at the entrance to the warehouse area. Sean pulled out his papers and showed them to the sentries. Reluctantly they let the company pass and returned to the small fire that they had been standing by for warmth before the marines had interrupted them.

Sean pointed out the warehouse that the sentry had indicated to him, and Lanigan halted the men before it and had them face it at ease. He could hear voices inside the office. A fat face, then two others, appeared at the dirty, frosted windowpane.

"Sergeant, I want you, Julius Jones and Peter Svenson to come inside with me," Sean ordered.

"You 'eard him, you two, fall out and follow me." It was not lost on Lanigan that Sean had picked the two largest men in the company to accompany them. From the looks of the scoundrels in the window, and the way Sean had a grip on the handle of his cutlass, this was going to be fun.

The four men entered the warm office to the smell of fresh, hot tea and cooked pork. The three men that had watched them at the window had taken their places behind a counter made of crates, separating them from the marines. They each had a heaping plate of breakfast in front of them, and the portly man in charge already reeked of rum this early in the morning.

"Good morning, gentlemen, I am Lieutenant Taggert of the Marines here to gather our supplies allotted to us by order of Congress," Sean said as he passed the paperwork to the men in charge. He looked him square in the eyes as the man passed the papers to his assistant to his right without even looking at them. He continued to chew on a large chunk of pork that he had bitten off in a menacing way while sizing up Sean as if he was an opponent in a duel.

"They look genuine enough, Ebenezer. Boy, don't them boys look purty in their green coats! Too bad we can't give 'em nothin'." he laughed as he said that to his boss.

"What does he mean that you cannot give us anything? We have signed orders," Sean asked.

"Wot 'e means is we don't give nothin' out unless you got the proper forms, you know the kind that jingles in your pocket," the fat man said as he wiped his greasy hands on the front of his shirt. "I know you Taggerts got money. If you want your supplies, you'll have to pay us our 'andling fee in gold."

"Handling fee…gold…humpf," Sean replied. "These men are about to go out and fight for the new nation that you will benefit from and you are going to sit there and tell me that we cannot have our legally ordered supplies without paying you a bribe?"

"Yep, that about sums it up nicely there, governor!" smiled the man. "Now if you want to pay our fee, we can do business. If not, you're interrupting our breakfast," he said as he put another chunk of pork into his mouth.

Lanigan sensed the ball was about to start, turned to the two men behind him, and whispered, "Get ready, lads, things are about to get very busy here in a moment."

"I am going to ask you for the last time, get our supplies--now!" Sean ordered.

The man did nothing but return his stare, and chew on his mouthful of pork.

Sean turned to Lanigan and said, "Have the men take his two assistants outside, and hold them at sword point. If they try to cause a problem, run them through."

In a flash the two big marines bodily lifted the two rat-like assistants from behind the barricade, and threw them out into the street, and followed them out, cutlasses bared. The other marines drew their cutlasses and gathered around the two hapless men who stayed sitting on the cold ground. Their heads constantly revolved as they watched their captors while they shivered from the cold.

Inside, Sean was about to reach out for the fat man's lapels, when the man pulled a pistol from under his shirt and pointed it at him. Before he could pull the hammer back, Sean kicked the crates in front of him, sending them and the man crashing backwards. The gun went off harmlessly in the air when he hit the ground.

Before the man could pick himself off the floor, Sean drew his cutlass and smacked the man across his ample rump with the flat of the blade. "Thought you could bribe me, did you?" he sneered at the man as he was sent sprawling again. Sean stepped behind him and smacked him again across the buttocks with the flat of his blade.

"Thought that you could hold supplies from fighting men, while you made a profit off their needs did you?" The man tried to get up a third time, and Sean repeated his actions. After the fourth time, the man gave up and turned to sit on his now painful posterior.

"I'll have ye busted for this! I got connections. I'll see ye go down, Taggert!" he yelled at Sean.

"I don't know what you're talking about, do you, Sergeant? All we are doing is having a conversation. There are no witnesses to back you up, just your word against ours. Now we will take our allotted supplies whether or not you approve, and we will not be giving you a penny. If you get in my way, if you dare make a move against me, you'll end up as fish bait, I swear it!" Sean said as he put the tip of his blade under the man's chin and let it cut him.

"All right, all right, you can take what you want, just don't hurt me. I won't do anything, please just leave me alone," the man begged.

"Get Jones and Svenson back in here to keep a personal eye on him. The others can come with me while we gather what is due us. Bring those other two in here; they can help us find our things."

Within minutes, the two helpers were showing Sean and Lanigan where everything was. They had the wagon backed into the warehouse so that the gear could be loaded up. The men made fast work of it as Lanigan checked off everything on the list.

"That's it, sir." he said as the last of it was loaded. "Fifty stands of muskets, each to include musket, bayonet and scabbard, cartridge box, powder flask and belt. Twenty-six canteens, twenty-five pouches, twenty-five pistols, twenty lead bars, five pounds each, twenty-five bullet molds, a sheaf of cartridge papers, twenty-five tomahawks, twenty-five pairs of shoes, one box of candles, six extra ramrods, twenty-five pairs of mittens, twenty lead bars, and a one-hundred- pound keg of fine powder for the muskets and pistols. That is all that we are due except for the knapsacks, they had none."

"Thank you, Sergeant. Have the men fall out. We will be leaving this foul place now. You three, if I hear of you doing this again, you better not be here when I get back, for I will keep my promise to you," Sean said as he turned on his heel and walked out the door.

"All roight lads, you 'erad 'im, fall out!" Lanigan ordered. The men all complied, several stepping over and on the three wretched figures sitting on the ground. All enjoyed the march back to the wharf as they reveled in their victory and the attention that they received as they marched down the streets.

When they returned to the wharf, they could see the other companies drilling down the way. Most were still in their own clothes, although some were now in uniforms. Sean had the men unload the wagon and pass out the supplies. Each man tried on his new shoes, and they put on their pouches, cartridge pouches, bayonet and scabbard, and inspected their new muskets. The gunner and gunner's mate took the powder and lead on board and stowed it away. They also locked the pistols and cutlasses back in the arms chests.

The extra stands of muskets were stacked neatly with the belts hanging from the stacks. Nicholas came riding up on his horse as they finished stacking arms. "Well now, you men do look like real fighting men. And you even got extras for the other company. I will not ask how you managed that. I'll have them come right over and claim the weapons. Good show, men, good show!" he said as he trotted off to the other company.

"Here, sir, I latched onto this at the depot for you," Lanigan said to Sean as they stood before the men. He brought out a bundle and handed it to Sean. "An officer needs to have a proper sword, not just a cutlass, and since I noticed that you haven't had one to use, I picked one out for you."

Sean unwrapped the cloth and pulled out a fine officer's sword. Not too heavy, and not too light. "Thank you, Sergeant, that was very thoughtful. Now I, too, have all that I need."

The other marines came over and helped themselves to the muskets and gear. Since it was not quite lunchtime, Sean and Lanigan started drilling the men in the manual of arms. They took to it with a passion, now that they were in uniform and armed. They all felt a difference in themselves this day.

The rest of the day was spent in drill, manual of arms, and in how to prepare and fire by volleys, first one rank then the other, both advancing and retiring. Sean and Lanigan were pleased with the men's attitudes and their ability to keep their movements together in the complex moves.

"Tomorrow, men, we will be going for a brief march out of town to take some target practice. I've had the carpenters and work party set up a suitable target range for you. We will spend most of the day there, so make sure you fill your canteens, and bring some extra food in your pouches. I have spoken with the sail maker, and he will be making knapsacks for everyone out of some of the older sails that we have on hand," Sean announced, as they were ready to quit for the evening.

"Look at 'em, sir," Lanigan said to Sean as the men left for the day. "They are proper marines now, they are. Once they've had a chance to fire their weapons, they'll be ready to take on the enemy. We'll have to watch them close tomorrow though, sir, we do have some lads that have never fired a weapon, and I seen a few of them that were quite nervous handling the muskets today."

"You're quite right. We'll work the two squads separately so that the four of us can be right there with them and watch closely. I think that you'll be impressed with what the lads set up for targets tomorrow. They'll have the ability to learn how to shoot straight ahead, and from the height of a fighting top as well. I'd like to get them some practice with the grenades, but we just do not have enough. Once we get under sail, we can get them some practice with the cannons."

"Don't worry about the grenades, sir, I have a little trick that I have used in the past. We have plenty of fuse cord in storage, that'll do the trick." They sat and talked a while before they went their own ways for the night.

The next morning the men formed up in the cold before the sun came up. After the roll was called, they loaded several baskets of food and other supplies into the wagon, and marched from the wharf. The men strutted through town, and they all perked up whenever they passed any onlookers. The sun came up as they reached the outskirts of town as they made their way to the farm where they would have their practice. Two men had taken the lead with fife and drum, and kept up a lively tune once they were out of the sleepy town.

After crossing a cleared field, Sean brought them to a halt at the base of a rock face about thirty feet high. Fifty feet out from the base of the small cliff were several five-foot logs standing on end, some in groups of four, some individually.

"These are your targets, men. Stand over against the cliff, and you will see that they are situated as if they were men on an opposing ship. Those in groups represent gun crews. The others represent officers and others. One squad will start from the top, giving you the experience of shooting down from a high perch, such as you will be firing from the fighting tops. The others will start at the base of the hill, so as to imitate shooting from the rail of the ship. You will each have the opportunity to do both. You will find that it is quite different shooting from on high," Sean instructed.

"Now, you see that there is a square of logs midway in between the groups. That represents the main hatch of the other ship. Topside, you will find a large pile of grenade size rocks. You will practice throwing them from up there at the hatch. That is your main target with a grenade from on high.," he continued.

Lanigan looked over the layout and was impressed. "Sir, I must say, this is quite a remarkable layout. This will do nicely for practice. Now, if I may before we get started shooting, I would like to run them through my little grenade exercise. I have cut up several feet of the fuse cord, two for each man." He held up the short lengths of fuse. "Now you men may 'ave the opportunity to 'eave a grenade at one time or another, and they tend to scare a person once the fuse is lit. So this little exercise will get you used to handling a sputtering fuse in your hand, since we don't have enough grenades for each of you to try," Lanigan said as he had the corporals pass out the cords.

"Roight, now I am going to come along in front of you and light your fuse. You will hold it in your fingers, count to six, then you may drop it. This is how long you should 'old onto a lit grenade before throwing it. Throw it too soon, and it may get thrown back at you. Hold it too long and it may go off in your 'and," he said as he stood in front of the first man.

He lit the fuse and moved down the line, lighting each one as he went. Several of the men dropped them fast, afraid of being burnt. This incurred the sergeant's wrath, which caused them to hold onto the second one the proper length of time. Once they had each had the opportunity to hold two burning fuses, Lanigan took one squad to the top of the hill to begin firing practice. He and Sinclair tutored each man in the loading and firing from the top, while Sean and Beckett tutored the squad on the ground.

After the first few rounds were fired, Lanigan peered through the smoke at the targets. A few of the bare logs had hits on them. There was also one ramrod sitting in a log, half buried in the wood.

"Jaysus, Mary and Joseph!" he swore. "Which one of you beef-witted, sheep-biting louts fired 'is ramrod? Look and see. Which one of you did it?"

"It was me, Sergeant," came the meek answer.

"Simon Betts! Come 'ere, lad. Now, you see that I have a few extra ramrods 'ere for them that don't load properly and shoots their ramrod at the target. Now load your musket with just powder," he instructed as the nervous Betts complied.

"Now prime your piece and put it to your shoulder." As he did so, Lanigan placed a new ramrod into the barrel of Betts' musket and pushed the weapon even higher

"I want you to fire your musket, and then go run after your new ramrod. The run will do you good, and it might help you to remember to remove it the next time!" Lanigan sneered at him.

Betts squeezed the trigger. They all watched as the ramrod arched high into the sky and sailed two hundred yards away till it bounced across the frozen ground.

"Now, laddie, go fetch your ramrod, for your other one has been ruined after being shot into that log!" Lanigan ordered. As Betts held his musket at the port arms position, he ran down the hill and out towards the ramrod, amidst hoots from his friends.

"Now I understand why you grabbed the extras yesterday, Sergeant!" Sean called up to him from below.

Only one other hapless individual had to launch and retrieve a ramrod the rest of the day. After each squad had the opportunity to fire several rounds from each position, they had to break for lunch and clean their muskets. The cooks had come along and heated the food for them. They also boiled a large kettle of water so that the men could flush the black powder residue from the barrels.

Once the men were fed and their weapons had been cleaned, they were marched out in the field to practice fighting as a unit in the field. They advanced on the log targets firing by rank, and then they fired by rank in a withdrawing direction. The rest of the afternoon was used in these maneuvers. Satisfied that the men had learned the maneuvers well enough, they again cleaned their muskets.

The sun was getting low on the horizon as they formed up for weapon inspection. This task finished, they formed up and marched back to town. The streets were busier than they were in the morning. They drew a crowd of onlookers and were followed by several boys imitating their marching. After they returned to the ship, Sean dismissed them as soon as the gear was stowed away. They had done well today, he thought, as they walked away. After a few more days, they and the *Osprey* would be ready to set sail.

Lanigan had suggested having them practice boat actions, and boarding hostile ships which they might find themselves doing in a matter of days. It would be cold work, practicing that in the harbor with the frigid winter winds blowing off the river. However, it would be better to get them practiced in the maneuvers in the relative calm, then have them do it for the first time in the open ocean in rough seas. A miss-step climbing down the side of the ship in rough water meant a dunking for sure, and in this temperature, it would mean very little chance of survival in the cold Atlantic waters.

Before they retired for the night, Sean and Thomas poured over the purser's tally of food stores that would be loaded in the morning "This looks complete enough for two months with the size crew we'll be carrying, don't you think, Sean?" Thomas asked as he handed the list to Sean.

"Let me move closer to the stove. I've been out in the cold all day, and won't be able to hold this still long enough to read it." Sean responded as he took the proffered list from his brother while moving towards the stove.

"Let's see here, what do we have?" he paused then read the list aloud, "Three thousand pounds of bread, twelve-hundred-fifty pounds of beef, same in pork, same in potatoes, eighty gallons of peas, three-hundred-fifty pounds of cheese, fifty pounds of butter, twenty-five gallons of rice, ten gallons of vinegar, two-hundred-fifty gallons of rum, fifty pounds of coffee, and two barrels of sugar. This should do. If we run short, we will help ourselves to the stores of the enemy vessels that we take," he smiled.

"Good, we'll be finished loading this the day after tomorrow. Will your marines be ready by then?" Thomas asked.

"The last thing we are going to work on is small boat maneuvers, loading and unloading, catching on to moving vessels, which we should be able to do with the ship traffic on the river. We'll be as ready as we can be. The only thing we haven't been able to do is to have them fire the cannons. How are we fixed for powder?" Sean replied.

"We have a ton-and-a-half of powder, that's thirty kegs of one-hundredweight each with enough wads, empty serge cartridges, one reel of slow match, and flexible ramrods, which should be enough to keep our ten guns and swivels in action for a while. We will need to confiscate at least another ton of powder for ourselves. With the extra guns we have now, we'll be using more of the stuff than we ever have before. I was thinking, there is that abandoned hulk a few miles down river, you know the one that ran ashore. That would make for a good target for your cannon practice on the way down river," Thomas added.

"You're right, we could get all the gun crews at least one round each at that old hulk. That would be just enough for them to get the hang of loading and firing the big guns. Well, that's enough for one day; let's go home. Tomorrow night will be our last supper ashore, so let's not miss dinner tonight.

They left the warehouse, climbed in the carriage, and James drove them home. Sean fell asleep on the ride home, exhausted from his full day in the field drilling the men. Thomas had to shake him awake when they reached the house.

That evening the whole family spent together, knowing that tomorrow night they would be parting company after dinner. Sean and Thomas would spend the night on board the ship with the men, for they would need to leave first thing in the morning the day after.

Morning came too fast for Sean, as he was shaken awake by one of the servants. He rolled out of bed, washed up, and put on an extra layer of clothing under his uniform to keep him warm. After a hearty breakfast, he was off to the wharf to start the men on their boat drills. When he arrived, those that had arrived early were building small fires to keep themselves warm. The fires grew larger as more men showed up.

When all were accounted for, Sean and Lanigan got the men busy loading into the cutter and longboat that members of the crew were manning. "Each of you will have the frizen on your weapon open as you climb down into the boat. This is so no one gets shot accidental like." Lanigan instructed. He inspected each weapon as the men climbed over the side into the waiting boats.

They practiced loading into the boats and latching onto the side of the *Osprey*, climbing back onto the ship as if they were assaulting her. They practiced with muskets, and later with pistols and cutlasses. As the traffic on the river picked up towards mid-day, the crew rowed them into the river. Sean hailed the captain of a schooner headed down river and got permission to attempt boarding her in motion. This presented a new twist to what they practiced earlier, as the schooner and boats being in motion made it more difficult to judge the jump to the side of the ship with the rise and fall of both vessels.

The men managed to board and depart the schooner without anyone falling into the cold water. They were far down river once they regained their boats, and Sean had the men spell the sailors on the oars for the experience. The sailors were unmerciful as the marines mis-stroked the oars and fell backwards when they did not get a good bite in the water with their oars. They finally got the hang of it when the experienced men among them set the pace.

They were able to 'attack' a small brig going down river, and again the marines managed to keep dry. The row back up to the harbor helped to warm them back up as the bitter cold wind was channeled right up the river.

Before they reached the harbor, Sean angled the boats towards a stretch of beach. "We'll have a landing on the beach there, Sergeant!" he called over to the cutter to Lanigan.

The old sergeant waved in acknowledgement and said to the men, "Get ready, lads, we'll try to run 'er up far enough so you don't get your feet wet. Get used to this, we'll be doing this a time or two in the near future," he grinned.

The men finished early. Sean addressed the formation before releasing them. "Tomorrow we will make final preparations for sea. We will all stay on board tomorrow night so that we can get an early start. We've trained all that we can, so now we'll be able to see how well we have learned. Get a good night's rest, and we'll meet here the same time tomorrow. Marines, dismissed!" he commanded.

The men gave a cheer and broke up for the night, some headed straight for home and families, others headed for the local taverns and brothels. They all felt the excitement and uncertainty of their upcoming voyage. They could come back with captive vessels to be auctioned off, giving them prize money if they were lucky, or they could be killed, or worse yet, wounded and suffer the rest of their life as an amputee.

The next day passed quickly as the marines joined in with the crew, loading the remaining supplies, cleaning ship, and preparing their living quarters. The *Osprey* would be crowded, but the men all seemed to get along. What petty rivalries or disagreements that had existed, were all past as they worked at the tasks that would ensure their mutual survival.

That evening, the cook fires warmed the ship inside along with the many men packed between decks. It took a while, but they all managed to arrange their hammocks to where no one was left on the deck. Sean, Thomas, Lanigan and the officers dined in the great cabin. They listened to the shipboard sounds all so familiar. The strains of a fiddle could be heard coming from the crew's quarters, while outside, a cold December wind howled.

Conversation was light, while all warmed themselves with the fine port wine that Thomas had brought on board. "We were to get a surgeon before we left, but I haven't heard from him. If he is not here by the time we are to cast off, we will leave without him," Thomas told the others.

"What do you know of him? Is he a rummy like so many of them are?" Sean asked.

"I don't know a thing about him other than I was told that he had a good reason for wanting to go to sea. Probably hounded by his creditors, or some jealous husband, I'd imagine," Thomas replied.

"Aye, all good reasons for leaving the land behind," Lanigan pointed out. "Gentlemen, I enjoyed the company; however, it is time for me to turn in. I'll have a turn around the decks, and then get to sleep. Good night to all of you." He gave a mock salute, tossed back the last of the wine in his goblet, and then left the cabin. The others followed suit. Within the hour, the ship was quiet, with just the sounds of the men on watch trying to stay warm and the murmur of the many men sleeping below deck.

The next day the *Osprey* was bustling with activity as the crew prepared to leave port. The wharf was overcrowded with townsfolk, members of Congress, friends and family members who came to the wharf to see them off on their journey. Nicholas had the other marine companies assemble and fired a salute as the ship slowly nudged away from the dock, being gently warped out by the crews of the longboat and cutter. The whole waterfront burst into cheers when the now- familiar "Don't Tread On Me" rattlesnake flag was hoisted.

"Wait for me!" a voice cried out from the crowd. Sean and Thomas stood by the railing, searching the crowd to see who was calling out. They could see the crowd parting slightly as a tall man forced his way to the front of the crowd. He carried a small trunk under one arm and a large seabag over his shoulder.

"Wait for me, I'm the doctor!" he cried out in desperation as the ship slowly started to pull away from the dock. The man set his trunk down and heaved his bag over the railing onto the deck. He then picked up the trunk, took a few steps back, and took a running jump at the side of the ship, landing headlong onto the deck through the entry port.

"Looks as if our doctor finally showed up, Thomas," Sean observed with a smile as the crowd cheered the man. The doctor was helped to his feet by a couple of the crew who took pleasure in jostling him as they brushed him off, making light of his obvious discomfort of having to make such a grand entrance.

He strode aft and presented himself to Sean and Thomas. "Good morning, gentlemen, I am Jonathan Faircloth of Boston, doctor by trade. I must apologize for my tardiness as the carriage that was bringing me here lost a wheel, and the dolt of a driver was forever repairing it."

"Welcome aboard Doctor, I am Captain Thomas Taggert and this is my brother, Lieutenant Sean Taggert, of the Marines. We almost gave you up for lost. However since you made it here, we will make room for you." Thomas shook his hand.

"Sergeant Lanigan here will show you to your quarters," Sean said as he shook hands and introduced his sergeant to him.

"Come along now Doctor, we will get you settled in. Have you ever been on a ship before?" he asked as the doctor retrieved his belongings and shook his head negatively. "Well, laddie, don't you worry, this is a fine ship, and you'll soon be fitting in here just like one of the family!" Lanigan cast a glance back at Sean as he led Faircloth below.

Sean smiled and just shook his head. He could tell that Lanigan would be talking the ears off the good doctor for quite some time, as he liked to with anyone new to the world of shipboard life. He would be telling the doctor sea-stories for quite a while.

The small ship turned slowly away from the dock and out into the current. Her sails were set and soon were filled by the gentle morning breeze. The longboat was recalled and hoisted on board, while the men in the cutter hoisted the sail to run ahead to inspect the abandoned hulk that would be their target.

"'Tis a fine send-off they have given us Brother," Thomas observed as the distance grew between them and the crowded wharf.

"Aye, that it was. "Tis good to be away from the land and headed for sea again. I was getting too much to eat at home, and will have to be running up and down the rigging for the next two weeks to work all of that extra ballast off of me."

"Yes, and I'll be right behind you!" Thomas quipped.

"It seems strange to be sailing without Father. This is the first time we have been out without him. I sure miss him," Sean said as he looked to the deck.

"It truly is strange. I half expect to turn around and see him there, or hear him yelling to the top men to 'Make more sail!' Remember what he said though Little Brother, we are not to go out seeking revenge. We are to do this for a higher purpose," Thomas cautioned.

"I've worked through that, so do not concern yourself there. My mind is clear. However, if we ever meet up with that bastard that killed him, I will be sure that he troubles no one else with his presence! Now I must go get the men ready for their gunnery practice. We should be coming up on the hulk within the hour."

Sean and Lanigan pulled the marines together, and went over the steps for firing the guns again. They had already been grouped together on their separate cannons, five to a gun.

"We should be able to get two shots off as we pass the hulk. Since most of you have never fired a cannon before, the most important thing to remember is to sponge out the barrel after every shot! You will be going through the rest of your life without your hands and arms if you do not do this, and push a fresh powder charge into the barrel of a cannon that may still have a burning ember of powder in it. So remember, stop your vent, and sponge out between firing and loading," Sean warned them.

"The cutter's returning!" the call from the forward watch rang out.

"Calhoun, run to the bow and call out to them, see if the hulk is clear to fire at."

"Aye, sir." Calhoun got to his feet and ran to the bow. He returned a few minutes later and said, "They called back and said that the hulk is all clear. We can fire on it till she sinks if we are a mind to... sir"

"Thank you, Calhoun. Now to your guns. Powder monkeys, go below and bring up the charges. Gun captains, take charge of your guns, and prepare to fire!" Sean ordered.

The men all jumped to their tasks. They had practiced this in port, but this was the first time they would actually be firing the guns. The gun captains each barked out orders to their crews as each one selected a ball from the shot garland.

The two powder monkeys came back on deck, gingerly carrying the powder charges for the guns. They carefully placed one in the bucket by each gun and returned below deck to get the next round.

The gun captains barked out their commands, and the men threw themselves into the task of loading and running out the cannons. Sean and Lanigan supervised the men and were satisfied with their progress.

"Hulk ahead on the starboard bow!" the shout from the forward watch bellowed.

"All right, men, you will fire as you bear. Take time to be sure your gun is laid on your target. Try for right at the water line. After you fire, sponge out, reload and fire again," Sean instructed as he drew his sword. He rested the blade against his shoulder as he watched for the hulk.

The ship glided slowly down river towards the wrecked ship. The men kept popping their heads up to see the approaching target. "Now stop that. Watch out yer gun ports!" Lanigan reprimanded them.

"Ready, men! Now fire as you bear!" Sean shouted as they neared the hulk. He had raised his sword over his head and brought it down as he stood behind the first gun crew. The cannon belched fire and smoke as it slammed back against the restraining tackle.

In succession, each of the five guns fired and were immediately reloaded and fired again. On the second round, a ball had struck what was left of the main mast, bringing it down over the side.

The crew of the fourth gun cheered as they claimed the shot as being theirs. The men lined the side of the ship to observe the results of their work. The hulk sported several holes in its side, most right at or above the water line. They watched as water rushed in the lower holes, and the hulk listed further over towards them. It did not move far, as it was grounded firmly on the sandy shore.

The acrid smelling gun smoke drifted towards the hulk as the *Osprey* continued on its way down the river. The men chattered excitedly as they sponged the guns out and secured them.

"That was not bad for your first time firing together. Nice shot on the mast, by the way, number four; however that was not your target. In the future you will fire at what you are told to fire at. It will make a difference as to whether we want to dismast the opponent, wreak havoc with the rigging to slow them down, or to sink her," Sean admonished them.

"When we go into action, most of you will be either in the fighting tops, or lined up along the railing back aft. Only some of you will be working the guns with the sailors. We will man the swivels and the twelve-pounders on the side of the ship that becomes engaged."

"You have all been acquainted with the different types of shot, round, canister, grape, and Landridge, or chain-shot. As we will want to capture and board the enemy vessels, we will be trying to disable them temporarily. Once done and we board them, we will most likely take command of them and sail them back to port, so it is important to only disable them briefly," Sean instructed them.

The men were released to go below. Sean watched as they went. He was satisfied that they were ready, they were working together. They were a fighting force.

Taggert of the Marines by David Ekardt

4

Osprey, Bird of Prey

The weather had taken a turn for the worse as the *Osprey* sailed down the Delaware River. Almost as soon as the guns had been secured, the snow started swirling down on the ship. All but the essential men of the watch were sent below.

Sean and Lanigan strolled the deck, bundled in their heavy boat cloaks. "I've got the lads busy rolling and tying paper cartridges. When the weather clears up, I'll have them fill them up here on the deck to avoid any accidents below. They are also preparing the sacks for the cannon charges. No sense in letting them be too idle. It is a fine bunch of lads that we have, sir." Lanigan stated.

"I think so too, thanks to all your effort. I have really learned a lot from you, Sergeant. The men we got were not all of seafaring background as we were supposed to have gotten. However, the ones we got were all stouthearted fellows."

"Aye, that they are, and thank you for your compliment. It feels good to be back in uniform again. I liked my life ashore, but I did miss the feel of the deck under my feet and the challenge of turning boys into marines. You'll see, sir; they will stand fast for you. They respect you because you have been right there with them all the while. Even Calhoun, who has been a thorn in my side since the very first day, will be a fine one. He shows leadership, and that will become very apparent as time goes by," Lanigan replied.

The two walked up and back the length of the deck several times. The snow started piling up, and their footprints were near filled up by the time they started their second turn around the deck. Sean looked up at the rigging. Snow was accumulating on the ratlines, crosstrees and fighting tops. From aft, the bowsprit could hardly be seen through the snow.

The bow watch nodded to them as they reached the bow again. He stamped his feet and kept his hands under his armpits to keep them warm as he watched ahead of the ship. His partner came forward with two steaming hot mugs of coffee.

"Have any of the boys started turning green on us yet?" Sean asked.

"No, not yet, but I'm sure that we'll have a few do that as soon as we get beyond Delaware Bay into the Atlantic where things are bound to get a bit dicey," Lanigan smiled.

"What did you learn of our surgeon? I haven't had a chance to talk with him yet." Sean pulled the collar of his cloak tighter as they walked.

"It seems the good Mr. Faircloth had a wee bit o' trouble back in Boston. He managed to get out of that fair city just before a jealous husband and a group of his friends caught up with him. The husband had called him out for a duel, and Faircloth had winged him. That did not satisfy the man who wanted to tar and feather him. It was his good fortune to know a gentleman on the Navy Committee, who gave him this posting. I watched him lay out his surgical tools and examine them as we talked, and he impresses me to be a notch above most of his trade."

"That's good to know, and hopefully we will not keep him too busy." Sean glanced at the shoreline off the starboard side. They were passing a small cabin and farm. The windows of the cabin glowed warmly through the falling snow.

"How many eyes at the dock this morning and along the way were watching us and are watching us now to report our movement to the British?" Sean mused.

"Ah, there were more than a few, I suspect. You'll soon learn that in war, there are few secrets. Too many people out there can be had for a few shillings, or a well-placed threat. Money and fear are two powerful motivators in the wrong hands," Lanigan replied. Now I don't know about you, sir, but that coffee smelled awfully good, and I'm getting a tad too cold up here."

"I agree, enough exercise for now. Let's go below and get with Thomas to decide on where we should go 'hunting,' to the north or to the south. With this weather, I'm partial to going south to a warmer climate," Sean joked.

The two descended the steps of the main companionway, picked up their mugs of coffee, and made their way through the crowded crew's area to the rear cabins. The crew and marines were busy with personal tasks, rolling the paper cartridges, or skylarking in the cramped yet surprisingly warm compartment.

Sean, Thomas and Lanigan poured over the nautical charts in the captain's cabin. The windows were already frosted over, and the subdued sound of the water rushing below the cabin made a relaxing sound. The three agreed on the southerly route, to patrol the Maryland, Virginia and Carolina coasts.

They would be most likely to have success unimpaired by British warships along there, rather than to go closer to the New York area. The shipping traffic between the islands to the south and the northern cities had picked up due to the British using their island ports to stockpile munitions.

Lanigan apprised them of different tactics of small boat action and how to board hostile merchant ships while keeping them under the gun. His years in the Royal Navy as a Royal Marine were quite an asset to the brothers. With his knowledge and their experiences dealing with Caribbean pirates, they were sure to succeed, Sean thought, as he sat back in his chair listening to the other two talk.

"Come in," Thomas said in response to a knock on the cabin door. "Ah, good evening, Doctor. It's good of you to join us for dinner. Plato will have our meal ready in a few minutes. Care for some brandy?"

"Good evening, gentlemen. Yes a brandy would not be amiss at the moment." He shook hands with the other three and sat in one of the padded chairs of the cabin. He looked around after taking the proffered glass.

"Cheers, gentlemen." He raised his glass, the others did likewise, and all took a drink of the brandy. "I must confess, this is the first time I have taken a voyage, and I fear that I am a bit queasy. Does the sensation last long?"

"Have no fear, doctor, you'll have your sea legs in no time, Just you wait till we get out in the ocean," Thomas assured him.

"Doctor, have you had much experience working with bad wounds and such?" Sean asked.

"Well, not in the light of what can be expected in a military situation. However, I have had my share of broken bones, gunshot wounds, and amputations. Don't worry, gentlemen, you are in good hands, and I do not believe in using leaches." He smiled.

"Aye, now that makes me feel better already!" Lanigan replied.

"Tomorrow the doctor will examine the crew when they are off duty, so have your marines ready for that too. I had hoped to have this done before we set sail; however, that was impossible with your late arrival. You'll be glad to know that we do have plenty of fresh food and vegetables, with some fruit on board. We have always seen to having good food for the crew," Thomas stated.

"Ah, that is wise, a healthy crew and less grumbling about bad food. How long do you expect to have us out on patrol?" Faircloth asked.

"We can stay out for a few months. However, we need to be back in port by the middle of January. The fleet should be ready then, and we will join with them on some grand adventure," Sean answered.

"Adventure, 'tis hard to imagine what is happening." Faircloth paused. "This is all an adventure into something grand all right. The people of the colonies shaking of the control of the Crown, God help us all!" he mused as he took another drink.

The men chatted all through their dinner, and were treated to several sea stories of Lanigan's, while outside the wind continued to blow snow down on the diminutive vessel. The *Osprey's* motion had increased noticeably as it moved further towards the Atlantic.

"Gentlemen, you'll excuse me, but I believe I shall turn in for the night. The brandy and the rolling of this ship have a decided ill affect on my stomach." Faircloth rose unsteadily to his feet, grasping for the deck beam overhead to steady himself. Slowly he made his way to his cabin, just in time to grab the slop pail in the corner. For the next several minutes, the others could hear him retching as the ship rolled vigorously to the waves outside.

"Aye, 'tis a sad thing indeed when we get a doctor who is a landlubber for sure." Lanigan smiled as he excused himself and left the cabin.

"Well Brother, shall we take a turn around deck before turning in?" Thomas asked Sean.

"Let's be off," Sean replied, as he picked up his heavy boat cloak.

They went up the steps to the deck. The frigid wind caught Sean by surprise as he fought to keep his collar tight around his neck.

"How goes it?" Thomas near-shouted to the helmsman.

"We're holding course well, sir. The sails are fine; we should not have to take in another reef. She's a fine ship for running before the storms!" he called back to Thomas over the noise of the wind.

Thomas nodded and together with Sean, walked up the starboard side of the deck. They checked the rigging along the way, taking time to tug on one now and then to be sure that they were all taut and not working loose from the gale-force winds.

As they reached the bow, Sean could make out Edward George, his Delaware friend standing with the bow watch.

"Good evening, Edward. Quite a bit different than the forests back home, eh? We have not had much chance to talk lately with everything that has been happening, but it's good to see that you stayed with us. You could have returned home, you know," Sean said to his friend.

"Yes, I know that I could have returned to my homeland, but I wanted to see more of the wonders that the Great Spirit created. This storm, the wind, the snow, the movement of the waves, it is all so powerful, yet beautiful!" He almost had to shout over the crashing of the waves against the bow as the ship ploughed through them.

The Delaware reveled in it all, so enthralled in the majesty of the ocean and the storm. Heedless of the drunken motion of the ship and the heaving deck as it rose and fell on the crests and troughs of the waves, he held his arms outstretched over his head, and launched into a chanting song of his people.

The sailor of the bow watch cast a bewildered look at the Indian, and another back at Sean and Thomas, who just shrugged their shoulders and moved on. "He told me earlier that the weather would clear by midday tomorrow. Even Cameron was reluctant to give me his estimate of the passing of the storm," Thomas hollered to Sean.

Sean just nodded, not wanting to fight the wind in conversation. They finished their turn around the deck and returned below. Each went to their separate cabins and retired for the night.

"Deck below, sail on the larboard quarter!" The call came down for the lookout on the maintop. Sean looked up at him. The full press of sails had been set early in the morning when the storm died down. True to his prediction, the skies had cleared by midmorning, and the crew had commenced cleaning the snow off the cannons, fixtures and deck. The sun melted what was left, when it climbed high enough in the sky.

"Can you make her out?" Cameron called up to the man high above.

"She's a topsail schooner, sir. She's changed tack and is coming our way. It looks like she has the Union Jack flying!"

The words went through the crew like an electric shock. They ran to the railing to get a better look at the schooner that they may soon be fighting.

"All right, you men get back to your duties. Marines, get below and get ready to earn your pay today!" Sean called out.

"Thomas, I want to keep them out of sight for now. I'll have the gun crews load the cannons but not run them out. Let's see if we can get her in close enough to slow her down with the first volley."

"My thoughts too. Mr. Cameron, have the helmsman bring her over a few points to intercept her without looking like we are trying to do that. Hands to the braces if you please, bosun!" Thomas ordered.

The crew came alive, each running to fulfill his part in the upcoming struggle. Except for the gun crews, the Marines stayed below, weapons ready. The lashings on the boats were loosened for fast launching when the time was right.

The two ships grew nearer, with the schooner showing no signs of fear of the *Osprey.* "Mr. Stark, send a man aloft with a glass. We need to know what she has in armament and crew," Thomas ordered the master's mate.

"Saul Dundee, come 'ere!" barked Stark as he took a glass from its rack. "Get aloft with ye and tell us what ya see. I want to know how she's armed and manned."

"Aye, sir." Dundee took the telescope, slung it across his back and raced up the rigging to the maintop. He clambered out over the futtock shrouds and down onto the top beside the lookout.

The men below waited for his report. "Deck below, she's got six guns, four-pounders by the looks of 'em. Ten maybe twelve crew, none manning the guns," he called out.

"Thomas, it looks so far as if he is not worried about us. We should get a lot closer before we hoist colors," Sean suggested.

"Aye, I think we'll let her get within a cable's length before we do that. Then you gun crew can put one across her bow," Thomas agreed.

Sean stood by the rail, partially shielded from view of the other ship by the shrouds. He watched his men crouched down by the guns, nervously chattering to each other. The sailors went about their usual routines, trying not to look over at the approaching schooner. The palms of his hands were wet with sweat, as he tried to keep a calm look about him. All was in readiness. The men had their instructions; all that would happen now only depended upon how long it took the two ships to close the gap between them.

He looked across the water again; the gap had narrowed. The signalman stood ready aft with the flag at his feet ready to be hoisted. Thomas nodded back to Sean and smiled. He, too, felt the uneasiness that sets in upon you prior to an attack.

The minutes passed, the distance shortened between the ships. It was time. Sean stood up from behind the rigging and called aft to Thomas. Thomas gave the order, "Hoist colors!"

The rattlesnake flag raced to the top of the halyard and burst out in the breeze.

"Number one gun, put a shot across her bow!" Sean shouted.

The gun crews stood up, when the foremost gun belched out its flame, throwing itself backwards against its tackle. The crew hurriedly reloaded as the smoke from their gun wafted back towards the others.

"She's pulling away!" Someone shouted as the crew of the schooner tried to change her course after the warning shot hit the water in front of her.

"All right, gun crews. We want to slow her down, not hole her, so fire at the rigging on the up-roll!" Sean commanded.

The crews acknowledged and waited for the ship to rise up on the next wave. The sound of the guns was tremendous when they fired. Sean was used to just four-pounders, not the guns they had now. As the smoke cleared, the crews had already reloaded, and the schooner had slowed to a near halt when the mainmast came crashing down and pitching over the side. It remained tangled to the ship by all the trailing ropes, which made it into a giant sea-anchor of wood and canvas.

"Man the braces, bring her about! Get the cutter swung out over the side, and prepare to reduce sail!" Thomas shouted out the string of orders, spurring the men to their tasks as they all tried to get a good look at the devastation that the guns had wracked on the schooner.

The crew jumped to their jobs. Within minutes the *Osprey* had come around to a position half a cable's length from the stricken ship. The marines came up from below and lined the rail, muskets pointing across at the ship. The schooner's crew lowered sail and colors to acknowledge defeat. The crew of the *Osprey* let out a collective cheer as they saw the Union Jack come down on the other ship.

Sean watched as the cutter was swung out over the side of the *Osprey*. The boat crew climbed down into it to prepare for the short pull to the other ship.

"Sergeant Lanigan, I will take the first squad over if you please. Get them over the side," Sean announced.

"Aye, sir, you 'eard 'im, lads, off with you, and don't forget what I told you about boarding a hostile ship. Leave yer muskets 'ere, and take pistols and cutlasses only. 'Ere, Calhoun, you take this swivel gun and mount it forward on the cutter. Keep yer eyes open and pay attention to what's going on around you," Lanigan instructed, as the marines climbed down into the pitching cutter.

"You watch yourself over there, Lieutenant, I know the lads will do you proud!" he said as Sean prepared to climb down the side.

"Thanks, Sergeant. We'll be back in no time." He shook his hand, then climbed down to the last step and jumped into the stern sheets of the cutter.

Sean watched the activity on board the enemy ship. The hands were chopping loose the wreckage, but made no hostile actions. He could no longer see the captain, whom he had spotted before the warning

147

shot was fired. Perhaps the falling debris wounded him.

The crew put their backs into the sweeps, bringing the cutter to the side of the stricken cutter in just a few minutes. Calhoun stood behind the swivel mounted on the bow and watched the faces above him, as one of the men behind him used the boathook to hook the chains.

"All right, men, draw cutlasses only until after you're on deck, then draw your pistols also. We want to get them grouped together aft, since most of them are there already. Betts, you keep them covered with the blunderbuss. Be loud in your orders to them, Make them fear you," Sean instructed as his men started climbing up the side of the ship.

Once on deck he was pleased to see his men herd the crew aft by the tiller. The captain lay on the deck before them, bleeding from the head. His attendant knelt beside him, trying to bandage the wound with an old cloth. Sean saw no other injured men.

"Corporal Beckett, take Baum and Potts below with you and search for others. Then determine what they have on board," Sean directed.

"Aye, aye, sir. Come on, lads, let's get it done," Beckett called to the others.

"Now you men, what happened to your captain, and where were you bound?"

"Ferguson struck 'im down, sir, he wanted us to turn and fight you. None of us wanted to get killed today, it ain't our fight. I'm O'Malley, sir; I'm second on board the *Dancer* here, sir. We was bound for Charlestown with sundry items for the army there and some dispatches. 'E didn't have time to 'eave 'em overboard, they's still down in 'is cabin."

Sean sized him and the other up for a moment. They were all able-bodied seamen typical of their lot. O'Malley stood straight up, no fear in his eyes or voice, a proud man. "You men have nothing to fear from us as long as you cooperate. Refuse to work the ship, or try to retake this ship, and you can well imagine the consequences. This ship will be sent up to Philadelphia to be auctioned off in prize court. Any of you men that want to sign on with us, now is the time. If not, you will be free to go once you reach port." Sean looked each man in the eyes as he talked to them.

"What about the captain?" came the shaken voice of the man attending the injured man.

"The same goes for him. If he causes trouble, he will spend the voyage below in chains and be treated as a prisoner of war back in Philadelphia, with possibility of parole," Sean replied.

"Sir, there is no one below. She's carrying a mixed cargo of non-military stores. I did find this satchel in the captain's cabin. It has several sealed documents and a lead weight in it. I figured it must be important to have that in it for throwing into the sea," Beckett reported.

"Thank you, Corporal. You have a good background in seamanship, having been one of our crew. I'm going to put you in charge of the prize crew. I want you to take her back to Philadelphia for auction. The satchel you will turn over to Captain Nicholas or the Marine Committee when you return. You and the others can consider yourselves off duty once all those matters are taken care of, pending our return. I will give you written orders once you have picked your men," Sean informed him.

"Thank you, sir. I'll not be needing much. I'll keep Baum, Potts, and Richards should do, oh, and three of the hands in the cutter, just in case this crew gets lazy on us," Beckett replied.

"Fine choices, all. I'll have your kits sent over, along with your orders. How much powder did you find below?"

"They have four hundred-weight barrels," Beckett reported.

"Good, we'll offload three of those to the *Osprey* to bolster our supply, and that will leave you more than enough. Start the crew bringing them up, and I'll send the cutter back over to bring it across. Hoist no colors until you enter the bay. Then hoist ours above the Jack so everyone knows," Sean cautioned.

"Let's go, men, back to the ship," Sean called to the others. Once they were in the cutter, the three crewmen climbed up the side to take their places as the prize crew. They carried their own cutlasses and pistols.

Once they returned to the *Osprey*, Sean had the men's personal gear loaded into the cutter as soon as a new crew prepared to go back across for the gunpowder. When all was accomplished, both ships hoisted sail and went their separate ways. *Osprey* headed south, while the captured schooner, one mast short, turned north for Philadelphia.

After they were under way, Thomas, Sean and Lanigan met to review their actions. "Aye, that was a neat piece of work, it was," Lanigan commented. "It went like clockwork, and very few go that easy. Not one of our lads hurt, and only one injury on board the enemy."

"Yes, they should all be so easy, but we all know

that they will not be. It surely has put the heart into the men though. They are all walking a bit taller today," Thomas added.

"'Tis good to get an easy victory right off for a new ship and crew; it pulls them together quicker than anything." Lanigan agreed.

"That crew had no stomach for a fight, and I wouldn't be surprised if Beckett doesn't get them all to change sides once they get back home," Sean chimed in. "Well, Sergeant, I think that once we've inspected the weapons, it will be time to pipe up spirits, don't you think?"

"That it will be, sir, and we better go back up on deck, for the lads should just about be ready by now," he replied.

The two formed the men up, and slowly went down the line, inspecting all their weapons prior to them being put back in the arms chest. Once done, Sean motioned to the bosun, who in turn piped up spirits. The men hustled below to stow their weapons and appear back on deck with their tankards to line up for their tot of rum.

Sean sipped his rum as he stood by the rail. The men were still all excited over the day's events. He just hoped they would stay that way. The training had paid off. He had observed each man's reaction during the engagement, and although a few were outwardly nervous, they had all performed exceedingly well.

He gazed out over the open ocean; the glare of the sun on the water was near blinding. He watched as a few errant seagulls hovered overhead, riding the wind currents. They were only two miles off the Delaware shore, almost to the Maryland coast. The deck had finally dried up from the melted snow. The wind was still crisp, but the sunlight beating down, combined with the rum, took the edge off the cold.

The rest of the day, the Marines spent on deck filling the paper cartridges with powder and shot. Sean had one detail fill the serge cartridges with powder for the cannons. The tasks were delicate, and all precautions were taken to prevent any sort of spark from igniting the powder. The men removed all metal from the area to include the removal of their shoes to make sure that the cobbler's nails in them did not spark against anything.

While the others worked on the musket and cannon cartridges, Lanigan and Calhoun along with the gunner, prepared the grenades. They had managed to get a supply of empty ones that needed to have the powder and fuses attached.

"Sergeant, why did you pick me for doing this with you? I thought that you didn't like me?" Calhoun asked the older man.

"Ah, you see, laddie, 'tis not a matter of likin' or not likin', 'tis a matter of making sure that you don't blow us all up doing this work!" Lanigan smiled as he replied.

"Calhoun, you're a good lad, just a bit misdirected. You've been a thorn in me side ever since the first day, but I know that you have the spirit for what we are about. You'll be a good Marine some day in spite of yourself. Just don't be so pig-headed about being contrary all the time and you'll do well," he advised.

"I know you're right, it's just that I've had some tough times growing up, and don't trust those in charge too well. I ain't ever seen people in charge like you and the lieutenant, doing the same things as everyone else. You take the same risks as us, and that confuses me. I never experienced that before," responded Calhoun.

"Well, lad, that's just the kind of people we are. That's what being a Marine is all about. When it comes right down to the real hot action that you'll find us in, we need to be able to trust and rely on each other to get us through the tough times. It's important to know that when you're in the thick of it, the lads on either side of you are going to protect you as much as they do themselves," Lanigan advised him.

"I see. You know, I kinda felt that today going over to that ship, not knowing what was going to happen, were we going to be all right, or were they luring us in to open fire on us? Somehow I knew when I saw the others in the boat with me, and all looked the same way, that things were going to work out just fine. I imagine this is what having a family is like, everyone being there for each other. I never knew what it was like, having been out on the streets since I was a youngster. I always had to fend for myself."

Calhoun fixed the fuse in the grenade he was working on as he looked down. He had never told anyone about his youth before, never trusted anyone enough to let his guard down. Quietly he placed the grenades in the bucket for the gunner who took them below to store.

Lanigan looked at him. *You'll do, lad*, he thought to himself. He had finally gotten through to him, although he had pretty much figured him out long ago. It was always good to make these boys think for themselves and figure things out. *Yes*, he thought, *this one will do just fine from here on.*

The next day as the crew was cleaning the upper deck, the call from the masthead lookout stirred them all. "Sail on the starboard bow! There's two of 'em!"

"Secure from cleaning, all hands prepare for action. Man the braces, we've got the wind, so let's beat down on them!" Thomas shouted out. The men sprang to their duties, and within minutes, the ship was headed on an intercept course with the two unidentified ships, and the marines were busy loading the cannons and taking their places in the fighting tops and along the aft railing.

"That was well done, men, that took just under ten minutes," Sean called out to the whole crew as they all stood watching their prey looming closer. The two ships came on not the least bit concerned for the ship coming close towards them.

Sean walked along the deck behind the gun crews. "Stay down, lads, we don't want them to see too much just yet. Looks like two schooners, probably coming up from the islands. We'll be letting them know who we are in a few minutes now," he advised them.

"They seem mighty confident that we are friendly, don't they, sir?" one of the men asked.

"Yes, they do, and why not, they think that the worst is behind them- the pirates in the south that is. They'll know better shortly," Sean replied.

"We have the weather gauge on them, so let's show them who we are. Hoist the colors!" Thomas ordered.

The rattlesnake flag broke out in the breeze as it hit the top of the halyard. The schooners were just out of cannon shot when the flag was raised. The result was almost immediate. The two ships altered course

154

towards shore. Both raised the British colors as they did so.

"They mean to close on the shore that is not a good choice for them." Sean observed to his men. "All right lads, run them out and get ready to fire. Remember, we want to stop them, not sink them," he laughed.

The ships closed the distance, as the shoreline loomed closer. The furthest schooner was closest to shore, so it had a better chance to escape. The closer one tried to angle harder towards the Maryland coast.

"All right now, lads, we're close enough. On the up roll, fire at her rigging!"

The *Osprey* plunged into the next trough, and as it rose to the crest, all five of the guns belched out their fire and smoke. As the smoke blew away from the ship, the men could see the nearest schooner as they reloaded.

"Her mizzen's been hit!" someone called out.

"Let her have another round, lads. Bring that mast down all the way!" Sean encouraged them as he watched the stricken ship's mizzenmast sway drunkenly, held up from the break by the rigging. The Landridge that the guns were loaded with should cut it free with this round, he thought.

The guns spoke again. The crews hurriedly reloaded as they peered through the smoke and saw the mizzen and the top of the foremast go over the side.

"She's coming around. Get ready, lads, they are going to fire on us!" Sean shouted out.

As he turned back around, the enemy ship fired off its broadside of four guns. The ragged shots went high, and only parted a few lines. The men cheered from relief, as a few men scrambled up the shrouds to repair the rigging.

"We won't be so lucky next time, lads, so fire true this time. We need to cripple her guns." Sean told the men. "On the up roll, aim at her side."

The blasts of the guns were matched with those of the other ship. Sean felt the breeze of grapeshot whisk past him as one of his men took a full measure of it, exploding his head, splattering blood and brains across the deck.

A sailor fell from above, also hit by the grape. Several others were hit, but not killed. The men reloaded and fired again. This time they were not fired upon themselves, as the enemy guns fell silent. Sean looked up to the fighting tops and saw his men busy firing and reloading their muskets. Lanigan was on the main ratlines directing their fire. The others along the aft railing had stopped firing as they helped a few of the wounded men below at Thomas's direction.

"They've struck their colors, cease fire!" a voice cried out from forward.

"Stand easy, men. Those of you that were hit, get below to the surgeon. You two, here, get Hadley's body out of the way, poor soul." He looked at the expression on their faces as they saw their dead messmate's headless body.

"The other one has run aground!" the lookout called, "The crew is running away on shore," he reported further.

Sean put his telescope to his eye and could see the second schooner, with both masts snapped off half way up, beached on the shoreline. The crew was indeed running across the beach and into the tree line.

"Why would they run aground like that, Sir?" asked Timmons.

"To avoid a fight, and possibly deprive us of her cargo. You see, if we cannot off load their cargo to our vessel, then we would have to leave it, giving them the chance to return and retrieve it themselves and possibly re-float the ship. But we will not give them that opportunity, for we will fire that ship if we cannot get her off ourselves."

"Look there, someone threw a satchel out the window of the cabin. She must have been carrying some important messages," one of the marines at the first gun called out.

"All right, you men stay at your guns, we have to board that ship. After guard, prepare to disembark!" Sean called out as he stood out of the way of the crewmen who were busy hoisting the cutter over the side.

The men eagerly climbed down into the bouncing cutter. Sean assessed the schooner as they approached. The wreckage of the two masts trailed along the side of the ship.
Blood trickled down the pock-marked side, giving it a ghastly appearance. They were across to the enemy schooner in minutes, but most were not prepared for the sights awaiting them on the deck of the foundering ship.

The first man up almost slipped over the side when he stepped in a pool of blood. The others were aghast at the sight of the carnage on deck. Only a few of the crew remained, all were wounded.

The deck was a macabre scene, with upturned guns, broken spars, cordage and bodies strewn about in disarray. Sean ignored the sounds of two of his men retching over the side. He had seen this before in his fights with the Caribbean pirates.

"You wounded men, we have a doctor who can look after you. Get down in the boat, and they'll take you across. Is your captain still alive?" he asked them.

"He were wounded pretty bad and went below, we haven't seen 'im since," answered a man with a bloodied face and broken arm.

Sean watched him as he shuffled towards the side with the others, the look of defeat about them. "Pitch the bodies over the side, and check for anymore survivors. Svenson, come below with me," Sean ordered.

The big Swede followed Sean into the darkness of the lower deck. They found the captain lying across his pallet in the rear cabin, blood pooled on the deck beneath him. The man was dead, yet looked fierce even in death, hand gripping his sword. Sean grabbed the logbook and checked the manifests. They were carrying a load of rum to the British garrison in New York. They'll be without their spirits for a while, he thought to himself, as he paged through the papers.

"Let's go check out the cargo hold," he said to Svenson, who stood there gaping at the corpse. The two made their way through the cramped hold and found nothing other than what had been on the manifests.

"They have plenty of fresh fruit just from the islands. Get a couple of the others down here to load this onto the cutter. No, forget that; let's get out of here. The water is rising;, he must have blown a small hole in her bottom, not enough to sink her fast, but sink her just the same."

The two regained the upper deck, and Sean ordered them into the cutter that had just come back across from delivering the wounded crewmen. Sean picked up a smoldering slow match and returned below. In the captain's cabin, he wadded up all his papers and set them afire. By the time he was back on deck, smoke was billowing out of the cabin windows and up from below.

He quickly clambered down into the waiting cutter and ordered the men to cast off. By the time they reached the *Osprey*, the enemy ship was engulfed in flames and settling down in the bow.

"Sure is a shame to burn all that rum. Brings a tear to me eye's!" one of the men lamented.

"It is indeed, but we'll see what the other one had on board it's in less of a chance of sinking under us," Sean replied light-heartedly.

Once on board, Thomas worked the ship around to get as close as they dared to the grounded schooner. "We have plenty of time to determine if we can get her off or not, so let's see what we can do, he said to Sean.

"What was our cost on this one?" he asked his brother.

"We lost your man and Carter, a top man. Eight men wounded all told, none too seriously from what Faircloth has told me," Thomas replied.

"This was a costly one. We'll do better next time." Sean said.

"They cannot all be easy Brother, remember that. This is a risky business. Men are going to die and be hurt. You do the best you can to avoid that, but expect it all the same," he counseled.

"I know you're right, but it doesn't make it any easier. Looks like they're ready; we'll go across now." He left his brother's side and again climbed over the side into the cutter. The grounded schooner appeared to be intact except for the broken masts. There was enough of them to be ably to jury-rig small sails on if they could get the ship off the beach.

On board he and his men inspected the cargo and the hold. Indeed the hull was still watertight and should float. The crew's quarters and captain's cabin looked as if the crew was just up on deck. Personal belongings and coffee mugs were just as they left them when they were called on deck. Sean found nothing of importance in the captain's quarters. The manifests indicated the cargo of this schooner was rum for the army in New York also. That'll make the lads happy that we won't have to sink this load, he thought.

Back on deck, he conferred with bosun Sharp who had come along to inspect the schooner's situation. "Looks worse than it is, Lieutenant. The tide should be backing around in a couple of hours. With that, and a tow from the *Osprey*, we should be able to get her off. Right now, we have the waves working against us, but with the pull of the *Osprey* and the tide, she should slide right off."

"Good, you stay here and get the preparation under way. My men can help you with that. Rig the towline to the stump of the mizzen, and have the others help to rig sails. It will be rough going, but it should make it back to Philadelphia. I'll go back across and get things going from that end. We're in luck, even the wind is coming around; that will be a big help."

Back on board the *Osprey*, Thomas had the crew prepare to run the towline across. True enough when the tide started turning, the grounded schooner did slide off the beach with the help of wind, tide and the other ship.

Eight men were sent off on the prize. Its cargo would fetch a hefty price back in Philadelphia. The *Osprey* sailed on with its depleted crew. The weather had warmed slightly as they went further south. Thomas did not want to go too far south and run afoul of the British Navy presence around Charlestown.

For three days they beat back and forth without sighting any more ships until they were off Cape Hatteras. The lookout reported a sail from the south coming towards them, flying no colors. "Sean, take a look," Thomas said as he passed him his telescope. "Do ya know whose ship that is?"

"Looks like the *Gull*, old man Harris' ship, the filthy bastard. We should be smelling her before too long. He must have sold off his cargo in Charlestown and is headed home to put his blood money in the bank the bloody blackbirder that he is." Sean replied.

Two of the men standing nearby listened in on their conversation as they watched the approaching ship. "Hey, Hyland, vat's a blackbirder?" Heinrich nudged his companion as he asked.

"Why you thick-headed Kraut, it's a slave ship. They buy those poor devils from their own kind in Africa. They chain 'em up below on racks, laying in their own filth, not able to move except to be fed slop. They stay like that for the six weeks' voyage to some Caribbean or southern port to be sold. Them that dies along the way are the lucky ones. Wouldn't be surprised if the Lieutenant has us sink 'er."

161

"Aye, it vould be a blessing to do that," he agreed.

"Hello, *Osprey!*" The shout came across the water as the two ships came within hailing distance. "Can you spare some food? Our stores got ruined during the storm a few nights ago."

"Stand off Harris, or we'll put a shot into you. You know damned good and well that we will not aid you who deal in misery and death. Be off with you! Put into port and buy more food with your blood-money!" Sean shouted back with the speaking trumpet.

The captain of the other ship replied with a gesture, and yelled at his men to set more sail again. "Father once put a round right through his cabin one time to keep him away when they had fever on board. We came up from behind them, following a trail of bodies in the ocean. They dumped nearly a hundred bodies into the sea, not all of them were dead when they did. They were so afraid of contracting the fever their black cargo had that they were throwing them over dead or alive," Thomas said to the men standing there.

"God, what is that awful smell?" one of the men queried.

"That's the smell of death; I imagine Hell itself must smell that terrible!" Lanigan spoke up. "They will never get the smell out of that ship. "'Tis a dirty business; no man should be treated like that."

The day after the run-in with the empty slaver, the lookout called out from above. A schooner was headed towards them from the south. The men were rousted from their midday meal and sent to battle stations. The schooner kept on its course right up until she was within range. "Fire one across her bows,

162

Mr. Sontag," Sean directed the stout Dutchman on the lead starboard gun.

He put his slow match to the touchhole, and the cannon hurled itself backwards against its tackle as the shot ploughed through the wave tops towards the frail ship. The effect was immediate. The captain of the other ship turned towards shore. The *Osprey* gave chase, and the men all made bets as to whether she would run aground in the shoals, or if they would be able to fire more shots at her to dismast her.

They did not wait long for the answer. Even as far away as they were, they could hear the sharp cracking noise of both masts of the schooner snapping when it impacted on the rocks in the shallow water. The masts pitched forward and crashed down on the deck.

Thomas ordered the men aloft to shorten sail. The *Osprey* was of deeper draft, and he would not take her any closer for fear of ripping her bottom out in the shallows. "Look there, they're putting their boat in the water. They're abandoning the ship!" one of the men exclaimed.

"Bosun, have the cutter hoisted out. Sean, you and your boys see if there is anything worth salvaging off that wreck. If not, you can take target practice at it to sink it."

"All right, lads, secure those guns. It's your turn to go," Sean called out to his men. They hurriedly lashed the guns tight, put their muskets in the racks, and stood back as the cutter was swung out over the side of the ship. Within minutes, they were bouncing in the craft as the crewmen rowed towards the grounded schooner.

They hooked onto the chains and without a misstep, were up over the side, cutlasses and pistols drawn. "Betts, Rodrigues and Schultz, check the hold to see if it's taking on any water, and if there is anything we can use. I'll go to the cabin and check the manifests."

The men jumped to their assignments while Sean entered the captain's cabin below. It was in disarray from the impact. The former inhabitant had hastily gathered some belongings to take along when the ship was abandoned, as evidenced by the clothes strewn from a sea chest to the cabin door.

The cabin was bleak, even more so than the *Osprey's* living quarters, he mused to himself as he rummaged through the small desk. He paged through the manifests that were in a pigeonhole in the upper part of the desk. "Interesting, we have most of the baggage and spare uniforms of one of King George's Highlander Brigades. Well, those lads are a bit overdressed, so we'll just make sure to change that. They'll be a bit chilly this winter," he said aloud.

The others had gathered back on deck. They had brought up what weapons they found in the arms chest. "Nothing but a lot of uniforms down there, sir." Rodrigues reported.

"Yes, lads, the manifests indicate that we have captured the spare uniforms of the Highlanders. We are going to burn them. You two lads go up to the cable tier and see if they have any paint or tar stored up there, anything that will get a fire going real good. Rodrigues, go below and make some pile of those pretty red coats for them to douse. Use anything that you can find. I want this to be seen as far as possible."

The men hurried about, dousing the piles with the flammable liquids that they found. The ship was ready to be fired. They passed the captured weapons down to the men waiting in the cutter as Rodrigues, Betts and Schultz set them alight with torches. The men raced up to the deck after setting the below decks ablaze. Sean motioned for them to get into the cutter while he put his torch to the piles of canvas from the broken masts on deck.

He went back to the side and tossed his torch into the open hold, as great masses of black smoke came billowing out of every opening in the ship. Sean took his place in the stern sheets as the crewmen pushed off from the burning ship. The men watched in amazement as they rowed back to their ship. The fire raced up what was left of the rigging, along the entire length of the schooner, and out along the bowsprit.

"Them Highlanders won't be lookin' too pretty for a while, I'm thinking!" Betts spoke out. The others in the cutter all laughed. Not a great victory, but Sean knew that the loss of their uniforms would be a serious blow to the morale of the troops that were expecting and needing them.

As soon as they were back on board and the cutter was once again in its place on deck, they headed south again. The men were allowed to fire the cannons at the burning hulk as they left the scene. Each gun managed to hit the schooner as it burned.

Once again they beat back and forth along the patrol route for two more days before any other ships were sighted. They had gone far offshore to be out of sight of anyone on shore, or in fishing boats along the coast so that their movements could not be reported. They were getting closer to Charlestown and the British Navy.

As they headed back in towards the coastline again, two sails were reported heading north. "One's a big 'un, an east Indiaman. The other looks to be a smaller one, maybe a bark. They're standin' in about a mile offshore," reported the lookout.

"All right, lads, jump to it. Stay low out of the sight of prying telescopes. Run up the Union Jack; we don't want those nervous boys turning rabbit on us!" Thomas shouted as the men all turned to their tasks.

"Sergeant, see to it the men stay down, out of sight as before. You top men get ready to race up to your posts as soon as the order is given. Stand easy, lads, we've been through this before," Sean cautioned.

Time seemed to stand still, Sean thought, as he watched the other ships coming towards them. The smaller cargo ship was off the aft port quarter of the big Indiaman separated by a cable's length. The ruse worked; the other ships did not alter course.

"Get ready, lads, not long now," he called down to his men.

Thomas held course as the distance between the ships decreased. They had to time this just right or the other vessels might run off towards shore before they could be stopped. "Sean, get ready to fire one across the lead ship's bow as soon as I swing her over," Thomas called out to his brother.

"Hands to the braces, put the helm over!" came the command. The crew snapped out of their carefree positions, grabbed the ropes and pulled with all their might as the bow of the *Osprey* swung across the path of the Indiaman.

"Fire your gun, Mr. Sontag, if you please." Sean ordered the gun captain.

"Aye, aye, sir." He replied as he touched off the gun. The Union Jack was hauled down and replaced by their defiant flag. The men came up from the hold to climb to the fighting tops. Some carried only their weapons while others were loaded down with sacks of grenades, swivel guns and the charges for them.

The shot bounced across the sea in front of the big ship, which instantly swung hard over into the wind. The other vessel nearly collided with its companion, not aware of the show of force from the *Osprey*. "Prepare to fire!" Sean called out as his men stood up behind their guns and the others had taken their places at the tops.

The crew of the Indiaman made no attempt to run their guns out as the two ships passed port side to port side. So complete was the surprise, they lowered their colors, knowing full well that their decks could be raked clean by the guns of the rebel ship.

As they glided past the now immobile ship, their captain shouted desperately to them with his speaking trumpet, "Don't fire on that ship, it's loaded with gunpowder, and you'll blow us all up!"

"Heave too and have your crew assembled on deck; prepare to be boarded!" Sean called back. He looked over towards the powder ship; they had already lowered their colors and taken in sail. Several of the crew waved any piece of white cloth that they could find, so worried about being fired upon.

The *Osprey* was brought to a halt between the two ships as both boats were lowered into the water. As the marines prepared to disembark in both craft, members of the ship's crew took their places at the cannons.

"Sergeant, you and your boys take over the powder ship, while we take the Indiaman. Muskets and bayonets this time; there are too many of them, we need to make an impression on them" Sean ordered as the men were climbing over the side.

"Aye, aye, sir. You watch yourself over there though, the John Company lads generally don't give in so quickly as they did. They may have something up their sleeves," Lanigan warned.

"Thanks, Angus, you take care over there. Don't want to see you go up with a ship full of black powder."

Sean climbed down into the cutter taking care not to miss timing his stepping off the side of the ship as the ship and boat rose and fell in the waves. He timed his step just right and stood in the stern sheets and watched the Indiaman for signs of activity. There was none as the cutter neared the ship. The crew had indeed all assembled aft as instructed.

"Lads, be careful on this one, they do outnumber us." Sean cautioned them as the bosun's mate in front hooked onto the chains of the ship. The marines clambered quickly up the side and fanned out across the deck, muskets held waist high, ready to fire or charge with bayonets.

Sean drew his sword and walked with his men as they approached the crew within fifteen feet of the massed men. He could see by their eyes that they were terrified. It was a mixed crew made of the sweepings of every port that the ship had put into, most likely. Better paid than ordinary seamen of the Royal Navy, they were also not the most loyal at times.

"Who is the captain, and where are you bound?"
Sean barked out.

A man in his late fifties came forward and spoke,
"I'm Captain Wells, and we are bound for New York
with military stores and powder." He nodded his head
towards the companion ship.

""Ere's the manifest. Look, we want no trouble
and mean you no harm. There are two more ships in
our convoy, a frigate and a ship-of-the-line. They are
following far behind, having chased off after two
unknown sails that were sighted earlier today."

"Thank you for that information. Now just stand
easy while my men search the ship." Sean turned and
nodded to Betts and Svenson, who took that as their
cue to go below. No wonder they caved in so fast; he
probably thinks the other ships will get here in time.

"Take the flints out of your muskets and pistols
now, lads, we don't want no sparks setting off the
powder in that ship. Leave your shoes in the boat
also, the nails in the bottom of them can make sparks
too, and make sure that you don't hit anything metal
with those cutlasses either, I don't care to meet my
maker today!" Lanigan ordered his men as the launch
approached the powder ship.

The men climbed aboard and herded the crew aft.
"Now will the captain please come forward?"
Lanigan asked.

A burly man in felt slippers came forth, face and
shirt greasy with his meal that was interrupted. "I'm
Captain Elders. We are not going to be any trouble,
just have your men be very careful. This is the worst
cargo I have ever carried, and I don't want it to kill us
before we get home," he pleaded.

"Fine, now we will be wantin' to offload some of this powder to the *Osprey* before we get under way, so we'll be needing the help of your lads. If everyone cooperates, it will be as if we were not even here. If any of you harms my men, attempts to retake the ship or blow the powder, you'll be thrown to the sharks! Is that understood by all of you lads?" Lanigan asked the men of the ship as he walked in front of them. He cast a scolding look at one of his men that chuckled at his theatrics.

"Sergeant, there's not a man here who will oppose you, they are all family men who want to see their loved ones again," came the captain's reply.

"Good, now let's swing your boat over the side, and prepare to load it with powder. Captain, if you would be so good as to direct your lads to turn to?" Lanigan directed a stern look to the captain.

"Right, you 'eard 'im lads, hoist the boat out, remove the main hatch cover, and get the cargo net ready down there! Come, hop to it, boys, you all know what to do!" the captain cajoled his crew. They all got busy with their appointed tasks. Within minutes, the ship's longboat was along side, and the crew was gingerly rolling kegs of powder onto the outstretched cargo net below.

"Corporal Sinclair, I'm putting you in charge of the prize crew. I want you and the lads to get this ship to Philadelphia. The stores on board her will supply General Washington's army with much needed supplies. You'll keep these men with you. The ten of you should be able to keep watch over the crew and get her home. I'll send your kits over right away so you can get started. We'll be along shortly after we

170

get some powder off the other ship."

"Aye, aye, sir! We should have no problem getting it done, sir!" The lads were just saying how a change of pace would do them some good, now weren't you, lads?" he responded.

"Aye that we were Lieutenant!" came the enthusiastic response.

"Good, now I'm going back to the ship, and will have your gear and orders sent across," Sean said as he stepped towards the entry port.

"Deck ho, sail on the southern horizon, frigate by the looks of 'er!" The cry came from *Osprey's* lookout. The men on all three ships heard his report.

"Don't get your hopes up, Captain. You are leaving for Philadelphia now. That frigate will not catch up to you in time to prevent that!" Sean gave the captain the sternest look he could muster as he warned him.

"Aye, it won't, and I wouldn't want it to. The bastard in command of that ship is a demon in human form, he is. That ship is cursed; no wonder they named it *Charon*!"

The word sent a chill right down Sean's back. That was the ship commanded by the man who killed his father. Sean said nothing more, but turned and climbed down to the cutter. Back on board the *Osprey*, he reported to Thomas what he had learned.

"We need to get the powder loaded and get under way before she gets much closer. If we weren't so low on powder, I would wait to transfer it until we were safer, but we need to replenish our supply before we run into any more trouble. We can always destroy the powder ship if it looks like we are in danger," Thomas observed.

"Right, I am having the men's gear sent right over so that they can get under way immediately in the Indiaman. I'll go across to see how Lanigan is coming along. The first load of powder is coming across now." He went below to write out the orders for Sinclair to be sent across with the men's kits that were being loaded into the cutter.

Once back on deck, he passed the orders down to the bosun in the cutter. "After you unload, row over to the powder ship to pick up a load. Be quick now."

Sean went forward to look for the frigate; he so wanted to come face-to-face with that bastard out there. It was just visible from the deck now, so they still had plenty of time. He stood back as he watched as the first load of powder kegs were swung up over the side and into the hold. The crew handled the load with the utmost of care. They were all too well aware of what would happen if something ignited the powder.

He climbed down into the boat, which was manned by the crew of the powder ship under the watchful eye of private Shultz. "Are they behaving themselves, Schultz?" he asked the stout German.

"Ya, dat dey are, zur. If not, then I vel club dem and trow dem overboard!" He broke out into a maniacal laugh which visibly unnerved two of the sailors.

"That bloke ain't roight in the head 'e ain't!" Sean heard one whisper nervously to his companion. Sean smiled and turned his head so that they could not see him trying to control his laughter. Schultz was known for his wildman act on board ship, and he was putting it to good use on these men.

On board the captured ship, Sean could see that the crew was busy hoisting another load of kegs up from the hold. His men were arranged along the deck out of the way, but close enough to quell any trouble. The captain stood by the wheel, guarded by Sheldon.

"Sergeant, that is the *Charon* coming towards us. Will we have the powder off-loaded in time to get under way with both ships?" Sean asked Lanigan. The captain stood as though he was not listening; however he was straining to hear every word.

"Aye, Sir that we will. These lads and I have an understanding. They will not slow us down, and I'll not feed them to the sharks," Lanigan beamed as he answered.

"Blimey, you Continental Bullocks are as crazy as the Royal Marines!" one of the crewmen remarked as he worked.

Sean and Lanigan looked at each other and smiled like conspirators. Everything was going smoothly, almost too smoothly. As they stood and talked, there came a shout from aft. Sheldon and the captain were locked in a struggle over Sheldon's cutlass. As Sean and Lanigan turned to see what was happening, the captain broke the cutlass free from Sheldon's grasp; and hit him in the head with the hilt, sending him sprawling.

"Don't shoot him, go after him!" Sean shouted to the nearest marine. Before he could reach him, the captain brought the cutlass down with all his might on the rudder cables, parting them, rendering the rudder useless.

As Sean and Lanigan ran aft, Hyland got up to the captain and tried to subdue him, only to be knocked senseless also. The captain had a wild look in his eyes as he saw Sean racing towards him. Before he could reach him, the man chopped through two of the mainmast backstays. The ropes sprang free of the tension they were under, snapping upward.

Sean reached the captain, and with one swift punch, sent him falling backward, tripping over a coiled pile of rope. Sean dodged the backstay rope as it came swinging back down. "Lookout, the maintop is giving way!" Lanigan shouted.

Everyone on deck ran for cover towards both ends of the deck. The maintop came crashing down, blocks and cordage raining down with it. Miraculously the debris hit no one, although everyone was stunned by the suddenness of the turn of events.

As the men all came out from their cover, the captain regained his feet unsteadily. He looked at Sean and said, "I just could not let you take the ship. You rebels have to be stopped!" Two of Sean's men grabbed him and tied him up. The rest of the men got the crew busy with bringing up another load for the launch.

"Sergeant, we will not be able to make repairs in time to get this ship under way, but I'm not going to let the Lobsterbacks get this powder back. We'll blow this ship to kingdom come before they get here!" Sean swore as he regained his composure.

"Aye, sir, that we will. Now that ship has that awful individual on it that you have sworn revenge on I understand?" Lanigan asked.

"Yes, he commands that ship, why do you ask?"

"Well then, sir, why don't we try to knock out two birds with one stone, so to speak. I can set a fuse on this ship timed to about when they will be getting here. We can bend on a signal that we need assistance; they will come close by, and BOOM! Both ships go up in flames." He gestured with his hands, indicating an explosion.

"I like the way your mind works. Now lets get the last load over to the *Osprey*, and I'll stay behind to light the fuse," Sean replied.

"No, sir, that just won't do. Setting a fuse to blow a stack of powder kegs is one thing. Setting a fuse in a ship, bouncing all over on the waves, out of control, takes something special. Besides, you have our mind fogged up with revenge. I, on the other hand, have the experience in doing this, and have no reason to have anything but a clear mind and am able to concentrate on the job at hand."

"But I cannot order you to stay behind to do this. I should be the one," Sean protested, knowing that Lanigan was right.

"Laddie, one of us has to be there for the boys, and that is you. I'll need one volunteer with me, and that will be Calhoun, I'm sure. Now as soon as the boats come back across after unloading, you and the lads get off with the crew. Have the mast and yardarm set on the cutter so that we can sail away from this ship as soon as the fuse is lit. This is tricky business to get it timed just right."

"All right, you win. I'll get you your volunteer. Do you need anything else?" Sean surrendered.

"No, I saw some coils of fuse down below, so we have what we need right here." Lanigan smiled. "You're learning, laddie, you're a grand officer, and that is no mistake!"

Sean gathered the men together and explained what was going to happen. As expected, Calhoun volunteered without hesitation. "I just can't let the

175

Sergeant get all the glory now can I? Besides, if 'e's good enough to stay behind, so am I!"

The boats made their last delivery and came back for the crew and marines. The cutter's sail was prepared for the two volunteers. "You only have about an hour, Angus, don't cut it too close," Sean cautioned.

"Don't you be worrying about us, you just have a big tankard of rum ready for the both of us when we catch up to you." Lanigan waved as the launch pulled away. The men all called out farewells and insults as they pulled away.

"Come now, laddie, we have our work cut out for us now." Lanigan slapped Calhoun on the back, took one last look at the approaching frigate, and led him below. "This is tricky work, you did leave your shoes off, good. You'll need to open a keg there, there over there and one here," he pointed out to Calhoun. "You do that while I get the fuse measured out and laid."

"I'm sweating already, and it's cold in here," Calhoun said nervously as he took the first keg from the stack where Lanigan had pointed out. "How many times have you done this Sergeant?"

"This is actually the first ship that I had to lay a fuse in." He grabbed the post by him as the ship lurched to a wave that hit it broadside. "I have blown up fortifications, buildings and some powder magazines though. You look kind of pale there, lad. Don't worry, if you make a mistake doing this, you'll not live long to regret it! You'll be staring Saint Peter in the face before this ship finishes burning up!" He laughed as he unwound the fuse from the spool.

The two men worked in the dim light until the powder had been poured out on the deck where the sergeant had instructed, and the fuse was stretched along the deck from the companionway stairs to the first pile of powder in front of the opened kegs.

"Now find a broom or take a shirt, and brush the deck clean of any stray powder. We don't want to ignite any stray powder before the main charge is ignited. That would ruin our little surprise, now wouldn't it? While you do that, I'm going to check on our guests."

Lanigan tread lightly up the stairs to the main deck. He walked to the side rail and looked towards the approaching frigate. It was closing in on them, and its crew had already taken in some sail so as not to overshoot the stricken vessel. He turned and looked towards the *Osprey*. It stood off a few miles, and beyond it, he could make out the Indiaman, already to the horizon.

"Calhoun, hurry up. Come on deck when you are finished!" Lanigan called out. He took off his green frock, stepped up on the railing, and grabbed hold of a brace. Holding his frock turned inside out, he waved it vigorously towards the frigate. The glint of sunlight on the lens of two telescopes showed that they were watching the ship for signs of life. Satisfied that they were not going to chase after the *Osprey*, he jumped down to the deck.

Lanigan was bent over massaging his knees when Calhoun came on deck. "I've got it all cleaned up. What's wrong, Sergeant, are you hurt?" he asked as Lanigan straightened up and put his frock back on.

"No, I'm not hurt, just getting too old for this business, maybe. Now get down in the cutter while I go below and light the fuse. Be ready to hoist that sail just as soon as I am over the side. We won't have much time to get away before she goes up."

Calhoun turned to go, then looked back around to say something, but Lanigan had already started back down. He clambered over the side, almost missing his step as he climbed down into the cutter. He checked the lines on the yardarm and sail to be sure that he could unfurl the sail as soon as the sergeant was on board.

Lanigan cupped the smoldering end of the slow match in his hand to be sure that no sparks fell into the deck as he descended into the hold. Twice, he was burned by it as he made his way to the end of the fuse. He walked the length of it twice to satisfy himself that there was no stray powder in the path of the fuse.

Silently he crossed himself, and blew on the end of the slow match until it glowed bright orange. He lowered it slowly until it touched the end of the fuse. Bright white sparks and smoke leapt from the fuse, as it took on a life of its own.

Lanigan watched it for five seconds to be sure that it was burning properly, then turned and walked up the stairs, straightening his uniform as he went. As much as he wanted to run as fast as he could he was determined to show Calhoun what courage under fire was. *No sense in scaring the poor lad more than he already is*, he thought to himself.

As he stepped out on deck, he took one more look at the *Charon* bearing down on them. He could make out individuals better now, working the sails and scurrying around on deck. They did not seem the least bit concerned about approaching the vessel.

He stepped over the side and climbed down into the cutter as if he had all the time in the world, and took his position in the stern sheets, hand on the tiller. He looked at Calhoun, who stared back at him in disbelief as he brushed some imaginary dirt from the sleeve of his uniform.

"Well, Mister Calhoun, are ye going to set that sail, or just stare at me all morning?" He smiled, hiding his own nervousness.

"Good gawd, Sergeant, we're about to be blown to bits and you're worried about yer uniform?" Calhoun responded, eyes wide open, as he worked the sail. He took his seat as the sergeant laughed at him.

Once unfurled, it billowed out like a shot as the cutter sprang to life. Lanigan laid the tiller over and grabbed the bulwark with his other hand as the cutter lurched over in response to the wind and rudder. Calhoun was taken by surprise and thrown across the boat.

As the boat was pushed out from the lee of the ship, it gained more speed and bounced lively across the waves. Lanigan looked back when Calhoun pointed, and he could see the masts of the *Charon* through the rigging of the powder ship. They had made their exit just in time. He looked forward toward the *Osprey* and noticed that they had taken in some sail to slow down for them to catch up with them. If they did not, and the *Charon* decided to chase the *Osprey*, the two men would be stranded in the cutter.

Lanigan resisted the temptation to keep looking back at the powder ship, as he watched Calhoun bouncing around trying to watch it to see the coming explosion. "Calhoun, why are ye so jumpy? You look like a hare in the springtime, bouncing all over like that. We're plenty far from that ship by now."

"Are you sure? That was an awful lot of powder in that ship. I just don't want that thing coming down on our heads when it blows! Look there, the *Charon* has taken in all sail and has come to a stop alongside!" he stammered.

Just as Lanigan turned to look, there was a brilliant flash and the tremendous sound of the ship exploding. The shock knocked Lanigan and Calhoun from their seats. As they regained them, they could see debris and parts of the ship veritably hanging far up in the sky, as they lazily stopped the ascent and came plummeting down into the sea.

What was left of the ship was on fire; the blaze and smoke filled the air. Sparks and burning embers falling from the sky caught the *Charon's* sails and rigging on fire. From across the water, Lanigan thought he could hear the men of the *Osprey* cheering madly. The *Osprey* had been turned around and was heading towards them.

"Straighten up your uniform and look sharp there, laddie. Yer a 'ero now, and yer messmates are a comin', so show them what a real 'ero looks like!" Lanigan could not contain the smile and the excitement he felt deep inside after witnessing the destruction that they had caused.

Through the billowing smoke and flames, they could see, crewmen of the *Charon*, desperately fighting the fires aboard their ship. Neither hurricanes nor monster waves were feared aboard ship as much as fire was. There was no forgiveness in a shipboard fire. Lanigan knew that from experience.

As the *Osprey* bore down on them, they could hear the men cheering. Not only had they kept the treasured powder from falling back into the hands of the enemy, they had also struck what appeared to be a mortal blow to the frigate.

On board the *Charon*, Jennings regained his footing as he clawed his way to his feet digging his fingers into ropes dangling from the rail. He looked around the deck, seeing only shear madness. His once orderly ship was in utter turmoil.

The blast, when it came, had taken them completely by surprise. They had approached the small vessel, one of his charges, to answer the signal for assistance. When they had pulled within hailing distance, his bosun could get no reply from the ship as he hailed it with his trumpet.

Someone from the mast had called out that there was cutter under sail just beyond the ship, and in the distance they could see the rebel ship apparently chasing the Indiaman. Then the blast from the powder ship shattered the cool morning air. The shockwave from the blast knocked several of the crew from the yardarms.

Everyone on deck had been blown from their feet, and as Jennings regained his footing, he saw that his crew was coming back to life. The officers, bosuns and quartermasters were driving the stunned sailors to their posts in an effort to subdue the flames.

Everywhere he looked, burning embers were falling onto his ship. Above him, several of the sails had caught fire, and flames were racing up some of the tar-coated rigging lines. Men formed bucket brigades up the ratlines to douse the burning sails, while others raced to get the cleaning hoses hooked up and others manned the pumps. He stood there stunned, digging in his ears trying to get his hearing back.

He tried to walk forward; and caught his foot on the body of the helmsman; a large splinter of wood had come down out of the sky and embedded itself into the top of his head. Jennings let out a gasp as he looked down and spied blood on his coat. He frantically tore at his coat to see if it was his own blood, but it was that of the hapless helmsman.

Pathetic fool, he thought to himself as he tried to regain his composure. He started yelling orders to his men, yet could not hear himself. He looked up in time to jump back out of the way of a burning mass of sail that came plummeting down from above.

Jennings and the officers drove the men in frantic haste to control the fires everywhere. It was fortunate that they had not as of yet brought powder on deck for the cannons; otherwise the flames surely would doom them.

Damn those rebels! I will hunt them down and have them beaten within an inch of their lives! He thought to himself as he struck a dazed sailor with the butt of his pistol. The man looked at him with wide-eyed terror as he jumped out of his way and took his position at the hose pump.

"You scurvy swine better not let my ship burn up!" he yelled as he dodged flames and men scurrying about with buckets of water and wet blankets trying to douse the flames. Jennings looked out through the smoke and could see nothing. There had been something familiar about that rebel ship.

"Get a line run aft and secure the cutter. We will not take it aboard just yet!" Thomas called out to the men at the side. They had just helped Calhoun and Lanigan up on deck and were thumping them on their backs and shaking their hands, congratulating them on their adventure.

"Come on now, lads, hop to it. We are going to give them Lobsterbacks another surprise!" Sean coaxed the men. They all broke away from the side party and took up their battle stations. "Welcome back, you two, wonderful job there. Now get to your stations, we are taking advantage of the smoke, and are going to blast that frigate right out of the water while they are too busy fighting fires to fight us!"

"Aye, aye, sir, now that's the kind o' thinking that I like. Come now, Calhoun, 'tis off to the fighting top for you. Get yer musket over there and get up there. Remember always shoot for the officers, beg pardon there, sir." Lanigan smiled.

"No need to, Sergeant. That is what they should do. You kill a snake by shooting its head, not its tail. Now instead of the top for you, I want you to take charge of the forward guns; I'll take aft. We have some sailors standing in on the gun crews since we have so many of our men gone now, so make sure they do the job for us," Sean instructed him.

"Aye, sir, that I will, those lads will shoot straight if they want their rum later." Lanigan laughed as he went forward.

"Steady now, lads, it will be our turn soon enough," Sean reassured the men on the aft guns. They all stood by the railings and peered into the dense smoke still coming from the wreckage of the ship. They could see some flames on the masts of the frigate beyond the burning hulk.

Sean glanced over at his brother standing by, next to the helmsman. Thomas nodded back to him. They both were trying to control the anger welling up inside, knowing that the man who killed their father was standing on his deck through the thick smoke. If not, then he lay dead on his ship; they would soon know.

The crew watched in silence as the *Osprey* glided past the burning wreck. In moments, they would be coming 'round and firing into the frigate. Sean ordered the men back to their guns to prepare to fire them as they made the turn and had the enemy's backside open to them. Time seemed to come to a halt, Sean noticed, as he tried not to pace and fidget.

The sound of Thomas' voice shouting orders brought him out of his reverie. The *Osprey* made a wide slow turn around the end of the wreckage. There, through the drifting smoke, they saw the stern of the *Charon*. The gilt-covered ornamentation around the stern cabin windows was about to be blasted away.

Sean watched as Lanigan brought his raised cutlass down as he yelled, "Fire!" He braced himself as he watched each of the forward guns lurch back against their tackle, and spew forth their deadly message. The guns were all double-shotted with grapeshot added for good measure.

Sean saw the ornate stern of the ship blown into tiny pieces, filling the air as if in celebration of some fancy party. The ship moved on, and as the forward crews frantically reloaded, Sean's crew prepared to fire. He stood with his sword raised as he watched the deck of the other ship. "As your guns bear, fire!" He yelled as his sword came slashing down through the cool air.

He saw the grape and shot tear through what was left of the stern. If men had been below deck, they surely would be cut to ribbons by the grape of five guns. Sean heard a loud crack, and saw the mizzenmast of the frigate sway drunkenly, before it tumbled over the port side of the ship. The last shots must have struck it below deck and broke it off.

"Sponge out, reload, prime your guns!" He heard himself calling out automatically as his eyes desperately searched the enemy deck for his nemesis. "Fire as you bear, this round at her deck, the next at her waterline!"

They would not give the larger enemy any quarter since they had them at such a great disadvantage. If it wasn't for the surprise and the fact that the entire crew was engaged in fighting the fires on board the ship, they would never had stood a chance against the *Charon*.

Sean was still searching intently when he heard the forward guns speak out delivering more iron and grape into the stricken ship. Finally a lonely gun replied from the other ship, then a second. Both were fired so frantically that the shots went wild, passing harmlessly over the main deck, hitting nothing.

There! There he was, hatless, his features blackened by the smoke, but Sean could make no mistake, it was the bastard that had killed his father. "Keep firing as long as you have them in your sights," Sean ordered his men. He heard the muskets of the men in the tops barking out as rapidly as they could be reloaded. The forward guns bellowed out again, and again two shots from the enemy.

Sean watched with dismay as musket balls hit the deck around Jennings repeatedly, yet none hit him. "Give me your musket!" he ordered Sontag, who was one of the afterguard.

Sean looked down the barrel of the heavy musket. He had Jennings in his sights. Slowly he squeezed the trigger, until he felt the musket kick his shoulder. Smoke filled his field of vision. He looked through the white smoke and saw a crewman stand up in front of his target just as he fired, and was struck in the side of his head.

He took the proffered paper cartridge, bit off the end and rammed it and the ball down the barrel, never once taking his eyes off the British officer. He took Sontag's powder horn and charged the flash pan. As quickly as he could, he raised the musket to his shoulder and took aim as his guns spoke out again. He felt the impact of two cannonballs hitting the side of the ship. Someone called out that they were well above the water line.

He told himself to settle down, took a deep breath, exhaled and once more squeezed the trigger. The musket spoke out again, and again; the luck of the other man held true as a yardarm came crashing to the deck next to him, deflecting Sean's shot. "Damn, that bastard has the lives of a cat!" he swore as he handed the musket back to Sontag, who looked at him dejectedly, not having the chance of firing his weapon but once.

"Go back to the aft rail and take another shot or two, you boys. You might hit something." Sean had seen the look in his eyes, and felt guilty for depriving him the opportunity. "You men of the gun crews can do the same," he added. They all jumped at the chance and lined up across the transom. The men took their time and fired back at men at the bow of the incapacitated ship.

Just then the lookout at the masthead called out, "Sail on the horizon! It's a ship of the line!"

"That's the other escort. We have to get out of here now!" shouted Thomas.

The *Osprey* was moving faster now, and there was no chance of getting off another good shot. He cursed himself silently for not bringing his hunting rifle topside with him earlier; he would not have missed with that.

He stood at the rail, watching the *Charon* fall behind them. Most of the fires were out except for two high in the tops of the fore and main masts. The reefed sails of both masts were still blazing. It appeared that most of the sails had been burned up, and a goodly amount of the rigging. Sean thought he noticed a slight list to starboard on the ship as they headed away from it. They watched as the stern of the burnt hulk of the powder ship shot into the air and then slid beneath the waves amid an explosion of frothing bubbles. Just as suddenly, the smoke from the burning ship dissipated, leaving only a thin pallor of smoke from the frigate.

The men in the tops broke out in a loud cheer as the ship slid beneath the sea, and it carried along the deck from each man on the *Osprey*. Sean could not hold back, and as he turned to face his brother, he too had joined in the cheering. They may not have killed their foe, but they had stricken his ship a mortal blow.

They all watched the *Charon* until it became a blur on the horizon. As soon as the men gathered themselves back together, the after-battle tasks of cleaning weapons, and checking for casualties and damage commenced. The men finished long after time for the noon meal had come and gone, but they all were treated to a double tot of rum once the tasks were all complete.

The only casualty was a lone sailor who had run below decks. Fearful of the sounds of battle topside, he sought refuge below deck. His timing proved fatal as he was cut in two by one of the balls that had come crashing through the side of the hull.

"Well, Thomas, I tried, but just couldn't take him down," Sean lamented to his brother as they sipped their rum.

"Don't worry, Little Brother, I don't think we'll see him again. Just think, he has to explain how he managed to lose two ships to our little *Osprey* and have his ship damaged beyond use. He'll be lucky to still remain an officer after this. Privileged personage or not, I can't imagine the admiralty putting up with such a loss. His own ship, if it does not sink, will be useless even if he manages to get it back to port. No, we have struck him a mighty blow today, and I'm sure that Father would be proud that we did not lose our heads with revenge."

"Aye, that he would, I think." He paused as he strained his eyes to catch sight of the Indiaman far ahead of them on the horizon. The men on board her had apparently slowed to let them catch up to them. "We should catch up to her by nightfall. Are you thinking about heading back to Philadelphia with her?" Sean asked his brother.

"Yes, I think it time. We have accomplished much on our first patrol, plus paring prize crews out of them has depleted our crew and your detachment. It's time to go back into port, collect our prize money, and pick up the rest of our crew. By now the fleet must be ready to sail out for whatever plot the Naval Committee has dreamed up."

"Yes, you are right. The men have pulled together like they had been shipmates for years instead of just weeks. It will be good to get home for a few weeks. I'm going below and write up my report. Call me if anything happens," Sean said as he turned to go below.

"The fires are all out now, sir!" a blackened and weary bosun reported to Jennings. He looked at the man and dismissed him with a nod of his head. He had no officers and only two boatswains to help him control the crew, or what was left of it.

At least half the crew was dead, and half of those remaining were wounded or injured, most of whom had worked frantically to contain the fires before giving in to their injuries. The ship was not much more than a hulk. The masts above the fighting tops were gone. The mizzen had gone over the side. There were three shot holes at the water line leaking water, and the rudder cables had been shot away.

The stern of the ship was open to the weather, as the cabin windows and much of the framework had all been blown to bits. Five cannons had been upended, damaged beyond use. Most of the upper deck had been scarred by fire, and much of the railings were gone. Below decks had not been spared from the vicious attack of the rebel ship. The broadsides fired into the ship as the rebels crossed the 'T' behind them had wreaked havoc below.

Jennings surveyed his ship as he sat on what was left of the skylight above his cabin. Men had dropped, exhausted, where they finished fighting the fires. He himself could barely move, more from rage than exhaustion. A few of the men closest to him looked at him, waiting for him to give an order or to say something to them. He sat there and stared back at them.

"Bosun, if the cook is still alive, have him get some food cooked for the crew. He can have a few hands to help. The rest of you men, while you are waiting for your meal, start throwing the bodies and the debris overboard. I want to be able to walk on this deck before dark!" He literally spat the words out.

The men were taken aback by his harsh attitude towards their fallen messmates, but none dared to oppose him or question his orders. Slowly the men dragged themselves up from where they lay or sat, and started to shuffle about.

"Yew 'eard the Captain, Crenshaw, get three men and get your galley fires lit, I want hot food for the men in thirty minutes. Brown, you take five men, bring up two spare spars and jury-rig one to each of the two masts. The rest of you men, split into two parties; one work the port side, the other the starboard. Get this deck cleared off," the bosun ordered the men, his voice nearly cracking from weariness.

Jennings, satisfied the men were responding, eased his pistol back into his shirt. He had started to withdraw it when it appeared the crew might balk at his orders. He stood up and walked to the companionway. He had to step over the bodies of his after guard to get there. The grapeshot of the rebel guns had cut them down.

Below, he entered what was left of his cabin. The wind whipped through the empty space. He looked through the remains of the cabin and saw the body of his servant. He bent down, grabbed the body, and unceremoniously lifted it up to the open stern and pushed it out. He turned to find what he could of clean clothes as the body splashed into the water below.

He stepped into the lazeret, where he found fresh water in a pail. Slowly he took off what was left of his soiled uniform and washed himself until he had all the black soot off him. His sea chest with fresh uniforms was untouched. He dressed himself in his clean uniform and found a bottle of brandy and one of his chairs. He up righted the chair near the blasted window, sat down and took a long swig of brandy straight from the bottle.

He remembered the rebel ship. It was the Scotsman's ship. The old man that had thrown him into the sea! Those two in charge of it must have been his two whelps! He would not rest until he hung them from his yardarm! His agitation welled up inside of him till it burst out when he heard a knock on the door.

"Enter, damn your eyes, and be quick about it!" he yelled at the cook's assistant. "Well, what is it, man?"

"Sir, I brought you your meal Sir.' The man stammered.

"Well just don't stand there, give it to me, then set that table back up so that I have something to eat it on," he commanded.

191

The crewman obeyed meekly yet quickly. He brought the small table from the corner of the cabin and set it before the captain. The captain set his brandy and dinner on the table. "Now you get busy cleaning this mess up. I want to be able to move around in this cabin by the time I am finished eating this slop!"

"But, sir, I was supposed to get right back to help get the crew fed." The crewman knew he had made a mistake as soon as he finished saying the words.

"Are you questioning my order to you?" he snarled at the man, who cowered against the wall as he waited for the captain to chastise him further. Jennings said nothing more; he just pulled his pistol out of his waistband, cocked it and laid it on the table next to his plate.

Nervously, the sailor obeyed his captain and said nothing more. Slowly at first, eyeing the pistol, the frightened man began pitching the debris out the open window. He stayed as quiet as he could as he set the cabin to rights.

Jennings ignored him. All he could think of as he ate was what he would do with those that had humiliated him like this. He would have to accept a tow back into port if the rudder could not be re-rigged. There was little doubt in his mind that he would face a board of inquiry and possibly be thrown out of the Navy for his humiliating defeat here this day. He would get those damned Scotsmen if it were the last thing that he ever did, he swore half aloud, startling the sailor who was working as fast as he could.

The next day passed uneventfully until close to dark. The weather had gotten colder, a stiff breeze coming out of the northeast. A sloop was headed toward them under full sail. "This one is a little one, boys. Let's grab her before it gets dark!" Thomas called out to the men.

"Sergeant Lanigan, have the men man the guns, if you please, and have Calhoun put one across her bow as soon as he has his gun loaded, if you please!" Sean ordered.

The men were already on their way to man their stations when Lanigan began barking out his orders. Within minutes, the guns of the port side were loaded and run out. Calhoun put his portfire to the touchhole of his gun as Thomas brought the ship over, giving him a clear shot.

As soon as they saw the shot hit the water in front of the sloop, the sloop's captain put her hard over on a course that took it towards shore a league off in the distance. Thomas was not prepared for the sloop making such a hard turn that he ran past it before he could bring the *Osprey* around to give chase.

"Damned near took the sticks right out o' 'er! Sean heard one of his men exclaim as they all watched the stately sloop race past, showing them her tail a cable length's distance off.

"Give her another warning shot, gun number two!" he ordered, not taking his eyes off the little vessel.

The gun next to him spoke out, sending the ball plowing through the water just to the starboard side of the ship. "That was so close it got 'em wet, it did!" the gun captain exclaimed.

The sloop pulled ahead of the larger ship, racing before the wind. Thomas had to change course after a thirty-minute chase, as he knew they were about to enter shallow water. "Hate to let that one go, but I don't want to rip the bottom out. Signalman, signal the Indiaman to continue without us," Thomas ordered. The Indiaman had taken up station behind the *Osprey* after they had caught up to it following yesterday's battle.

"He'll be hiding in the mouth of that creek over there for the night. That's a good place for them. They know we cannot come any closer. He is a cagey one, that one," Sean remarked as he and Lanigan came aft to discuss a plan of action.

"I was just telling your brother, this would be a good time for the lads to get the experience of a boat-action and cutting-out party. If the *Osprey* were to hold position here for the night, they may think we are going to wait them out. Instead, as soon as it gets dark, we should lower the boats, row inshore and capture her. They can't have much of a crew on that small a vessel, so it should go fairly well," Lanigan suggested to Thomas.

"That does sound as reasonable of a plan as can be. I would not like to see that one get away. They turned tail just a little too fast for my liking; might be trying to hide something important. Good, then get your men ready, select the crewmen that you need to row, but don't take too many as short-handed as we are now."

Sean and Lanigan got the marines together and discussed their plan, while the crewmen took in sail in preparation for taking position off the mouth of the creek for the night. The splash of the anchor reached them as they talked. The galley fires were lit, and the men were fed a hot meal with an extra tot of rum in preparation for their raid.

As soon as it was dark, the boats were hoisted out as quietly as possible. The crewmen had already gathered rags and old clothes to muffle the oarlocks so that their approach would not be heard. The men were armed with pistols and cutlasses, and two men had blunderbusses for good measure. Both boats had swivel guns mounted in the bow.

Sean had the men wait until an hour after dark to get loaded and shove off from the ship. They were aided by the fact that it was a moonless night and darker than most. The men settled in the boats and shoved off. The breeze had slowed down after the sun had gone below the horizon, so they did not have a hard pull to the shore.

The boats glided silently into the mouth of the creek, aided by an incoming tide, pushing the flow of the creek back upstream. The warm glow of candlelight spilled out of the stern cabin windows. There were lanterns hung at the bow and stern, showing them their destination. Sean and Lanigan had the boats hang back out of the reach of the light.

They watched the deck of the ship for any movement, and finally could discern two men standing by the rail talking. They would not have been seen had not the one man taken a draw of his clay pipe, which lit up their faces.

The sloop swung to its anchor rope, as the tide had pushed the stern upstream so that the bow was facing out to sea. This would be tricky, but they would have to row around to the other side of the sloop, just out of reach of the light.

Sean whispered over to Lanigan to take the stern, and he would take the bow. Lanigan nodded barely visible in the darkness, and as one, both boats pulled away from each other headed for their appointed positions.

Sean watched the men on deck as the crewmen pulled silently on the oars. They rounded the bow and came in close and fast to the port bow. The sailor in front hooked onto the sloop's chains with his boat hook and quietly pulled the cutter alongside. He and the man on the tiller held the boat tight to the ship while the marines readied themselves for the assault.

The side of the sloop was not high, so they would be able to vault themselves over the railing once they stood up on the benches of the cutter. Sean looked at the men; all were ready. "Now!" he yelled as the men jumped up the side of the sloop, yelling and firing their pistols in the air as they ran for the two watchmen.

The surprise was complete, and as the men on watch threw down their weapons, Lanigan's squad leapt up the side of the sloop from portside aft, just as men started pouring out on deck from below. There were a few shots fired, and within moments, all had settled down as the men of the sloop threw down their weapons. Lanigan detailed two of his men to run below quickly to be sure they had everyone.

They returned a few minutes later with the sloop's captain and a weighted satchel that he was attempting to throw overboard through his cabin window when they apprehended him. All told, they had fifteen crew and five passengers, all Royal Army officers, none above the rank of captain.

"You are all prisoners and will be treated fairly as long as you cooperate. You'll be taken to Philadelphia and be held there for possible prisoner exchange. Sergeant Lanigan, any casualties?" Sean asked.

"None of our lads are hurt, and only three of these buggers have gotten their heads stove in, but they'll survive. Shall we get under way, sir?" he asked.

"Yes, the boat crews can hook on aft. We'll tow them out to the *Osprey*. The officers will go below and be held in the cabin under guard. The rest of you men get this ship ready to sail out of here. Sergeant, you and the men watch over them. I'll take the helm."

Without any resistance from the captured crew, they raised anchor and set sail. Within minutes, they pulled alongside the *Osprey*. They held position there while the boats were hoisted onboard. Sean went back across with five men, leaving the rest with Lanigan. Thomas's second-in-command came across to take charge of sailing the sloop back to Philadelphia.

"This has been a worthwhile endeavor tonight, Thomas. The men did extraordinarily good out there. We have made a good haul on this one. The hold is full of muskets and six mortars and shells for the mortars," Sean exclaimed to his brother once back on board.

"This whole voyage has been quite fruitful indeed. But for now, we must get back to join the fleet. I think we are stretched much too thin now to take on anyone else, so let's hope we do not run into any of the Royal Navy." Thomas replied.

The rest of the voyage home was uneventful. The three vessels entered the mouth of Delaware Bay early in the morning. Thomas had the Indiaman go in ahead of them to ward off the large chunks of ice floating down the river. The tiny sloop came in behind the *Osprey* trying to stay in the larger ship's wake to avoid the damaging ice floes.

The procession made its way to Philadelphia. They had to take in sail and crawl up river to avoid hitting any of the floating ice too hard. Sean and Lanigan stood at the starboard railing watching the ice flow past them. He had come back across from the sloop the day before entering the bay, having put Calhoun in charge.

"Listen to the sounds of the ice breaking up over there in that inlet sounds almost like cannon fire," Sean observed as they listened to the cracking and buckling of the sheets of ice as they passed the inlet.

" 'Tis fortunate indeed that we have that Indiaman ahead of us clearing the path for us. I had the pleasure of going to Denmark in the dead of winter once. We were to deliver a party of diplomats there and reached port as it was freezing over. We stood just outside the port, the captain not wanting to be locked in by ice. We stayed there for a few days, and I tell you that the sound of a ship having its sides crushed in by ice is not a pleasant sound at all. We ended up having to come back home with those gentlemen, who had to wait till spring time to go back."

"Aye, that it isn't. I have heard that happen in Philadelphia one winter. We watched it happen the next wharf over from ours, as a ship did not get out in time. Not a pretty sight either."

Toward evening the little flotilla reached Philadelphia and was met at the docks by a crowd of curious townsfolk. The reunions of family and those returning from the sea were as they had been for centuries: treasured moments until it was time to set sail again. It was good to be home.

Taggert of the Marines by David Ekardt

5

The Marines Land

"Sir, the *Fly* has signaled. She collided with the *Hornet* last night. The *Hornet* suffered major damage and has to return to port. The *Fly* is going to escort her," the signalman reported, removing the ice-cold telescope from his eye.

"Not an auspicious start to this endeavor, eh Brother?" Sean said to his brother as he stomped his feet to improve the circulation in the bitter cold.

"First we sit in port for a month waiting for the ice to break up, then the gale we got blown around in last night, and now to find out two of our ships are damaged and returning home," Thomas quipped. "Acknowledge their signal," he ordered.

"Do you think the rest of the fleet fared well last night?" Sean asked.

"We should know in a few hours. That sail on the horizon should be the *Alfred*. We'll signal her as soon as we are in range," Thomas replied.

They looked up to watch the top men in the rigging splicing ropes and making other minor repairs necessary due to the beating they took in the storm last night. The wind was still blowing heavily from the northeast, and the whitecaps were lively. The marines busied themselves cleaning the deck and helping to hoist up a new mizzen sail to replace the one ripped the night before.

Suddenly everyone stopped to look for the source of a scream. The men saw one of the top men fall from the mainmast top. Sean watched, as his body seemed to fall in slow motion until it hit the side rail with a sickening crack and toss below into the sea. Men ran to the side in time to see the body sink below the surface.

"Who was it?" Sean asked.

"It was Jason, the new man that just signed up!" replied a sailor.

"Ain't we gonna stop and look for him?" asked Sontag, one of the marines not familiar with the ways of the sea.

"There is no use in it; if he did not die on impact with the railing, he'll be dead by the time we could turn the ship around. That water is too cold to stay alive in for but a few minutes," Sean replied.

It's a sailor's lot," said one of the sailors standing at the rail as he removed his hat. The others followed suit.

"May his soul rest in peace, may the wind always be at his back," Thomas said as he put his hat back on. Slowly the men returned to their work.

A couple of hours later, they caught up with the *Alfred* and relayed the information about the other two ships. On the horizon they could see the rest of the small fleet. By sundown they fell back into formation and resumed their course for the Bahamas.

The ships beat back and forth before the wind for weeks as the contrary weather hampered their progress. They were to attack the British outpost on New Providence and capture as much war material as they could.

"We should be off the southern tip of Abaco Island by nightfall. That is the pre-arranged rendezvous point for the fleet, had we stayed separated. Commodore Hopkins will want a council of war when we heave-to there," Thomas said to Sean as they took their mid-day meal in Thomas' cabin.

"Sam told me that he wanted to sail right into Nassau harbor and take the town. He argued that we would be better off landing on the other end of the island, taking Fort Montague by land, and then assaulting Nassau from inland, rather than by a direct attack on Fort Nassau," Sean replied.

"Let's hope that he takes the latter course. It will produce less casualties amongst the men. No sense in needlessly wasting lives."

"No sense indeed. Sam said that the garrison of British regulars had been withdrawn from the island, and only the militia was left to defend the place. That is still at least a couple of hundred able-bodied men who can put up a stiff resistance. From what I remember of our last visit there though, they are not too likely to put up much of a fight." Sean observed.

"Let's hope not, but I suppose we will find out soon enough." Thomas quipped as he refilled his empty goblet.

The deck tilted over slightly as a fresh breeze filled the sails, and Sean caught the plates and decanter of port from sliding off the table as it happened.

"Nice save there, Little Brother, I just hope you're that quick when the time comes ashore," Thomas said.

"Don't worry about me. I will be in good company. Now we should go back on deck; Sergeant Lanigan is going to have the men practice with the bayonet this afternoon, and I need to be there to observe," Sean replied.

"You have a good one in that Sergeant, he was a godsend. He certainly doesn't let the younger ones show him up. It still amazes me how fit he is," Thomas observed.

The rest of the afternoon Sean assisted Lanigan in running the men through bayonet practice and finally some drill as was possible on the crowded deck. Sean looked to the masthead when he heard the lookout announce their approach to the island of Abaco. He strained his eyes to see it in the haze on the horizon. They would be able to anchor off the island by nightfall.

He looked across at the other ships. The flagship, *Alfred,* stood out to the starboard followed by the *Columbus.* Behind them came the two sloops captured this morning by the *Cabot,* who brought up the rear behind them. Ahead of the *Osprey* was the brig *Andrew Doria*, and behind the *Osprey* were the sloop *Providence* and the schooner *Wasp.* The ships made an impressive sight, all sailing together.

Commodore Esek Hopkins had worked the ships as they sailed together in changing formations so that they would be able to work in unison if attacked. Except for a time when the *Cabot* and *Wasp* got their signals mixed and nearly collided, the maneuvers had proceeded very well, considering that most of the ships' officers had never sailed in formations such as they practiced.

Sean had watched the marines on the other ships, especially the ones on the *Alfred* and *Columbus* as they practiced drill when the ships were close enough to see. From what he observed, his own lads were no less capable than the others, and may actually be better, considering Lanigan's tutelage.

The fleet dropped anchor two hours before sunset. The anchors barely had dropped into the emerald waters when the signal from the flagship beckoned all captains and marine officers to the flagship for a council of war.

Sean stood and watched as the crewmen swung the launch out over the side of the ship and gently lowered it to the water alongside. The oarsmen were decked out in their finest uniforms to make a good impression on the commodore and the officers who were gathering.

The evening breeze was refreshingly balmy, considering the cold winter storms that they had passed through on the journey here. Sean removed his hat to feel the waning warmth of the tropical sun. The oars of the launch raised and dipped in perfect unison as the craft was propelled to the *Alfred*.

"Up oars!" commanded the bosun as he put the tiller over. As one, the oars raised straight up, glistening in the sunlight from the water running down them. The launch glided to a perfect stop alongside the ship. One of the men in the front caught the chains with the boat hook and pulled the launch closer to the ship. Sean looked up as he grabbed onto the steps and hauled himself up the side. He passed through the side port and stepped aside for Thomas to gain the deck. The side guard of marines snapped to and presented arms as they were piped on board.

"Request permission to come aboard," Thomas asked as he saluted.

"Permission granted. *Osprey* aboard!" announced the greeting officer.

"Welcome aboard, gentlemen. Glad to see that you weathered the passage to this place!" exclaimed Lieutenant John Fitzpatrick, junior marine officer of the *Alfred*. Sean and Thomas returned salutes and shook hands with the affable officer. They had known each other briefly as the marine battalions were formed.

"Captain Saltonstall and the commodore are below in the cabin, along with Captain Nicholas and Lieutenant Parke. Being the junior man, I am the official welcoming committee. Captain Whipple is already down there with them, while his marine officers are forward, walking the deck."

"Sean Taggert, come forward!" called out Lieutenant Trevett of the *Columbus*. Sean waved and walked forward to meet them as Thomas went below.

"Good to see you again, Sean. You know my commanding officer, Captain Shoemaker, and this is Lieutenant Cummings." The men all shook hands as Trevett made the introductions. "I was just telling them about your exploits in the *Osprey*. That was quite a successful foray that you were on, capturing all that shipping and battling the *Charon*! It's too bad she made it back into port. I heard that the British are repairing her, even after you all but sank her."

"I hadn't heard about that. Are you sure that you heard correctly about the *Charon*?" Sean was stunned as he asked.

"Yes, there was no mistake. My cousin came up from Charles Town where the ship put in. He saw it and heard the details of your attack with using the powder ship to attack the *Charon*. He could not believe the ship was still afloat from the damage. The captain was livid, and unharmed."

"That man is a pox to us, and has unbelievable luck. I had him dead to rights in my sights, when one of his men stepped in the way as I fired." Sean shook his head as he recalled the battle.

The men continued their conversation as they watched the boats from the other ships deliver their officers. The last of them arrived, and they all adjourned below to the great cabin. There was barely enough room for the twenty-three officers, so after pleasantries were exchanged, Commodore Hopkins got straight to the plans for their attack.

"Gentlemen, it is good to see you all here safe from the storms. I congratulate the men of the *Cabot* in their successful capture of the two sloops earlier today. Apparently they thought she was British, so they didn't try to run. Those two vessels will be the key to our attack tomorrow." He paused to take a drink from his goblet.

"I have come to the conclusion that we should attempt to assault Fort Nassau in the morning by sending all of our marines and some sailors ashore in the two sloops covered by the *Providence*. We have the element of surprise, and no one knows that the sloops have been captured. The *Providence* will move in a league out with the *Wasp* a league behind her to pass signals to the rest of us, who will be over the horizon until the fort is taken. With us out of sight, the surprise should be complete."

"Sir, do we have anyone familiar enough with the waters around the island so that we don't have to rely on the locals as pilots?" a voice from the back of the room asked.

"Yes, we do. Lieutenant John Paul Jones is the most familiar and will guide the attacking vessels

from the *Providence*. I believe the Taggert brothers
also are very familiar with these waters. Is that not
right, Thomas?" he looked for him in the crowd.

"Aye, sir that we do." Thomas replied.

"Good, so we have another guide if necessary.

"Sir, may I point out something about the islands
here?" asked Thomas.

"Certainly, Captain, go ahead."

"We may feel as if no one knows of our
whereabouts and that the sloops are merrily on their
way. However, with all the fishing skiffs about and
other small vessels sailing these islands, the people of
Nassau will know what we are about long before we
have the fort and town in sight. Remember, these
people have been dealing with pirates and navies of
several countries trying to invade them for years, and
they are very well informed of strange vessels in their
waters," Thomas pointed out.

"He is correct about that, sir, there are few secrets
among the islands," offered Lieutenant Jones.

"That would make an attack on Fort Nassau
suicide. Maybe we should attack from the other end
of the island," offered Captain Welsh, marine of the
Cabot.

The officers bandied about many other comments.
Hopkins let them talk for a few minutes before
continuing.

"Gentlemen, please; understand that I have no
ideas for glory here. I came to do a job. I do not wish
to see many of our men killed in a careless attack. We
will attempt this, and if it appears that the fort is
manned and ready for us, we will pull away and
assault Fort Montague by land on the other end of the
island. That will leave the backside of Nassau wide

open. The decision to change the attack will lie with the officers of the attacking force."

There was a murmur of approval from the officers. "What are we going to be up against as far as the natives, cover and the militia forces on hand?" came a question from the back of the cabin.

"Sean Taggert, that would be for you to answer, since you have been there and are part of the assault force," Hopkins directed.

Taken somewhat by surprise by the commodore, Sean spoke up. "Yes, sir. If we go around to take Montague, we should put in here by this small stream at this small village called New Guinea. That part of the island is mostly low, scrubby cover. The road goes along the shoreline, and on the inland side there is scattered-to-heavy growth, which we will have to be careful of ambush through there. The cover opens up before we will get to Montague." Sean paused and saw that the other marine officers were listening intently as they studied the chart of the island as he pointed out the route they would take.

"The buildings in the village and town are mostly of wood, no chimneys and very few glass windows, on small plots that are separated by rows of bushes and trees. The villagers are mostly divers and fishermen, and in Nassau there are plenty of petty officials and owners of the larger plantations. The locals there are mostly ship builders, carpenters, merchants and laborers. There are several slaves on the larger plantations. There is one main street with houses on it and there is also the church, and the gaol. The governor's mansion is on a hill just outside town. There's probably at least two-hundred men of militia age; however, most of them are family men who want to enjoy the comfort of their homes, not fight."

"Are you saying they won't fight?" came a voice from the back.

"No, I'd say the men there are used to having a garrison there to protect them, so they are not the best trained or enthusiastic. They will put up a fight if they feel they are protecting their families, but may not be so interested in protecting the Crown's interests."

"In that case we should try to make it clear to them what our intentions are if we get a chance to parlay with them," Nicholas summarized.

"Right, that may make our job easier here," reinforced the commodore. "Now, we should get moving. I want you marines to have your men fed and transferred over to the two sloops by sunup. Volunteers from the other ships will man the sloops. The *Providence* will go in with the sloops to give them support, and Lieutenant Jones will direct the movements from the *Providence* in regards to the approaches that he is familiar with. The rest of the fleet will stand off the mouth of the harbor to prevent any ships from leaving." He paused long enough to make sure all were listening.

"We want to make contact with the governor as soon as possible to demand his surrender of the forts and militia. The sooner we get them to surrender, the fewer casualties we will have. Captain Nicholas will be in charge of the campaign once the marines land, while keeping me abreast of the situation. Now if there are no questions, Sam, why don't you take your officers on deck and finalize your orders while the rest of us get our loose ends tied up here. As soon as we finish here, we will raise anchor and sail on to New Providence. Good luck to you, men!"

With that, the marine officers squeezed out of the cabin, climbed the stairs and gathered in the warm evening air on deck. They chattered amongst themselves until Nicholas stepped to the front of the group and cleared his throat.

"Lads, tomorrow we will find out how well we trained our men. If we go in to Nassau, we will disembark on the wharf if our deception holds. If not, we will sail to the other end of the island and land at the spot that Sean pointed out. Once ashore, the first men need to spread out and take up defensive positions until all of the men have been ferried ashore in the boats." He looked each man in the eyes.

"As soon as everyone is ashore, we will march to Fort Montague and lay siege to them and induce them to surrender. Once we have taken the fort, we will determine our next moves then. Any questions?"

No one spoke up. "Good, you have your orders and know when to have your men on board the sloops, so as soon as you get back to your ships, get your men prepared and make sure they are fed before leaving in the morning. I see the others are coming on deck, so good hunting to you all tomorrow!"

The officers disbursed to their ships as their boats came alongside. Sean and his brother sat in the stern sheets of the launch and rode back in silence. A hundred details of preparation raced through his mind as he watched the shape of the ship grow larger as the launch approached. The sun had set and the night air began to cool.

As they gained the deck, Thomas shouted for the anchor to be raised. The anchor party sprang to the task while others raced up the rigging to set sail. Sean watched as the silhouettes of the other ships of the fleet began to move to the south. The great stern and bow lamps were lit so that the ships could stay in visual contact with each other. Below deck, Sean waited while Lanigan rounded up his men. They gathered together, eager to hear what Sean had to tell them of the operation that they were to participate in. Somehow, word had already gotten to them or they had guessed the plans.

"Lads, you all know we have work to do tomorrow. We are going to be transferring over to the two captured sloops in the morning before sunrise. We will sail into the port of Nassau, disembark and take the fort there." He stopped while the men absorbed what he said and spoke excitedly about the mission. He let them banter about for a few moments then continued.

"There is a possibility that they may know what we are about, and if that happens, we will sail to the other end to the island, land, then take the other fort. Our intention is to confiscate all war material on the island. We in no way are to molest or harm the inhabitants there."

"What if they put up a fight?" one of the men asked.

"If they fight, then we fight. Now get your equipment together and get some sleep. We'll be up at four to get breakfast and boat over to the sloops. Give your pouches to the cook tonight so that he can pack them with extra biscuits and bacon for you to take along. Fill your canteens in the morning. Sergeant, do you have any suggestions?" Sean asked.

"You lads make sure that the flints are out of your muskets until we are headed for shore. Being packed below decks with all those other men, we don't need to have someone getting their head blown off for nothing. Tomorrow, follow orders, act on your orders immediately and you will all live through this. Do your duty."

"Have you ever done anything like this, Sergeant?" came a voice from the group.

"Aye, that I have. There is nothing more exhilarating than to go charging against the enemy with as large a group of men as we will have gathered tomorrow. Now off with you and do as you have been instructed. There's an extra tot of rum for you now, and then get some sleep. It will be a long day tomorrow."

The two left the men's quarters and took a stroll on deck with their rum. "They're a good lot, sir, as good as I have ever served with. They will do you proud, don't you worry," Lanigan said to Sean.

"You've done a wonderful job with them, Angus. You have transformed them from boys to marines, and I thank you for all your effort. Now, I must go and prepare my equipment. Good night to you," Sean said as he shook Lanigan's hand. The older man had nothing to say to the unexpected praise.

The two men parted and returned to their cabins to get ready. After he had his things ready, he stretched out on his pallet. His mind was racing with the details of his job, not expecting to get any sleep.

"Sir, sir, it's time to get up," Lanigan said as he shook Sean's shoulder.

Sean looked at him, not realizing that he had fallen fast to sleep. The smell of food cooking greeted him as he sat up. He had fallen asleep fully dressed. As quickly as he could, he washed and shaved. He finished as Thomas' orderly came to invite him to breakfast in his cabin. He grabbed his pistols, sword pouch and canteen and went to the great cabin.

"Good morning, Brother. Are you ready for this?"

"As ready as I can be. I'm anxious to get under way. I'm glad that the commodore listened to everyone about having a second landing plan in case things go sour at Nassau. I really think that they already know about our fleet. It will be better to land unopposed on the other end of the island and take Nassau from land were it is unprotected," Sean responded.

"Yes, I think that will be the better plan. You take care out there; I know you'll be in good company," Thomas said.

"I will be in good company indeed. It sounds like the crew has put the boats in the water, so I must go now. See you ashore, Brother." Sean stood up and hitched up his sword and pistols. He slung his shot pouch and checked to be sure his powder flask was inside, and then left the cabin.

There was much activity on deck as the crew bustled about, preparing to disembark the marines. Sean saw that the fleet had shortened sail and could see several lanterns bobbing about on each of the ships. The boats were manned, and his men were starting to go over the side, Lanigan barking orders in the midst of it all.

"Good morning, Angus. Have the lads been fed?"

"Ah, good morning, sir, that they have. The lads are full of the Old Nick this morning. I pity those militia on the island if they oppose us; these boys will rip their heads off," Lanigan laughed.

"Good, let's hope they are as eager after they've been packed into the holds of those sloops for a couple of hours. Sun will be up soon. It rises fast down here. We will have to make good time to get there shortly after it comes up. Well, Sergeant, it's time. You take the launch, and I'll take the cutter. Over the side with you," Sean ordered.

The cook handed Sean his pouch of food to take along, as he was about to step over the side. After he slung it over his shoulder, he stepped through the entry port and climbed down into the tossing boat.

He could make out boats from the other ships making their way to the sloops, oars dipping up and down, looking like water beetles. They reached the one they were assigned to and had to wait in line as other boats disgorged their charges.

Finally it was their turn. The men eagerly climbed aboard the sloop and climbed below into the already crowded hold. Sean looked for Sam and found him standing with the sailing master from the *Cabot* at the tiller.

"Good morning, Sean. It won't be long now, eh," Nicholas greeted him.

"Good morning, Sam. It's great to be under way. The lads are chomping at the bit to be about the day's business," Sean replied.

"The other officers are at the aft hatch of the hold. Get with them and take my coat along. I'm going to stay on deck to make sure all goes well. You'll be able to hear me if anything happens. There's the signal, the other sloop is all loaded, and the boats have been transferred to the *Providence* to haul in for us in case we need them to land ashore. All right, lads, hoist sail! It's on to Nassau!" he called to the sailors.

The crew quickly went about their business of hoisting sails and getting the sloop under way. Sean felt the sloop heave forward as the sails caught the early morning breeze. He sat at the top of the steps leading below, his head just below the coaming around the hatch. The sky was just showing a slight lightening. It would not stay dark long, for on the tropical sea, the sun rose quickly.

He watched as Nicholas scanned ahead with his telescope, watching for the lights on the shore. It would take them at least an hour or more to reach their objective. Sean listened to the sounds of life below deck. No lights were allowed, so he could barely make out any shapes in the darkness. There was a constant murmur of many hushed conversations among the men who were packed in tightly in the small hold.

"Blast, listen to that! One of them is retching in there. That will get others to retching and then we won't be able to stand the stench. Someone get a bucket passed up to the deck to get some seawater to throw on that!" came the voice of Lieutenant Cummings of the *Columbus*.

There was the sound of much shuffling about and mild cursing as those nearest the sick man tried to get away from the mess, while others searched for a bucket that eventually was found and passed to the sailors on deck. It was returned in a few moments and passed down to the ailing man. He sloshed the contents of the bucket on the deck; that brought more curses and the sound of two more men retching.

"Damnation, before too long, they'll all be heaving their innards out!" another of the officers speculated as he pressed upward toward the fresh air of the open hatch.

"Stay low lads, I see the harbor. It won't be long now," called out Captain Nicholas, oblivious to the problems below. The sun had been up for a few hours, and the heat in the hold was getting intense.

Sean looked below and could see now just how cramped the men were. They sat and stood shoulder-to-shoulder along the hull and back-to-back up the center of the hold. He could make out faces in the dim light. The faces told much about the men. There were the stoic looks on some the nervous-rabbit look on others. Still others showed the look of false bravado, while others looked truly bellicose.

He could see and hear a few men close by working their Rosary beads, saying their 'Our Fathers' over and over, while some just prayed in silence. There were those coarse toughs who sneered at those of faith. He saw one such man sliding his bayonet blade up and down a whetstone, much to the chagrin of his neighbors. The sound of the blade scraping the stone sent chills up the spine of one such nervous fellow.

The smell of tobacco wafted up towards him as several of the men lit their clay pipes to help cover the odor of the sick men. The smell did not bother some of the others, who eagerly ate at the biscuits that they carried in their pouches.

Time seemed to drag on; finally Nicholas announced, "We're rounding the tip of Hog Island now, lads; the fort is in view. The other sloop and the *Providence* are not far behind us now. Get ready, we'll be at the wharf in about ten minutes!"

"Do you hear that, lads? Make ready to depart in ten minutes! Keep quiet now!" Sean passed the word forward below deck. He eased up on the step and loosened the pistols in his belt. They were loaded, but like the men with their muskets, the flints had been removed to avoid any accidental shootings as they were below or when they disembarked. The flints would be put back in their weapons as they got on deck.

Sean looked at the sun in the sky; it was almost noon. He craned his neck to see if he could see ahead, but could not. Just then he heard one, then two more cannon shots. He could hear the sound of a cannonball splashing down alongside the sloop.

"They are on to us! They are firing from the fort! Prepare to go about!" Nicholas shouted, as the sailors jumped to his orders. Flawlessly the little ship turned and headed out toward the entrance at the tip of Hog Island. The other two ships turned at the same time, having seen the shots fired by the defenders of the fort.

"Steady, men, stay quiet," Sean called out to them.

"Sir, the *Providence* is signaling the fleet to let them know we're changing landing sites," the signalman called to Sam.

"Relax down there, lads, it won't take long to get to the other end of the island. The *Providence* is coming in closer now to lead the way in through the shoals. You'll be out of there in no time!" Nicholas encouraged his men as he stood by the hatch so that they could hear him.

Sean looked up at him and admired his steadiness. He had known him a long time, but this was the first time they would be under fire from an enemy together. He exuded confidence to those around him, no matter what the circumstances.

"There she comes now! The *Providence* is taking the lead. She is a glorious sight under full sail indeed," Nicholas, remarked, standing with his feet apart and hands on his hips. "Pass me my coat, Sean, there's no need in trying to pass off as an island trader now. The whole island must know what we're about by now."

"At least we will stand a better chance now of taking both forts without many casualties," Sean said as he passed Sam's coat up to him.

"You officers can come on up deck now. Look there, the *Providence* has cast the boats loose for us to pick up. The men in them can cut the distance to us as we tack over to them. You lads over there, prepare to throw them a line as we come by. There's no turning back now!" he smiled as the other officers came on deck.

"You men know your orders. Don't try to separate the men as they come on deck. Get them ashore first, and we can separate them there as soon as everyone is ashore. Just take over the nearest group of them as you get ashore to set up a defensive line. Once everyone is ashore and there is no threat, we will form up by ship's companies and march to Montague. Remember, no harm is to come to the citizens as long as they do no harm to our lads, is that clear?"

"Yes, Sir!" came several replies.

"Good, now get ready to move the men to the boats when it is time," Sam ordered as he strode to the rail to watch the shoreline.

"Right up there, Captain. See, the *Providence* has taken in sail. That is where we go ashore," Sean pointed to him. Nicholas scanned the shore with his telescope, looking for enemy troops, but saw none. The sailors had finished lashing the towline that they had thrown to the boats that had been assigned to the sloop, and the men manning them sat back as they were pulled along. They were almost to the *Providence* when signal flags went up the halyard of the other ship.

"It says to approach to a cable's length and anchor," the signalman stated.

"Helmsman, come about. Anchor party, prepare to let loose. Prepare to lower sails!" the orders were called out, and men ran back and forth to their duties. The signal was given, and the sails were lowered and anchor dropped as in one smooth movement. The sloop came to a halt as the anchor bit into the coral below.

As soon as the sloop glided to a halt, the boatmen brought the boats alongside for the marines. Sean watched as the men prepared to make the assault. With the five boats secured alongside, it was time to get the men from below and disembark them.

"All right now, men, get topside with you and form lines at the side. As soon as you get into your boats, replace your flints so you are ready to fire if necessary when you land. Keep your weapons pointed skyward at all times until you hit the beach!" called out Nicholas, as he and the officers starred down at the men at the main hatch.

They stood aside as the marines climbed up the stairs and onto the deck. Many showed signs of cramped muscles, and all were glad to be out of the stinking hold. They chattered excitedly as they stood ready to climb down into their boats. Many went straight to the scuttlebutt to replenish their canteens that they drained in the hot hold. The officers stood at the railing until they had all settled down. Each of the five officers would take charge of a boat.

Sean looked across the water to the other sloop. The deck was alive with activity as they, too, prepared to make the assault. He gazed over at the *Providence*, which also lay hove too, its gun ports open, cannon muzzles protruding out, ready to fire over the heads of the attacking marines if necessary. A noisy gull flapping above him caused him to look skyward. It circled around with several others, masthead high, watching all the activity below them. The sloop had obviously interrupted their morning fishing.

"Listen up, lads. You all know your orders. Listen to your officers, and all will go well today. I want to see all your smiling faces when we get done here on this island, so be careful." Nicholas paused while the men laughed at his remark. He looked around at their faces, seeing the nervous, the frightened, the uncaring, the shocked looks on them. "Look, the others are starting to disembark! Let's not let them beat us to the beach! Hurry, lads, into the boats! Keep your muskets up, your powder dry, and replace your flints. Hurry now!"

The men all gave out a cheer, as he and the other officers climbed down into the waiting boats. As soon as they took their places, the others followed. Sean watched the men climbing into his longboat to be sure that no one dropped a weapon or got careless.

The sailors at the oars got crowded as the benches filled up. Sean saw that only a few of his own men were in this boat, but could see that most of his men had made it into the other boats. He could see that the boats would have to make a second trip to get everyone ashore.

"Shove off!" he commanded, as soon as everyone had been seated. The oarsmen dropped the oars into the water, and the men pulled heartily against them to propel the boat away from the sloop. The marines all strained their eyes towards the shore to see if they could spot any enemy soldiers. Sean, too, watched as he stood next to the man at the tiller.

He watched to his left and right as the other four boats from his sloop and the five boats of the second sloop all raced towards the shore. The men called back and forth to each other as though they were on a lark; and not an armed assault on foreign land. The officers ordered them to stop and pay attention. The men settled down and got busy replacing their flints.

Within minutes, the boats were closed in on the beach. Sean steadied himself as he felt the keel of the boat grind to a halt in the sand of the shallow water. The men looked to him as the boat came to a stop.

He stood, drew his sword, waved it over his head and shouted, "Over the side men, and take up positions at the line of dunes across the beach!" With that, Sean leapt off the side of the boat. He landed in knee-deep warm water and started to slosh his way to the beach. Behind him, he heard his men.

"Let's go, boys!" one of them hollered out. With that, the men rose with a shout, jumped over the side of the longboat into knee-deep water and charged ashore, yelling at the top of their lungs. Sean was surprised to feel the madness of the moment take over him, and he, too, was raced across the water and beach yelling along with the men.

The feel of the sand and shells crunching under his shoes felt strange as he ran. A flock of resting seagulls took to the sky, squawking as they rose. Two small boys peered over the dunes at the madmen coming their way. They thought better of waiting and took off running down the road in terror of the green-coated strangers.

The marines of Sean's boat stopped on top of the dunes and waited for the men of the other boats to reach them. Sean looked out over the area in front of them. Palms, palmettos, sea oat clumps, and a myriad of other plants spread out before them. There was a road running along the beach through the growth that lead to Fort Montague.

He looked over his shoulder and saw the boats returning to the sloops for the second group. The men around him settled into the warm sand as they waited on the others to arrive. The colors had come ashore in the boats from the second sloop and had been carried to the dune next to the one that Sean was standing on.

The color bearers stood on the top of the dune and uncased the banners. As they unfurled the flags, one the Rattlesnake flag and the other the new Grand Union flag, the men on the beach let out a cheer.

"*Huzzah*! *Huzzah*! *Huzzah*!" they shouted so that the men on the sloops could hear them, and from across the water, their cheers could also be heard.

"It's good to see you made it here safely, sir," Sergeant Lanigan said to Sean from behind.

"Good morning to you, Sergeant, and it is good to see you also. Isn't it grand? Just think, we have carried the war to the enemy's land now."

"Aye, that we have, sir. Look at these lads, will you? Just moments ago they were grumbling and complaining about being packed into those ships like herring and upset at being herded onto the boats, but now there is pride in them that no one will ever take away from them. They know that they are a part of something important. They know that they are making history. Now, I'll get back to watching my group. Make sure that they don't drink all their water, sir. We don't know when we can refill the canteens," Lanigan suggested as he saluted.

Sean returned the salute. He was never bothered by Lanigan's suggestions, for he knew that he had years of experience that was priceless. He knew that even small details that might be overlooked could adversely affect the men and the mission.

Nothing moved in front of them as they waited for the second group to come ashore. He turned to watch them as the boats were beached. As did the first group, the newcomers charged across the beach, shouting all the way. The group of sailors who had rowed the boats joined them. One boat was kept ready to take messages back to the *Providence*. As soon as all the men were accounted for, Nicholas stepped down from his dune, took up a position twenty feet back and called for all the officers.

As they gathered about him, he addressed them. "Gentlemen, congratulations on a superb landing; let's hope the rest of our operation goes as smoothly. Now we will reform by ship's company and move towards Montague. It is only a couple of miles' march from here, so we should be there in no time. Sean, you have your man, the Delaware, and a few woodsmen in your company, so I want your men to protect our flank. Get them spread out in that brush and a little ahead of the column to protect us from ambush. We will have the sea to our right, so we are safe from that direction. Any questions?"

No one spoke; all were eager to get under way. "Good, bosun, take a boat back to the *Providence* and tell them to signal the fleet with this message: 'The Marines have landed!' Now then, you men take up positions on the beach in marching order as we have already laid out and rally your men. As soon as they are formed up, we move out. Now go!" Nicholas ordered excitedly.

The officers' voices rang out with a hearty, 'Aye, aye, sir!' and after saluting, they turned away from Nicholas and took their positions while the bosun ran to his boat and chastised the men in it to launch it.

Sean stood off to the side of the line of officers and called out, "*Osprey* Marines, rally to me!" as he waved his sword in the air. From down the beach he could hear the other officers call out their ships' names.

"*Columbus* Marines rally here! *Cabot* Marines, rally to me!" the calls continued down the line. Pandemonium reigned on the scene for a few minutes while the two hundred and seventy marines ran to and fro at the bidding of sergeants, corporals and officers shouting orders, until they had found where they needed to be. The company of seamen formed up at the end of the column.

Sean took the opportunity to instruct his men on what was expected of them as the column formed up. "Now, lads, we have an important place in the advance. It's up to us to protect the flank of the column from ambush. We will spread out from the road as far as we can at an angle and move through the brush. Keep alert watch for any movement in the brush and ahead of you that might indicate troops hiding in ambush. Edward George, you anchor the far end of the line. With your instincts and hunting skills, I'm counting on you to warn of any possible attack. Sergeant Lanigan will take the center of the line, and I will be our anchor on the road to be available for any orders from the column. Now take your positions."

As the column was taking shape, Nicholas and the color guard took position at the head of the column. As soon as the men were in place and silence fell over the gathering, Nicholas stood out from the side of the column to take a look down his command.

After he saw that the column was formed, he drew his sword, held it above his head and shouted, "Marines, attention!" He listened as his command was repeated by his officers, then continued, "Right shoulder arms!" he paused again as that ordered was repeated. The sound of two hundred and seventy muskets being slapped and popped into place was impressive.

"Marines, forward march!" he called out at the top of his lungs. He watched as the column started in motion, and took his place back at the head of his command. He glanced over and could see that the *Osprey* marines were off to the left moving ahead and to the left through the tough underbrush.

Sean and Lanigan had placed their men in a wedge formation winging out from the road. He had a good vantage point to watch as the column took shape. He was impressed to see all those men move as one as they snapped to attention, shoulder arms and move forward. He started his men forward at the same time. It gave him an immense feeling of pride to see the column of green-clad men with flags flapping in the breeze moving toward him.

"'Tis a pretty sight, eh, sir?" He heard Calhoun's voice from next to him. He was moving through the brush with his musket pointed forward, moving the palmetto fronds aside with the bayonet on the end of it.

"'Tis indeed, Mr. Calhoun. It's a fine day for this little walk, wouldn't you say?"

"Oh, it is indeed, sir. Yes, sir if you have to go to war, this is the way to do it with a nice boat ride, nice beautiful beaches and sunny warm weather. Yes, sir if we have to fight a war, this is the way to do it. None of that mucking about in the mud and cold, bitter, winter weather."

"Didn't I tell you this, laddie? And I also promised you pretty dark skinned lassies. Look up there in the village," Lanigan kidded his protégé.

"Spread out men, be watchful for any armed men. Treat them kindly unless they put up a fight," Sean called out to his men. He walked forward towards a group of three men who appeared to be of some importance in the village. He looked around at the inhabitants who stood in their doorways and peered from behind their windows.

He returned his sword to its scabbard and saluted the three men as he approached. The people were mulattos and freed slaves and were dressed in colorful dresses and shirts. He stopped in front of the three elderly men and greeted them.

"Good morning, gentlemen. How are you?"

"Good morning, suh. May we ask, are you Spanish goin' to attack the town?"

227

"No, sir, we are American Marines. We are not here to harm anyone in your village, or in Nassau. We have come to take charge of military stores left here by the British, and then we will leave." He stepped back and laughed as a piglet ran across his feet.

It was enough to break the tension as the three elders broke out laughing also. "We welcome you to our village and will not give you any cause for concern. We did see the militia out of the fort earlier. They had come through here, and when they saw your boats coming ashore, they ran back towards the fort. They did not go all the way back though; they are waiting up ahead behind some sand dunes up there," the old man said, as he pointed to the dunes in the distance.

"Thank you, sir, we will go now and leave you in peace." Sean took a step back and saluted them. The three men all gave him a salute in return.

"Private Calhoun, run back and report to Captain Nicholas that we expect to run into the militia about two cables' length ahead," Sean ordered his man.

"Aye, aye, sir!" he replied, as he spun on his heel and trotted back down the road. The fort was less than a mile off, and the militia was half that distance away. He moved his men ahead until they were just out of musket range.

Sean took out his telescope and scanned the dunes ahead of him. He counted the number of heads he saw peering over the dunes at him. He counted about sixty in all. Behind them he saw a small column approaching the dunes from the direction of the fort. They halted before reaching the dune. He could see sunlight glancing off the lens of a telescope as he watched.

He saw the column as it reversed and headed back in the direction of the fort. Sean turned around and saw the column of marines approaching. Sam walked up beside him as the column came to a halt.

"What have you got, Sean?" he asked.

"That column you see moving away, about eighty men, had just come up, saw you coming and turned back for the fort. There are only about sixty men still behind the dunes. Look there, they have raised a white flag!" Sean replied.

The two watched as two men carrying a sword with a white cloth tied to it and raised high cautiously approached the marines. They were in shabby brown uniforms and came to a halt a few feet from Sean and Sam.

"Sirs, we are Lieutenants Burke and Judkin of the island militia. Governor Browne has instructed us to inquire as to who you are and what your intentions are on our island," Burke stammered out timidly as he looked down the column of marines.

"We are American Marines here to take possession of all war materials on this island that belong to the Crown. We are not here to harm anyone, nor harm the property of the citizens of this island. We only want the supplies left by the army. Tell your governor that if he surrenders, there will be no harm to anyone, nor to any property. As soon as we take possession of the military stores we will sail away."

"We will report this to the governor. He is a stubborn man, loyal to the Crown, and may not surrender the provisions." Burke stammered.

"You tell him that if he does not surrender what we came for, then the deaths of his men, your friends,

229

will be on his head. Now be off with you, and let us take possession of the fort at this end of the island," Nicholas replied.

"We cannot hand over the fort, but we will send word to the governor," Burke said. He could tell by the look in the marine's eyes that he meant business. The two officers saluted sloppily and returned to their men.

Sam and Sean watched as the militia argued amongst themselves as the officers told them of the intentions of the invaders. A few turned away from the dunes and headed back towards the fort. The officers shouted at them to halt, but their efforts were in vain as the rest of the force joined in the slow retreat to the fort.

Finally the officers joined their men. When they were out of sight, Sam said, "Let's move forward. After what we just witnessed, it appears that the militia is not going to fight. Let's press on to the fort and convince them to relinquish it to us."

"I'll get the boys moving again, sir." Sean said as he saluted and turned to his men. "Move out, lads, on to the fort!"

Nicholas signaled for the column to advance. They were within musket range of the fort within minutes. "Spread out, men, and take cover!" Nicholas shouted.

He stood in sight of the fort as the men spread out to the left and right of the road and hunkered down behind sand dunes and clumps of vegetation. The British flag flapped in the breeze above the ramparts of the redoubt. There were many militia men running back and forth along the ramparts, and little by little their number decreased.

Twenty minutes passed without much movement on the fort walls. "Up men, and move towards the fort. We will take it by force!" Nicholas shouted.

Up and down the line, the marines leaped to their feet, muskets at the ready, and started forward. They stopped as one as three cannon were fired. They turned and watched the badly aimed shots rip through the tops of the nearest dunes and go bouncing harmlessly beyond them across the sand.

Before they started forward again, they saw the flag lowered. Nicholas signaled for them to halt and waved at Sean.

"Sean, take a few men and circle around the fort and report back what you find," Nicholas ordered as Sean approached. He quickly turned and went back down his line.

"Edward George, Calhoun, Sontag, follow me!" he called out. Together with his three men spread out, they cautiously made their way around the fort. As they approached the opposite side, they could see several of the militia far down the road, running for the safety of Nassau.

There was a small sally port door on the rear wall. However, when they tried to open it, it would not budge. "The last ones out must have jumped down from the wall," George surmised.

They completed their circle of the structure and returned to Nicholas who was standing with the other officers.

"It appears that they have abandoned the place, sir. We'll have to climb the walls, as they left the gates locked and climbed down from the wall," Sean reported.

"All right, lads. Then it's over the top! Get your men going, find what you can to get some men over the top, and open the gates. I want at least twenty men on top, in case they left a force inside to attack us. Let's go!"

The officers returned to their men and encouraged them forward. Several men boosted their comrades up the wall, while grappling hooks with rope went sailing up to the parapets thrown by some of the sailors. Men scrambled up the ropes and raced down inside the fort. As most of them went running through the structure searching for the enemy, a few threw open the gates, and the rest of the men came charging in, yelling.

It became apparent that the defenders had left the fort to them. "Private, come with me." Nicholas barked the order at the nearest man. He led him to the flagpole and pulled out a flag from his pack. Together the two hooked the flag to the halyard and with dramatic gestures, Nicholas hoisted the Grand Union flag by himself as the men stood and watched.

As soon as the flag reached the top, it was caught in the breeze and snapped out fully. The whole crowd of marines and sailors let out a hearty cheer and threw their hats in the air. Their response was a mixture of pride in their flag and relief from the anticipation of a bitter fight and possible death.

Sean stood and admired his friend and the accomplishment of the men this day. They had landed and attacked a fortress on a foreign shore without a shot fired and without a single casualty.

The rest of the day was spent trying to find food for the men and setting up a guard duty schedule after the premises had been thoroughly searched. Only

Sean's men had brought some along, and it was now near dark. The rest of the men had not eaten since way before sunup. A patrol was sent back to the village with gold coins to purchase as much as they could from the villagers.

They returned with some villagers an hour later, loaded down with fruits and dried fish. There was not enough to make a normal size meal for the men, but it was enough to take the edge off their hunger. A detachment of sailors was sent back to the beach to row back out to the fleet that had reached the landing site to bring back food, water and a few cooks. Once the supplies were unloaded, the fleet moved to the mouth of the harbor to block shipping.

"Sean, since your men have their food, once they have eaten, I want you to take them out and patrol between here and the town. There is no sense in letting them catch us napping tonight. The men are exhausted from the heat and from spending so much time cooped up in the holds of those ships. Your men are in better shape than the rest, so I'll make sure that they are relieved after midnight when some of the others are fed and rested up some."

"You know you can count on us, Sam. We won't let you down." Sean returned to his men. They were gathered in the shade of the wall of the fort and had rounded up enough firewood to cook their slabs of bacon.

"Men, as soon as you are done eating, we will go out to patrol the area. The enemy might try to take the fort back after dark, so we have to be on our guard to make sure that does not happen. So eat up and then we will move out. You all did excellent today"

Sean joined them for supper. Once their bellies were full, they gathered their equipment and headed out the main gates. Sean split them into two groups. He would take one group to the left of the road, and Lanigan would take the other on the road and beach. He intended to patrol as far as Nassau and back, a distance of a league.

The sunset that evening was a spectacular combination of reds, gold and pinks. The men marveled in it as they walked their patrol. As soon as the sun went below the horizon, they all perked up for in the darkness there were many unfamiliar shapes looming around them.

The men moved in perfect unison and in total silence. They had taken to this ground warfare as readily as they had taken to fighting on the deck of a ship. The night was calm, and the air was slightly chilled. The sound of the waves hitting the beaches on the other side of the road was a comforting sound. The only other noise came from the night creatures and from his men as they pushed their way through the underbrush.

They took their time, since there was no need to hurry. They paused after they had gone halfway. The light from the village glowed on the horizon in front of them, and occasionally they could hear the sounds from the village. A dog barked, a gull cried out. All seemed so natural, yet so strange at the same time. Sean looked overhead to a cloudless sky full of stars. He smiled as a shooting star crossed low across the sky, burning bright green.

After they moved on, they had gone but a few minutes when they spotted a small number of shacks alongside the road. Several chickens and ducks came to life as the men approached. The occupant of one of the shacks came out the front door, the ground in front of him suddenly bathed in the soft glow of candlelight from inside. As soon as he saw the men approach, he hurried back inside and the lights went out, and the sounds of children were hushed up.

The men moved on ignoring the people in the shacks and the scurrying fowl. They reached the outskirts of Nassau and stopped at Sean's whispered command. Sean turned to look out across the beach as he spotted movement from the corner of his eye.

"Sergeant, look there!" he whispered to Lanigan as he grabbed him by the arm and pointed seaward. Out in the middle of the channel between New Providence Island and Hog Island, a ghostly packet silently and without lights glided past them.

"Buggers are probably loading supplies to ship them out before we can get to them! What shall we do, sir?" Lanigan inquired.

"We need to alert the men at the fort. Who are our fastest runners? Tyree, Monacelli, come here quickly!" Sean called out. The two men raced up to him. "Lads, I want you to run back to the fort as quickly as you can. You may not make it in time to alert them to that ship moving out the channel, but try. If they can fire on it, get them to do so. I believe they are sending out some of the stores that we came here for. Now go!"

The two men turned and sprinted off in the direction of the fort. Sean did not think they would make it back in time to loose a few shots at the ship, but at least they would be alert for anymore that might try to pass under the guns of the fort later in the night.

"Angus, I want you to take half of the men and go halfway back to the fort. Set up across the road and in the brush to watch for anyone trying to get to the fort. I am going to take the rest of the men into Nassau and see what is afoot. If they are trying to load anymore goods to get out of our grasp, we shall stop them."

"Aye, you be careful there, sir. They may be civilians, but there are many more of them than there will be of you. Don't be doing anything rash now," he cautioned in a fatherly manner.

"Do not worry. You know me, I'm the epitome of caution," Sean said jokingly. "Now be off with you. We'll try to get back by midnight, depending on what we find."

The patrol turned back toward the fort while Sean gathered the other men around him. "We are going to go into the town to see what they are up to. I'd wager that packet that just slipped by was loaded with the supplies we came to confiscate. We will be mindful of the civilians. However if they threaten us, we will respond, but wait for my orders. If anything happens to me, Corporal Beckett will take over. Any questions?"

"What will we do if they want a fight?" a voice came from the dark.

"We're marines, so we'll fight better. Now let's move out. Edward George, you and I will take the lead. Corporal Beckett, you bring up the rear. Remember, lads, those people are as fearful of you as you are of them, so keep your wits about you."

The men moved on in silence, weapons at the ready. They crept along the houses that lined the street heading into the main square. They could see movement and the flickering of torches towards the wharf.

They slipped along the wall of a warehouse and watched from the darkness as several men, by torchlight, unloaded kegs of gunpowder from the backs of two wagons and rolled them down the wharf to a waiting schooner. The crew of the schooner was lowering a ramp in place for the men to roll the kegs onto the deck.

Sean pointed out to his men that the men laboring to load the craft had stacked their muskets off to the side of the dock. "Listen lads, we need that powder. There are twenty-three of them, so what we need to do is rush over there, knock their stacked muskets into the water and hold them at bayonet point. We will prevent them from moving anything off the island tonight."

"Let's hope the rest of their friends are all home snuggled in their beds! That's almost twice as many of them as there are us, sir," observed Hauser.

"Check your priming lads." Sean ordered. He pulled his pistols out and checked the priming on them as his men checked their muskets. He kept one in his hand and drew his sword in his other.

"Ready lads? Now be real loud, and let's charge." With that he let out a yell and ran for the wharf his men hollering and charging past him. Timmons reached the stacked muskets and slammed his weapon into the four stacks sending them splashing down into the water.

The workers looked up, startled by the sudden clamor and sight of green-coated men rushing them. They all threw their hands high in the air as the marines drew up in a line across the dock, muskets held level with their waists.

"You men move over here, now!" Sean ordered loudly and pointed towards the wall of a warehouse. The men climbed down from the wagon, and those who were rolling kegs along the dock, turned them upright and walked to the wall. The crew of the schooner did not know whether to hoist sail quickly or come off the ship. Sean sent two men over to the side of the schooner to convince them of what to do. The six crewmen came off their craft and meekly joined the others.

"Who's in charge here?" Sean bellowed.

"I am, sir, Lieutenant Burke."

"Ah, yes, we met this afternoon. Well, Lieutenant, what shall I do with you now? Should we shoot your men for opposing our intentions?"

"No, sir, please do not do that. We were just doing what Governor Browne ordered us to do. He wanted to get all the powder off the island tonight before you tried to take the town."

"How much powder is there?" Sean asked.

"This is the last of it, twenty-four eighty-weight kegs. The *Mississippi Packet* that just left took one hundred and nineteen barrels, and the *Saint John* that left just before her took forty-three barrels. This is all that is left. The governor knew that we could not move all the cannons out in time, but that we could get the powder out of your reach by sunrise." Burke explained.

"Well, that was a good attempt on his part. Now as for you, I want you men to restack all the powder kegs along this wall, and when you are done, I will let you go home if you give me your parole that you will not try anything else to hinder us tonight or tomorrow, agreed?" Sean offered.

The men talked amongst themselves for a minute and then Burke turned to Sean, "We accept your offer; it is most generous. I believe your captain was sincere earlier when he told us you mean no harm to the inhabitants here as long as they do you no harm. We will do as you say and you have my word that we will do nothing more to oppose you."

"Fine, I will take your word on that. Now get that powder moved and go home." Sean looked at the islanders as they eagerly hastened to do his bidding. Within ten minutes, they had the powder neatly stacked and then headed for their homes.

"Do you think they will be back, sir?" asked Beckett.

"No, I think they have had enough of this business. However the governor may have other ideas. Get one of the men down in the water to retrieve their muskets. We'll pull and replace the loads in them in case we need some extra firepower here tonight," Sean instructed.

Beckett and Hauser removed their equipment, stripped to their breeches and got down in the water. The tide was low, so it did not take long to locate the muskets in the water. After they retrieved them all, the men set about pulling the loads out of them, swabbing the barrels and reloading them.

They stacked crates across the neck of the dock for protection and stacked the extra muskets close at hand. They kept the torches lit and away from the powder. Satisfied that they were in as good of positions as they could be under the circumstances, Sean let half the men curl up behind the crates and get some sleep. He suddenly realized how tired he was and knew the others must be the same way.

A few hours later, he heard a commotion up the street. He roused the sleeping men, and they took up positions behind their barricade. He strained his eyes, peering into the darkness, and could see several uniformed men cautiously coming towards them.

"Lieutenant Taggert, is that you?" a voice called out quietly. It was Lanigan.

"Over here, Sergeant," Sean called back.

"It's good to see you alive, sir! Is everything all right?" Lanigan asked as he, his patrol and a relief column of other marines came up to them.

"Yes, we're fine. We put a stop to the townsfolk shipping their powder out of here. We have confiscated these kegs here, but they managed to slip out two ships with loads of powder on them," he replied.

"When you didn't come back, I sent a runner to the fort to bring a reinforced relief patrol out when it was time so that we could try to find you. These men will stay here, so we can go back to the fort, sir," Lanigan reported.

"If it's all the same, Sergeant, the lads are worn out. We can bed down in that warehouse instead of marching all the way back there tonight. Send a messenger back to the fort to let them know what we have been about, then get your men bedded down also."

"Roight, sir. The other lads will be along tomorrow anyway to take the other fort here." Lanigan padded off to his men and picked one of the relief marines to return to the fort to let the others know what happened. He conferred with the sergeant of the relief patrol as to what to do and then led his men to the warehouse, where Sean and his men had already sacked out on top of bales and crates.

The night passed without incident. In the morning, several vendors showed up to sell the men fruits vegetables and bread. Sean allowed them to make their sales and then they hurried them off. At least the men had fresh food for breakfast, including some smoked fish and eggs.

Shortly after they finished eating, a messenger showed up and searched out Sean. "Sir, the captain gave me this message for you," he reported, and handed Sean a note.

"It says the men are headed for the governor's mansion to demand the keys to Fort Nassau and the governor's surrender," He said to Lanigan and the others who had gathered around. "We are to stay here until they come by to take the fort, then the *Osprey* marines will go with them and you other lads will remain here to guard the powder. Any questions?"

No one replied. Sean and Lanigan had the men line up and then inspected them and their weapons. All was in order so he let them relax until their time came. "Stay alert, lads. It appears the townsfolk are getting curious," Lanigan pointed out as several people had come out of their dwellings.

Several curious children wandered over to inspect the green-coated strangers as people tried to go about their daily routines as well as they could. A few came over to talk with the men in an effort to determine what was truly happening. They were relieved when Sean assured them that they meant no harm and only wanted the military supplies. As the morning progressed, several of the ladies brought out more fruit and breads to the men.

Suddenly, everyone scattered off the streets. "Get ready, men," Sean ordered.

From around the end of the row of houses came the column of marines, flags fluttering in the morning breeze. Nicholas was in the lead; he called a halt to the column when they reached the docks. Sean went out to meet him.

"Good morning, sir. Out for a stroll on this fine morning?" Sean said with a smile.

"Good morning, Sean. Good catch last night. I congratulate you and your men. Well done, lads!" he said louder and waved to the men behind the barricades so that they could hear.

"What is the plan, sir?" Sean asked.

"We have just come from the governor's house. He was a little reluctant, but finally gave me the keys to Fort Nassau. We are on the way there to take possession; the governor promised that there would not be any resistance. Come along, let's get it over with," Sam said.

He waved for his men, and together with the column, they marched to the main entrance of the fort. Nicholas called out to the men inside to open the gates and lay down their weapons. The men did not hesitate to do so, and when they swung the gates open, hastily withdrew to their homes.

The marines entered, and as before, Nicholas raised the flag over the fort. The men spread out and inspected every inch of the place. Unlike the guns at Montague, these had not been spiked and were still loaded with round shot and Landridge shot. The men at Montague had so hastily tried to spike the cannons;

they used nails that were too small to do any damage and were easily removed.

Sean and Sam inspected the guns on the ramparts. Three of them had fallen through their rotted carriages. "These are the ones they fired at us yesterday, from what one of the men below said before leaving. Several more of the carriages are just as rotted, yet the guns themselves are in good shape. Look at all the mortars and cannon here. This load will certainly help General Washington," Sam observed.

"Look out there. The *Alfred* and *Wasp* are entering the harbor. I suppose that means the commodore will be coming ashore to inspect the place," Sean said.

"Right. Let's go get the lads ready for his entrance. Get a detail to fire a salute with the better of the guns," Nicholas ordered.

Sean took charge of the guns and had his men fire a salute that was returned by the *Alfred*. The rest of the day was spent inspecting the warehouses and storerooms of the public buildings of the island. The governor was held prisoner and kept under guard at his mansion. The marines and sailors started the moving and cataloging of all military stores that were uncovered.

Sean was busy with his men pulling the loads out of the guns in the fort when the commodore and his party arrived. They made a cursory inspection of the fort and congratulated the men. They left to go to the governor's mansion, but before doing so, the commodore had three kegs of rum brought in for the marines and sailors who had taken the two forts.

Sean watched as the men worked on the guns. The barrels were indeed in very good shape and they would take them all along. All told, they had captured forty cannon and fifteen mortars in this fort alone. There was a great quantity of shot and shells for all the guns stored in the fort also. This made up for the fact that they were not able to capture all the powder. What they did capture was just enough to distribute among the ships of the fleet.

After the commodore took his leave and returned to the *Alfred*, Nicholas sought out Sean. "The commodore is pleased with our success. The only flaw in the operation was in not blocking both ends of the channel between the islands to prevent those ships from slipping out. However, he thought it best to have a show of strength off the mouth of the harbor to convince the locals to yield. He didn't count on the governor as being so crafty." Nicholas told Sean as he took a break from helping the men move one of the fort's guns in preparation for lowering it to the ground.

"Well, at least we are going to leave this place with enough artillery to give General Washington's army more teeth. We can always get back to attacking the British shipping to obtain more powder," Sean said as he wiped the sweat from his brow.

"We should be finished here in a couple of weeks. The commodore wants to be gone from here before the British get wind of this and mount an attack. We'll probably return to New London, Connecticut. That is the best place for these guns to get to Washington and for us to get re-supplied. What happens to us then is anyone's guess," Nicholas replied.

"Here's a list the Sergeant has compiled for you of the contents of this and the other fort," Sean said as he pulled the list out from under his coat that was laid across the wall.

Nicholas unfolded the list and read, "Forty cannon, fifteen brass mortars, five thousand three hundred thirty-seven cannon shells of various sizes, one hundred-forty hand grenades. Also nine thousand eight hundred and thirty-one round shot, eleven canisters of grape shot, various rammers and worms, copper ladles, scrapers, measures and cannon trucks. This is all from this fort. Then from Montague, we have five twenty-four pounders, six twelve-pounders and one nine- pounder. Twelve hundred forty round shot, and one hundred and twenty six-inch shells. Cannon trucks, brass measures, and etcetera. This is an incredible haul, no doubt about it," Sam beamed.

The two drank from their canteens as they watched the men moving busily around the fort, moving shot and shell, cannon and other supplies to move them to the docks for loading. There was a steady stream of marines and sailors moving the supplies to the wharf.

They looked out over the harbor where the *Alfred* and the *Wasp* rode at anchor, surrounded by local boats with men and women trying to sell all manner of things to the sailors on board the ships. The other ships were on station outside the harbor and patrolling the other end of the channel and around the immediate surrounding islands. The ships would be loaded one at a time to avoid having the entire fleet in the harbor and possibly being trapped by the British who may be lurking about.

True to their word, the islanders did nothing to oppose the work of the Americans. Several opened their homes to them and invited many for meals in the evenings. While off duty, the men enjoyed the warm, sunny weather, fishing and visiting with the friendly ladies.

There were always many children playing around the men as they worked, always looking for some kind of trinket from them, or trying to sell them fruit or services, such as shining their shoes or taking their clothes to the local women who did their laundry.

The local taverns and working girls were always open to serve the visitors, and the men were happy to make use of their services. The other merchants benefited from the influx of potential customers to the point that they tried to encourage them to stay longer than they had planned.

The ships were loaded one at a time, and before long, the last two were ready for receiving their cargo. Sean had been summoned to the governor's mansion, where Nicholas had made his temporary command post.

He walked up the road leading to the imposing building. Out in front stood four marine guards and two four-pounder cannon that had a clear range of the fort and town below. He returned the salute of the guards and entered the house. He was lead into the study by a servant who had formal manners and dress that was the custom in European homes of the well-to-do families.

"Good morning, Sean, I'm glad that you could take breakfast with me this morning. We will be leaving in a few days, and I wanted to let you in on an excursion that I have planned," Sam said to his friend as they sat down to eat at a side table in the study.

"Ah, what have you got up your sleeve this time? I can tell by the look on your face that it is not duty-related?" Sean asked.

"You know that we cannot go back home and go to our fishing club without having tried fishing here. Unfortunately I didn't think about bringing my rods and reels, and I'm sure that you did not either. However, I have located a local guide with equipment for us to do a little fishing. He promises we will fill up the boat where he is going to take us. How about it, are you game?"

"Just name the time and I'm ready. You're right, we have to get a fish tale or two to be able to tell the others when we get back." Sean smiled as he sipped his tea.

"Good, then it is settled. Meet me down on the dock in the morning. The guide will be there with his boat and equipment. We'll fish the morning away, and from what he said his wife will cook up the best of our catch for us." Nicholas replied.

"So, has the commodore said anything to you about what we will do once we deliver our spoils back home? Are we to go back out to sea, join the armies, or what?" Sean asked.

"The commodore is keeping his ideas to himself, and rightfully so. We don't need anyone around here hearing what our plans are and getting the information to the British when they come back, and they will come back. No, I think he will let us know either after we get under way, or after we return, since there may be orders awaiting us when we get home."

"Yes, there are a lot of over-eager ears around here, willing to take the chance of picking up information to sell to the British or just get them in better standing when they get back. This has been a grand adventure, hasn't it, Sam?" Sean inquired.

"Yes, it has. I'm sure that these lads will long remember the date of March the third 1775, the day we landed on this foreign shore. We have taken the war to the enemy and have succeeded most admirably. The folks at home could use some good news, and the army can use the supplies we are bringing them. Let's hope our journey home goes without incident,. We have been lucky so far, not having lost a man to the enemy," Nicholas observed.

"Yes that is amazing. Our ship's doctor has actually been complaining that he has nothing to do. The men have been so healthy here with the sun and wonderful fresh food. The only thing he has been treating anyone for is sunburns and a few cases of the pox from one of the sporting ladies in the tavern by the dock," said Sean.

"I'm not surprised. A few of those trollops are rather poxy-looking. Well, they'll think twice next time after he gives them those painful injections," laughed Sam.

"We can only hope so," Sean said as he laughed.

The two reviewed the watch lists for the two hundred and seventy marines and the work details for the next two days' worth of loading at the docks. When they were done, Sean returned to his men at Fort Nassau to supervise the removal of the last of the cannons from the fort walls.

The next morning, Sean met Sam at the dock just as their guide rowed his boat in and back-paddled to bring it to a stop without bumping the pilings. The marines clambered down into the skiff with their food pouches. They examined the fishing rods the man had neatly laid along the gunwales of the small craft.

After a brief discussion over what they could expect, the two took up the oars as the fisherman took control of the tiller. The sun was just above the horizon, and the air was cool as they rowed out through the harbor. The exercise felt good to Sean, as he had always liked rowing boats along the river back home. He looked overhead as a formation of twelve pelicans flew effortlessly overhead, going out to their fishing grounds for the day after sleeping on the wharf all night.

They rounded the tip of Hog Island, and within ten minutes they were where the guide wanted them to be. "You each take up a rod and fish from the same side of the boat. We're gonna drift here a ways, and you should get some good sea bass along the bottom here," he instructed them.

The man watched them with keen eyes to see if they really knew what they were doing, and after he watched them cast and retrieve a few times, gave a grunt of approval and filled the clay pipe he had pulled out of a satchel he had at his feet.

True to his word, they both started reeling in the fish. After an hour at that spot, they had pulled in over twelve of the bass of various sizes, the largest of which was thirteen pounds. The guide had them put the rods down and take up their oars. They rowed out further in the emerald green waters and again cast to one side of the boat, letting it drift parallel to the beach.

Sean gazed into the water. It was so clear he could see the bottom as the shadow of the boat moved along the sandy bottom. He pointed excitedly to a school of stingray as they glided through the water between them and the bottom. They were a strange sight, as they flew more than they swam along in the water.

"Strange critters, they be" observed their guide. "Good eatin' though, if you have nothing better."

They drifted on for another hour, pulling in more fish as they went. Their collection grew as they pulled in several trout, a couple of small sharks and a two-foot-wide stingray. The men took up the oars again and rowed further out, as they were close to beaching the boat.

After another hour in the increasingly hot sun, they had almost filled up the bottom of the skiff. Satisfied that they had caught enough and would have a great fishing story to tell their fishing club members, they laid their rods to rest and took up the oars.

They had a long row back, as they had gone pretty far out, but the tide was in their favor, so they were not too exhausted when they returned. They did not go to the dock, but put into the beach just outside of Nassau where the man lived. His wife and five children met them at the beach, and they marveled at their catch.

They took the six largest fish out of the boat and after cleaning them, two of the children carried them to the house where their mother was ready to cook them. The other children helped the men clean the rest of the fish and put them on drying racks close to the shack.

The men drank rum and swapped stories as they waited for the fish to be done. When the meal was served, they all sat around a large rough-hewn table outside the house under a thatched canopy. The children chattered giddily all through the meal, much to the amusement of the adults.

When time came for Sean and Sam to leave, they gave the man twice what he had asked for and shouldered ten of the larger fish of the catch on a pole to take back to the fort. They enjoyed the peaceful walk back to the town, taking turns carrying the load.

"Ah, 'tis good to see you made it back in one piece, sirs!" beamed Lanigan as he saluted the two officers, who looked more like townsfolk in their breeches and shirts with rolled-up sleeves. "I see that you have had a bit o' luck this day," Lanigan said as he examined the fish on the pole while he helped Sean to lower it to the ground.

"Sergeant, you should have gone with us. It was a beautiful day to be out on the water fishing. Make sure our cook gets these for our men," Sean said as he rubbed the soreness from his shoulder.

Lanigan signaled two of their men to retrieve the fish and take them to the cook. "See to it that the lads eat well the next couple of days, Angus, for we will be leaving as soon as the last ship is loaded. Then they will be back on ship's rations," Sean advised his sergeant.

"Ah, the lads will appreciate this meal tonight that you have provided. And don't you worry about them; they will be ready for sea just as soon as the word is given. They have been here long enough to have enjoyed all that there is to enjoy. If we stay any longer the men, will lapse into boredom, and then trouble will start," Lanigan mused.

"That they have, and it is fortunate for all of us that we have had so little trouble between them and the locals. I did hear yesterday that an angry father was looking for one of the *Cabot's* men that had dallied with his daughter. He had come looking for him with a blunderbuss, and it was with a great deal of diplomacy that Captain Welsh got the situation defused," Sean added.

"Yes, I had the opportunity to see him in action," interjected Sam, "the good captain had that blunderbuss pressed right into his chest as he stood the man down. He did not even flinch while they were standing there in that manner. Finally he managed to get him to settle for a case of good port from the governor's private stock and a brace of pistols that Lieutenant Wilson offered. Well, gentlemen, duty calls, and I must leave you. Carry on," Nicholas said as he turned and departed.

The next two days were busy ones for everyone. The last two ships were loaded, and the detachment of men that were guarding the other end of the island at Fort Montague was withdrawn to Nassau. The evening of the second day saw all the marines and sailors back on board their ships, which rode at anchor in the harbor and just outside the bay.

The next morning, the seventeenth of March, the much-laden small fleet raised anchors, set sails and with a thunderous salute of their guns, departed from the island of New Providence. The ships headed northeast for their destination of New London, Connecticut.

Sean walked the deck with his brother, observing the men getting back to the daily shipboard routines of holystoning the deck, attending to the cannons, splicing rigging and mending sails. As they reached the bow, they looked out across the ocean at the other ships, their sails billowing out in the breeze and all tacking in unison.

"Now that is a pretty sight indeed, Little Brother," Thomas exclaimed as they watched the ships change tack. "It is incredible to think about what we have done in so short time. From nothing, we have put a small naval force together, attacked a foreign land, and are returning home with the spoils of war weighting us down."

"Yes, and it is amazing to see how everyone has pulled together. Just look at how the men responded to the hardships and uncertainty of going into battle. Now look at how well the fleet responds to the signals of the flagship. They move out there as if we had been doing this together for several years instead of mere weeks."

"I still do not know what lies in store for us when we return. The commodore wouldn't say although anything that he might have planned could change in an instant as soon as we drop anchor," Thomas observed.

"We have been fortunate so far, as we have had better success than Washington has had. Let's hope that we continue to have such luck. We have such a good crew, and it is to them that we owe a lot of our good fortune." Sean said.

"Like Father said, set a good example, lead them properly and they will exceed your expectations every time," Thomas pointed out.

The two continued their conversation as they walked. They hadn't had much time together since they had landed on the island, as Thomas was busy on board ship while Sean's duty kept him ashore.

The fleet sailed on without any trouble from the enemy or the weather. On the morning of April fourth, they were off the east end of Long Island. They saw the *Columbus* approach from windward with a schooner in her lee that she had captured in the early morning hours.

"We're coming up on Block Island in an hour," Sean said to Lanigan as he joined him at the railing.

"I understand that the commodore has ordered us to work back and forth to try to pick up any other stray ships that we can," Lanigan inquired.

"Yes, the signals have been passed, and the *Andrew Doria* is going off toward Rhode Island to try to entice some of the enemy fleet out of port," Sean replied.

"It is a grand haul we have, and we could be risking all of it if we try to tempt Wallace's ships to come after us. The man is very active and is likely to send a sizable force out after us," Lanigan warned.

"Yes, it would be too bad to suffer losses so close to home after what we have done," Sean said. The two chatted at the railing as the men were busy with their daily tasks. The remainder of the day passed without incident.

In the morning, the *Alfred* was seen far ahead of the fleet, bearing down to leeward after a small sail. The rest of the fleet remained in formation as instructed by the flagship.

"Sir, the flagship has signaled us to take up the chase!" the call from the masthead sang out.

"Man the braces, all hands to quarters!" Thomas shouted out, sending every man into motion. Sean raced below to get his weapons and ran back up the stairway as he buckled his sword belt and slipped his pistols into it.

The sails were brought around, and within minutes, the *Osprey* was racing across the choppy ocean on an intercept course for the enemy vessel that had stood out from shore to avoid shallow waters and was heading straight for the *Osprey*.

The men had the guns loaded and run out in just under ten minutes, and each gun captain raised his hand to signify that he was ready for action. Sean acknowledged their signals and glanced to the fighting tops. The men were all in place and were busy loading their muskets and securing their buckets of hand grenades.

"That is a strange looking craft there, Sergeant. What do you make of her?" Sean asked as he handed his telescope to Lanigan at the starboard fore rail.

Lanigan took the telescope and put it to his right eye. After a moment of swirling it around to locate the ship and focus the lens, he studied the ship. "Why, that, sir, is a bomb-ketch, I'm thinking. See how it appears to be missing the foremast? Look just to the front of the mainmast, and the large dark object there would be two large mortars," he said as he handed the telescope back to Sean.

"Yes, I can make them out now. That is a strange rigging set-up they have with the foremast gone."

"It is indeed. I had the opportunity to serve on one of those many years ago. The bomb-ketch is an unwieldy vessel in hard weather, but very well designed for its main purpose. You see the large anchors at the back? When they anchor off the fortification or city they intend to bombard, all four anchors, two fore and two aft, are positioned carefully. By pulling in and letting off line from one anchor to the other, they are able to adjust the direction of the mortar shells," Lanigan explained.

"I can see how that could have a devastating effect on the target area. I wouldn't want to be trapped in a fort that has one of those anchored off-shore." Sean exclaimed.

"No indeed. The aftermath of that kind of shelling is a terrible thing to see. We had to go ashore after our enemy surrendered, what was left of them, to evaluate the effectiveness of our bombardment. It was an awful sight to behold," Lanigan replied.

"It appears that other than the mortars, the ship itself is lightly armed. It appears to only have about eight four-pounders on board," Sean observed.

"Yes that would be about right. They don't put much on those things because of the weight of the mortars, powder and the fifteen-inch explosive shells that they carry. Most often the bomb-ketches are protected by larger ships in transit."

"Look there, the *Alfred* has fired a couple of warning shots across her bow! She has struck her colors! Look sharp there, men, we will go alongside of her to be sure that they do not try anything," Sean called out to the marines.

He looked overhead to see the crew taking in sail as the ship bore down on the surrendered vessel. The *Alfred* took up position at a distance, letting the smaller *Osprey* do the honors of accepting the enemy's surrender. Several men already were in the process of hoisting the launch outboard.

"Angus, you take charge on board here. I'll take the boarding party over so that I can take a closer look at the vessel," Sean ordered as he walked back towards the entry port. He tapped eight men as his boarding party as he made his way aft, and by the time he got there, the boat had been lowered, and the boat crew was already down in it preparing the oars.

He and the others climbed down and took up their positions as the sailors cast off. They pulled hard in the chop to close the distance to the other vessel. Sean studied the rigging of the other vessel as they approached.

"Spread out across the deck and hold your muskets level at the hip once we get aboard. I don't expect they'll give us any trouble with the rest of the fleet in sight, but stay on your toes just the same," Sean cautioned his men.

They reached the other vessel, and in an instant the marines boarded the vessel and herded the crew to the bow. "Corporal Beckett, go below and search the Captain's cabin, although I do not expect you'll find much, as I saw a pouch thrown out the cabin window as we approached. Who's in charge here?" Sean barked.

"I am, Lieutenant Edward Sneyd." Came the answer from the officer not much older than Sean. "What do you intend to do with us?" he asked.

"For now, you are to consider yourselves prisoners. If there are any of you men that wish to end your service with the King and wish to join us, now is the time to speak up!" Sean said to the crewmen, who nervously eyed the muskets that were pointed at them. "Those of you who join us will have better conditions than what you have experienced, and will share in any prize monies that we collect. Those of you who do not will be transferred over to the flagship and will be put in irons for the rest of the journey. When we return to port, you will be put in a military prison."

"Count us in, sir!" came a voice from the crowd. "Henry and me will join ye!"

Sean looked at the two men who stepped forward of the group. The one who spoke was a toothless, older man with disheveled hair and appeared not to have bathed in months. The other man was a mousy fellow who had more the appearance of a clerk than of a sailor.

"You two, come over here. Private Julius Caesar Jones here will be your companion for now. You do as he says," Sean instructed the two.

"They're a fine lot for you, a loggerheaded impertinent dolt and a weakling! Take them, you deserve the likes of them you traitors!" sneered Sneyd.

"That we will, and I'll ask you to keep a civil tongue in your mouth,Sir!" Sean ordered.

With that said, three more men stepped forward and offered their services. "The rest of you line up at the entry port. The boat from the flagship is approaching, and you will be taken back with them," Sean said as the men were sorted out, those who would stay and those who would go.

As they waited for the boat to arrive, Sean took the opportunity to inspect the massive mortars. They could hurl fifteen-inch shells packed with explosives and a lit fuse a couple of miles inland. He went below to inspect the hold and the reinforced beams that were underneath the heavy mortars.

He saw the huge timbers that were used to shore up the deck beneath them. They had to not only hold the weight of the guns, but also absorb the tremendous recoil of them when they were fired. It was a marvel of engineering that kept this ship from being torn apart when those things were fired.

Once the prisoners were transferred and volunteers from the *Alfred* ferried across to man the bomb-ketch, Sean and his men returned to the *Osprey.* The enlarged flotilla continued to tack back and forth off Block Island for the rest of the day. Toward evening, a sloop and brigantine from New York were captured and taken under guard.

"If we keep this up, we'll own half the British merchant vessels and half their fleet!" Thomas exclaimed, as he and Sean took their evening pipe and grog by the wheel. "We have to head for port soon or we will not be able to keep watch over so many extra vessels."

"We are now a fleet of twelve and can still grow by the time we reach New London," Sean observed. "Look there, they have made their tack perfectly this time. The volunteers on the bomb-ketch have finally gotten the knack for sailing her with that cumbersome sail plan."

"I want to get a chance to go on board her and inspect that for myself once we get into port. The latest signal was that in the morning we will discontinue our maneuvers here and head on into port," Thomas informed his brother.

The two talked for a while before turning in for the night. Sean settled in for a good night's sleep, but at one-thirty in the morning was roused from his deep sleep by the duty watch. "Sir, we hear gunfire to the north of us. It sounds like the flagship has tangled with another vessel!"

"Have you awakened my brother and called for all hands to quarters?" Sean questioned the man as he grabbed his coat and threw it on as he tried to get his feet into his shoes.

"Aye, sir that we have and the captain has just now gone on deck," he responded as he turned to race up on deck.

The night air was cool, and the crew was pouring out of the hatches towards their respective duty stations. Sean saw that his men were all going about their duties as he walked to the rail and listened to the sound of cannons in the distance. The horizon came alive with bright flashes that could be seen coming from two distinct vessels locked in combat.

The men had the guns loaded and run out when the lookout reported the signal from the *Wasp* as she relayed a message with her lantern. "That's the signal for us to remain on station," the man called out.

The men of the *Osprey* waited in silence as the battle continued. From the sound of the guns, it seemed as though the *Alfred* had bowed out of the fight and one of the other vessels took over. A while later the sound of the gunfire changed again. The fighting continued through the rest of the night.

The crew was kept on deck but allowed to rest as the night wore on. Most of them curled up between the guns and slept part of the night. By dawn the firing had ceased, and a signal was passed down from the flagship to maintain positions.

The cook had breakfast prepared for the men, and they were given an extra tot of rum to warm their bones after having slept on the hard rolling deck all night. The rest of the day was quiet, and the fleet slowly headed for port. Word had been passed that an enemy ship had engaged three of the fleet and was finally driven off at daylight.

The rest of the voyage went quietly, and on the morning of the eighth of April, the fleet sailed into New London harbor and dropped anchor. A crowd of cheering spectators and several officials of the town greeted them. They all came to see the victorious fleet and all the prizes that they had captured.

It would take several days for the holds of the ships to be unloaded of all the artillery and shells and then be restocked with victuals for returning to sea. The men had all stood proudly at the rails as they glided into port and saw the welcome that the people of the town had for them. It was a proud moment for all in the fleet.

They had been in port for a few days, and it was *Osprey's* turn at the wharf for unloading, when Nicholas came aboard to find Sean. "Good morning, Sean, how goes the transfer of supplies?" he asked as he returned Sean's salute.

"They are making a fast job of it, and should be done tomorrow. We have the artillery shells in our hold, so they are taking their time handling them very gently. Sam, you look troubled. What is the matter?" Sean inquired.

"Come to lunch with me so we can talk. There are too many here who might hear what I have to say, and there are enough rumors afloat already," Nicholas warned.

"Right. Wait here while I inform Thomas and Angus that I'm leaving the ship with you. There's a decent steak house a couple of streets over from the docks," Sean said as he turned to go below to report to Thomas.

Once he found him and Lanigan, he let them know he would be gone for a while and returned to the deck. The two men saluted the flag and left the ship. They walked in silence along the waterfront amidst the men scurrying everywhere with handcarts full of cannonballs and shells. Two wagons were being loaded with cannon barrels that were brought back from the cannons that had such rotten carriages as to be of no use to bring along. They would have new ones built by local craftsmen and be put to good use in the field.

Once they cleared the area onto a quiet side street, Nicholas turned his head to see that there was no one in sight and said, "Have you heard any of the stories floating around the fleet about the investigation that the Navy Committee and Continental Congress wants to have in regards to the *Glasgow* incident?"

"No, I haven't heard that, just that some of the members of Congress were upset with Commodore Hopkins for having three ships shot up during the engagement with the *Glasgow*. But I didn't think that it would go as far as having an inquiry," Sean responded.

"Well, they are, and I have been called to return to Philadelphia with Commodore Hopkins, Captain Hopkins, Captain Whipple and Captain Biddle. It's almost as if someone is trying to prevent us from returning to sea and taking more of the enemy's shipping," Nicholas lamented.

"Here we are. Let's go in and find a place to sit where we won't be overheard," Sean said as he steered Nicholas towards the door of the tavern.

A buxom waitress greeted them, once they stepped inside, and led them to a corner table. The men ordered their meal before continuing their conversation.

"Sam we haven't had a chance to talk since we left New Providence. Tell me just what happened that night. I have heard the stories going around and they all are a little different," Sean asked.

"All right. It was about half-past one that morning when we heard the 'all hands to quarters' call and went on deck. The *Glasgow* had come up on the *Cabot* thinking we were all British ships, and when they hailed the *Cabot*, a marine on the fighting top threw a grenade down on the deck of the *Glasgow*, and then the *Cabot* let fly a broadside at her, and received two in return. The *Cabot's* men were too slow in reloading, and the *Glasgow's* captain was well trained." Sam paused to take a drink of his ale that the waitress placed in front of him.

"The *Cabot's* hull and rigging took a beating, and she had to haul off for some quick repairs. We then came up in the *Alfred* and took on the British ship. We exchanged fire side-to-side for over an hour. In the first broadside that hit us, my second Lieutenant, John Fitzpatrick, was struck down by a musket ball to the head. I shall miss him; he was an excellent officer and a good friend, " Sam took another swig of his ale.

"We then drifted off when our wheel-block and tiller lines were severed by a cannonball. The *Andrew Doria* and *Columbus* both took turns in the fight, but both of them were out-gunned and did little damage. Just at daylight, we did hit the *Glasgow* a few more good ones, and as the sun came up, she broke off and headed to Newport. I lost three more of my people, and two others were wounded. Captain Hopkins of the *Cabot* is wounded and he lost two others dead.

Not a good ending for such a grand voyage and success that we had in Nassau." Nicholas lamented.

"The British captain is a trained fighter and has experience at ship-to-ship fighting. Our captains are mostly merchant men who have had limited experience against pirates, and only one or two had any fighting experience in the last war, so mistakes were bound to occur," Sean reassured him.

"Well, the Navy Committee is not inclined to be so gracious. We accomplished so much, yet we had such a poor showing against one ship. However, since being here in port we have learned from a post rider that the *Glasgow* barely made it into port. She came in listing with men working both pumps trying to keep her afloat. Her rigging was ripped to shreds, as were most of her sails, and her hull was in pretty bad shape, and half her guns were knocked out of commission." Sam shook his head as he said it.

"Surely they will not hold you responsible for any of this?" Sean asked.

"Probably not. I think they just want me as a witness. I tell you though, this will keep half the fleet in port for an extended length of time for no reason. When you get your ship loaded, get out of here as fast as you can so they don't hold you back too. I think the commodore will be talking with Thomas later to tell him the same thing. There are members in Congress who will have some of their business hurt if we manage to slow down the British flow of goods on the high seas, and they may try to hamper us if they see us succeeding at it," Sam cautioned.

"That is hard to imagine, that all of us are working so hard to achieve independence and there may be some of our own people trying to hinder our efforts although they are with us in the struggle," Sean mused.

"There are always those who will put profit ahead of anything else, so don't forget that. Well, here comes our food, so enough talk of business. Let us devour this heavenly smelling food before it gets cold," Sam smiled.

The two ate heartily and returned to the docks. They parted company, and Sean went aboard to talk to Thomas. He had been summoned to the flagship, and Sean filled him in on his conversation with Nicholas before Thomas left for his meeting with the commodore.

When he came back an hour later, he looked grim. "Sean, as soon as we have unloaded the cargo and gotten our supplies on board, we are to get out of here and resume our patrols off the coast. The commodore recommends that we hit the southern routes, as they may prove lucrative in capturing supplies meant for Cornwallis in the south. Now let's go see if we can hurry things along. I wish to be gone from all this political in-fighting."

"I agree with you, Brother. The lads will be willing to get away from here and get busy capturing more of the enemy's goods. It does them good every time that we take a prize. They can hear the coin jingling in their pockets even before we get them auctioned off in the prize courts."

Two days later, fully stocked with food, water and supplies, the *Osprey* cast off from the dock. The cutter and launch were manned, and together they warped the ship out into the river current. The wind caught the topsails, and their towlines went slack. Within minutes, the two boats were hoisted on board, and the *Osprey* once again was headed out for the Atlantic under full sail.

6

The Hurricane
and the *Charon*

Sean stood with his hand on the tiller, straining his eyes to see what the last man aboard the grounded schooner was doing. "Steady on your oars, lads. Take us in closer." The men resumed rowing toward the beached ship.

They had chased the schooner for several miles before she turned in towards the coast, and she was driven right onto the beach. The mainmast snapped at deck level as she struck, and the crew jumped onto the beach and ran off into the woods a hundred paces from the water's edge.

"Look, smoke! He's lit a fuse, sir!" shouted Edward George standing at the swivel gun on the prow of the launch.

Sean saw the man hold the fuse and slow match above his head for them to see. He lit the fuse, dropped it to the deck, and ran to the bow. The man leaped down onto the sand and ran off to catch up with his mates already hiding in the woods.

"Back oars, fast! Dig in, lads, hurry!" Sean shouted. The men responded, sending the launch backwards. Once they had put some distance between them and the stranded ship, he had them reverse again, and swung the bow of the boat towards open sea and the *Osprey*.

The men rowed for their very lives as they put more distance between them and the schooner. Sean turned to see more smoke rising from the ship. The burning fuse had apparently started small fires below. He gauged their distance, still too close. If the ship had a full cargo of powder, they might not survive the impending explosion.

The flash and blast wave hit them before the deafening sound of the blast. Several of the men were knocked into the bottom of the boat; Sean and George had instinctively ducked down from where they stood as they saw the explosion.

One of the sailors rowing made the mistake of standing up while everyone else ducked down. He was instantly impaled by a large section of railing that came flying over the launch, sending him overboard, screaming into the water.

The air and sea around the boat came alive with chunks of wood, burning canvas, and all manner of ship's items flying overhead and splashing into the water around them. "Stay down!" Sean called out. He glanced up in time to see a black mass falling from the sky. It appeared to be coming right down onto them in the boat.

The gun carriage of one of the schooner's six-pounders came crashing down amidst the out-stretched oars on the starboard side of the craft. When it hit, it shattered the oars, and the inboard ends angled up violently, knocking three oarsmen straight up. They fell back unconscious into the boat as a large wave of water rained down on the boat from the gun carriage hitting the water.

The raining of debris and water finally came to an end. Sean looked at the men in the boat who were starting to sit back up. "Help those three there, stretch them out, and you men move to the side. Even out the oars, get some from the port side moved across to even things out. Now, are we missing anyone besides Burger?"

"Looks like 'e's the only one, sir," called out Beckett. "Look there's 'is body. Do you think 'e may still be alive?"

"We'll row over and find out, though I doubt it," Sean responded. The men regained their composure and started dipping their oars into the water. All were trying to make their ears pop, as the force and noise of the explosion rendered them a little hard of hearing. They steadied the oars as they came alongside the corpse.

"Bloody 'ell!" said Tyree as he reached out and rolled it over, the two-foot long splinter jutting out from his heart like a mast. "'E's dead, sir, lucky for 'im 'e must 'ave died instantly," he said as he pushed the body away from the boat.

The men doffed their hats in respect, each mumbling a prayer under his breaths. Without encouragement, they regained their oars and began rowing for the ship. Sean looked back to see what was left of the schooner, now that the smoke was blowing towards the trees. There was a tremendous amount of debris washing on shore where moments before the ship had been, just moments before.

The largest pieces left appeared to be what remained of the masts rolling about in the surf. He turned back around and watched, as the *Osprey* grew larger in front of them. Just beyond and behind her were another schooner and a bark about the size of *Osprey*. They had captured them a few days earlier

269

and were headed back to Philadelphia with them when they came across the schooner that had eluded them until it was beached and destroyed.

They reached the side of their ship and passed up the wounded men who were just regaining their senses. Doctor Faircloth had them helped below by some of the crew. Once the launch was swung back on board, the small flotilla set sail and headed north for Delaware Bay and home.

Later, in his cabin, Sean put his quill and ink pot away as he re-read the entry he had made in his personal journal for today, the seventeenth of July 1776. He paged back through it to review his other entries since the raid on New Providence.

The past few months had been good for the men on board. This was the second time they had headed for their homeport with prizes. Since April, they had taken five vessels, sunk seven others, and had successfully defeated a British ship slightly larger than *Osprey* but with the same amount of guns. In the running battle that lasted for two hours, they had finally struck a mortal blow to the other ship when they had managed to cross the 'T' and send a full broadside down the length of the ship from astern. One of the shells must have set off an explosion in the other ship's magazine, as it suddenly blew apart.

They had been hailed by the *Fly* a few days back, bearing news from the Congress. The representatives of the colonies had declared total independence from Britain. No longer now were they thirteen colonies, but thirteen individual states, banded together to form a nation they called the United States of America.

All on board welcomed the news warmly, yet many did not realize the full impact of what that meant to all of them. Thomas had explained to them as they met after supper that no longer were they just rebellious citizens, but now they would be treated as traitors if Britain won the fight. They all stood to lose their lives if captured. Even with that sobering thought, they were still imbued with a new sense of purpose and pride in what they were about.

"Sean, the Captain of the *Fly* told me that the British have built a battery on the tip of Cape May. It is a log and earthen structure with a battery of twelve and eighteen-pounders. Now, we don't have to sail close to them to get into the bay, but I was thinking that maybe we should pay our respects as we pass, and shell them with some of the munitions of theirs that we have captured." Thomas approached Sean at the rail close to dark.

"Why, I think that is a grand idea! We know the water at the Cape, so why don't we sail past in the dark, and let loose a broadside or two from each of our vessels just to liven up their evening?" Sean asked.

"That is a splendid idea. We'll space the other two ships behind us. We'll go in close; the next in line will come by farther out, and the third will come in close also. We have a moonless night ahead of us, and that will help to confuse their gunners as they try to set their range."

"Good idea. I'll make sure the lads are ready. I think we should send a few more men to each of the other two ships to be sure everything goes smoothly."

"Right, now let's get ready. We should be passing the Cape at about three in the morning."

The three ships hove to after they crossed the mouth of the bay after dark. Coming from the south, they had to position themselves to the north of the bay so that they could cut around the tip of the peninsula where the redoubt was built.

The bosuns that had been put in charge of the two captive ships had come on board to be given their orders personally by Thomas. They returned to their charges with five extra marines each to ensure that the bombardment went as smoothly as possible.

They were four miles out when they hove to so they would be out of sight and have time to make their preparations. Each of the two ships in the lead would have a shielded lantern hung from the stern to guide the ship behind them; all other lights would be extinguished. It was a moonless night, and they wanted to make it as difficult as possible for the enemy gunners to be able to aim their guns properly.

When all the preparations were complete, the signal to proceed was given. The night sky was alive with stars, which provided some light but not enough to help the enemy. From a mile out, the British position could be clearly seen from the glow of the campfires within the fort walls and the torches lit on top of the walls for the sentries.

Sean stood next to Lanigan by the forward guns. No one spoke, for as light as the breeze was, every little sound would carry a great distance across the water. The dark outline of the fort and surrounding woods grew larger in their sight. They would be close enough in just moments.

From somewhere aft a man tried to stifle a cough. Lanigan turned and went aft to take charge of the aft guns. Sean looked at the men of the two forward guns. They all stared intently at their target. The gun captains made their last-minute changes in the elevation of their guns.

The fortification was a mere one hundred and fifty paces away. "Steady lads," Sean whispered. "Give it another minute now." Sean strained his ears to pick up on any sound from the fort that would indicate that they were seen. Nothing. He counted the silhouettes of four sentries against the light of the torches. They were either very careless about giving away their location, or just overly confident that no one would fire on them. He watched as the distance between the ship and the fort shrank until it seemed that they would end up on the beach.

It was time. "Fire!" he whispered. The two guns crashed out, brightening the forward portion of the deck momentarily. "Stop your vents, sponge out, reload!" the commands seemed to blurt out automatically as Sean watched the fort to see where the shots hit. The aft three guns fired, lighting up the ship. Sean could make out geysers of dirt and wood from where the five shots had impacted on the walls of the redoubt.

From across the water came shouts, a bugle call to arms, and the staccato beat of a drum, rousing everyone in the fort to action.

The gun crews were ready and managed to get off a second round before the men in the fort responded with hastily fired shots that flew off into the night, nowhere around the *Osprey*. The crews got off a third round as the cannons in the fort fired a second time, again to no avail but closer this time.

The *Osprey* was out of range yet before the inhabitants of the fort could recover from their attack, they were hit again from the second ship. The six-pounders could not do much damage except upset the men in the fort. Sean watched as the fort's guns belched out flame in the direction of the ship. As planned, he could see the shots hit in the water, far short of the ship. That indicated the gun crews did not realize the second ship was further out.

The men in the fort and on the other ship both got off second rounds. The fort's shots fell short again, and the shots from the ship thudded into the earthen wall of the redoubt. The third ship now opened fire from closer in, and again the fort's shots missed, as they had adjusted for a further range. After each had exchanged a second round, the night grew silent once more with the exception of the creaking of cordage and spars in the wind.

The men of all three ships let out a cheer, then secured their guns. They may not have caused much more than an annoyance to the British there, but it gave heart to the men. The rest of the voyage up the Delaware was uneventful, and they reached Philadelphia after sunrise.

The ships were tied up to the Taggert docks, and the crew undertook the countless tasks of securing from sea. Many friends and family members came to greet them, and after a brief reunion, the men returned to work so that they would be able to leave the ship for time with their families.

Just when the officers were making the final inspections, Sam Nicholas showed up. "Good morning, gentlemen. It's good to see you safe at home again. I have it on good authority that sometime during the night, that the British battery on Cape May was shelled. You lads wouldn't have had anything to do with that, now would you?" he asked grinning, knowing full well it was them.

"We just gave those lads a little something to write home about, them being stuck out there all alone like," laughed a sailor nearby.

"Well, Sam, looks like you got promoted! How does it feel to be a major now?" Sean observed as he shook his friend's hand.

"It would feel real good if we could get all the men and supplies that we need. It seems like I spend most of my time trying to get what we need out of our impoverished Naval Committee," he responded.

"What have you there; that looks like quite a document you have rolled up there?" Sean asked.

"Sean, Thomas, have your men gather around for a moment before they go ashore. I'm sure that you may have heard about the Congress declaring our independence, and I wanted to take this opportunity to talk to everyone about this. Commodore Hopkins is away, so I have the honors."

The brothers called for the crew to gather on the quarterdeck and sent runners to the other two vessels to have the rest of the men assemble with them. It took a few minutes for the scattered crew to come together. Finally when all were accounted for, Sam stood up on one of the guns for all to see him.

"Lads, first of all, welcome back from another successful hunting trip. I have here," he said, holding up the rolled up parchment in his right hand, "what many are calling our Declaration of Independence, signed by Congress on the fourth of this month. Let me read to you." He paused while he unrolled the paper.

"When in the course of human events, it becomes necessary for one people to dissolve the political bonds which have connected them with another, and to assume among the powers of the earth, the separate and equal station to which the Laws of Nature's God entitle them, a decent respect to the opinions of mankind requires that they should declare the causes which impel them to the separation," he paused to let his words take effect.

"Lads, this means that we no longer consider us to be British subjects, no longer colonials, or Continentals, but we are now to consider ourselves to be free men, men of the United States of America!" he stopped while the men cheered.

"Let me continue," he called out, as they grew quiet. "We hold these truths to be self-evident, that all men are created equal, that they are endowed by their Creator with certain unalienable Rights, that among these are Life, Liberty and the pursuit of Happiness. —That to secure these rights, governments are instituted among Men, deriving their just powers from the consent of the governed, --That whenever any Form of Government becomes destructive of these ends, it is the Right of the People to alter or to abolish it, and to institute new Government, laying its foundation on such principles and organizing its powers in such form, as to them shall seem most likely to affect their Safety and Happiness." He paused again and lowered the paper to his side.

"Gentlemen, probably not since the founding of Rome has any such government been laid out. Our Congress of the Colonies has just instituted the groundwork for a government of the people, not of some monarch that inherited his position from his father to rule as he sees fit, but as the people see fit. This is a momentous occasion, and all of you here are a part of this undertaking."

He held the document high facing them so that they could see the bold signatures of the men who signed the declaration.

"Look at the names on this paper; each one of these men has, by signing this, made himself a hunted man. Each of them is now a criminal as far as the Crown is concerned. They have put all that they have, not the least of which is their lives, in jeopardy by this action. You see the largest signature there, John Hancock? They said that when he signed this he declared, 'I shall sign this so large that the King will not need his spectacles to read my name!' So there you have it, not only are you risking your lives, but those that are running our government are also."

He was satisfied to see the men nodding their heads in agreement as they looked and pointed at the document.

He continued, "Lads, you are no longer a band of outlaws or renegades from a tyrannical government, you are now part of a new nation. You are no longer British subjects; you are citizens of the United States. You are now sailors of the United States Navy, and marines of the United States Marines!"

Nicholas was taken back by the loud cheering that sprung from the throats of the men before him. The outpouring of elation was not to be curtailed. He gave up any further attempt at trying to quell the men to read on. They had heard what was important. They were now free of the chains of subjugation to the Crown.

"Lads, let's break out a cask of rum to celebrate together!" Thomas shouted out over the cheering. Two men were sent below to bring up a fresh cask and tankards for all. The men drank several toasts to their new nation, the ship and many other things that none would remember.

After the impromptu celebration, the men were allowed to go ashore to be with families and friends. They would have a few days rest while the ship's stores were replenished. Sean looked at his friend and said, "Well Sam, with this I suppose there is no turning back; we either win our independence or we hang!"

"There is no doubt about that, old friend. Anyone that signed this or who is an officer in our rebellious military forces will be hanged as traitors if Britain wins this war," he said grimly. "So it's up to men like us to make sure that that does not happen. When the men lose heart, you must be there to bolster them up. When they want to turn and run, you must be there to inspire them to face the enemy. The life of our nation is in the hands of men like us—you, me and Thomas-- we are the ones who will make sure those men out there win this war, win this independence!" He held up the document. Sean took it and read the rest of what Sam did not finish. It would truly infuriate King George for in it the document listed all the dastardly actions that he had taken against the people in the colonies.

Put together in a list such as this, it was quite clear that the King had overstepped the boundaries of British Law where it concerned the citizens of Britain, be they in Britain or in the colonies. The King had prevented the Colonial Governors from signing laws that were necessary in the colonies. He had passed laws that were unjust, levied taxes without proper representation, tried to prevent the colonists from buying goods produced from anywhere outside of Britain, and forced the housing of troops on the people.

The King would not relent when this was read to him. He would only send more troops to seize control of his former subjects. This would be a hard-fought war from this point on. Sean rolled up the document and passed it to his brother, who took it to read later. Nicholas took his leave of the brothers, and they took a carriage to their home.

The past months had flown by, Sean thought as he stood by the railing. They had put into Philadelphia at the end of September with two more prizes in tow and stayed in port for a week to have minor repairs taken care of, and some caulking done to the decks and upper hull. The entire crew worked on pounding the oakum into the seams to prevent leaking.

Also while they were in port, Major Nicholas showed up with a couple of crates for the marines. He was wearing the neck stock on his green uniform that had been authorized by the Marine Committee. They kept the green coat and round black hat, but added a high leather neck stock to the uniform such as the British Marines wore. It was uncomfortable to the wearer, yet protected the neck from saber cuts.

The sail maker and his assistants were kept busy while in port, attaching the buckles to the neck stocks Nicholas brought them for the *Osprey's* marines. They grumbled at the new addition and put up with the jibes of the sailors and civilians who made fun of them.

He ran his finger around the inside of the stiff leather as his brother walked over to him. "Still not used to it eh, Brother?" Thomas kidded him.

"You'd think that the leather would soften up a bit, but it sure doesn't. The wind is kicking up a bit much, don't you think?" he replied.

"Yes, we are in for a bad blow, I'm afraid. The barometer has been slowly falling since last night, and when I just checked it now, it has dropped way too far for my liking. I believe we are in for a hurricane. That is the only thing that I have ever seen make the barometer drop so rapidly. We need to make preparations before things start kicking up much more. What do you think about our prize?"

"It may be best to get the men off and sink her. If we are in for a hurricane, I would rather not have to worry about part of our men being on another ship, and one that is in need of serious repair. We should get within hailing distance while we can and give them instructions to scuttle the ship and get back to the *Osprey* fast so that we can prepare for heavy weather before it gets here."

"I think that is an excellent idea. Once we have done that, if you would, have your men take charge of securing the guns. Have them remove the swivels and take them below. When they finish that, they can help the crew rig safety lines across the deck. The rest of the men will be aloft, reefing the sails and rigging the main, fore and mizzen storm staysails," Thomas instructed.

Sean went below to roust his men out. Once he had given them their instructions, he and Lanigan went on deck in their foul-weather gear to supervise the securing of the guns.

As they were about that task, the prize crew and prisoners arrived on board from the schooner that they had captured. Sean and the others watched in fascination as the other ship started sinking. The men had opened the seacock, and for good measures, moved one of the four-pounders to the main hatch and fired it into the hold, punching a large hole in the bottom of the hull.

The schooner was down by the bow when suddenly the stern shot straight up in the air. The glass in the stern cabin windows burst from the air pressure built up inside, and the ship quickly slid beneath the waves.

It had taken an hour to prepare the ship for heavy weather, as the wind grew stronger and the seas rougher. Overhead the sky was alight with great bursts of lightning arcing across the sky in every direction.

"By the eternal, look at that! It's the apocalypse for sure!" exclaimed one of the seamen when he saw a tremendous explosion of lightning cover the entire horizon. The clouds were lower and moving much faster as the seas kicked up.

"We'll keep her headed west as long as we can; the wind is coming steadily from the south-southeast," Thomas shouted over the howling wind to Sean, as he clung to a safety rope that had been rigged across the deck.

There were several ropes rigged fore-and-aft, and port-to-starboard in a grid across the deck so that the men would have something to grab hold of if they were swept off their feet by the waves that were crashing ever so frequently across the deck.

"I have sent all the men below that are not needed on deck. It is pretty miserable for them down there, with things flying back and forth every time the ship lurches. Look at those clouds! I can no' remember ever seeing clouds such a dark green color before!"

"It's the worst I have seen, Sean. The last hurricane that I went through when you were out west, we saw the clouds turn green, but never as intense as those look. I'm afraid that we are in for a real tough go of it with this one!" Thomas shouted back.

Just then the ship dropped down into a deep trough, throwing the rudder hard over, which in turn jerked the wheel out of the hands of the helmsman, and threw Nelson, who was helping the helmsman control the wheel, clear across the top of it, into the bulwark.

Sean and Thomas both jumped for the wheel and brought it under control while Wilson checked on Nelson. "He's coming too, sir, but 'e 'as a bloody 'ead."

"Come take the wheel, and I'll take him below," Sean ordered. He let go of the spokes when he was sure that Wilson had a good grasp on them. He then helped Nelson to his feet and carried more than supported him to the aft stairway. "I'll send two more men up to relieve you," Sean called out, as he was halfway down the stairs.

Hands reached out and relieved him of the injured man as he reached the bottom of the steps as remnants of a wave came splashing down after them.

"Me and Dundee will go topside and help at the wheel, sir," offered Thompson.

"Fine, be off with you then. Wilson is about played out. The rest of you stand by to take a turn at the wheel. It is beating them pretty bad up there. How are the rest of you holding up down here?" he asked as Faircloth helped the injured man to the other end of the crew's quarters, where a lantern danced madly from its hook in the overhead.

"We're getting tossed around pretty good down here, sir, but I imagine it's better than being on deck," Seaman Young replied.

No sooner had he said that than the ship lurched over heavily, throwing everyone standing or sitting toward the opposite side of the ship. The men who were in their hammocks merely swayed in the direction that the ship rolled. The men were pelted with tankards, clothing and everything else that had not been locked up.

He went below to the hold to check on the water level. It appeared that the pumps were keeping up with the influx of seawater from above. There appeared to be about a foot of water down below in the bilges. He went back up to the crew's quarters.

Sean could see fear and apprehension in the eyes of the men crowded together. They were all wet and shivering from the water that came crashing in the hatches whenever someone came in or went out. He took Lanigan aside and whispered to him, "I'm going to go topside to help Thomas. It looks like the lads could use some distraction. Have any good sea stories to tell them that they haven't heard yet?" he smiled.

"Aye, that I have!" he turned and stood in the middle of the men and smiled. "Did I ever tell you laddies about the lassies up in Denmark?"

Sean did not wait to hear the rest. Instead he picked four men to go topside with him to relieve the men on the pumps. The four marines donned their tarpaulin coats and hats and followed him topside.

When they got on deck, they all were amazed to see how low the clouds were. They were at mast-top level and moving faster than any they had ever seen before. The men at the pumps were elated to be relieved and almost too worn out to make it to the hatch to go below. The replacements started pumping as soon as they had lashed themselves to the safety lines.

Sean struggled to get back to the helm to his brother. "I checked the bilge, and it appears that the pumps are maintaining about a foot of water below." He shouted above the shrieking of the winds.

"Good, if it gets much higher, we will have to use the emergency pumps." The storm is at its worst right now; I don't know how much longer it will last. It has been an hour so far!" Thomas shouted back.

Just then they heard a loud crack above them and saw the main yardarm split in two and dangling above the deck. Several lines snapped, and rigging was snapping back and forth in the wind, sending a block hurtling at the men by the wheel. They ducked in time, and it crashed into the bulwark, punching a hole through it.

"We need to get some men aloft to cut those pieces free or they could fall and punch holes in the deck!" Thomas warned.

"I'll get some men aloft!" Sean replied. He went to the hatch and called for eight volunteers. The men came rushing up, coils of rope and hatchets in hand. Sean directed them to try to lower the pieces to the deck and roll them overboard. Four men went aloft to hack away the ropes holding the two pieces aloft as soon as they were lowered to the deck. The pieces of shattered yardarm swung madly back and forth as the ship lurched with the wind.

The men on deck frantically tried to loosen the ropes holding them from the pin rails, but with all the weight from the free-swinging pieces on the ropes, they could not do so. They had to latch onto the pieces with their own ropes and take the strain off the others. For fifteen minutes they struggled to accomplish this, and when they finally did, the yardarm sections were lowered to the deck and rolled over the side with ease.

The men came down from aloft and were about to go below when the ship heaved high in front as it climbed a wave and came crashing down again. They all lost their balance, yet managed to grab onto the safety lines; one man almost was swept overboard. As they regained their footing, a sickening sound of cracking wood from forward was heard above the howling of the wind.

They turned in time to see the starboard forward twelve-pounder running loose on the deck its ropes trailing behind a portion of the bulwark. The men scrambled to control the gun and lash it down before it caused great damage.

The cannon charged back and forth with the pitching of the deck like a maddened beast. The men had to be quick to avoid being crushed by the heavy gun. One of the men got a rope around the muzzle of the gun, and before he could loop it around one of the other guns as an anchor, it dragged him off his feet.

The ship heaved upwards again, sending the gun rolling at the man with the rope. He regained his footing as the cannon charged at him, but it was too late. The cannon hit the truck of another gun, and up righted itself as the ship plunged into the trough of a wave, sending the gun crashing down on top of the man, with the barrel landing squarely on top of him full-length.

The man's horrid scream of pain could be heard over the wind's chorus. The others jumped at the gun and rolled it off the man and wedged it between two of the aft guns, where they managed to lash it securely before the next wave threw them about.

They gathered around Young, whose eyes looked as if they were about to burst forth out of their sockets. Sean bent down over him and felt his chest. The ribs were crushed into many small pieces, and he had stopped breathing. He felt no pulse, and a growing pool of blood under the man made it evident that he was no longer alive.

Four of his messmates picked up the lifeless body and dropped it over the side. Once they saw it sink beneath the madly churning sea, they went below. Sean returned to his brother's side.

"It looks as though the weight of the gun pulled the bulwark apart. It was still lashed to the very wood that it had been secured to. The ringbolts were still imbedded in the wood that had torn loose. Young never stood a chance poor fellow. He died trying to save his shipmates."

"He was a good fellow and a good seaman," Thomas replied.

Sean suddenly felt very weak from the constant exertion of fighting the wind, waves and loose cannon. He was about to go below when the wind abruptly died down. He turned away from the hatch and looked at the sky. The men on deck looked all around. The clouds were no longer racing past them, although they were still as sickening-looking green as before.

"I think we have entered the very vortex of the storm. See how the clouds in the distance are moving fast way over there? We have punched through to the center of the storm. We will have a brief period of no wind, and then it should pick up from the other direction. Get some men aloft to start splicing the severed rigging. We won't have much time, so they will need to be quick about it."

No one had to go below to relay the order, for the men had come up the stairway to see what had happened to the storm when the wind had dropped away. The ship still was pitching wildly about from waves that were slamming in from every direction.

"Thomas, come over here and take a look at this!" Sean shouted from the port side railing. The men came over to see the strangest sight that any had ever witnessed.

The waves in the vortex of the storm were acting as though they had gone mad. They were coming in from every direction, crashing into one another, making the sea appear to be like boiling water, hopping all about but in no particular direction nor from any particular source of wind.

"Aye, it's as if King Neptune himself is stirring up the kettle!" exclaimed one of the bewildered men. They stood staring in amazement until Thomas hastened them aloft.

"We may only have less than an hour, lads, so be quick about it. Watch your footing up there. We'll be getting thrown in every direction during this lull in the wind!"

The others watched the sky. They could see the winds off to the port side as the clouds kept racing along in the distance. Lightning again started arcing all over the horizon, yet above them the clouds seemed to stand still.

Thomas had gone below for a few minutes, and when he came on deck again, he said, "We were running before the wind for just over two hours. This old ship sure has done wonders for us today. I just hope she can hold together for the rest of the storm, which we should be feeling pretty soon. Look over there, the clouds are moving in the opposite direction. We must change tack and get ready. It won't be long now!"

The men overhead were watching the clouds too, and when they felt the ship change course, they doubled their efforts to finish their work. As the individual men finished their tasks, they started to come back down to the deck. Two men remained aloft as the wind started to pick up from the opposite direction. Xing Xao, the Chinaman, and Mathew Ross were attempting to finish their repairs when the wind started blowing hard again.

The men that were not needed returned below deck to get out of the weather. The two men aloft were about ready to come down when a wave that hit from abeam threw the ship way over to the starboard side. The ship swung over so fast that Ross lost his grip, and he was flung far out into the sea.

Xing Xao, who had been on the inside of the shrouds, was jerked loose when the ship righted itself, and he was caught on a dangling rope that had wrapped around his ankle. He was left hanging upside down and was being swayed back and forth like a pendulum as the ship was tossed about. He desperately grabbed for the shrouds each time he was swung toward them but could not grasp the slippery lines as he bounced off of them.

Sean tossed his tarpaulin coat down the hatch, kicked his shoes down after it, and ran for the starboard main mast shrouds. He was knocked off his feet by a wall of water that came sweeping across the deck as the intensity of the wind increased. He had a hold of his safety line and was kept from being swept back towards the aft of the ship.

Once again on his feet, he heaved himself over the railing and pulled himself out onto the shrouds as the ship dropped into another trough. He clung to the slick ropes as he tried to keep from being thrown into the sea.

As the ship steadied itself, he climbed up a few rungs and held tight again as the ship swayed way over to starboard, to where he felt he was hanging backwards over the churning sea beneath him. He was thrown hard against the shrouds as the ship righted itself, and he managed to climb a few more rungs as the ship swayed far over to port.

This went on for what seemed to be an eternity until he was at the same height as Xao. Sean braced himself as best he could for the next upheaval of the ship, and when it swayed over again to starboard, he clung to the ropes with both his arms through them, ready to catch the hapless seaman as he was thrown back over to him.

The two men reached out their arms to each other, but they could not grab hold before Xao was slung back the other direction. Sean could not turn his face into the wind, which was at the peak of its fury, without being blinded by the driving rain.

He looked past the swinging man to see the very crests of the waves being virtually sheared off by the force of the wind, and sheets of spray from them were driven horizontally for hundreds of feet. As they hit Sean as he clung to the rigging, it felt as if he had been hit by a charge of buckshot. His shirt had been ripped to shreds by the wind, and every bit of his exposed skin felt as if it were on fire from the stinging seawater droplets.

Xao was slung back towards him again, and again they could not hold onto each other. Sean's arm was bleeding from the deep gouges of the man's fingertips as they dug into it when they tried to connect. He looked below and saw the difficulty that the two helmsmen and his brother were having trying to control the unruly wheel. If it weren't for the fact that they were lashed to the uprights, they would have long ago been swept away by the four-foot-high walls of water that swept down the length of the deck.

Once more the ship took a deep plunge into a trough, and it felt to Sean as if the ship had fallen away from him. He could not feel the rope rung beneath his feet, until the ship slammed into the bottom of the trough. Sean's feet slipped through the rungs, and he fell through until his fall was rudely stopped when his crotch hit the rung. The pain caused him to lose his grip, and he fell backward. He caught the rungs with his feet, stopping his fall over backward, but it, too, left him hanging upside down on the shrouds, looking into the angry green sea boiling below him.

"Bloody 'ell the Lieutenant has done for 'imself!" exclaimed Calhoun as he watched the scene unfold from the top of the gangway on his way out to relieve the men at the aft pump. "Come on, Julius, we got to go help 'im!" shouted Calhoun as he stripped off his jacket and shoes. The big freeman behind him did likewise and followed him out onto deck.

They reached the shrouds and started climbing, stopping to hold on tight when the ship plunged again into a trough. The two marines got up to Sean and waited for the ship to go through another plunge downward, then heaved Sean up with their shoulders until he could grab a hold of the lines himself. "I'll say this for you, sir," shouted Calhoun as he held him tight against the ropes, "My life certainly has not been boring since I met up with you and the Sergeant!"

Jones grabbed a hold of Sean's belt from behind and lifted him so that his feet could regain the rung. Once they had him held tight to the shrouds, Jones reached both arms through the shrouds in anticipation of Xao's next swing towards them. The Chinaman was hanging limp when he swung close, and Jones grabbed a hold of him.

He pulled the unconscious man around to the outside of the shrouds and heaved him onto his shoulder. With his other hand, he removed his knife from between his teeth, and with one deft motion, sliced through the rope that was wrapped around the man's ankle, and replaced the blade in his mouth.

Timing their descent to the movement of the ship, Jones carried the Chinaman down the shrouds while Calhoun climbed down over the top of Sean to keep him from falling off. As they reached the railing, several hands reached out to help the men down to the deck.

Sean was more carried than supported to the gangway, and as they started down, a wall of water virtually flushed him and Calhoun down the steps to the deck below. Jones and Xao followed, and all four landed in a heap. As they sorted themselves out and the other men came down, Faircloth was at hand to aid the battered men.

Calhoun and Jones faired well; however, Xao, who had regained his senses, and Sean had swallowed massive quantities of saltwater. Both of them started retching it all out. Buckets materialized in front of them as they heaved until they could heave no more. "Get them some fresh water from the scuttlebutt. They need to flush out their insides," Faircloth directed as he bandaged Xao's head.

Sean gulped down the cool water until he could hold no more, then it all came right back up. Xao suffered the same fate. The two men were helped into hammocks, where they fell straight to sleep.

Sean was not sure what awakened him first, the shout of "Ship off the starboard quarter!" or the dead silence from no more howling wind or waves crashing against the hull. The crew's quarters were deserted, as everyone was on deck except Faircloth, who was attending the Chinaman.

Sean pulled himself upright very slowly and swung his feet to the deck. He was very unsteady as he stood. "You had better lie back down. They can do without you for a bit. How are you feeling?" asked Faircloth, who walked over to try to put him back down.

"I feel as though I swallowed half the Atlantic Ocean and had been beaten by a hundred men. My skin feels like it is on fire from an intense sunburn from being pelted by the spray, but other than that I am fit as a fiddle," Sean responded half-jokingly.

He saw his shoes and coat on the small table and put them on. Every muscle ached as he pushed his arms through the sleeves. Slowly and unsteadily, he climbed the steps out of the wet and malodorous compartment.

Once on deck he looked around to take in his surroundings. His head pounded as he looked aloft to see most of the crew trying to undo the damage that the storm had wreaked on the rigging. Besides the main mast yardarm, they had lost the mizzen top and the jib boom. The deck was askew with rope and shreds of canvas that had once been sails.

His men were busy trying to right the stray cannon and get it back into place where the carpenter and his mates had nearly finished replacing the part of the bulwark that had been ripped away. He walked to the railing where Lanigan and Thomas stood, both examining the ship off the starboard side with their telescopes.

"It's in worse shape than we are, yet it looks as though there is no one left on board her," Thomas said as he turned to see his brother standing there. "Sean, you should not be on your feet after what you have been through, now get below," he barked, looking as drained as his brother before him.

"No, if I lie back down, every one of my muscles will stiffen up, then I won't be able to move at all," he argued.

"You look awful, if you don't mind me saying so, but 'e is right, if he doesn't get to moving around, he won't be able to move at all tomorrow," Lanigan interjected.

"Let me see what we have here," Sean said as he took Lanigan's telescope. "Yes, it does appear that she is deserted, yet her boats are still on the boat tier. Maybe her crew got washed overboard in the storm. We should go check it out there may be injured on board," Sean observed.

"The wind is staying steady, and the seas are down to a normal level. All right, we will lower a boat. Sergeant, you lead the boarding party though, Sean is in no condition to do that," Thomas ordered. Sean was not about to argue.

"Look, there is another squall line headed this way. That's the second since we came out of the storm. It looks to be about the same strength as the last one, so it shouldn't bother us much," Lanigan observed.

The crew working on deck stopped their work to swing the cutter over the side. Lanigan and six marines disembarked with six sailors to row the boat over to the damaged vessel. The going was not too rough, for the seas had calmed down. Once they hooked on to the chains, Lanigan led his men up the side. They drew their pistols and cutlasses as soon as they stepped on board.

Lanigan looked around at the wreckage strewn over the deck. Here and there they could see a body sticking out from under the cordage, broken spars, woodwork and canvas. "Look lively, lads. Two of you go below and check for survivors. The rest of you spread out and check these bodies for any signs of life."

The men went about the grisly task of checking the bodies. Lanigan strode to the wheel and took a turn of it. The wheel and rudder seemed to work fine, so they had steerageway. "There are no safety-lines rigged," he observed out loud. "The stupid lubbers didn't rig the ship for heavy weather. It'll be a wonder if we find anyone left alive on board."

"Sergeant, here's one still breathing!" called out Schmidt. Lanigan stepped over wreckage to where the marine knelt beside a sailor while he lifted a broken spar from across his body. "He is barely alive, yet he is whispering something," Schmidt said to Lanigan as he knelt down beside him.

"The lad's ribs are all stove in; he won't last much longer. See how e's spittin' up frothy blood? 'is lungs are punctured. Laddie, can ye tell me what happened to the rest of your shipmates?" Lanigan called out to the man as he turned his head to face him.

"Waves, giant waves, washed them all away! The captain, the captain made us all stay on deck. "E was afraid to 'ave us below deck in case we sunk. It's what done us in, don't you see? The giant waves took them away three, four, ten at a time; they didn't stand a chance. They that didn't get washed overboard were trapped like me beneath debris."

"Sergeant, we found two more below that are alive, but barely. They said they ran below and hid from the captain, then when the seas got really rough, cargo broke loose and they were run over by barrels of water that were bouncing around after being ripped loose from their tie-downs. They don't look like they'll last much longer. They said the captain made everyone stay on deck for fear of having them trapped below deck if the ship rolled over," Calhoun reported.

"Well, lads, get them into the boat. We'll take them across to see if the sawbones can make them comfortable before they die. I want four of you to stay behind and try to secure the deck. This is still a good prize, so we can take her in tow. Get the bodies overboard though, before they start stinking up the place. Corporal Sinclair, you take charge," Lanigan instructed.

The rest of the men returned to the *Osprey* as the last of the squall passed them. Lanigan reported, "'Ere's the log book. She's the *Daphne*, a Royal Navy supply ship. It appears 'er captain wasn't very good at running before a strong blow. He had no safety lines rigged and had the crew stay on deck through the whole thing. The only ones not washed overboard that are still alive won't make it another day, I fear."

"She appears to be sailable, and you say her hull is not leaking, so we can take her under wing to make up for the one we had to sink before the storm. As soon as we make most of our worst repairs and replace the torn sails, we'll send some men across to get her ready to go along with us," Thomas responded.

"Deck there, I think there is a ship out there to port. She's there. No, now she has disappeared back into the squall!" the lookout cried.

"Sean, another ship so close to this one will most likely be the enemy. Get the guns manned and ready. I'll get the rest of the crew down from aloft, but quietly, we don't know what we're up against or if she knows we're here," Thomas ordered.

Sean and Lanigan rounded up their men and gave them their orders. The port side gun crews were to load and run out with the men from the starboard side to hold tarps over the guns to protect the touch holes and slow-matches from getting wet if more rain came.

The crew managed to set two sails before returning to the deck. They were able to get the new spar and sail put in place on the mainmast. They cleared as much of the deck as they could as quietly as they could. An extra lookout was sent aloft with a telescope to help look for the phantom ship.

"Listen, does that not sound like gun trucks and someone shouting orders?" Sean asked. The others around him strained their ears for any sound to alert them to the elusive ship. To the starboard, another squall line of rain was quickly headed their way.

Minutes passed, and as the rain caught up to them, the previous squall line moved further away and they saw the ship. "It's British all right, a twelve-gun brigantine, from the looks of her. She's not headed our way, but I think they saw us," Thomas said.

"At least this rain storm will hide us from them briefly. We need to get under way with or without our prize as soon as possible," Sean suggested.

"Her belly is loaded with muskets and flints, from what little I saw of her manifests. We should make every attempt to save her, even if we have to tow her," Lanigan observed.

"Cameron, take ten men and row over to the *Daphne*, and get her under sail as best you can. Stay off our starboard beam for now until we get clear of that British ship. We'll try to hide from her in these squalls that keep hitting us," Thomas ordered.

The master turned and singled out ten men to follow him. They went over the side into the cutter and rowed across to the *Daphne*. As soon as they secured the boat with a line, the men dashed to set some sails on the damaged ship.

They got two undamaged sails set and the ship made some forward progress, as did the *Osprey*. There was still no sign of the enemy ship in the steady rain. The men stood as still and quietly as they could, trying to hear or see anything through the rain. The rain passed the *Osprey* and moved away. They could see another line of showers headed towards them from starboard.

The last line of showers was about a hundred yards off when they caught a glimpse of the ship again. As suddenly as it appeared, it turned and went back into the rain shower, lost from sight. "This is a cagey one; he's playing cat and mouse. Two can play that game. We'll change course as soon as we are hidden by the next line of showers and try to stay with them till we put some distance between us and this place,' Thomas whispered to his companions.

They waited until the next line of showers hid them. Thomas had the helm put over and they moved in the same direction of the showers. "This should take us past them and keep us hidden," he smiled.

"By the Eternal, look out, she's headed straight for us!" called out a frantic voice from the forward port bow gun.

The point of the other ship's jib boom pierced the rain at the port bow, and swung over till it was parallel to the *Osprey*. Before anyone could react, cannon fire broke out, and the sounds of lines parting and the foremast cracking could be heard through the din.

"Fire!" screamed Sean at the top of his voice, and three of the five guns spit out flame in the direction of the slow-moving ship. The other two must have gotten water in the touchholes, as they misfired.

Sean watched as the crews reloaded in what felt like an agonizingly long time, yet it was as fast as they had ever done. The flame of the other ship's guns could be seen through the rain, pointing down at the hull, and they felt the thuds of at least four hits in the hull.

A man came running up from below. "We've been hit below the water line, and we're taking on water fast!" Several men ran below to tackle the task of plugging the holes, while others jumped to the pumps.

The *Osprey's* guns started to fire back. Sean ran to the last gun and had them hold their fire. "Wait till their stern comes by and shoot at the rudder. We must disable her or she'll be back to pound us to kindling wood!" The men crouched under the tarp by the aft twelve-pounder acknowledged and adjusted the elevation on their gun to be ready for their shot.

They watched as the stern of the enemy ship was passing their gun port, and when they had a clear shot, they fired. Sean stood looking over the rail in the rain, and could see the rudder had been blasted away. "Great shot, lads. Now reload just in case she does get back to us." As he looked back at the stern of the ship once more, he noticed the name across the stern windowsill. It was the *Charon*! The man who killed his father had just passed them by!

Just as he said that, they could hear shouts from the other ship calling out that they had lost steerageway. Sean looked towards the bow and could see a work party chopping the lines holding the remains of the foremast to the ship. It had fallen over the starboard side and was slowing down the ship. As the last of the lines were chopped away, the wreckage fell into the water and the ship leaped forward free of the debris that had acted like a sea anchor.

He turned as bosun Sharp came up from below. "Sir, it's pretty bad. She's been holed four times just below the water line, and two of the ribs have been stove in. We have the holes plugged with canvas for now, but there's still plenty of water coming in, and I don't know if the pumps can keep up with the flow."

"Damn!" swore Thomas. "Well, we should be closing in on shore soon, and it will be dark before much longer. We do have the *Daphne*; if we have to, we can lash onto her alongside to keep us afloat until we can careen her in shallow water. "We'll never make it as far as home," Thomas thought out loud.

"That we can, but where? We have to find a secluded spot or we'll be a sitting duck for any British ship that comes by," Sean warned.

"Remember that hidden stream where we used to go fishing when we were younger? The mouth of the stream is almost hidden from view from river traffic, and there is a small bay with a big enough beach to where we can careen her to patch up the ribs and holes," Thomas explained.

"Yes, but we are at least two days away from there, and the *Charon* will not be out of action that long. Thomas, it was his ship. I saw the name on the stern myself. The bastard almost did us in again."

"All the more reason to get moving as fast as we can. If he realizes who we are, he will waste no time hunting us down. Now let's get moving; we need to take advantage of our cover as long as it lasts."

"Right, I think we can throw him off of the pursuit. He won't take long to repair the rudder. and be back after us. There's still enough debris on the *Daphne's* deck, and we can add to it. If we throw enough flotsam over the side to make it appear that a ship sunk here, he may not try to locate us. We can set the bodies from the *Daphne* afloat on gratings to make it look even more convincing," Sean suggested.

"Good idea. As soon as the *Daphne* comes alongside, take the rest of your men over and take care of that while we get the two ships lashed together " Thomas looked to the rain-filled sky above, then at the men standing around him waiting for orders, "If this rain holds up, we may stay hidden in it until we reach the coast; that will give us cover. Now get to it men, we have not much time, and keep the noise down. We don't want to let them know where we are!"

The men jumped to their jobs with a renewed sense of urgency. The *Daphne* was signaled to come alongside the port side so that they could lash on. As long as the seas did not get any rougher than they were now, they should do all right. The *Osprey* had already started to list to the port, and before the

Daphne could come alongside, the crew had to readjust much of the ballast and cargo in the hold to bring her upright again.

It took the men almost an hour to complete the job of running lines between the ships and making them fast. Sean and his men finished up making the decoy wreckage when the ships were ready to get under way.

They moved on through the rest of the afternoon until the darkness finally overtook them. Their position was off the coast of Delaware when they finally sighted land just before dark. They hove to in a small bay and waited out the night and next day to give the exhausted men some rest.

Once the ships were secure for the night, many of the men literally dropped in their tracks from exhaustion. The rigors of being tossed about from the hurricane and the exhaustive work of repairing the damage and fighting the other ship left them drained.

Sean posted a deck watch on both ships and turned in for the night. His body ached all over from the beating he took aloft during the storm. Xing Xao was finally back on his feet, but not able to do much, as he was almost beat to death as he had been slung about by the storm when he was hanging from the rope.

They would need a full night to get to the hidden stream and would need everyone to be alert. The next morning, the men had their first hot meal that they had in over a day. They had to settle for cold food the day before since the cooking fires could not be lighted in the storm.

Sean awoke to the steady clanking of the pumps. The men took one-hour shifts on them, and they had not stopped since the storm hit them the day before.

Although they had stopped some of the flow of water thought the shot holes, a considerable amount was still leaking in, filling the bilges.

He put on the last of his dry clothes after washing. Then he got his plate of food and coffee and went on deck to eat. The air had turned much colder than the day before, as the cold November air of Delaware had replaced the tropical air of the hurricane. It was hard to imagine that it would be December in a few more days; so much had happened this past year.

The appearance of the deck had returned to normal, yet the missing jib boom, foremast, and mizzen top made the ship look bare. The men at the two pumps were working them steadily, clouds of steam coming out of their mouths as they pumped.

"It's going to take a month, maybe two, to get her back in shape again. We'll have to have the two ribs replaced, and that will take the longest. Stepping a new foremast will be easy compared to that," Thomas said to Sean as he drank coffee from his tankard.

"With luck, we should be safe here for the day. We really should have kept going, but I'm not sure the men would have made it after all we went through yesterday," Sean replied.

"If that bastard had fired at the hull with his first round of shots, he would have sunk us on the spot yesterday. We were very fortunate indeed. We have no more suitable wood that we can make patches of for the hull other than what the carpenters have managed to do Rather than start pulling the *Daphne* apart to do that, I'd just as soon get to a safer place first. Even if we could take her as far as Philadelphia, we will surely get frozen in for the winter. We need to get back out as fast as we can," Thomas added.

The crew got as much rest as they could; many fell asleep on the deck below when they stopped for the night. Most of them needed dry clothing. The cooks dried clothes over their fires all day until everyone had dry garments to wear.

Late in the afternoon, they were surprised to see a ship come straight in on them. It was the *Fly*. "Lord, you lads are in terrible shape!" exclaimed Lieutenant Hacker when he came on board. "We were up Delaware Bay and got nothing but rain from that storm. You must be careful going up the Bay. The British are in and out of it on a regular basis now. They are driving Washington's army back across New Jersey toward the Delaware and everyone in Philadelphia is worried that they will be attacked. It is possible, so you don't want to be going there for repairs."

"We don't intend to go that far, as we were worried about getting iced in for the winter. Any other news for us?" Thomas asked.

"I have been asked to relay the message that Washington has ordered Nicholas to recall all his marines to the defense of Philadelphia. Sean, that means you too. Nicholas specifically asked me to try to locate you and your lads. Once you get your ship to safety, you are to get to Philadelphia by whatever means are available. He has most of the men assembled there now, but he was most anxious to get your lads there too. Washington runs the risk of losing most of his army since their enlistments run out at the end of December."

"I'm not sure that I'll be able to do that, what with the ship being in the condition that it is," Sean replied.

"Sean, as soon as we get the ship secure and careened, there is no reason for you and your men not to go. We'll have enough men to carry out the repairs, and if we need more help, we'll get James to hire some more. With what we have to do, too many men would just be in the way, and they would be consuming supplies that the workers need," Thomas interjected.

"Well, I suppose that settles it. Once we get the ship to safety and you set up for the winter, I'll take the men to Philadelphia," Sean concluded.

"Good, I'll go back up river to let them know, and then get on with my patrol. Do you have any messages that you want me to take to your brother James?" Hacker asked.

"Yes, why don't you come with me to my cabin, and I'll give you a list of supplies for him to start purchasing. We have need of several pieces of timber cut to replace several parts of the ship, and I have the dimensions. He can get busy having the pieces cut so that we'll have them when we need them," Thomas replied.

Hacker left with his list and other messages. They watched the small schooner sail off towards the Delaware Bay. They would head in the same direction as soon as it got dark to avoid being seen by anyone on the bay. It would be tricky sailing the rest of the way hooked to the side of the damaged *Daphne*. The pumps were just able to keep up with the flow of incoming water still seeping in through their hasty patchwork.

Having to stay hidden for the daylight hours was a blessing for the crew, as they were spent from the day of fighting storms, the *Charon*, and all the pumping and repair work necessary. Close to sundown, the men were fed an extra big serving of beef, peas and potatoes plus an extra tot of rum to bolster them for the arduous trek ahead of them.

"It's time, lads," Thomas announced as he took the last swig of his tankard of rum. He had joined the men below deck for the big meal. The others tossed back their drinks, and together they all went up on deck.

Twelve men stepped across the railing to the *Daphne* so they could set the makeshift sails and tend to the wheel once they were under way. The two ships were held in place by the *Osprey's* anchors, and as soon as everyone was in place, the crewmen took up the bars on the capstan and set a lively pace walking around it, hoisting the anchors.

Once the anchor party secured the great anchors, sails were set on both ships. The breeze caught the patched up canvas, and the ships moved forward. *Osprey* still had a slight list to her, but managed to move forward without any trouble.

"This is going to be one long night, sailing like this. I had the men grease the pumps good.No sense in giving our position away as we sail past the British battery at Cape May. I think we'll forego shelling them this time as we go by," Sean said to his brother.

"The lads were looking forward to doing that, I'm sure. But in the condition that we are in, if we were to draw the attention of any enemy ships to us, we should not be able to out-maneuver them," Thomas agreed.

"I have had the outboard guns of both ships loaded and manned though just in case. I have men picked out to go with me in the cutter to find the mouth of the stream when it is time. It has always been hard to see during the day, so this will be no easy task finding it in the dark," Sean replied.

"No, it isn't. But at least the landmarks near to the stream are easy to spot day or night, so I don't expect to have too much trouble as long as it is not too overgrown," Thomas suggested.

The ship sailed on in silence. The clouds blocked the moon, so they did not cast a silhouette across the water. The men had extinguished all lights and pipes, so they were in total darkness.
Only the quiet lapping of the water against the bows and the muffled sound of the pumps could be heard, as most activity along the shoreline had ceased due to the cold weather.

They glided into the mouth of the bay, giving the British redoubt a wide berth. They encountered no other vessels as they sailed up the bay. They were getting nearer to the head of the bay, which grew narrower as they went by.

It was after midnight when Thomas had Sean summoned. He had gone below to get a few winks of sleep before departing in the cutter to find the mouth of the stream. As soon as he pulled on his heavy boat cloak, he went into the crew's quarters to see if his men were ready.

"Good evening, lads, are you all bundled up for our little trip?" he asked with a smile.

"Aye, sir that we are," Replied Beckett.

"Fine! Let's be about it then. We'll cast off as soon as they take the headway off of her, so get your last cup of hot coffee before we go," he said as he poured himself a hot tankard of the brew.

He went on deck to see if all was ready. The cutter had been hoisted over the side, and the sailors were just climbing down into it. He was taking six men with him beside the six sailors who would row the boat.

"Ah, it's a fine night for this, sir," exclaimed Lanigan in a whisper. "I have been on many a cutting out party or landing parties on nights like this. Always gets your blood a-pumping!"

"I can vouch for that, Angus. The men are ready; take my mug if you would, please. All right, over the side with you, lads," he said as Lanigan took the mug and had each of the men show him their flintless pistol as they came by.

"You lads stay warm out there tonight. Now be sure that you have your flints close at hand if you need them. Don't be putting them back in unless you are told to do so. No sense in giving yourselves away out there by accidentally firing your pistol or having it go off by dropping it," Lanigan advised them.

"See you soon, Angus," Sean said as he stepped over the side.

He watched as the boat silently moved away from the ship. They had only rowed a few strokes and Lanigan could no longer see them in the darkness. *Good luck to ye laddies*, he thought to himself. He wished that it was he leading the boat party, yet he knew his time for that was almost over, as he was getting too old for all this foolishness. At least he had many fond memories of his several years of doing such things.

"Raise oars," Sean whispered from the bow of the cutter. The men quietly lifted the oars just above the water. Sean watched the shoreline as they started to drift. They would notice a change in current when they reached the mouth of the stream.

"Continue," he said as he strained his eyes to see ahead in the dark. They continued on for another fifteen minutes when Sean had them halt again. He thought he saw a break in the shoreline. This must be it; the cutter was being pushed gently back out towards the middle of the river.

"Angle to the starboard," he directed Beckett. The bow of the cutter swung right and then straightened at Sean's signal. In the starlight he could make out the opening. They had found it.

"This is it, lads. We'll go make a complete sweep around the inlet to make sure that it is clear. Be very quiet from this point on," he cautioned.

The men pulled on the oars with renewed vigor, knowing that their work would soon be done. They cruised along the entire shoreline to observe it. After they made the first pass, Sean had them put in towards the beach. The leadsman in the bow next to Sean took soundings as they went all the way around the bay.

The boat glided to a stop on the hard mud. "Edward George, it is up to you now. We'll back out into the bay while you search. Give us the hootowl call when you are ready. Good luck," Sean instructed his friend as he stepped off the bow of the boat and disappeared into the darkness.

The crew pulled the boat out into the bay and waited for what seemed to be an eternity. Then from where they had beached the boat, they heard the call of an owl.

"Lively lads, put her into shore again." Sean directed them. The boat surged forward and ground to a halt on the shore. Edward George clambered back on board and reported to Sean.

"There's an old hunter's cabin there along the tree line, but it does not appear to have been used this season. I found no fresh tracks along the beach, and only one path through the woods that was nearly grown over. I went upstream a bit but found no signs of anyone having been along there in a long time. I think we should be safe here," he reported.

"Fine job. In the morning, after it gets light, I want you to take a few men and scout around further out. We need to know if we need to put out a daily patrol, or if we should be all right without one. Let's get back to the ship, men," he said as he turned back to them,

The men used the oars to turn the boat around in the bay and headed back into the river. Sean pulled the cover back on the shielded lantern and waved it back and forth twice. He watched in the darkness until he saw the same signal from downriver.

They swiftly returned to the ship, and once on board, Sean reported to Thomas and the other officers.

"The bay is clear and suitable to our needs. It appears that no one has been about there for quite some time, as Edward George reported that the only path through the woods there was pretty grown over. The entrance from the river is too narrow for both ships to go in side-by-side, so we'll have to cast off here and go in. There is enough room for both once we're in there, and the soundings we took indicated that there is ample depth there also."

"Good, then let's get with it. You men all have your assigned tasks, get with your men and get them moving. Have extra men on the pumps until we get situated. As soon as we cast loose from the *Daphne*, we need to get her up against the beach as fast as we can before we take on too much water," Thomas instructed.

"I'll get my men in the launch and cutter to warp her in, while you do what you can to stem the water flow when she settles lower after casting off. The lads are rested up and should be able to pull the ship into shore. We'll lose the wind as soon as you cut towards the entrance."

As soon as all the work parties had their instructions and were in place, the work began in earnest. The marines were in the two boats with the tow cables in place, ready for the signal. The cables were hove short, ready for them to pull as fast as they could once the *Osprey* was freed from the other ship.

"Get ready, lads. Once they are cut loose from the *Daphne*, the ship will settle lower on that side, putting the shot holes below water again. Just be glad you're not below decks with the work party standing by, ready to shore up the patches when that happens. If you hadn't noticed, the river water is mighty cold, and those lads are going to get soaked," Sean said as he watched the masts of both ships silhouetted against the star-filled sky.

The men watched for the expected roll of their ship when she was cast off. "There she goes! Pull hard, lads, now!" Sean encouraged them as he grasped the tiller bar.

They saw the masts of the *Osprey* swing over, and they heard the sounds of gear tossed about when that happened. The marines dug the oars deeply into the water. It took a few strokes for them to see that they were making headway.

There was just enough breeze to fill the sails, as they were set for one last push into the bay to make their job easier. True to Sean's estimate, the wind was cut off as soon as they entered the bay. Once more the rowing was tough, as the headway of the ship was matched by the flow of the water.

As the ship entered the mouth of the stream, the men heard the cracking of tree limbs as the yardarms broke all that was in their way. Once they had pulled the ship into the bay, the current helped push them off to the left toward the beach.

The sounds of the pumps grew louder as the ship glided closer. The men rowed ashore and dragged block and tackle across the beach to the bases of three large elms. They rigged the tackle in place and then ran the towing cables through them and rowed the other ends back out to the ship, where they were passed up to the deck and run around the capstan. The men in the boats got clear of the ship and watched as it was slowly pulled broadside to the beach by the large windless.

The ship ground to a halt against the shore and settled into the mud. Sean had the crews of the boats pull out to the *Daphne* to warp the damaged ship in past the entrance. By the time they towed her in, there were torches in place on shore, as many figures moved about on shore running lines between the ship and shore.

Lines had been fastened to the main mast just below the fighting top, to the stump of the mizzen and to what was left of the bowsprit. The marines put the boats ashore and prepared to help pull the lines to careen the ship over.

When all was in readiness, every man of the ship's company and the marine contingent hauled on the lines. The blocks and tackle squealed as the strain was put on them. From the ship came what sounded like moans as it started to lean over toward shore. When they had pulled enough to raise the shot holes back above water, they secured the lines.

Two work parties ran more lines to make sure the ship was secure, while others clambered back on board to start off-loading the cannons and cargo so they could careen the ship further.

"Now that the holes are above water again, the pumps should be able to get the water out of the bilges, and she'll ride higher," Sean said to Lanigan as they supervised the men.

"Aye, when we cut loose of the other ship, so much water rushed in, there must be at least five feet of water down there. Have you been down there lately? It smells like a whorehouse at low tide!" Lanigan smiled.

"I know, it will take awhile to get the inside of the ship dried out and that stench out of there. We'll stay here as long as it takes to off load the ship and make suitable quarters for the men, then we'll have to head to Philadelphia," Sean said as he looked towards the sky, which was starting to turn a faint gray.

By noon that day, the crew had off-loaded the cannons and some of the barrels of food and supplies from below. The cook had his galley moved ashore and was busily cooking a hot meal for the men. Sean and Lanigan, with some of the men, rowed out into the river to see how much of the activity could be seen from the river. A narrow finger of woods shielded the bay. Most of the trees had shed their leaves, yet there were many cedars growing amongst them to block the scene in the bay.

"We'll get a work party busy gathering scrub and bushes from inland and plugging the gaps there as much as possible. That should shield sight of them from this angle. The mouth of the stream is quite another matter. Only from one angle can you see into the bay from the mouth of the stream. I think if we anchor a log raft piled high with brush to look like bushes, we should be able to block off all view of the bay," Sean observed as he and Angus inspected the area from all angles.

"That should do. We can lash logs together, about three wide and two long, that should reach across there and give us enough of a base to erect a sufficient screen across there. By giving them enough slack, the whole raft will be able to rise and fall with the water level. I'll get the lads right on it. We'll tackle the landside first and then the raft. I imagine we can be done with it all by tomorrow night."

"Good. I am going to have a few of the men that are injured come out into the river to wait for James. They can do some fishing to not attract any attention and be able to intercept James when he gets here," Sean added.

The two rowed the *Daphne's* dingy back into the bay and assigned tasks to the men. They gathered up their boarding axes and headed into the woods in two parties, one with Sean and one with Lanigan, to start the camouflage work.

By nightfall, the men had erected a solid screen of bushes across the finger of land. They had woven saplings between trees in the bare spots and used that to support the bushes and cedars that they dragged from inland. They would tackle the raft the next day. Sean and Lanigan inspected their work from the river and were unable to see any of the activity beyond their screen.

The next day the cove was a flurry of activity as the offloading continued, and the marines started work on the floating screen. Most of their day was spent felling six trees, dragging them through the inland forest and floating them in the stream. Once they had them chained together in the middle of the entrance to the cove, the ends were secured by chains to two large oaks on either side of the stream.

A detail dug up the roots of six cedars, all about seven feet tall, dragged them to the raft and inserted the roots between the logs to help keep them alive, to give a more natural appearance. By nightfall they had the rest of the raft filled in with bushes, small trees and other scrub plants. When they were finished, it had the appearance of the rest of the riverbank from the river.

On the third day, the men who were keeping watch from the dingy came into the cove through the woods. Behind them came James and twelve men carrying an assortment of hams, beef quarters, barrels of flour and sacks of fresh bread.

"Oh lord, she looks terrible!" he exclaimed as he met up with Sean and Thomas. "They said that it was the same ship that you thought you sunk with Father's murderer on board; is that true?"

"Yes it is James. The man has the nine lives of a cat! But we prevailed. The hurricane and that maniac were unable to sink the *Osprey!*" Thomas replied.

"It's good to see that you didn't come empty handed, Little Brother," Sean said to James. "Over half of our food got soaked during the storm and is ruined. How much more have you brought?"

"I hired a twenty-five-foot gondola and loaded it to the gunwales with food and as much spare canvas as we had in the warehouse. These men are part of our ship's crew, and six will stay behind to assist you. They are all good seamen; one is a carpenter."

"What about the list of cut timbers and other items I sent you?" Thomas asked.

"I have one of the shipyards working on those items. They are running short-handed and short-supplied, so it will take awhile for them to fill the orders. Try to use as much as you can from that hulk that you have there," James said, nodding towards the *Daphne*.

"We are trying, yet she is older than the *Osprey*, and her timbers are not exactly fresh. We can use some of her deck planking, but the wood in her hull is beyond trying to use. There is quite a cargo in her for you to take back with you," Thomas stated.

"Yes, there is a large shipment of six-hundred stands of muskets, camp equipment, tents and uniforms. The shipment was meant for the Fifty-Fifth Regiment of Foot. They will be sorry that their equipment did not make it to them, for there is a large quantity of blankets, mittens and woolen stockings for them. Now, those things will be keeping my men warm when we go to join up with Washington's army."

"Yes, he will be in Philadelphia soon, from the sounds of it. The British have chased him almost all the way across New Jersey, and the people of

Philadelphia are near to panic-stricken, thinking that they are going to keep coming until they take the town. I think they will retire for the winter once they drive Washington from New Jersey," James informed them.

"I have received orders to take my marines to meet up with them there. We will be leaving in another day or two, once we have Thomas and the others situated. We'll help you to load the gondola with the muskets to take back with you. When can you come back to take the rest of the cargo?" Sean asked.

"We should be able to get back here in two days. I'll try to send a few wagons down for your men to ride back in. Come up on the Pennsylvania side; do not try to come up this side of the river. The British have patrols all over, and you may be attacked," James warned.

"Good. Most of the men weren't looking forward to that fifty-mile march from here. With the British loose on the river, I didn't think it prudent to try to take boats all the way up there," Sean replied.

"No, that would not be wise. We were stopped but not searched on the way here. But since we looked like fishermen, and gave them a jug of rum, they let us continue downriver. We have another jug for the trip back, just in case; however I want to get back upriver during the dark, so as soon as we are loaded, we will hoist our sail and head back," said James.

The three brothers walked around the beach so that James could see the extent of the damage from the storm and attack. They watched as the cutter with a work party of men attacked the weed growth on the exposed part of the copper hull. The weed had reached a length of three feet and was overdue for being scraped off.

The other men were all involved with unloading the ship. The barrels and kegs were being stacked two-high and covered by the sails to create cabins for the men to live in. One was complete. Inside, with the fire burning in the center with an opening in the canvas overhead, it was nice and warm, with enough room for fifteen men.

"Corporal Beckett, after you have the men transfer the cargo to the gondola from the *Daphne*, have them select enough tents for themselves and set them up in a row along the tree line. They may as well get used to living in them now, for I don't know how long we will be ashore with the army."

"Aye, aye, sir. 'Tis fortunate indeed that we have captured such a supply as we did. I'll have the lads take extra stockings, mittens, breeches, and blankets from the ship also. No telling when we will be able to get new ones," suggested Beckett.

"Good thinking. Make sure that you pull enough for Edward George and the others out on the hunting party. I do not expect them back until after dark, so get tents set up for them also." Sean returned the salute as Beckett went off to herd the men towards their tasks.

By nightfall the gondola had been loaded with as much of the spoils of war they could fit in her without sinking it. James and his men shoved off from shore. They extended the long sweeps to gain control of it in the river's current before three of them hoisted the large sail, giving the craft the look of a Viking ship of old.

Once Sean was satisfied with the evidence of their landing and the trail through the woods was once again blocked with dead bushes, he returned to the encampment that his men had erected using the captured tents and cooking equipment. The smell of roasting ham greeted his nose as he walked up.

"Here you are, sir," Calhoun said as he handed Sean a plate heaped high with ham, bread and potatoes. "As it turns out, Private Julius Caesar Jones is a pretty fair cook besides being a fearsome fighting man!"

"Indeed he is. This is the best meal I have had in a while. When the hunting party gets back, you'll have to cook us up whatever they bring in," Sean beamed.

"That I will, sir." Jones said, enjoying the extra attention. The men gathered around the three campfires that had been lit to keep them warm.

"They set up a right proper camp, wouldn't you say there, Sergeant?" Sean asked as he accepted the tankard of hot rum from Lanigan.

"Aye, that they did, and I didn't have to bust any heads to get them to do it right either," he joked. The men laughed at his remark, chiding him in return. They relaxed around the fires as much as the temperature would allow them until it was time for the night watch to take up their posts, and the rest turned in for the night in their new tents.

"We won't know what is in store for us until we get to Philadelphia Angus, so if the men ask, that is all that we can tell them. I'm sure the city will be safe for the winter." Sean said to Lanigan as they sat by the dying embers of the fire in front of their tents.

"It should be. As I recall, army officers are not inclined to fight in the dead of winter! They will probably settle down for the winter in New York City and some of the larger towns in New Jersey for the winter and have parties all season!" Lanigan said in disdain.

The hunting party came into the camp around nine o'clock, tired from their long day. They brought in three deer and several turkeys that they carried on poles between them. They had cached six more deer far out in a clearing three miles out and would retrieve them in the morning. After they turned their loads over to the cook and his mates, they had a hot meal and retired for the night.

The next day, Sean's men continued to help unload the *Osprey*, while the hunting party went back out to retrieve the rest of their game. The men would have fresh food for a few days. When they unloaded the barrels of gunpowder from the ship, they discovered that the water that had flooded the hold during and after the storm had ruined it.

"You have enough for about two shots apiece for each gun, Thomas. When we discovered this, I had the supply on the *Daphne* checked, and it too, is bad. We opened several casks, and the powder was nothing more than black, runny slop. You may be able to recover some of it when it dries out, but it may all be useless," Sean reported.

"We'll have to see if James can bring us some, although if we get to the point of needing the cannons, it may be too late for us anyway. You have enough for your men, don't you?" Thomas asked.

"There is a small keg that was in your cabin for the muskets and pistols that did not get wet, and we have another one for us to take along. Their powder flasks are all full, so we should be in good shape when we leave," Sean summed up.

They stayed on, helping the crew for another day when James showed up with another load of food and supplies. The wagons that he promised showed up across the river at the same time. After the men packed their gear, they were ferried across the river in the gondola where they loaded their camp equipage and themselves into the wagons for their ride back to Philadelphia.

The weather turned bad, and they endured the cold and snow for the two-day ride, stopping along the way to eat and pitch camp after dark to spend the night in a field. They reached the city after dark and continued on for the Taggert warehouse, where they would disembark.

The city was quiet as they rode in through the driving snow. Most of the townspeople were indoors as was evidenced by the warm glow emanating from the many windows that they passed. As soon as they had unloaded the wagons, Sean dismissed those with families for the night. Those who had no families in town were given the night off to revel in town or just sleep next to the large stove in the warehouse.

He decided to wait until morning to send word to Nicholas that they were back in town, and climbed on board the wagon for the ride to his home. Once there his brothers, sisters and his mother greeted him. They stayed up late to hear of the adventures that he and Thomas had had, especially their ordeal in the hurricane. By the time Sean went to bed, he was totally exhausted and fell asleep no sooner than his head hit the pillow.

The next morning he found that his uniform had been cleaned and was still warm from being dried by the hearth in the kitchen. He quickly washed, shaved and dressed and went downstairs to the dinning room.

"Good morning, Mother," he said as he bent over and kissed her head while she sat at the table sipping her coffee.

"It's still snowing, so bundle up when you go out," she said in a matter-of-fact way, knowing that she could not keep her son from attending to his duty.

"I have to find Sam Nicholas to see what he has in store for us. I hope that you are not upset that the British may be coming to town?" he asked.

"That's all that anyone has been talking about the past few days. They called up the Associators yesterday, and if we have to depend on those shopkeepers and clerks to protect us, we may as well surrender now. They apparently have been given some of those muskets that you had sent up a few days ago," his mother replied.

"Well, don't worry, Mother. Those boys are the last line of defense, and if it comes to them having to fight, you know it is time to get out of town."

"Rubbish! I will not leave my home no matter who comes to town, so don't even try to talk me into leaving. They wouldn't dare to molest women and children," she responded.

"There's someone at the door," he said as he stood to go answer the knock. He heard James come down the stairs and open the door. He could hear from the dining room that it was Sam.

"Welcome home, Sean. It's good to see you safe and sound! I hear that you had quite an ordeal in that hurricane, but you look like you have recovered from that," Nicholas said as he bowed to Sean's mother and took a seat at the table.

"Yes, we had quite a go at it that is for sure. The ship is in pretty bad shape, but Thomas should have it ready for sea in a month or so. You look like you've been run through the mill; what's afoot?" he asked his friend.

"I'm on my way to the assembly house now to get our orders. They did not have them written up last night, but I can tell you part of what we are to be about. We'll assemble all the men down at your wharf by nine a.m. and get them ready to move out. We'll have about a hundred and thirty men, now that you and your lads have arrived. We'll be boarding gondolas to go upriver to Trenton to assist Washington's army in case of British attack," Nicholas explained.

"Is he really being pursued by an army, or just being harassed by small units?" Sean inquired.

"A little of both. The main army is being slow in following him, probably afraid of Washington laying an ambush for them. The Safety Council here in town passed orders out last night for the Associators to form up today. They also called for schools and shops to be closed so that the city can prepare its defenses. Already this morning, I saw people loading wagons to leave town as fast as they can."

"If the members of the Safety Council are not careful in how they handle this, there could be a full-scale panic on their hands by the end of the day. My men will be ready. I told them to be at the warehouse by eight this morning. We fell into some supplies on the last ship we took, so we are fully outfitted with tents and other camp equipment for the men," Sean stated.

"Good. They'll need it. Look, Sean, I do not know when or if you'll be able to get back to sea. This may keep you and your company busy for quite awhile. From what I have been hearing, Washington is not in favor of keeping a separate Marine Unit; he is more in favor of us being a part of his army. So we'll just have to play along and see what is to become of us," Nicholas warned.

"There is never any certainty about anything, old friend; the important thing is that you know that you can count on us to be with you, no matter what," Sean assured his friend.

"Thanks for that. Now I have to be off to meet with the Council. I'll see you at the wharf at nine. Try to get yourself a wagon for your gear and food. Each company will be allowed one wagon, each if they can find one," Sam said as he walked towards the door.

The two shook hands, each knowing that they were about to face a severe test, not only by the enemy but also by the bitter winter weather. Sean watched Sam ride off into the swirling snow, losing sight of him by the time he reached the gate. This was a bad day to start off on a mission; however, they would prevail. He just knew it.

7

With Washington's Army

The driver brought the wagon to a halt in front of the Taggert warehouse on the wharf. Sean climbed down, his boots almost slipping out from under him as he stepped down into the snow-covered cobblestones. A few of his men were outside drinking their coffee, gathered around a fire that they had built. Looking down the wharf, there were a few other groups of green-coated marines of other companies doing the same.

The driver attended to his horses as Sean joined the men at the fire. "'Tis not much warmer inside, sir," Lanigan said as he saluted Sean and handed him a mug of coffee. "Most of the lads are here, but there is still plenty of time for the others as long as they don't get run over by some damned fool trying to get out of town," he quipped.

"I know. We had a couple of close calls on the way here. Some of the folks out there are really in a panicked state of mind. It's just half-past seven, and the other companies are to meet here at nine. Is there enough wood to keep the fire going until then?" Sean asked.

"Yes, there is quite a pile around the side, plus your brother pointed out some near-rotten barrels that we can break up if we have to do so," Lanigan replied as he sipped the hot drink.

"We're to disembark onto gondolas and head up to Trenton to help cover Washington's retreat. We should be under way by noon if the weather doesn't get any worse. Get the men busy loading their tents and equipment into the wagon. There is half a side of beef, four hams and some fresh loaves of bread in the wagon already. I'm going to go inside to see what else we can take of use to us," he said as he set the empty mug on an up-ended cask.

He went in and talked with James to see if there was any other food or powder available for the men. They inspected several of the crates and bales of goods in the warehouse. "There is an unclaimed consignment of tools that have been sitting here for the past month. Shovels, picks, axes and hatchets," James said as he pried open the top crate on a stack in the corner.

Sean reached in and withdrew two of the hatchets. "These are tomahawks, not hatchets. You know, these would be good for the men. Help me take this crate over by the door. I'll pass them out to the men, once they are all here. I'll want to take at least six of those shovels and an equal amount of axes and picks. Lord knows that if we are going to be with the army, we'll be needing those. You know how they love to dig everywhere they go," Sean joked.

They carried the crate over to the door and then piled up the other implements to be put in the wagon. Sean picked out a tomahawk for himself and examined it in his hands. It was about the same as the one he had brought back from out West, where he had gotten to be pretty good throwing it.

He and James sat in the office talking for half an hour when Lanigan came in to report that the last of the men had shown up. The two men went outside to pass out instructions to them. They stopped at the door and picked up the crate of tomahawks.

Once outside, they gathered the men around and passed out the weapons. "A tomahawk can be a good weapon for close-in fighting when you cannot swing your musket around. Edward George and I will show you how to handle them and throw them when we get a chance. You lads here grab those shovels, axes and picks and load them into the wagon. Corporal Beckett, I want you to select three other men to accompany you with the wagon," Sean instructed.

"I'll take Jones, Svenson and Betts. We'll make sure that no one gets into our supplies; don't you worry, sir." Beckett assured him.

"Good, I'll write up orders for you before you leave. Once the other companies get their wagons loaded, you will all go together to the ferry and cross to the New Jersey side. Once across there, you will proceed to Trenton. We will probably get there ahead of you, but if we do not, find a place out of sight and out of the storm if you can, and wait for us," Sean said.

"Sir, I have made sure that the men are properly fitted out, dressed warmly, and have given each one a day's ration of the meat and bread that you have brought. No sense in them going hungry if we don't meet up with the wagons. I have put your food in your pouch," Lanigan told Sean.

"Thank you, Sergeant. The men can stand easy until the companies are assembled. Look, it won't be long now; here comes Major Nicholas," Sean pointed out.

Nicholas climbed out of the carriage and pulled his gear out behind him. He waved at Sean, who walked over to give him a hand. "I want my things to go into your wagon, if you don't mind," Sam said to Sean.

"No, not at all. We are honored to have you with us. It appears that we only have three companies out of four?" Sean asked.

"That's right, I had to send Captain Shaw's company to man the *Randolph* again," Sam said as he glanced around at the gathering. The men were excited to be together again and were meeting up with old friends and skylarking in the snow.

"Don't you just feel the excitement in the air, Sean?" he asked as he grinned at him. "The men are chomping at the bit to get at the enemy, even if it is cold and snowy out. The men who were not on board a ship, as your men, have had their fill of guarding the shipyards and the stockpiles of supplies here in town. To tell you the truth, I am just as glad to get out of this town for a while. There is just too much politics in all of this for me. Look out there in the river. Here comes our transportation." Nicholas pointed to the three long, wide gondolas with their large sweeps, coming in towards the dock, looking like three big water beetles.

"It's about time to assemble, Sam. Do you want us to get the men in formation?" Sean asked.

"No, the supply wagons should be showing up any minute. We'll need to have them transfer the food, powder and other supplies to our wagons as soon as they arrive. Let them have a little more time before we get them assembled," he advised.

Within a few minutes, two wagons showed up laden with food for the three companies. Each company unloaded its share of the supplies into their wagons. Once that had been accomplished, Sam got a drummer of one of the other companies to start beating out "assembly" and in two minutes the chaos on the wharf had been transformed into three quiet and neatly assembled companies of marines.

Nicholas addressed the men. "It's good to have you all together again. We haven't been all together like this since we took that excursion to the Bahamas. Unfortunately, I can't promise you warm weather and sunshine on this assignment." He paused as the men laughed at his comment.

"We have an important role to play here this time, lads. We have to go and help cover the withdrawal of General Washington's troops at Trenton. There is a real possibility that we will run into some red-coated gentlemen that may object to our being there, so I expect you to let them know how we feel about them being in our country." He paused again as the men cheered at what he had said.

"Now Marines, let's go get the army out of trouble! Into the boats with you, and let's move out!" With that said, the men all let out a throaty cheer that even the falling snow could not muffle.

Sean turned to Lanigan and ordered, "Sergeant, let's go to war! March the men over to the first gondola. Corporal Beckett, you have your orders; lead the wagons on out of here," he called over to Beckett with his detachment.

The wagons started rolling out as the men of the three companies climbed down into the waiting craft. The journey upriver was uneventful but cold. The men took turns at the sweeps in an effort to stay warm. When not so occupied, they sat bundled up in their greatcoats covering their uniform coats and wrapped their blankets over that. The sails were hoisted, yet there was not much breeze to help them along the way.

They were fortunate that the river had not started freezing over, for that would mean they would have to march to Trenton. Lanigan had made sure that a small cask of rum found its way into their boat, and after a few hours, the men were given some to warm them up.

The boats were put into shore twice along the way for the men to cook their food and stretch their legs. They had gotten an earlier start than planned and were making good time. A fresh breeze pushed them along quicker after their second stop. They kept on past dark, and finally, just before midnight, the glow of lights from Trenton could be seen in the distance.

The men at the tillers angled the big boats into shore at the landing. A sentry came out of the dark and challenged them, and was answered back with so many cat calls and disrespectful questions about his parentage from the marines as they stood up to exit the craft that he did not know what to do for a moment. Since the new arrivals did not shoot at him, he decided they were on his side and did not cause them any more grief.

"You keep the men together, while I go find out from the persons in charge where they want us," Sam said to his officers. He wandered off into the night in the direction that the sentry had pointed him.

Sean let the men stroll around the immediate area to loosen their muscles and warm up. The snow had stopped falling, and the night had an eerie appearance to it, with everything blanketed in snow.

Nicholas reappeared in thirty minutes and announced that they were to relieve the men that had been positioned on the other side of the town guarding a bridge. One of the men in Mullan's company was familiar with the area and was given the lead. The men marched to their area, and arrived in about fifteen minutes. Sam awakened the officer in charge to apprise him of their arrival and to find out where the men could bed down for the night. They were pointed to a barn that they could use since their tents had not arrived yet.

The men strolled over to the barn and were glad to have plenty of hay with which to make their beds. They bedded down in their blankets for the night. In the morning, they would take full charge of the position from the army unit that was in charge of it for now.

The next morning, the marines formed up to formally take charge from the Continentals who would be moving into Trenton with the rest of the army. Sean looked at their haggard faces as they marched past them. Their uniforms were in tatters; some had their feet wrapped in clothes for warmth, as many did not have wearable shoes. They had the look of a defeated yet defiant army.

Behind them they left a six-pounder field piece for the defense of the bridge. Sean and Lanigan inspected it as the men ate. It was in serviceable condition; and only had a dozen charges left for the six-round shot and six explosive shells in the ammunition boxes on the carriage. As they inspected the hastily constructed earthen parapet that they had dug, Nicholson came up the road from town.

He signaled Mullan's drummer to beat out "officer's call" and walked over to where Sean and Lanigan were standing. "Good morning, gentlemen. It's good to see that the snow has stopped for a bit. As soon as the others get here, I'll explain what we are to be about."

The other officers and sergeants assembled, and Nicholas had them gather around. "Gentlemen, we have been given the responsibility of this bridge and two crossroads here, and here," he said as he pointed to them on a map that he held up in his other hand.

"Sean's company will remain here to cover the bridge, while you two men will take your companies to the other checkpoints. They are just a mile's distance in either direction. Once there you will relieve the Continentals that are presently guarding them. These lads have seen a lot of fighting in the past several months and are suffering from it. We are to give them a break while they recuperate. Lads, it is very possible that we will see some action here ourselves. There have been reports of British dragoons and mounted Hessians patrolling close in and making harassing attacks. Engage them if they show themselves, and capture some, if you can, for the intelligence they may provide," Nicholas instructed them.

"Do you think we will stay here for the winter, or will we withdraw to Philadelphia?" Mullan asked.

"I'm not sure that the general has made up his mind yet. He has ordered the Associators to join us here along with the men from the frigates *Delaware* and *Washington*. The British have ships at the mouth of Delaware Bay, so the frigates cannot go anywhere for now. We will all be under the command of a Colonel Cadwalader, whom I understand that the general holds in high esteem. They should be joining us in a few days to hold this position. Now, if there are no more questions, move out to your positions. I will make sure that your supply wagons find you. Also, each company will be given four horses for the purposes of patrolling further out from your positions.
The general wants as much advance warning of any enemy movement as we can give him." Nicholas rolled up his map and returned the salutes of his subordinates as they left. Sean signaled for the men to join him at the cannon.

"Lads, this is home for now. It is our responsibility to protect this bridge, and patrol from here to gather what information we can. We may be seeing the enemy, as they have several probing mounted patrols in the area, so stay alert. We will be receiving some horses shortly, so I will need to know who among you can ride." He paused while several of the men raised their hands.

"Good. Sergeant, make note of those who raised their hands. We'll set up a rotating watch schedule, and when the wagon arrives, those not on watch will set up a proper camp. We'll need some volunteers now to go and gather more firewood. Sergeant, see to that, while I'll take the first watch with those who take the first shift," Sean instructed.

Sean took the six men who volunteered for the
first watch and walked them around their position.
There were two earthen parapets, one on either side
of the bridge, on the town side of the creek. The
cannon was in place on the left side of the bridge and
commanded the entire field and road on the other side
of the creek. The open fields stretched two hundred
yards from the creek to the tree line, with the road
running in a slight arc from the tree line to the bridge.
They had an excellent field of fire, should anyone
approach the small, stone bridge.

Lanigan got the others busy gathering firewood.
By noon, they had amassed several cords of it,
enough for a few days. The men on watch kept a fire
burning on both sides of the road to keep warm.
Shortly after the men cooked the last of their food for
lunch, their wagon and escort arrived. The men on the
wagon looked chilled to the bone. After they reported
to Sean, they immediately crowded around the
nearest fire.

The watch changed, and Sean stayed with the new
group while Lanigan got the men busy setting up their
tents and cooking gear. Shortly after lunch, two
Continentals rode into their camp with four horses in
tow behind them. They turned them over to the
sergeant and accepted a hot meal from the men.

Sean joined them and listened to them tell their
tales of fighting under Washington. They held the
marines spellbound with their stories. Sean looked in
their eyes as they talked; they showed no emotion, no
life in them. They truly had been in some of the worst
that warfare had to offer.

The two soldiers mounted their horses and trotted
off. Sean looked at his men and asked, "Well, who

among you is up for a ride this afternoon? Now that we have some mounts, we might as well make use of them." Immediately all who could ride raised their hands to have something to do that would relieve the boredom of sitting around the camp.

"George, Monacelli, and Baum, get your weapons and mount up. We'll go for a ride in the country and see what we can see," he smiled.

Sean retrieved his rifle and picked out a horse. It was a fine bay, although it was a little underfed. He fixed his sword in the straps on the saddle and mounted. He rested his rifle across the saddle in front of him, after checking the powder charge in the flash pan.

"Angus, see to it that the lads stay warm. We should be back before dark, so watch for us." he instructed the sergeant.

"Aye, sir, and don't you go getting into trouble over there; those dragoons are not a nice group to run into, you know," he warned.

"Don't worry, we are going to reconnoiter only. Ready, men?" he asked of the others who had mounted their horses and had gotten situated.

The four marines trotted off across the bridge and set a steady pace down the road on the other side. Sean adjusted his scarf high on his face, as the wind was very cold as they rode. He looked to make sure that his men had mittens on, as he did, and was gratified to see that they did. All four men wore their heavy boat cloaks over their uniforms.

They slowed down and conversed with everyone they saw along the road, and at every farmhouse. No one had seen any British about. Sean was about to turn around and head back, but first wanted to see what was beyond the next rise. They stopped at the top of the hill and gazed out over the valley before them.

"Look down there, sir!" Monacelli exclaimed, as he pointed down at an isolated farmhouse. There were six horses tied up, and three men in red coats holding two men at gunpoint at the small barn. One of the soldiers struck the older of the men in the face with the butt of his musket.

"Quickly, men, get off the road into the trees!" Sean ordered. The four turned the horses into the trees alongside the road and headed down for the farm. They would be in the trees until they were about fifty feet from the house. As they approached, they heard a woman scream repeatedly and was suddenly silenced.

"Sir, we got to help them people," Baum whispered.

"I agree Baum, we'll dismount and go on foot from here. We'll get to the farmhouse and see what is happening inside and decide what to do then," he said as they dismounted and tied their horses to saplings.

The men spread out and approached the edge of the clearing. They stopped, and Sean motioned for them to follow him. There was no window on this side of the house, so they would not be seen. The men lined up on the side of the house while Sean crept around the corner and looked in the window. Inside were three more dragoons. He could see a woman and her two teenage daughters being manhandled by the dragoons.

"This is what we will do. This has to be done quickly, lads, or those people may get killed. There are three more inside molesting the women. Edward

George, you and I will charge in and attack them. Baum, you and Monacelli take our rifles, and when we break in the door, you two shoot the three at the barn. Don't miss; you have to take down all three as quickly as you can. Any questions? Good, George check your pistol, and let's get in position."

The four men crept around the corner, staying below the window. They watched the three men at the barn kicking the farmer and his son, laughing at them each time they heard a scream from inside the house.

When Baum and Monacelli got into firing position with the rifles, and with their muskets at hand next to them, Sean looked at his friend, who nodded at him. Sean cocked both his pistols and saw that his friend had a pistol in one hand and tomahawk in the other.

They stood on either side of the door. Sean stepped out and kicked in the door. He and George rushed in, firing their pistols at point-blank range. He heard his men outside fire, as he realized that only one of his pistols had gone off.

The dragoon that he missed grabbed his saber and charged at him. He only took two steps before the tomahawk that was thrown by his companion felled him. The man dropped to the floor dead, with the weapon stuck in his skull. The woman pulled her ripped clothing up to her neck while she grabbed her two frightened daughters.

"Sir, we got them all!" Monacelli shouted in the door. "One of them is only wounded, so we may get some information out of him."

The three hugged each other while they broke out in uncontrollable sobs. "Let's get these bodies out of here. These women have been through enough without having them to look at," Sean said as he

337

grabbed one by the feet and pulled him outside. He looked over at the barn. The farmer grasped his son as the boy kicked and beat the wounded soldier. He managed to drag the boy away from him and bring him up to the house.

"You had better go inside, they need you in there," Sean said as he stepped aside for George to pull the third dead man from inside. Baum and Monacelli stood guard over the wounded man. Sean looked at George and said, "We better get these bodies away from here in case there are any more patrols about. Find some rope, tie them to their horses, and drag them off into the woods. We'll take the weapons and horses with us."

He walked over to the other men and instructed Baum to assist with removing the bodies. "Private Monacelli, let's question our prisoner to see what he can tell us."

"Sir, if you don't mind, this man is scum, a rapist like his friends. You should not be involved with the questioning. It ain't fittin' that a gentleman as yourself be a party to the way I will question him," he replied as he pushed the man towards the open barn door.

Sean was about to object, but after what he had seen inside the cabin, he thought better of it. The ways of the men of the 'lower deck' were sometimes the best methods of dealing with situations.

He walked back over to the cabin and stepped inside. The farmer stood up from where he was sitting on the edge of the bed comforting his wife and daughters. He walked over to Sean and shook his hand.

"Thank you. Thank you for what you did. They were going to kill us all after they had their way with the women. They wouldn't leave us alive to report them to their commanders. They said that this is what all rebels deserved! Who are you men? I haven't seen your kind of uniform before," he asked.

"We are marines, sir, and always glad to be of assistance. My men are cleaning up the yard out there and will hide all evidence of those men having been here. You had best do the same in here. Better to not say anything of this to any British that come around here; they may hold you responsible for what happened. We will leave no trace of what happened here today," Sean advised them.

Sean stepped back outside to let the family console themselves. He saw Baum and George returning from the woods with the dragoons' horses and their own. They rode in and stopped in front of him.

Monacelli came out of the barn and came over to them. "There's one more inside the barn to drag off. His wounds got the better of him, being shot through the lung and all. He did tell me that the British are out in force, scouring the countryside, looking for any remnants of Washington's army. They are planning to move a larger force back into the area, to occupy the bigger towns on this side of the Delaware."

"Good job. Now, we had better finish our work here and be gone before any more arrive," Sean ordered. Baum dragged off the last body behind his horse, while Monacelli packed all the weapons onto the dragoons' horses. George went back to the trees and chopped down a large bush. He roped it and then dragged it over their trail that they left from dragging the bodies into the woods. He then dragged it back and forth, all around the farmyard wherever there were boot prints or blood.

Sean mounted his horse, and from where he sat, he could see that the area was smoothened out. He and the others rode back out to the road, followed by George and the bush. When they had gone as far as the top of the rise, he angled off the road and left the bush back in the tees.

The men headed back for their lines, as the sun was close to going down. They set a good pace as they led the horses behind them. When they came to a small crossroads, they looked down the road to their left and saw a group of mounted men.

"Kick the hell out of them, boys! Those are dragoons down there, and we are at least a league from our lines!" Sean ordered. The men wasted no time as they kicked the sides of their horses. The animals did not balk, but jumped ahead, racing for all they were worth.

The dragoons must not have realized that they were not one of their groups until they reached the crossroads themselves. Sean looked back and saw them as they, too, kicked their horses into pursuit. The marines had a good half-mile lead on them and kept up the pace and the lead that they had.

The horses were eager to run and did not disappoint the men. Sean kept watching over his shoulder as they raced through the countryside. The dragoons were gaining on them. He looked ahead and saw one of the farmers that they had talked to earlier. He was on his wagon, plodding down the road. The man looked back and quickly angled his team of horses off the road.

He waved to the men as they raced by, and then deliberately pulled back onto the road and stopped. Sean looked back to see the dragoons going off the road to get around the wagon. He heard the crack of a pistol and saw the farmer duck as the shot went wild. He had bought them just a few moments of time, enough to give them a greater lead on their pursuers.

They rounded a bend in the road, and Sean could see the bridge ahead of them. They spurred their mounts on, as they saw the men on the other side of the bridge come to life and man the parapets.

They were almost to safety. Just then, Baum's horse stumbled and fell, dumping him on the ground, as the horses that he was leading kept running, trying to keep up with the others. Sean halted his horse and swung him around. They were about eighty yards from the bridge.

He raced back to Baum. As he reached down and grabbed his arm to swing him up behind him on the horse, he saw the dragoons race around the bend. As soon as Baum was on the horse, Sean kicked it into motion. The animal needed no more encouragement, as the sound of several muskets fired behind them helped to quicken its pace.

They were nearly on him as they were halfway to the bridge. The horse shuddered, and Sean thought he had either been hit or was about to give out. He spurred it on; just as they thundered across the bridge, the horse collapsed on the other side, spilling Sean and Baum onto the ground. They rolled to a stop, and several hands were there to pick them up.

Sean steadied himself and then stumbled over to where Lanigan was standing by the cannon, a burning portfire in his hand. "Ah, 'tis good to see you lads back safe and sound. I just knew that ye could not stay out of trouble!" he laughed.

Just then the twenty dragoons formed up in the field across the bridge, just within musket range. They shouldered their weapons and fired a volley at the marines. "Hold your fire, lads," Lanigan called out. "Now ain't it just like those beef-witted cavalrymen to show up at a cannon fight with muskets?" he exclaimed as he touched the glowing portfire to the touchhole of the gun.

The cannon roared, sending an explosive shell screaming towards the dragoons. As soon as they saw the smoke from the cannon, they turned to ride off, but the shell burst behind them, sending four horses and riders crashing to the ground. Three other men dropped from their horses as their mounts ran off.

The marines let out a yell as they watched the enemy ride off, leaving their wounded and dead behind. "Corporal Sinclair, take ten men with you and go bring those lads back here. Bring the bodies in, and we'll find a spot to bury them," Lanigan ordered.

Sinclair picked his men, and with muskets at the ready, they went across the bridge to claim their prisoners and dead. They marched the men back across the bridge, carrying the three dead men between them.

"Just march them on over to the headquarters. They can take charge of them and the bodies," Sean called out to them as they came across the bridge. "It's been an exciting day, Angus! I hope we're not too late for supper and a bit of rum?" Sean asked as he shook his hand.

"No, in fact your party is just in time. Calhoun has been roasting a large cut of the fresh beef all afternoon, and it should just about be ready. Let's go get a spot of rum for you and the lads, and then ye can tell us what ye did to get those dragoons so riled up at ye!" Lanigan laughed as he guided Sean back to their camp.

The men gathered around as they had their tankards filled with rum. As soon as they had been served, Sean and the others told them of discovering the six dragoons attempting to rape the woman and her daughters and how they rescued them.

After Sean finished his supper and recounting their run-in with the dragoons, he took his last swallow of hot rum and left to report to Nicholas. He mounted his horse and rode into town past encampments of the Continentals. The mood in the camps seemed subdued as the men huddled around fires for warmth. He noticed that the uniforms of many of the men were threadbare. They supplemented their uniforms with pieces of blankets and parts of uniforms from their fallen enemy.

He reined in his horse in front of the house serving as Nicholas' headquarters and tied the reins to the fence in front. He saluted the shivering guards at the door, as they presented arms, and went inside. He found Sam in the sitting room at a desk pulled close to the fireplace.

"Come in, Sean, and have a seat. I just got back in myself and am trying to get warmed up. The men are having such a terrible time staying warm that we are changing guard every hour. Now tell me about your little adventure this afternoon. They just gave me a rough report of it when I got here. It sounds as if you got to that farm just in the nick of time today. Nice job!" Nicholas commented.

Sean took the next ten minutes retelling the story of how they discovered the enemy patrol attempting to ravage the women on the farm, and the information that Monacelli extracted from the dying cavalryman. He also retold of their narrow escape from the larger patrol on the way back.

"Good show, and you brought back some good horseflesh as I understand also. Keep them in your area; I'll want you to continue to scout out the other side of the river. I'm afraid that no one else took it upon them self to cross over there today, so what you learned was all the information that we received today."

"So, what are the plans for us? Are we to just stay here while the British make up their minds what they are going to do?" Sean asked.

"Things are pretty much up in the air. In case you did not know, most of Washington's volunteer army may go home after the thirty-first of December, when their enlistments run out. This is something that I am sure the British are well aware of, and may be just biding their time until that happens. That may give them the opportunity to just cross over into Pennsylvania without any opposition," Nicholas replied.

"Those men look so wretched out there; they have been through so much with so little in return. Yet there is still a glimmer of fight left in those eyes. Washington may not have a large permanent type of army as the British do; however, he does have the ability to have his ranks filled with volunteer militia that springs up wherever they are needed," Sean pointed out.

"Yes, and so far that is the only thing that has saved him. However, he may be left with no one to command if all his men go home for the winter, leaving just the militia and us here to hold them off. Cadwalader and the rest of his command should be here tomorrow to join us. We will then be under his operational command," said Nicholas.

The two talked on for a while until the clock in the next room chimed nine o'clock. Sean got up and bade Sam a good night. He stepped out on the front porch and was amazed at how quickly he felt cold as he was blasted by a frigid wind carrying more snow with it. He pulled the collar of his boat cloak up, threw his scarf around his face, and walked down to his horse.

He rode back to his camp, led his horse into the barn, and made sure it had water and fresh hay. Several of the men were in the barn, out of the wind, playing cards and dice. Sean declined their offer to let him sit in and went out to the men standing guard at the bridge. They had two large fires blazing to keep them warm with two large woodpiles nearby to make sure they did not run out of fuel for the night.

Sean looked out across the frozen creek to the snow-covered fields. At any other time, the scene before him would be rather beautiful and peaceful. Yet he knew that danger lurked beyond the trees out there, and it was quite possible that there were enemy eyes watching them at this very moment.

The next morning as Sean and his men ate around their fires; a messenger arrived carrying a crude map of the area across the river for Sean. It had a note from Sam detailing where he wanted him to scout today. There were several crossroads and towns within ten miles of the bridge, and Sean was to attempt to enter all of them to question the residents about enemy troop movements.

"Angus, since we have the extra horses now, I want you to take a patrol to the south of here, and I'll go north; that way we can cover more ground. There is a path that goes along the creek in both directions, not that you can find it with all that snow, but go as far as the next ford, and go inland from there. Try to cover as much territory as you can and still get back here by dark, and I'll head towards Maidenhead, which is halfway between here and Princeton. The major is having a squad of Mullan's men come here to beef up the men we leave behind, just in case of trouble," Sean instructed his sergeant.

As soon as the reinforcements arrived, Sean and Lanigan led their patrols out. The sky was still overcast, and snowfall blew down on them for a while then stopped, then resumed again. Sean and his group watched the road for signs of recent traffic in the snow, but although they did see depressions in the snow, it was near impossible to tell how old they were with the constant snowfall.

The men rode on, careful to watch all around them. "Sir, what is the meaning of the red rags nailed up to the doorpost of that farm we just went by?" Baum asked.

"That is the signal for British troops to know that the occupants are loyalists and not rebels. I'd wager, however, that there are many rags posted on the doors of men who belong to the militia fighting the British. There's no real way of knowing just who is and who is not on our side," Sean explained. "All the same, we will avoid those places just so we keep them guessing who we are, since there are no other troops in green uniforms."

The men made several stops at farms along the way. Most of the people reported seeing British patrols and hearing them go by during the night. So far they had not seen any yet today. The marines pressed on in the direction of Maidenhead.

As they rounded a bend on a hill overlooking a valley, they drew up their horses and pulled back into the woods alongside the road. There ahead was the town of Maidenhead, and there was a mounted patrol headed their way about a mile away.

Sean led them off the road into the woods. They led their horses into a thicket of bushes so that they were out of sight. Sean and Baum then went to the edge of the woods so that Sean could look the town over with his telescope. They watched the patrol as it plodded along. The men appeared to be reluctant to continue their patrol. When they got to the top of the hill, they turned into the woods on the opposite side of the road and dismounted fifty yards back into the trees.

In a few minutes, Sean could smell wood smoke. The men were forgoing their patrol for the warmth of a fire where they were in hiding. They had pulled off the road before they had come upon the tracks in the snow of Sean's men, so they were safe for now.

Sean turned his attention to the town below. He could see a considerable amount of activity in the town square and outside the town where several wagons had pulled into a field. There was no mistake; this was a large contingent of the British army taking over the town.

He studied the scene below him for several minutes. It appeared that there were at least two thousand men in uniform in the town. They would have to find out who it was and what they were doing, and the only way to do that was to take prisoners.

He motioned for Baum, and the two backed through the trees to where the others awaited them. "There is an entire column of infantry, artillery and some cavalry in that town. We need to try to take at least one prisoner, and we have some candidates right across the road in those trees that we can try to take. It is obvious that they are hiding from their officers as much as they are from the weather. We can slip out of here, away from the road, cross over and then enter the woods on their side and come up behind them They obviously will be watching the road toward town in case someone comes looking for them, so we should be able to get right in on them before they know it," Sean instructed them.

"We should leave the horses here and go on foot; we will make less noise that way. No sense taking a chance that one of the horses makes a noise," suggested Edward George.

"Good. Let's move out. Stay low; the snow should muffle our footsteps," Sean said as he checked his rifle and headed out.

The four men crouched over and made their way through the woods until they were below the crest of the hill, crossed the road and entered the woods on the other side. The men moved stealthily, homing in on the smell of the fire and the sounds of the men talking. From the loudness of their talk it was evident that they were drinking.

Sean held up his hand for the men behind him to stop. "We will rush them and use your muskets to knock them over. We want to take them all alive if we can. Remember, any shots could bring help to them," Sean whispered to them. He signaled for them to spread out, and they moved forward.

They got within sight of the men who were all looking the other way. "Now!" shouted Sean, and all four of them leaped at the surprised enemy soldiers. The four British all tried to reach their stacked weapons, but were not fast enough, as they were all brought low by the butt-strokes delivered by the marines with their muskets.

The fight was over as quickly as it started, and Sean and his men stood over their prisoners, all writhing in pain. They stripped the men of their swords and pistols and then tied their hands. "You have a choice. You come quietly, or you stay here to die in the forest by yourselves. What will it be?" Sean offered the men.

They looked at each other dejectedly, then the corporal stammered, "We'll go with you," and hung his head.

They gathered the weapons and led the men and their horses out of the woods while Baum ran ahead to retrieve their horses. Once they were all gathered together, the marines and prisoners mounted the horses and rode away from the town.

"We'll keep up a steady pace and not stop until we get back. There's too much of a chance that we'll encounter enemy patrols with their main body so close," Sean told his men as they trotted off.

The men did not slow down until the snowfall increased, so they had a hard time seeing ahead of them. They knew that it was mid-afternoon as they plodded on; they should be only a half an hour from their lines.

They were about to pick up the pace when one of the prisoners kicked his horse, and wheeled it around, crashing into Monacelli's horse, sending him tumbling into the snow. He charged off with Baum in close pursuit. Sean and George lowered their rifles at the other three men, who showed no inclination to resist.

Sean watched the road behind them as Baum caught up with the prisoner, and clobbered him over the head with the blunt end of his tomahawk. The man fell into the snow bank alongside the road while his horse kept running. Baum made the decision not to chase after the horse and waited until the man on the ground started to move.

"Get yer arse up! On yer feet now, or I'll cleave yer head wide open with this!" he ordered, waving the weapon wildly around his head. The man slowly got to his feet and walked back to the group.

"You there, corporal, he'll have to ride double with you, and the next one of you who tries that will be shot. We are closer to our lines than yours, so there is little danger for us to fire upon you now," Sean said sternly to the prisoners.

The man climbed up behind his corporal and they set off again for their lines. It was almost three in the afternoon when they got back. They rode on into town to turn over their prisoners. As they passed through the Continental camp, Sean deliberately slowed down as the soldiers got to their feet to stare at the prisoners.

The Continentals shook their fists at the men and shouted threats and laughed derisively at them. Sean looked back and saw the fear in the eyes of the prisoners. "Would you like for me to turn you over to them?" he asked

The question and the reaction of the Continentals had the desired effect on the men. When they got to headquarters, they took the prisoners inside. One at a time they were led away by a marine officer and sergeant into a back room for questioning. Sean and his men stood at the fireplace warming up.

As they were finished with each one, the prisoners were led off separately out a side door to the compound where they would be held. When the last one was led away, the two marines came into the room where Sean and his men were.

The lieutenant came over to Sean and introduced himself. "I'm Lieutenant Bawers, and may I say that whatever you did to those men, they sang like meadowlarks. They told me everything that I wanted to know. It appears that the unit that you ran into was part of Cornwallis's army. They had orders to set up their headquarters in Maidenhead, and await General Grant to move on Trenton. He is apparently behind time and should have been here by now."

"Good, that means we have some time to either decide to defend this place or withdraw across the river," Sean suggested. He took leave of the young lieutenant and led his men back to their camp.

They were just settling in around the fire and warming up with some coffee when they saw Lanigan's patrol heading in. After they came across the bridge, Lanigan dismounted and passed his reins to Calhoun.

"Good day to you, sir. How was your hunting trip?" he asked. "We saw several mounted patrols, and were even chased by one until we turned and fired on them. We hit two of the six, and the rest just tucked their tails between their legs and ran," he reported.

"We bagged a few, just got back from headquarters after turning over the prisoners. It appears the British may make a push towards us here, so make sure the men are extra alert standing watch. I found out that Cadwalader and the rest of his command has arrived and set up camp. He's going to hold a council with all the officers tomorrow, so I will not be going on patrol in the morning. Let Sinclair take a patrol out in my place, Beckett can take over your patrol, because I want you to take charge of the protection of the bridge," Sean instructed.

"You're right about that. The lads will need a steady hand if the Lobsterbacks show up. What do you think? Will we stay or go away from here?" Lanigan asked.

"I'm not sure, but we most likely will go back across the Delaware. The British are too well supplied and too numerous to resist an attack here. Better to go into winter quarters on the other side and start anew in the spring when everyone is fresh," Sean answered.

The next day the officers of Cadwalader's new command met. There were the Marines, the Associators, an assortment of clerks and townspeople, and the sailors from the two frigates docked at Philadelphia. The group spent the morning covering the command structure, needs of the various units, and the responsibilities of each group.

"General Washington and his men have left for Princeton to reinforce that area and to try to force the British into a fight. We should know by tonight the outcome of his move. So for now, we are to hold this area and be prepared to fend off any attacks by enemy forces, and be prepared to cover the Continentals if they have to fall back here," Cadwalader announced.

The meeting over, the officers returned to their commands. Sean apprised Lanigan and his men who were not on patrol of what was expected of them. "He has a lot of amateurs under him, as only we marines, the sailors and only a handful of his militia have any fighting experience. It is up to us to provide the backbone of the brigade since we have the experience, Nicholas said as much also."

"Don't worry, sir. Our lads and the other companies with us will not let them down," Lanigan assured him.

The next day before noon, the head of the column of Continentals was observed heading back to camp. Riders had come in earlier to inform the men at Trenton that it had been discovered that the British had laid a trap for Washington's army near Princeton. Washington's spies had uncovered the trap and convinced him to return to Trenton.

By late evening the army was once again encamped around the town. That night, Washington called a war council, and he and the officers decided to withdraw across the Delaware and fortify the other side of the river. There was still too much uncertainty as to whether the British would brave the snowy weather and attempt to cross the river and attack Philadelphia.

"So we are to be the rear guard for the army to escape across the river, are we?" Lanigan asked Sean when he got back.

"Yes, we are. We will hold the positions around the town while the bulk of the army gets across. After they are safe on the other side, we will be transferred across also. We are to keep the field gun that we have at the bridge and the horses for now. Once we get to the other side, we will take up a defensive position somewhere along the riverbank.

The next day, the marines stayed at their posts while the army disembarked in every manner of watercraft available. There were rowboats, rafts, gondolas, ketches, bateaux, flat-bottom boats, and a few small schooners.

The crossing took all day. Sean rode around the area observing the activity. He had never seen so many people in one place in his life. He watched as horses, mules and oxen were forced onto the rafts and flat-bottom boats to the curses, kicks and whips of their handlers.

The militia that could be spared from guard duty was assigned the task of burning all the supplies that they could not take with them to prevent them from falling into the hands of the enemy. He was astounded at the wanton waste of valuable supplies, but it was better to destroy them than to let the British have them to their advantage.

By nightfall, only the militia and they remained on the New Jersey side of the river along with the units that were still trying to transport the rest of the wagons and supplies that were to go along with the army.

Early the next morning, the militia got to board the boats which were sent across, while the marines remained until the last. "It's our turn to go now, Sean. Get your men moving. There are rafts for the wagons and cannon, and plenty of boats waiting for the men," Nicholas announced as he rode into Sean's position by the bridge.

"And none too soon. It sure is quiet here with everyone gone. Sergeant, have the drummer sound the signal for the patrol to return," Sean ordered. "I've had a patrol out beyond the tree line since daybreak just in case."

"No need to, sir, Look there, they are riding like the devil 'imself was after them!" Lanigan exclaimed.

They all looked towards the tree line, and sure enough, the four-man mounted patrol was returning as fast as they could. They galloped to a halt in front of the group, and Baum jumped down and saluted. Catching his breath, he reported, "Sirs, the Redcoats are coming for sure! They are about a mile out. They should be here in about ten, maybe fifteen minutes," he stammered.

"Did you see any cavalry?" Sam asked.

"There was a small patrol, maybe twenty trottin' up the road when we come back. There's a huge column of infantry following 'em not far behind."

"Good report. Now take those horses and get them loaded onto the rafts. The wagons should be there by now. Sean, I'll stay here with you and your lads while the other companies get to the boats, if you don't mind?" Nicholas asked.

355

"We always have room for some company. Calhoun, if there is any more coffee there, bring some over for the major. Look, here comes the cavalry," Sean pointed out.

"We should welcome them, don't you think?" Sam asked.

"Yes we should; Angus, send them our compliments, if you please!" Sean smiled.

"Aye, sir that I will. "ere take the cover off the touchhole and stand back, lads," he said as he stood behind the field piece, squinting along the barrel as if aiming a musket. Lanigan gave the elevation a twist, stood aside and applied the portfire to the touchhole.

The gun crashed backwards, and the men watched as the explosive round exploded thirty feet in front of the massed cavalrymen. Their horses turned and tried to run in every direction. It took the riders a few minutes to calm the beasts and reform their line. They made no attempt to advance, opting to wait for the infantry to come forward.

A runner came up to announce that everyone else had boarded the rafts and boats, and the marines at the bridge were now the only ones left. Sean's men stood up and hoisted up their knapsacks.

"How about it, lads? Should we give 'em one more for them to remember us by?" Angus asked. The men cheered in agreement. The four who acted as gunners stepped forward and within a minute had the gun loaded and primed to fire.

"'Ere you go, sir. It's fittin' and proper that you should have the last word in this!" Lanigan said as he handed the portfire to Nicholas.

"Why thank you, Sergeant!" he said enthusiastically. He stepped behind the gun and did the same as Lanigan had, making a big show of turning the elevation one more partial turn. He then stepped to the side, blew on the smoldering end of the portfire, touched it to the hole, and again the gun crashed out.

When the smoke cleared, they saw that the shot had landed behind the mounted men, yet had created the same havoc on their horses. The marines let out a loud cheer and gave their enemy mock salutes. They then gathered around the gun and picked up the trails and pulled the gun to the river.

The men loaded into the waiting boats after securing the cannon on a raft and sat back while they were rowed across the Delaware. They unloaded onto the far shore, and after hooking the gun to a horse and harness, they fell in at the end of the column of Cadwalader's brigade and marched off to the south.

Sean looked back across the river as they marched off. There on the opposite bank sat the cavalrymen that they had fired upon. They sat astride their horses, watching as the column marched off. A militia unit guarded the crossing with four guns aimed across the river. Once the British saw the cannon, they turned away from the riverbank and headed into town.

The men marched the rest of the day, stopping at different river crossings as one company after another was doled out to take up their posts to protect the crossing places along the river. Sam came riding back to Sean as they marched.

"Cadwalader is making his headquarters at Bristol. We will be quartered there in the Quaker meeting hall. There should be enough room there for our three companies. Your men will take up position at Dunk's Crossing. You can keep the cannon with you, and I will try to get at least one more for you. We may be here for a while so have the men make themselves comfortable when they get there. Be sure that the engineers who are to make your fortifications do a good job for you. With Washington's army about to end their enlistments, we may be all that stands between the British and Philadelphia in a couple of weeks," Sam warned.

"We'll do everything within our power to prevent a crossing by us, you can count on that," Sean said as he saluted. Sam rode off to see to the other companies.

The men reached the Quaker meetinghouse and set up their kitchen area outside among the tents they set up for their supplies. After they stowed their gear, Sean took them to their post on the river. They brought the cannon along, placing it in the best position for preventing a forced crossing.

They set up a watch schedule, then those who did not take the first watch, went out to collect firewood for the guards and for their fires at the meetinghouse. It was long after dark before the men settled in for the night.

For the next several days, the marines endured the bitter cold, snow and sleet, guarding the several river crossings just to the north of Philadelphia. The Quaker meetinghouse that they used as a barracks did not offer much warmth from the outside, as it was drafty, and they could not keep it warm enough for fear of it catching fire and burning down.

Those not standing watch took turns crossing the river with horses on a raft to perform patrols for gathering intelligence. The British were active around the towns across the river, constantly making their presence known.

Sean and his men had heard several stories from the people living in New Jersey of the Redcoats and the Hessians beating people at random to impress upon them not to assist the rebels. They had even heard that several rapes had occurred at some of the isolated farms in the area, just as they had prevented weeks before.

"There's renegades in every army, and they should be shot like rabid dogs!" exclaimed Lanigan one day after he brought his patrol back across. They had come upon a farm about an hour after an enemy patrol had been there. They had looted the cabin, shot the farmer, and had their way with his wife before they killed her.

Lanigan and his men torched the cabin to create a funeral pyre for the two, since the ground was much too hard to try to dig graves for them. A neighbor had led them to the farm after seeing the Redcoat patrol approach the cabin and hearing screams and shots from within.

With each passing day, the food supplies started getting scarcer, and the men had to subsist on reduced rations. Sean had Edward George lead a few hunting parties on their side of the river to supplement their rations. With the several thousand men encamped along the river, the game had been scared away, and the men had to travel several miles away to find any deer.

The days passed rapidly. On the eleventh of December, Sean had the patrol out on the other side of the river. They had gone far inland and were on their way back without sighting anything. Sean halted them for a few moments outside of Bustleton, where they stopped at a farm to water the horses.

The farmer inside the cabin was reluctant to come out when he saw the five marines, but after he had called out to them and Sean answered back, he came out smiling. "Damned glad to see you. I saw the green uniforms and thought you might be them Hessian Jaegers! A friend came by earlier and told me he ran into them coming from Bordentown. He said they were wearing green uniforms like you boys. Once I heard you talk, I knew you weren't no Hessians."

"How long ago was that?" Sean asked, worried that the Hessians may trap them.

"He just come by here about an hour ago, so you fellas ought to get going. He said there was over a hundred of them," warned the farmer.

"Thanks for the warning. You watch out for yourself; we have heard that they have committed some terrible things where they have been concentrated. Being out on a farm like this, away from town, they may decide to be rough with you here," Sean advised the older man.

"Don't you worry about me, I have a hidden cellar under the floor. Put it in when we still had some trouble with the Injuns. It come in handy a time or two," he exclaimed proudly.

"Mount up men, we need to get away from here before those Hessians come around and see him talking with us," Sean ordered. The men got back onto the horses and headed back down the road. They were headed in the direction of Bustleton when they saw several wagons and carriages coming their way from the town.

"Looks like they must have reached town. Let's skirt around the town and see what we can see," he suggested to them. They turned off the road and cut across the fields, far enough from the town to be out of musket range.

They drew up to watch what was going on in town from a small rise in the snow-covered field. "Look there!" exclaimed Timmons. "Over by that fence, there are several armed men running towards that fence! They've seen us!"

"They are in green like us. They must be those Hessian Jaegers the old man told us about." stated Sean as he tried to count them.

"Don't get excited, Timmons. We are well out of musket range here," observed Hyland. Just as he said that, the fence where the Hessians were gathering disappeared in a cloud of gun smoke.

They heard the sound of the weapons going off at the same time that they heard the bullets cracking past them. Timmons spun out of his saddle and hit the ground with a thud. "Damn, they ain't firing muskets, they have rifles!" shouted Sheldon.

Sean and Sheldon jumped from their horses to help Timmons back up as the others took aim and fired at their attackers. "He's wounded bad. Come on, we'll get him onto his horse and take him back with us," Sean instructed Sheldon.

They passed their weapons to the other two men, who fired them before attempting to reload. Sean and Sheldon managed to get Timmons onto his horse; he was barely able to hold on. Sheldon picked up Timmons' musket and fired it at the Hessians, more out of defiance than of being able to hit them.

They remounted and got their weapons back from the others and spun their horses around to head back to the river. Just then the Jaegers fired another volley. Sean felt his hat jolt as it flew off his head and landed in his lap. He spurred his mount on as the others followed. He noticed a bullet hole in the brim of his hat as he returned it to his head.

The Hessians charged after their prey, but they knew they had no chance of catching up to them on foot. The marines reached the river and signaled for the raft to be sent back across for them. As they waited, they watched the road behind them, as Sean tried to bandage Timmons' wound.

The man had bled profusely from his chest wound, which outwardly did not look bad. However, as he peeled the layers of shirts and coat back from his chest, he saw that the clothing had sopped up a great quantity of blood. The man had fallen unconscious from his horse as they arrived at the river, and Sean did not hold out much hope for him living.

He finished his work on the wound and stood up as Sheldon said, "Here they come again Sir! Looks to be about fifty of them."

Sean looked to where he was pointing. There, coming around the bend in the woods through the trees, the column of Jaegers came at a trot about two hundred yards off. "Reload your weapons and prepare to fire. We can't beat them, but we can slow them down," he ordered as he started to reload his rifle. The others had rifles, except for the musket that Timmons had carried. Sean looked over his shoulder to check on the progress of the raft crew.

The raft was in midstream, slowly being maneuvered across by the large sweeps manned by four men. Sean called out to the cannon crews on the opposite shore. "There is a column of enemy infantry approaching at two hundred yards. Prepare to fire at my command!"

The crewmen waved to acknowledge his order. He could see Lanigan barking orders to them as he climbed atop the parapet to get a better view through his telescope. He turned to see that the Jaegers had narrowed the gap between them.

"All right now, boys. Take aim at the men in front and fire at will," he ordered. He watched as the three men knelt to take better aim at the approaching enemy. He brought his rifle to his shoulder, pulled the hammer back, and took aim. He and the others fired in unison, and as the smoke from their weapons cleared, they saw that three men had dropped, and the column had stopped in confusion.

The men stood and reloaded as quickly as their cold hands would permit. They watched as the column changed shape. The officer in front stood shouting orders in German that they could hear, and the infantrymen spread out into two ranks; the front kneeled and the rear rank remained standing.

Sean watched as they were forming up to prepare to fire on them, when he spun around and shouted at the cannon crews, "Fire!"

The two six-pounder field pieces spoke out as their smoke and flame shot out across the frigid river. The men watched to see where the shots impacted when they heard the guns. The explosive shells blew up, one about ten yards in front of the two ranks, and the other about five yards in back of the enemy. Dirt and snow flew up in the air like geysers.

The shots landed just as the Jaegers were about to fire in volley. That shook them up as they did fire, sending their shots wild around the four marines. Hauser called out as he was spun around and hit the ground. "Damn, they got me!"

He got back up, grasping his left arm. He had been hit in the upper arm, but it did not appear broken. Sheldon fired his weapon at the Germans again, and then took his scarf and bandaged up Hauser's arm. They fired another volley and reloaded as the cannons roared again.

The Jaegers retreated about ten yards as the shots had fallen short. They reformed and prepared to fire again as the raft reached the shore. "Hurry men, get your horses onto the raft. Petrov, give me a hand with Timmons." Sean ordered.

The big Russian slung his rifle, passed his horse's reins to Hauser, and helped Sean pick up the wounded man. They supported him with his arms across their shoulders, and dragged more than helped him walk to the raft just as the enemy fired another volley.

Petrov collapsed, and Sean felt his boat cloak jump as bullets tore through the skirts of the coat. He caught himself from being pulled down onto the two men and looked to see the Russian grasping his right leg. I can make it, sir," he stammered as he got back up, supporting Timmons again.

Sheldon came running back to them, grasped Petrov from his free side, and together they got to the waiting raft. Once again they heard the snap of bullets passing by them. Suddenly Timmons' horse shuddered, lifted itself on its hind legs and fell overboard into the river. They watched as the beast did not move again after it hit the water.

The men manning the sweeps needed no encouragement to put their backs into their work. The raft, slowly at first and then with more speed, moved out into the river as the cannons fired once more. Petrov had collapsed on the rear of the craft, where Sheldon helped him bandage his leg with his scarf.

Sean turned to see a few of them fall as the cannon shots landed just in front of their ranks. "That showed them! The dirty buggers!" swore Sheldon. He sat down next to Timmons to try to rouse him. The wounded man did not respond. "Sir, I think 'e's dead."

Sean took out his knife and put the polished blade under the wounded man's nostrils. The blade showed no signs of being steamed up by breathing. He put the knife away and felt the man's neck, but found no pulse.

"I'm afraid he has gone on ahead of us lads, He will be missed, for he was a brave man, and a good friend to all in our company," Sean lamented.

They all removed their hats and bowed their heads. The rest of the company stood on the shore, weapons at the ready, in case the Jaegers got close enough for them to fire upon. When the raft ground to a stop on the frozen riverbank, they rushed forward to assist the wounded men.   Four of them carried their dead comrade back to the graveyard at the meetinghouse and waited for the others to show up to bury him.

They got shovels and picks from the wagon, and without having to be told, attacked the hard ground in a spot close to a large barren maple tree. It took them an hour, but they finally got a hole dug deep enough to put the body in and cover it up. Sean had the company gather around, and after a brief ceremony, they fired a volley over his grave in salute to their fallen comrade.

As the men returned to their posts, or to the campfires to keep warm, Sean and Lanigan walked back to the gun emplacements at the river crossing. "That was a close thing for you and the lads today!" Lanigan observed as he pointed to the holes in Sean's hat and cloak. "Those Jaegers are hunters and woodsmen by trade, and they are a hard lot to tangle with. They are some of the best that the Hessians have to put in the field."

"I won't argue that, but they are mercenaries just the same. Hired killers. Hired by King George to rape and murder his own subjects! There is nothing honorable in that," Sean exclaimed.

The men fell into the daily routine of standing guard at the river crossing. The other marine companies and the rest of Cadwalader's militia did the same, while Washington tried to hold his army together for a little longer as the deadline for the end of the men's enlistments came near.

Sean received word on the twenty-fourth of an officer's council being held among the general staff. "What do you think it means, sir?" asked Lanigan as they warmed themselves by the fire at the bridge.

"I hope it means that we are going to take some action. Major Nicholas told me yesterday that Washington had been asking around as to whether the men would be able to go on one last offensive before hunkering down for the remainder of the winter. I think that he must have decided and has come up with a plan. Make sure the men prepare their equipment just in case, but do not let on to anything," Sean advised him.

Lanigan strolled back to the meetinghouse to get the men that were off duty busy preparing their equipment for inspection, and making sure that they gathered in as much extra supplies as they could. When that was done, he had them prepare extra cartridges with whatever paper that they could find.

Later that day, Sean was summoned to Bessonet's Tavern, where Nicholas was lodged and had made his headquarters. When he arrived, the other officers of the marine companies greeted him. They gathered around the hearth, warming themselves with hot-buttered rum.

Nicholas came into the room and called them to order. Sentries were posted at the doors, and the tavern workers were herded off to the kitchen so that they could not hear what was said. Nicholas waited until everyone had settled onto the benches at the tables before addressing them.

"Good afternoon, gentlemen. It's good to see you all healthy. I hope you are ready for some action, as the general has decided on one more offensive move before his army goes home for the winter. Tomorrow night, gentlemen, under the cover of darkness, while the Hessians are celebrating Christmas and imbibing as much drink as is available in the town of Trenton, the army will cross the Delaware in three divisions. Washington and his division will cross at McKonkey's Ferry, General Ewing's division will cross below Trenton at the Trenton crossing, and we along with General Cadwalader's division will cross the river south of them at Bristol. Ewing's forces will block the Hessian's at the Assunpink Bridge, while Washington attacks the town. We will be blocking them from being able to retreat to Bristol."

"The weather has not been very obliging lately, and the ice has been forming and breaking up, clogging the river with large floating ice floes. How are we going to manage getting troops across in those conditions?" asked one of the other officers.

"We have to do everything within our powers to carry through with this if we are going to prevent the British from crossing to this side. If that happens and the army fails to stop them, it is conceivable that we will never be able to drive them out of our lands. We must succeed, gentlemen. We need to end this season of fighting with a victory to ensure that fresh recruits will come forward in the spring to fight again," Nicholas explained.

The rest of the meeting was taken up with issuing orders and making sure that enough rations and ammunition was gathered and marching orders issued. The marines were to be towards the front of the column that was to be headed by Colonel Matlock's Pennsylvania riflemen, followed by the marines and militia. Continentals would bring up the rear of the column.

"We will leave after dark tomorrow night, gentlemen. Make sure that your men have been fed a hearty meal before we depart, for we may not have time to stop and cook a hot meal the next morning." Nicholas said in conclusion.

Sean bade his farewells as the meeting broke up and the men returned to their commands. He hurried through the cold, whistling wind to find Angus to see if he had gotten things prepared. They would be in far better condition with rations if he got a detail busy before the other units started. He had the feeling that the old Sergeant had spent the last hours wisely, as he had a sixth sense for these things and could generally tell when something major was about to take place. What tomorrow would bring was anyone's guess, but when he saw the excitement in his men's eyes when he returned to his company, he knew that they were ready to take on the enemy again.

"Gentlemen," he announced as they gathered around,"the hunt is on; we go after the British tomorrow night!"

Taggert of the Marines by David Ekardt

8
The Winter Offensive

Sean and Lanigan stood off to the side of their men as they waited in formation, ready to march. The men in the ranks were talking excitedly as they stamped their feet and rubbed their hands to keep warm. They had been fed shortly before forming up for the march to the river crossing and were now waiting for the final word to move out, as the company commanders made sure that they had all present.

"It is good to be on the move again, but a worse night for it, I can't imagine. We'll be lucky to get across before the river freezes," remarked Lanigan.

"I think you are right; the snow has been coming down heavier by the hour. The men are eager to be about this night's work, though. They want to tangle with those Hessian mercenaries. 'Hired killers' as they call them, and rightfully so. Nothing the Crown has done has rankled the men as much as the thought of these soldiers for hire," Sean pointed out.

"Listen, the call to march is being passed down the line," Lanigan observed as they heard the command, 'Forward March!' repeated by officers in the companies ahead of them.

"Well, I guess it is time, Angus. *Osprey* Marines, attention!" Sean called out. The men hurriedly fell into ranks and stopped talking. "Right shoulder arms!" he called out, hearing the slap of weapons being handled to the command.

"Forward, march!" he called out when they were ready. As one, the men stepped forward into the snowy night toward Neshaminy Ferry on the Delaware. Sean watched the companies ahead of them. He could see the other two marine companies in front of them, and Colonel Matlack's Pennsylvania riflemen ahead of them. He turned to see the militia companies starting movement behind them. After them came companies of Continentals, yet they were invisible to him through the driving snow.

"What was that? It sounded like a rifle shot!" exclaimed Sheldon as they marched along the frozen road. The sound was repeated off to the stand of trees along the road.

"Easy there, lads. Look over there. Those were tree limbs snapping off from the weight of the snow and ice. I imagine you'll be hearing plenty of that with this snow and sleet tonight, so don't get too jittery and start shooting," warned Lanigan. Just as he said that, a large branch from a stately maple tree loudly broke off from its trunk and fell right alongside the marching men.

They marched on through the bitter cold, trying not to turn their ankles on the frozen ruts in the road. "Sure, we will always go places on a ship, 'e says, you'll always fight on board a ship, 'e says, no marching, no mud, just nice sailing and brown-skinned lassies, 'e said. I joined up for that, not for playing soldier," Hyland complained.

"Why, laddie, I said nothing about taking walks through the snow, and look at it this way, there is no mud!" Lanigan said, laughing at the complaining marine hearing him repeat the things he had told him when he signed him into the company.

They finally came to a halt at the crossing and were met by boatmen waiting for them. The men fell out and stood around in groups, backs to the wind, trying to stay warm. Sean wandered forward to see what the holdup was. He joined the group of officers gathered around General Cadwalader as he spoke with the boatmen.

"General, look out there in the river. The slabs of ice could crush the sides of our boats, and they have been increasing in number coming down the river. The river is starting to ice over in some spots, and we stand a chance of losing everyone if you try to cross here," explained one of the river men.

The officers surveyed the scene before them. The boats they were to use were tied up at the bank. Ice was starting to form in the spaces between them. The river was clogged with massive ice slabs that were grinding into one another and in some spots, piling up on each other as they got wedged against the bank or jammed together.

"Things might be better downstream. As you see, there's not much moving just below that main ice jam over there. Dunk's Ferry might be better unless this breaks apart and flows down there." Just then they heard several loud cracks as the ice slabs crashed into each other.

"Men, I think we should heed his advice. To try to get the men across here in boats would be shear madness, and we would lose good men to the river. We shall turn the column and make for Dunk's Ferry. There are enough boats there for our purposes,"

Cadwalader announces. The officers ran back to their commands, and in moments, the lead companies of the column were marching along the rest of the column, headed in the opposite direction.

Sean explained to the men what happened and ignored the griping that ensued. Once he reminded them that they would only last about half a minute in the freezing water if the ice crushed their boat, the complaining subsided.

The column of men marched on in silence. The cold air tore at their lungs as they marched. The snow and sleet swirled around them as the volume of it increased. By the time they reached Dunk's Ferry, most of the men had pulled their blankets from their knapsacks and were wrapped up in them in an attempt to keep warmer.

Sean could not help but wonder at how the Continentals were faring in this cold, as many of their uniforms were threadbare, and many had nothing but rags and old clothes wrapped around their feet. His men were fortunate to have been so well supplied, having fresh uniforms and warm blankets and heavy boat cloaks over their uniforms.

He watched as Lanigan moved among the men, joking with them, encouraging them, bolstering their spirits. He was a fount of energy for them as they struggled along. Finally when they reached Dunk's Ferry, the snow and sleet was pelting them unmercifully.

Matlack's battalion was the first to cross in the waiting boats, as the rest of the men were permitted to do whatever they could to stay warm. The Pennsylvania volunteers fought their way across the ice-choked river. The last hundred yards or more, they had to cross ice that had formed from the opposite shore. Once there, they went inland and set up a defensive perimeter to cover the rest of the landing party.

The next to go across were two companies of the Associators. They, too, struggled to reach the other shore. When the boats came back across, the storm had unleashed its fury. The wind and driving snow made it next to impossible to see anything.

Cadwalader called a conference of the officers. Sean plodded forward to learn what was happening. It was nearly impossible to identify anyone under the heavy clothes scarves and blankets as they gathered around a roaring fire.

Cadwalader spoke to them as they gathered. "Men, the storm shows no let up and has gotten worse. The river has frozen over on the other side, and the men had to walk across it to get to the shore. We have cannon and horses to get across, and I am afraid that we will lose them and lives of our men if we try to proceed." He paused while he let his words have effect.

"With the troubles we are having, it is almost certain that the other two divisions are encountering the same. I propose that we abandon this crossing, have the men on the other side return to us and we return to camp for the night. In the morning, weather and river permitting, we can make the attempt again. Tonight, I'm afraid we stand too much of a chance of losing too many lives to the elements. What say you men to this?" he asked.

The others all uttered their agreement with the proposal. The weather conditions had indeed worsened beyond what was reasonable to attempt to overcome.

"Then return to your commands. We will wait for the others to come back across to return to camp, in case they have need for assistance," he ordered.

The boat crews cast off to retrieve the hapless men from the other side of the river. Sean returned to his men, who had managed to get a fire going, and reported what had been decided on. They all were thankful that the crossing was to be delayed, for even the heartiest among them were showing signs of fatigue from the struggle against the weather.

The men returned to their barracks after midnight, and once fires were lit in the stoves, many fell asleep still bundled up in their damp clothing. By morning the storm had lessened, and men came out of their shelters to start the cook fires for their breakfast. They stayed in camp that day to wait out the weather and attempt to communicate with the rest of the army.

Shortly after sunrise the next day, the division was on the march again. This time they marched to the river crossing a couple of miles north of Bristol and started across. The ice had broken up, and the crossing went well, including transporting the field pieces and horses across.

At one o'clock in the afternoon, when the last regiment was to start across, they received a message from General Washington and sent it across to Cadwalader. He had sent Washington a letter the day before, explaining that they had not been able to cross over the river but they were doing so this morning.

Once again the officer's call was sounded, and Sean joined them, gathered around a fire. General

Cadwalader held a letter in his hand as he read the news.

"Gentlemen, I have good news here from General Washington. His was the only division to make the crossing the other night, and yesterday morning his surprise at Trenton was complete. They defeated the Hessians and have brought back almost nine hundred prisoners, after killing or wounding a hundred others! The victory is complete." The men interrupted him by applauding and raising a cheer.

As the excitement died down, he continued. "However, he has returned to the Pennsylvania side and has asked us to do the same. Now that we are here, I think that we, too, should press the enemy and see what we can do," he explained.

"Why don't we proceed to one of the other towns being held by the Hessians?" a voice called out.

"They are entrenched in Mount Holly, Burlington, Bordentown and Crosswicks," Nicholas pointed out. "Any one of those places would make for a good objective, and we may be able to capture a good deal of their supplies at any one of those towns."

"I concur with the major," Colonel Matlack spoke out. "We need to get the rest of the men across and then move on to attack. There is no sense in staying here, now that we have finally gotten across. I say we move on Burlington; it was the least defended, as the last of our scouting parties had reported a week ago."

The discussion continued until all were in agreement to move on Burlington. It had a supply depot of the enemy; and also had the least amount of troops. The meeting broke up, and the men waited until the last of the division had come across the river before moving inland towards Burlington.

Sean was thankful that everyone agreed that they did not want to see all their efforts go to waste by returning to Pennsylvania without having done anything. He walked alongside his detachment as they made their way through the deep snow. The sky was overcast, yet it was not snowing, which lifted the men's spirits. They showed eagerness in their stride, now that they were finally on the way to strike against the enemy.

They marched on through the rest of the afternoon and halted long after dark while a scouting party moved closer to the town. The men had to make a cold camp, not wanting to give away their presence by the smoke of fires.

The scouts came back to report that there were no troops in the small town. Cadwalader ordered the companies to form into the column again, and they marched into the town. They marched to the other side of town and fell out to rest while Cadwalader and his officers questioned the townspeople. They told them that the Hessians had left earlier in the day and intended to move into Bordentown. There had been less than a hundred enemy soldiers in the detachment, and they had reports of the large American force headed their way, so they decided to fall back from Burlington.

Satisfied with what they had heard, the officers decided that they should move on to Bordentown at once and attack during the night. The Hessians most likely would not expect them to go that far since they had been on the march all day. Since Burlington had many barns, a meetinghouse and churches to use as barracks, it would seem that the Americans would stop for the night at Burlington.

The column of Americans once again formed up and headed off into the night towards Bordentown and a vast supply of military goods. The men had grown tired from the exertion of marching all day in the snow with very little food, and many had fallen behind.

Sean and Lanigan marched alongside their men, most of whom marched in the silence of total exhaustion. Their feet were nearly frozen from having snow encrusted on their feet as they marched. Many walked with their eyes shut as if they were walking in their sleep, the clouds of their breaths swirling around their heads as they moved onward. Sean swung his arms back and forth trying to get warmer, as the temperature had gone down since sunset.

"We should be there any time now, so keep it up, men. With any luck we should be able to bed down in some nice warm barns before much longer," Sean said to encourage them. He was impressed that none of them had fallen out. He had looked back earlier and had seen a large group of men who had fallen way behind the main body due to frostbite, hunger or fatigue. As he watched ahead, every so often one or two men would fall alongside the road until one of their comrades would come and help them back to their feet.

"Hold on now, lads. We seem to be stopping," Lanigan spoke softly. He looked forward to see the other officers and sergeants of the companies ahead of them motioning for a halt and silence. He turned his head as he heard several thumps in the snow behind him and saw that the men had literally fallen where they stopped.

"I'll go forward and see what is happening; stay here with the men." Sean ordered Lanigan. He made his way through the snow alongside the road and around soldiers who had fallen to the ground after the halt to take advantage of the break in the march to get a few minutes of sleep. He imagined that it must be at least three in the morning by now.

At the head of the column he gathered with the other officers; the faces that he saw all showed signs of near collapse. Cadwalader had sent a scouting party on into the town to find where the enemy was and to bring back a civilian or two who might aid them. The officers found an old fallen log to sit down on while they waited. Sean looked at his feet; he was glad that he had gotten his boots from home before they left Philadelphia. They were not much warmer than the uniform shoes; however, the tops were high enough to keep the snow from filling them.

He watched as many of the men nearby had to empty their shoes out, or unwrap the rags from around their feet that they used to keep the snow from filling their shoes and freezing their feet. He tried to take a drink from his canteen, only to discover that the water in it had frozen solid. The militia officer next to him saw that he was not able to drink, so he offered him a drink of rum from a flask that he produced from under his coat.

"Thanks. It's too bad we can't warm this up and add some butter to it," he said after taking a long drink and handed the flask back. His throat and insides warmed instantly as the liquid descended into his gullet.

"That would be just the thing to warm us all up inside!" the man replied as he took a swig and returned the flask beneath his coat. "When you get a chance to find some more, add it to the water in your canteen, and the water won't freeze," he offered.

They stood up as they saw twenty shadowy figures come running toward them across a snowy field. The scouting party returned with the news that there was only a small detachment in the town, according to what they saw and the people they had talked to. The enemy soldiers were housed in several homes of the families in the town.

"We're going to have to be careful moving in so as not to endanger the lives of the people whose homes the soldiers are in," Cadwalader warned the gathered officers. "I want some volunteers to go in as raiding parties to capture the Hessians as they sleep. That is the only way to ensure a minimum of gunfire so that we don't endanger the citizens of the town."

"My men are in good enough shape to go in there," Sean offered. A couple of others offered units of their commands also.

"Good. Now return to your commands and come back here ready to go in ten minutes. These gentlemen that the scouts brought back will guide you to the houses that the Hessians are staying in. As soon as you assemble your men, you can depart. Once you have secured the town and prisoners, signal us, and the rest of the column will advance into town," Cadwalader ordered.

Sean rousted out his men and returned with them ready to go. They had gotten their second wind and were ready for action. As soon as the other raiding parties were assembled, they marched out across the field towards the quiet town.

The night was silent except for the sound of the snow crunching under their feet and the occasional barking dog. They saw the silhouettes of the houses ahead, and only a few had candlelight showing from inside. The chimneys all had smoke rising from them; the scene was idyllic as they approached from across the field.

"Careful now, lads. We don't want to get any citizens hurt. Those going inside will use pistols and cutlasses only. This is going to be close work, and muskets won't be suitable for this. The others keep a watch out for any Hessians charging out from other houses or firing from inside others. Now let's be about this night's work," he instructed.

As they drew near the town, the other groups peeled off and went in different directions, all with a local guide. Sean's men came to the end of the street which they were to work. They split into two columns, one each on each side of the street. They had not gone far when their guide stopped them and pointed to a house.

"There's at least three in that house. It's an old couple that live there, and they are not happy having to shelter and feed those Hessians," the young man informed them.

"All right, I want three of you to go in on this one. Two more will wait by the door in case you need help. Keep it as quiet as you can. Get them bundled up, tied and gagged, so we can bring them along," he instructed Sheldon, George and Baum.

The three men passed their muskets to the others and checked the charges in their pistols. As soon as they were ready, they went to the front door, Hyland and Heinrich behind them as their backups.

Sheldon looked at Sean, and Sean nodded. Sheldon reached for the door, and it swung open. He and his companions charged inside quietly, and from outside they could hear muffled shouts; and a thud as someone hit the floor. Baum appeared at the door and waved.

The window was suddenly aglow from candlelight as the men inside trussed up their prisoners. They shoved three hastily dressed Hessians out in front of them, all bound and gagged. As they shoved them out to the end of their small column, an old man in his nightshirt appeared at the door.

"Take the dirty bastards out and hang 'em! They ate up half of our food that we had stored for the winter and gave us nothing but a hard time. Shootin' is too good for the likes of them! Thanks for taking them out of here!"

"We're only too happy to oblige, sir, keep whatever they left behind; you might be able to sell it to make up for your losses. Good night to you, sir." Sean said as he saluted the old man.

They went on to the next house, and the next. By the time they were done, they had rounded up fifteen soldiers and waited in the town square for the other detachments to gather with them.

They did not have long to wait. By four in the morning, they had made a clean sweep of the town, having rounded up eighty Hessians, including those standing guard. A runner was sent back to the waiting column to advise that the town had been cleared.

About half an hour later, Cadwalader and his division marched into town. The townspeople slowly came out to see what was happening to their town. They gladly showed the soldiers the warehouses and barns that the Hessians had used to store their supplies. There were no food stores being held here; however, the men were allowed to get whatever they needed from what was on hand.

The main body of troops took up position at the edge of town, after they had gotten what supplies they needed, and built fires to warm themselves. The sun was just coming up as they settled in around their fires.

Cadwalader and his aids conferred with the town leaders concerning what the Hessians had done to them and what stores they had left behind. He worked out a deal with several of the men who owned wagons to transport the goods back to the river crossing so that the supplies could be taken across to Washington's camp on the other side of the river.

Sean returned to his men after conferring with Nicholas and the other officers. He got in close to one of the fires that the men had built to warm himself. He looked around at his men huddled around their fires, cooking and eating the last of their food. He did not like to have to tell them what was in store for them now, as they were drained of all energy.

"Eat up, men, for the Hessians left no victuals stored here, and they had taken most of what the citizens had. The general has decided that we will push on toward Crosswicks, where there are several barns full of food that they had taken from the locals, along with several barrels of salt beef and pork that they had transported there for their army."

"Sir, we're pretty played out, with marching all day and night and having almost no food since yesterday morning. Most of us can go on, but I seen the way some of the militia boys have been dropping out all day and night long. I ain't sure that most of 'em are going to make it any further," Baum said as he took a bite out of his last biscuit.

"I have seen them too. There is a large group of those that fell out gathered on the other side of town where they stopped from fatigue. They will have to keep up the best they can, and those who are unable to move on will be taken care of by the townsfolk. How about you, lads? Have you all checked your feet for frostbite?" Sean inquired.

"I had them all show me when they had gotten warmed up a bit by the fires. They are a hardy lot, for none of them show any signs of frozen feet," Lanigan replied.

"Good! Get as warm as you can, lads, for we will be moving out in about an hour, as soon as they have the wagons loaded and on their way," Sean advised as he lay down with his back to a log.

He stretched out his legs so that his feet were near the fire, reached into his pouch and pulled out his last biscuit and dried beef. He took out the steel ramrod from his pistol, stuck the end in the ground by the fire and put the meat on the other end to heat it up. At least he would have some semblance of a hot meal before leaving. He ate his meal and settled back against the log.

"Sir, sir, wake up. It's time to go," Sean heard Lanigan say as he shook his shoulder. He got to his feet, a bit unsteady, and saw that the companies were falling into formation for the march to Crosswicks.

"I let you sleep as long as I could; I didn't get but a few winks me'self, but now 'tis time to move on again," his sergeant informed him as they walked over to the road.

The commands were shouted out and down the full length of the column. As one, the weary men stepped off toward Crosswicks. The sun had broken through the clouds, and the glare of its light on the snow was blinding as they marched.

They marched the four miles to Crosswicks and found no enemy there to oppose them. By noon, the men had gotten their shares of food from the stockpiles that they found there. The companies were assigned to several of the barns, meetinghouse and churches in the area for barracks. They gladly went inside the structures to get out of the cold wind and warm themselves by stoves or fires built inside the barns.

As soon as they had eaten, the men virtually collapsed, and sleep finally overtook them. The army stayed in the town for a few days while they waited for Washington to join them. They had gotten word that he had made a desperate appeal to his army to sign on for six more weeks, and Congress authorized the payment of a ten-dollar bonus for those who stayed.

He was successful in convincing half of his men to stay the extra time beyond the end of their enlistments. Once again he had an army, smaller, yet still an army. He intended to strike the British one more decisive defeat before they went into winter quarters.

During their recuperation at Crosswicks the men went out on regular patrols to gather intelligence. Cadwalader sent a force of militia to Allentown and Cranbury, only to find that the Hessians had left both towns alone.

One of the patrols led by Nicholas brought back word that the British were gathering a large force at Brunswick for the purpose of attacking Washington and bringing an end to the winter fighting.

"Well, Sam, do you think we'll ever get into a real fight with the enemy?" Sean asked as they walked out of the house where they had just attended another late night meeting of the officers. "We have done nothing but march all over the New Jersey countryside. The lads are getting restless; if we aren't going to fight the British army, they would rather get back out to sea on the *Osprey* capturing the enemy shipping. At least there we were making a difference to the war," Sean complained to his friend.

They had just been informed that they were to march the division back to Trenton to join with Washington's army. The officers had expressed their opinions of all the moving about the countryside and having little or no enemy contact.

"I think we're in for some hard times with the Lobsterbacks this time, Sean. It sounds as if Cornwallis is rather upset that the Hessians got so badly beaten; and is going to try to get his revenge before the weather gets any worse. It appears that Washington has upset his party plans for the winter," Nicholas laughed.

"Well, we'll just have to keep the old gentleman busy for a while. No sense in letting him enjoy himself in New York all winter attending parties," Sean replied.

"I just hope that the upcoming fight turns in our favor. The country cannot stand all the defeats that have happened this year and still hold out hope for getting our independence," Sam pointed out to his friend.

"The men are up for a fight, so we'll make a good accounting for ourselves," Sean promised. They had come to a barn that the *Osprey* marines had made their home. "I'll see you later, Sam., I have to break the news to my men now, and prepare for the march." Sean said as he saluted. Nicholas returned the salute and walked on to the house where he had been quartered.

Sean entered the barn and could see his men were already awake and nearly all packed to leave. He gathered them around and announced, "For those of you who have had not heard already by whatever means that rumors spread in this division, we are moving out to Trenton to join up with Washington. The enemy is massing an army at Brunswick, so we are joining forces with Washington to fight them," Sean explained as the men stood around him.

"More marching?" questioned Tyree. "I'll never complain about being crowded in the nether regions of a ship again!" he said, as the others both laughed at his remark and grumbled at the same time over the prospect of more marching in the cold weather.

"We move out in one hour, so gather your gear. Get as much hot food as you can, and pack as much as you are able to in your pouches before we leave," he instructed them.

"Yes, laddies, and be sure that you tend to your feet before we leave. It's warmer out there now, and the roads are going to be muddy, not hard as we've been marching on all this time," Lanigan said as he leaned on his spontoon. "That mud can suck the shoes right off your feet if you are not careful. This is worse than marching in the snow."

After the men had all eaten their breakfast, the men of the division once more fell into formation to march back to Trenton. They had gotten well rested and fed the last few days. At one o'clock in the morning on this, the second day of January 1776, Cadwalader's division of Marines, Pennsylvania woodsmen, and the clerks and shopkeepers of the Philadelphia Associators set off to the tunes played by the fife and drums in the lead of the column.

They had not gone far before the mud became their enemy. The snow was melting, and the roads were slippery, muddy mire that they had to pass through. Sean saw that the men in the companies ahead tried walking off the sides of the roads, but to no avail, as that bogged them down even worse.

He saw many men fall out and search for lost shoes in the mud. Several dropped alongside the road to tie them to their feet with rags that helped to keep them on their feet when they got sucked into deep mud.

Sean heard the men curse and fall, more fighting the mud than when they were marching through the driving snowstorms just a few days before. He hoped that they did not run into any enemy forces along the way, for this battle with the mud was wearing the men out faster than the snow did.

The column moved on slowly but steadily. Sean listened to the clanking of equipment, the curses of men, and the sounds of them slipping and falling in the mud. The scene in the darkness would have been almost comical if the situation had not been so serious.

The men struggled on for hours against the mud. Finally, as the sky was starting to brighten, they could see the town of Trenton and the campfires of the army in the distance. The men picked up their pace, seeing that their destination was less than a mile away. They marched through the camp of the Continentals, who were just crawling out of their tents and cooking breakfast.

Officers of the Continentals led the companies of the division to where they were to be quartered. The men fell out to build fires to cook their breakfast. Sean saw that they were plainly exhausted from the mud. He and Lanigan set up their own fire to cook their food.

They had just finished eating when they heard the staccato sound of drums being beaten to the call of *"To Arms!"* A rider galloped through the camps announcing that a British army was approaching the town.

Sean flagged the rider to a halt to hear what he had to say. "Cornwallis' army is out in force headed towards Trenton! Colonel Hand's Pennsylvanians at Shabakunk Creek have held them at bay for over an hour now, but they are getting ready to withdraw as more Redcoats are joining in the fight!" the rider explained excitedly. Having given this information, he moved down the road to the next units.

"Get ready, men. We will be moving soon. Take whatever hot food you can with you, since there is no way of knowing how long we will be engaged."

"Wouldn't you know it; here we have gone and marched all over bloody New Jersey looking for Lobsterbacks to fight, and now, just after we finally get some warm housing and get a chance to have a hot meal, the bloody bastards show up wanting to fight! There just ain't no justice in this war!" grumbled Calhoun.

"Stop yer grousing, Calhoun; you wanted to fight, now the whole British Army is headed this way to oblige you. What more could you ask for?" Lanigan laughed.

The others joined in while Sean took a slice of hot beef from the fire and juggled it in his hands, trying to cool it off. He saw Nicholas approaching, as he had just left the company to their left.

"Eat fast, gentlemen. We will be heading out in half an hour. We are to take up position in the field on this side of the creek, just beyond the bridge. The Redcoats are coming, and they mean business!" he said as he took a slice of meat that one of the men handed him.

He took Sean by the elbow and guided him away from the fire as he chewed the beef. "Sean, this is not going to be like what we have faced before. This is the cream of the crop; both British and Hessians are coming here. They are the best of the best. Your men have been in more actual fighting on board ship than the other companies have, so I want you in the center to act as an anchor for the others. They are less likely to run so the others will see them and take heart. We are to take up position in the field on this side of the Creek, just beyond the bridge. The Redcoats are coming and they mean business!" he said as he took a slice of meat that one of the men handed him.

"You sound a bit worried about this old friend; what are they saying at headquarters?" Sean asked.

"They all realize that this could be an important turning point of the war. If we do well, the ranks of

Washington's army will swell in the spring. If we do poorly, many of the men will stay home and not come back to fight the British. There is a lot riding on this today! We must drive the British back at all costs!"

"I understand; we will do whatever it takes to defeat them. The lads are fired up after seeing what the bastards did to the citizens of the towns and farms we passed. The bastards raped, pillaged and plundered the homes, businesses and farms of innocent people, even those still loyal to the Crown. The Hessians and Redcoats have turned more people in New Jersey against the Crown than ever before. They are ready to get even with them for what they did," Sean replied.

"Good, now go get them ready to move out. I'll see you after we take up our positions. Good luck to you and your men." They shook hands and Sean turned back to the men.

"Check your weapons and powder. Take extra food. Be ready, men. Today I feel that we will be earning our pay. Today, lads, we pay those Redcoats back for what they did to those people we saw hanging from trees, raped and beaten. Today, we even the tally!" he said loudly.

The men all cheered and shouted encouragement to each other. The camp turned into a scene of rapid activity as they all scattered to gather their equipment and load their pouches with food. By the time they finished, the other companies were just beginning to fall into formation on the road. Sean looked up and down the road. He could see the Associators, the other Marines, the Continentals and the other militia groups.

Once again they all stepped out in unison to be positioned for the upcoming fight. The men were both excitedly and nervously talking among themselves as they marched. They knew that they would soon face the best soldiers that Europe had to offer. There was plenty of reason to be afraid. There was also plenty of reason to be angry and stubborn, and that was what it was going to take to defeat the enemy today, Sean thought as he marched alongside his men.

He noticed that several of them were crossing themselves and mumbling prayers as they marched. They did not have far to go, and within an hour, they were formed up in their position in a field overlooking the Assunpink Creek. There was militia to their left, close to the bridge, and way to their right was General Mercer's men covering Phillip's Ford.

Sean permitted the men to fall out in formation as they waited. Far off they could hear the sounds of gunfire as Colonel Hand and his men fought to hold the British back. The other marine companies, as well as the militia, stood down as they waited for something to happen.

The gunfire ceased, and they kept their ears turned towards the wind to try to hear what was happening. Again they heard the sound of sporadic gunfire as the Pennsylvanians fought as they withdrew.

They soon came in sight of the bridge. The companies of militia came down the road headed for the bridge. The marines watched as Hitchcock's brigade charged across the bridge to take up positions to cover the retreat of Hand's men. As they got into place, the first red uniforms came into sight across the creek. As they marched down the road and cleared the tree line, the companies of Redcoats spread out to the right and left of the road and halted.

"It's good that we got 'ere in time to get front-row seats for the show, wouldn't you say, Sir?" Lanigan said as he stood next to Sean. The others gathered behind them as they watched the enemy soldiers falling into attack formation across the creek.

"They sure make a pretty sight, don't they?" said Tyree nervously as he gave up trying to count the hundreds of British and Hessians.

They watched and listened to the barely audible commands being shouted. Once again the Redcoats moved forward. The Hessians, in their blue and white uniforms also advanced toward Hitchcock's waiting men.

Sean watched as the last of Hand's men staggered across the bridge. It was apparent that they were about played out as they half-stumbled, half-walked across. Many men were being assisted by their comrades, but what struck Sean about them as they came across was that they walked tall, not like defeated men. These men had fought off the advance of the British for over three hours and finally retreated from fatigue and dwindling supplies of powder and shot.

"Look at them! See how they sway to and fro as they march all in step!" shouted Sheldon as he watched the enemy, mesmerized by the precision of their movements.

"Steady there, men. They are as afraid of dying as you are. This is more of a war of nerves at this point than it is a shooting match. That showmanship of theirs is to put fear in the hearts of their opponents," Lanigan explained.

"Yeah? Well it's working!" someone from the company next to them shouted, bringing a chorus of nervous laughter from those around him.

The men of Hitchcock's brigade opened fire with their rifles, as the men with muskets held their fire until the enemy got closer. Several of the Hessians fell to the ground. The Hessian Grenadiers were approaching them head-on with the British infantry on their right.

The advancing ranks of enemy stopped as one. The only sound for a moment was the fluttering of the battle flags. Suddenly, the stillness was broken by the sounds of commands being shouted, and the sound of several hundred pairs of hands slapping muskets as they shifted from shoulder arms to the 'Make Ready' position.

The militia across the bridge hurriedly fired off a volley toward the two groups of enemy, and through the smoke, several could be seen falling to the ground. They heard the command shouted by several voices; "Fire!" The whole of the enemy's front ranks disappeared in smoke as they fired a volley at the militia.

Many of the militia fell to the ground as they returned another volley at the British and Hessians. The enemy reloaded and advanced again, firing when they stopped within a hundred feet of the militia. They fired as the militia fired. Groups of men fell on both sides of the conflict. It appeared that many more British and Hessians fell, and their ranks crumbled and retreated.

Everyone watched as they regrouped and once again approached the bridgehead defenders. Both sides fired on each other again, and many of the militia broke and ran back across the bridge. The enemy retreated a short distance.

The British infantry charged the militia. Just before the lines clashed, artillery on the American side opened up, sending explosive shells down on top of the advancing light infantry. Once again they retreated.

Sean turned as he saw Cadwalader racing towards them on his horse. He reined the horse in and halted in front of the marine company to the left of Sean's. Nicholas stepped forward, and Sean watched as he spoke with the general. Cadwalader and his staff trotted off towards the other companies to the right of the marines.

"Marines, it's our turn now. We must hold that bridge!" Nicholas shouted. The company commanders called their men to attention, fixed bayonets, shouldered arms, and then ordered them to march at double time to the bridge.

Sean saw the looks on his men and saw the signs of fear. "Steady men, we will take up position across the river and drive the enemy back. They have had to march as far as you did this morning, so they are as tired and as fearful as you are. Don't crack; you've faced far worse from enemy broadsides, remember?" he encouraged them. He acknowledged those that shook their heads in assent and those that replied.

They started across the bridge. When they reached the other side, they slowed to the quickstep as they took up position in the center, while the militia broke to the right and left of them. This gave them a clear field between them and the Hessians, who were reforming en masse for another charge. Sean looked to see that the men dressed their lines. Lanigan was with the rear rank to watch for those who might break and try to run. He would be able to knock them down with his long spontoon.

Corporal Sinclair took the front rank and Beckett the rear. Sean stood in the middle of the front rank. He watched the Hessians, and then drew his pistols to check the priming in them. Satisfied that they were ready, he returned one to its holster and drew his sword with his right hand.

"Steady now, men, check your priming. They will be here directly, and you want to be sure to have a warm reception for them," he joked. The men laughed half-heartedly as they checked their weapons. Some poured extra powder into their flash pans to replace that which had been knocked out as they ran. They all kept an eye on the movements of their enemy to their front.

"Why are they just waiting? Why don't they just come ahead?" asked Sontag with his shaky voice.

"Stand easy there lad. They are just playing on your nerves while they try to get their own nerve back up to make another charge. This one will be a hard one. They have strengthened their center and will try to break the line right where we are standin'," Lanigan pointed out to them.

"They've been hit hard twice, men, while we are fresh; so if we hit them hard in return, they may break. Stand your ground and do not yield! Remember, those are the bastards who raped and beat those innocent citizens that we saw! Let's show them what happens when they attack those who can fight back!" Sean roared.

They stood motionless while they watched the Hessians. They appeared resplendent in their blue and white uniforms. They looked as if they were going on parade, not charging a stubborn enemy. Sean glanced down the line at Hitchcock's men. They had taken a beating, yet they appeared resolute, those who had not run.

He looked down at the ground before them. It was littered with the dead and the dying, weapons, canteens, and sundry other items strewn about. The snow that had not melted was stained a bright pink from the blood of the men who were hit.

A man lying on the ground at his feet stirred. Sean holstered his pistol and turned him over. His head had a gash on the right temple where a bullet had grazed him. He had regained consciousness, and Sean helped him to his feet. The man stood up, bent back down to retrieve his musket, then walked off, as he put his kerchief between his wound and his hat, to find the rest of his company of militia.

Sean watched him as he made his way to his company on unsteady feet. The man found his friends and took his spot in line with them. Sean admired the man's pluck. It was encouraging to see a man who was injured get right up and return to the fight. There was hope for them this day after all, with stalwart men like that here today. He hoped the others felt as he did. It was time to bring this to an end. It was time to drive the British out of New Jersey.

"Here they come again!" one of the others said. Sean turned to see the Hessians once again on the move. He watched as the whole body of men swayed in step, marching directly towards them as though they did not have a care in the world. He listened to the staccato beat of their drums and the shrill melody of their fifes as they came closer.

"Make Ready!" came the shouted command from down the line. The marines of all three companies snapped their weapons upwards. "Take Aim!" The muskets snapped forward as one.
"Fire!"

Sean leveled his pistol at the enemy and fired just as the muskets and rifles of his men discharged. They were enshrouded in smoke for a few seconds until it blew behind them. They looked at the advancing enemy while they reloaded. Those in the rank behind the front rank had quickly replaced those that had fallen in the front rank, so the wall of men headed toward them appeared unbroken.

The marines finished reloading, and as they prepared to fire, the Hessians stopped their approach and prepared to fire also. Both groups fired simultaneously and disappeared in a great cloud of smoke.

"Don't reload lads they are going to charge us with bayonets!" someone yelled.

"Charge, Bayonets!" Sean yelled out, without waiting for another command. The smoke from the Hessians had blown toward them after they had fired, blinding them longer than the Hessians. That is what they waited so long for! Sean thought. The wind had changed right before they started for them.

The men stood ready to receive the enemy, their weapons leveled, their bayonets pointed at the approaching men in blue. The Hessians came fast, yelling in German and smashing into the lines of the marines. They got no further, as the men held firm. Sean parried swords with an officer and swung around as he knocked the man to the side, drew his other pistol and shot him in the face.

The world around him had gone mad with men screaming from being stuck with the long blades, smashed by musket butts or trampled underfoot as they fell. The confusion increased as a militia company that had been sent over from the other side charged into the melee of marines and Hessians.

Sean had no time to shout orders as he fended off one bayonet after another. The blade of his sword snapped and it went flying through the air as he had brought it down on a bayoneted musket that was being jabbed right for his midsection by a maddened Hessian. Sean slammed the hilt of his useless sword into the man's face, sending him reeling backwards and underfoot of two men locked in mortal combat.

He drew his tomahawk and warded off another attack and dispatched the attacker with his hunting knife that he pulled from his boot sheath. He saw two of his men struck down, blood gushing from bayonet wounds to the chest and stomach. Lanigan was holding his ground with Calhoun, standing back-to-back covering each other. There were several Hessians on the ground around them as they slashed and parried with bayoneted musket and spontoon.

The fighting seemed to go on forever until someone shouted, "They're breaking; they're on the run!" Sean stabbed a soldier who had tried to club him with his broken musket. He whirled around as the man fell, looking for other attackers.

He stood for a moment with his chest heaving as he tried to catch his breath. He looked out over the field in front of their position, and indeed, the Hessians were running away. A cheer rent the air from the men around him and was echoed by the men across the creek.

Sean looked around him. There were bodies everywhere. Men in blue, men in green, men in the drab clothing of the militia, many of them moving as they cradled their wounds, calling out for help. It was a terrible sight to behold, and as he suddenly became aware of the stench of men's innards and blood spilled all around him, he felt the immediate need to retch.

His knees buckled out from under him, and he found himself on all fours, heaving his stomach empty. He was oblivious to what was going on around him until he could heave no more. He righted himself and tried to stand. He got to his feet and reached for his canteen.

He stood there shaking as he uncorked the canteen and took a drink. He swirled the water around in his mouth and spit it out, to get the awful taste of vomit from his mouth. Sean looked around and saw that he was not alone in retching, as several others followed suit.

He looked for Angus and saw the older man leaning heavily on his spontoon. "I'm gettin' too damned old for this!" he swore in his lighthearted tone as he looked at Sean. Just as he said that, he fell to his rump on the back of a dead man and just sat there looking around at the horrible sights before him.

The men started to come out of their trance-like state and began to search for their friends. "Get on your feet and form up ten paces toward the bridge," Sean managed to get out of his mouth.

Slowly the men obeyed. They searched for their weapons and equipment as they moved to the appointed rally point. Sean took a moment to take the sword and scabbard of the dead Hessian officer to replace his own broken one. He sized up his men who were attempting to stand in formation as he walked up. They appeared wretched. Lanigan walked up alongside of him.

"We have lost three dead: Sontag, Tyree, and Jarmolowski." He paused. "Eight more have wounds, but they can go on with us. This was a costly venture, but we held the day and beat those bloody bastards!"

"How are you, Angus? You look a bit pale?" Sean asked the old veteran.

"I've been better, and that's a fact! Here, sir, share a drink of rum with me. I can see in your eyes that you are starting to feel guilty for losing those men. There is nothing that you could have done to prevent that, sir; you must get that out of your head. It was their time to die, just as you will have a time. Here now, take a drink, the major is coming." He shoved the flask into Sean's hand and watched as he took a drink.

Sean handed the flask back to him as Nicholas walked up. "We took a beating here today, lads, but we showed them! Sergeant Lanigan, would you share a tot of that with me?" he asked.

"It would be an honor, sir, but don't drink it too fast; this batch took out the bottom of the barrel, so it may do the same to your gullet!" he laughed as he watched the major drink the rum.

"I see what you mean. That is not for the young!" he exclaimed as he fanned his breath and handed the flask back to Angus. "Sean, your men held the center against the worst of what the enemy had to offer, and for that I thank you. I thank all of you; you have all done a marvelous job here today!" he said louder to the men.

"What now, Sam, are we to move forward to go after them?" Sean asked.

"No, we will not pursue them; there is too much of a chance of an ambush. No, instead we will stay here and hold Trenton. We'll make them come to us. We have had enough marching around," he joked. "Now, move your men back to the other side and return to camp to rest. The others that were in reserve can take over here," Nicholas ordered. He turned and went to the other companies.

"Sergeant, form the men up, bring our dead so that we can bury them," Sean ordered.

The men gathered the bodies and the weapons of their slain comrades and marched back to their camp. They took the bodies to the cemetery and buried them before returning to their camp. Their feeling of loss for their dead friends overshadowed the pride that the men felt in defeating the stronger force of Hessians.

Once back at their encampment at the barn assigned to them, they fell out to rest. They stayed in camp the rest of the day, until sundown. The rest of the army returned, and Sean could tell that something was amiss.

"Lieutenant Taggert?" an unfamiliar voice called out.

"Over here," Sean called back. A sergeant came over and stood before him, where he sat on a pile of hay.

"Sir, I have orders for you and your men. You are to break camp and prepare to move out. It appears that Cornwallis and his entire force has arrived, and we are going to move out under cover of darkness to attack the remaining forces at Princeton. We are leaving behind men who will keep the campfires burning all night and make plenty of noise so that the British will believe that we are still here. Your men are to go with the main column."

"So, we are sneaking away from the main body of the enemy to attack his weaker forces. It sounds like General Washington is a cagey old fox," Sean replied. He dismissed the orderly. It made sense to fight on your own terms and not those of the enemy. Washington was making sure that he would have his victories for the winter by whittling away at the smaller forces of Cornwallis and avoiding a major confrontation when he was too weak to do so.

He got to his feet and gave the men their instructions. Within an hour they had packed up and returned to the road to march toward Princeton. "Sergeant Lanigan, are you up for a little stroll this evening?" Sean asked as he walked up alongside him. He noticed that he was favoring his left leg.

"Aye, sir, that I am. That little bit of rest did me a world of good, the lads too. One of those damned Redcoats sliced my thigh with his bayonet, which is smarting a bit, but other than that, I'm right as rain!" he replied.

"Cadwalader is now under General Greene, and from what I hear, Greene is quite the fighter. The army will be splitting in two when we get closer to Princeton. We'll cover the bridge on the Princeton-Trenton road in case the British try to break out in that direction. The other half of the army will attack Princeton from the east. We should be there about sunrise if the roads hold up as they are," Sean informed him.

"Yes, lucky for us that the cold has set back in and the ground has frozen again. Better to march in the cold on frozen ground than to be a little warmer and be on roads that have turned to mush like we have just done last night," Lanigan observed.

"Have you ever seen a darker night? There are no clouds overhead, yet it is darker than any night I have ever seen," Sean said

"Aye, it is uncommonly dark and that is for certain. It almost sends shivers up your spine, cold wind or no!" exclaimed Lanigan.

They marched on through the bitterly cold night. The column was halted in a field as the sky was showing the faint pre-dawn light. General Sullivan and his half of the army marched away, down the Saw Mill Road, while General Greene set off on the Quaker road. They were within three miles of Princeton.

"Listen!" Sean said to Lanigan, as he stopped him and cocked his head to one side. "Gunfire in the distance over there. Sounds like the ball has started," he exclaimed.

"That will probably be Mercer's men who are scouting in force in that direction, wouldn't you think?" Lanigan asked.

Before Sean could answer, Cadwalader galloped down the line, stopping at the company commanders shouting orders to march toward the sound of the battle.

"Look lively men, we are headed for trouble; check your priming and move out," Sean ordered. He watched as the men checked their weapons. He checked his pistols, and then ordered them to march along with the other companies.

As they crested a low rise, they could see Mercer's men before them, running for all they were worth, many stumbling along the way, some without weapons. The gunfire had stopped, yet they could see a large body of Redcoat infantry taking up a new position beyond where the main clash had taken place. The ground was littered with bodies, some crawling along a line in front of a small embankment.

"Form up to the right!" someone shouted from down the line. The Marine companies got on line to the right of the formation. Sean looked to their left and could see Matlock's men to their immediate left, with Morgan's men beyond them.

Sean stepped out in front of his company and could see the other commanders do the same. He looked to his left and saw Nicholas standing with the captain of the company next to him. He waved back as Sam tipped his hat to him. Sean looked at the men. They and the men of the other companies were nearly exhausted. They had marched all night two nights in a row, fought a major engagement and had had very little food to eat.

The artillerymen, who had taken over the guns that had been assigned to his men, wheeled the guns up in line with them and fired one round each. "Forward, March!" came the command. The brigade stepped off as one, arms shouldered as they approached the enemy from extreme range.

They watched the British as they approached them. They were busy reforming in preparation for the attack. Their every move appeared deliberate and well-practiced. They were well-trained and well-led, Sean thought to himself.

The artillerymen had hooked the cannons back up to their horses and moved up with the infantry. They were to set up their guns at close range to rake the enemy lines. Orders were shouted from down the line.

"Hear that, lad?" Sean asked as he turned to face his men as he walked backwards. "We are to fire and reload as we advance. Make ready." He waited to see that they obeyed. "Take aim, Fire!" he shouted as he turned to face the enemy to avoid getting any flakes of gunpowder in his eyes.

The men hurriedly reloaded as they walked; their first shots were fired at too great a distance and had little effect. The lines were halted so that they could take better aim. The brigade fired in volley and advanced while they reloaded. They advanced to within fifty yards and fired again; this time they stood in place as they reloaded. The artillerymen set up their guns and fired at the British.

The shells exploded behind the formation, and they adjusted the elevation as they reloaded. The brigade fired again, disappearing in a cloud of smoke. The Redcoats fired a volley, which tore through the ranks of the Marines and militia. Sean heard the screams of men torn apart by the musket fire that had ripped through their ranks.

The formation moved forward again as they fired, but were met by another devastating volley in return, with many more men falling, writhing in pain from their wounds. Sean saw that this was having a visible effect on the rest of the men. The cannons roared, the enemy fired again, and the men faltered and fell back.

"Steady, men! Hold your ground!" Sean shouted. Beckett and Sinclair shouted at the men and Lanigan tried to hold them back with his spontoon, but when they saw that the other companies had fallen back there was no stopping them.

The entire formation halted out of range and looked back at the enemy. They had come forward as the men had retreated and captured one cannon that was left behind by the panicked crew. Many bodies littered the ground between them and the enemy.

"What the matter with you, lads?" Lanigan berated them. "You faced far worse at Trenton. Why did you turn away here?" he yelled.

They sat and looked away from his stern gaze. Everyone was exhausted from marching two nights in a row, having fought a pitched battle yesterday, and once again under the gun, having had next to no food to eat in all that time.

Cadwalader came forward and tried to rally the men. The militia just sat where they were. Nicholas had gotten most of his men to their feet and dressed in ranks. Just then Sean turned and saw Washington and his staff ride up to the formation. He watched as the general talked to the men as he rode before them. Bullets hit the dirt just short of where they stood; the Redcoats tried to hit him. The men stood with their heads hung low, fearful of looking him in the eyes. Slowly the men got to their feet and started toward the enemy again, but as the two groups of men fired at each other, they fell back again.

Sean tried his best to encourage his men, but to no avail. They could hear the British taunting them as they hung back. Then the sound of cannons from atop the rise behind them startled them. Two guns were set up on the crest, and the gun crews started raining a deadly fire down on top of the Redcoats.

They watched as the formation of the British started to show holes in it as they weathered the cannonading. Bodies, packs, weapons flew into the air when the shots found their targets. A fresh brigade of troops came up from behind the brigade and halted in formation. They stood for ten minutes while the cannons mauled the enemy position.

"What say you, men? Look at them; with one more push, we can take the field!" shouted Cadwalader in front of the brigade. The men responded with a weak cheer and then shouldered their weapons.

The new arrivals took up position to flank the British left, while Cadwalader's men would press the center. Once again the formation stepped off, firing as it went. The cannons fired over their heads and they could see the shells explode amongst the British ranks.

They stepped over and around the dead and wounded men, a few who cried out for help, when they reached the first battle line and kept moving, firing and reloading as they went. The return fire from the British slowed and was less effective as they drew closer, as they had to fend off attackers from two sides now instead of just one.

The American line halted on command within ten yards of the enemy, and suddenly, the men just ran pell-mell straight into the Redcoat line, screaming madly at the top of their lungs. Most of the enemy broke and ran, while those who stood their ground were overwhelmed by the assault.

Sean's men ran right into a knot of about forty men who chose to stand and fight. They hurled themselves at the enemy, turning the scene into a fierce brawl. Sean ducked a musket that was swung at his head and fired his pistol into the stomach of the man who swung at him. He sidestepped another who had charged him and watched as Lanigan brought the blade of his spontoon down on the man's head.

He turned on his heel and sidestepped another bayonet, as the man charged past him and sunk his blade into the back of a Marine who screamed out in agony before Sean could run him through with his sword. Calhoun blasted three of them at point-blank range using his blunderbuss.

The sights and sounds of deadly combat surrounded Sean as he shouted to his men to keep fighting. He felt something strike his left arm and realized that a pistol ball had grazed him. Sean pulled his tomahawk and sent it hurtling into the face of the man who had shot him. The shouts and screams were deafening. As suddenly as the fight began, it was over.

The remnants of the vanquished threw their weapons to the ground and held their hands in the air. The militia and the reinforcements that had aided in the attack kept after the infantry that had retreated. They finally stopped when the orderly retreat of the Redcoats broke apart with every man running in his own direction. Many were run to ground and bayoneted; yet the Americans stopped when they finally became too exhausted to follow them.

Sean had the men fall in, to account for everyone. He looked around to see who was missing. He saw Sinclair sprawled on the ground, his hand still clenching his knife, which was stuck in the back of a Redcoat who lay across his body. Schmidt had fallen at the first volley of the British; a musket ball tore a hole right in his forehead as he walked next to Sean. Monacelli had taken a bayonet in the stomach and was lying dead, hands still clutching his gut, as he had tried to hold his innards from falling out.

The men of the brigade were too fatigued to go on, and many fell to the ground where they stood. With great effort, they took the time to tend to their wounded and bury their dead. As they attended to their tasks, a rider came up and informed them that the British had been pushed back to Nassau Hall in Princeton, and after two cannon shots, had surrendered. Washington had achieved another victory!

Instead of delaying at Princeton and having Cornwallis and his main army return and engage them, they took all the military supplies from the town that they could and marched to Somerset Courthouse, where they spent the night. The entire army was too exhausted to continue. The next day they went as far as Pluckemin, where they rested for two days.

As the men rested in camp, they were near to starving. "Lieutenant, the rest of the lads have agreed, we ain't above eating horse meat, and since we have one pack horse left, we don't want to wait no longer for the army's food to get here," Calhoun suggested as he stood in front of Sean and Lanigan, his uniform in tatters and hat in hand.

"Calhoun, I think that you are right," Sean said with a grin. "By the way, we were just talking about who should take Sinclair's place as corporal, and we have agreed that you are the man for the job. From this day on, you are now Corporal Calhoun!" Sean exclaimed.

"Now, sir, I don't think that I can..." he did not get to finish, as Lanigan stopped him.

"Laddie, ye have shown a good deal of leadership since we took you under our wing, so to speak. Sure, you were a bit of a pain when you first joined us, but you've gotten beyond that, and this thing is done; you are our corporal. Now go out there and see to it that the lads have a good meal of horse meat!" Lanigan interjected, as he took Calhoun's hand and shook it.

"Yes, sir!" He stepped back, saluted, turned on his heel and walked away.

"He'll do a fine job for ye, sir," Lanigan smiled at Sean.

"I believe you are right." Sean replied.

The men ate well for the next few days as they recuperated from the rigors of the cold, all the marching and the battles that they had fought. On the sixth they moved out again to Morristown, where Washington decided to make his winter camp. It was located on a plateau at Thimble Mountain and very defensible.

The marines were lodged at Sweet's Town, two miles from Morristown. There, like the rest of the army, they found it hard to obtain enough food to keep them fed. They went out on hunting parties to bring in what game they could, since the locals charged them exorbitant amounts of money for what food they would spare them.

Washington's army shrank when the men who had volunteered to stay on the extra six weeks went home at the end of January. "Sean, we have been given a new assignment," Nicholas announced as he sat next to Sean by the fire. "The artillery units have gone home for the winter, and that has left Washington with all his cannons and no one to man them. We have been chosen for that since most of the men have fired cannons before on ship. However, your men have the most experience, and I want you to make sure that all the men in the companies are trained."

"I'll do whatever I can, though I think Washington should release us to go back to sea again. I had a letter from Thomas that James had sent to us with some baked good and hams. He should have the *Osprey* ready for sea in at least another month, depending on the weather. They had delays, as the inlet froze up and they could not turn the ship to work on the other side," Sean replied.

"I know how you feel. We have done our part here and should be released for sea duty again. The general has other ideas, I'm afraid. I do not think he is in favor of keeping a separate force of marines. To him it is a waste of manpower for a separate force that should be released to the army instead. Cadwalader and I have had a few discussions with him on that subject, but for now he is adamant; we are to be the artillery until the men return in the spring," Nicholas countered.

"We'll get started in the morning then. How are the powder supplies for the guns?" Sean asked.

"They are well enough for a short campaign, so don't use too much in training," he cautioned.

The next day what was left of the three companies of marines turned to their new assignment. They were now to be under the command of General Henry Knox, Washington's chief of artillery. They relocated to Morristown and took charge of their guns.

Sean and Lanigan walked down the length of the artillery park. From the short, stubby barrels of the field howitzers on their carriages, covered with snow, to the squat mortars on their platforms, to the six and twelve-pound fieldpieces with their "Galloper" carriages and those that had the regular carriages, they had quite a few pieces to maintain.

For the first week, Sean and his men took groups of the other companies and trained them on the loading, aiming and care of the different pieces. They worked all day in the bitter cold learning how to lay in a piece on a target, and they practiced firing a few rounds with each type of weapon. After Nicholas was satisfied that the men knew how to handle the weapons, they positioned several pieces to cover the only approach to the encampment to protect against any possible enemy attack.

The men then started standing guard with the field pieces and did so for many cold, bleak weeks. Day and night, the Marines stood watch over the main approach to Morristown for an enemy that had finally gone into winter quarters, leaving only a few scattered, lightly defended posts in New Jersey.

The men endured the hardships of the cold winter, with barely enough food to keep them on their feet and barely enough warm clothes to keep them from freezing. Sickness took its toll, and many of the men suffered from the maladies associated with lack of nourishment.

February passed into March, and the weather started clearing. More supplies were able to reach the men, and their health improved. By the end of March, several of Washington's veterans, and several new recruits started to filter back into Morristown to rejoin the effort.

Nicholas came to Sean as he and Angus stood by one of the guns overlooking the road leading into camp. "Sean, a word, if you please." He turned and walked over to a massive, leafless oak tree. Sean followed him, and they sat on one of the large roots of the oak.

"Sean, things are not looking good for us to remain as an intact unit. Our strength is less than eighty men, and the general wants to split us up into other units. Some will stay with the artillery, but the rest will be divided into the other units as needed. I will soon command nothing," he said, trying to control his anger.

"I have spent all winter arguing this with him. However, he has the ears of Congress, and they are granting him almost whatever he wants. As soon as the enlistees all show up, and the army is ready to move again, I will be out of a job unless I take a commission in the army."

"That is terrible; how can they do this?" Sean asked. "What about us? The *Osprey* is almost ready for sea, and we should be rejoining her," he protested.

"That is the one bright spot in all of this; you may get to do that. You need to come with me to the headquarters to speak with a gentleman who has come here on the behest of the Congress. I do not know what he wants or needs, but he asked for you specifically. I managed to learn from the general's clerk; that the man is from the Secret Committee of Congress. If I were to venture a guess, I would say that you are about to be handed a special mission," Nicholas explained.

"Special mission? What could that be?" Sean wondered. The two got up, and after Sean waved to

Angus, they walked back to the headquarters. Sean waited in the anteroom, while Nicholas entered the general's office.

Sean saw the general when the door opened. He remembered the day outside Princeton when he rode up to encourage the troops to stand their ground. There was a presence about him that he could not explain, but it affected everyone around him in a positive way. Somehow, Sean thought, this man would achieve his final victory over the British, even if his army had to use rocks to do it.

Nicholas returned with a man dressed in riding clothes. He did not appear to be too pleased that he had to come way out here, away from the comforts of Philadelphia. "Sean, this is the gentleman that I spoke to you about. His name is not important; however, it is important for you to know that he is here representing the Congress and has the blessing of the general to make his request of you. Be assured that I will do all that I can to assist you in whatever you may need," Nicholas stated. He took a seat in the anteroom and turned Sean over to the stranger.

"I think it better if we go outside, Lieutenant. Walls have ears," the man said without any show of emotion.

The two walked in silence until they had gotten away from everyone, and the man stopped and leaned against the top rail of the fence bordering the road. "Taggert, I do not need to tell you that the war has not gone well, and we stand a very real chance of losing it unless we get assistance from the outside." He stopped to look at Sean, his eyes fixed on Sean's.

"We need the French. The French, however, are glad to see that their old foes are having such a hard time against the rabble we have put in the field against them. However, they are somewhat reluctant to join us. The aristocracy is understandably nervous that their people could rise up against them also. It would not be good for the French to see the monarchy of England toppled, for that could start revolutions against all the monarchies of Europe."

Sean did not reply but stood waiting for the man to continue. "We have had communications from them, and they have finally agreed, somewhat reluctantly to join us against the British. However, we must do something for them in good faith first." He paused as he stared at Sean again.

"And what may that something be, and how does that involve me?" Sean asked defiantly, somewhat irritated at the man's manner.

"Our sources have confirmed that your brother is within a couple of weeks of having his ship ready for sea. We have been keeping track of his progress, and have given him some additional aid. We want you two to take on a special mission, a rescue mission if you will, and that may induce the king of France to join us."

"Who are we to rescue?" Sean asked.

"It seems that a favorite cousin of the king and his daughter have become prisoners, or more appropriately, official hostages of the British, on some damned island in the Caribbean. It is his fondest wish to have them brought off by us to prove our good intent and worthiness of his assistance. He cannot send in his own men to rescue them, as that would be seen as an act of war, taking approved official hostages back, and the French public would not abide him starting a war. However, once the two are safely on French soil, he could be induced to join us," he continued.

"What of this island? Is it heavily defended? Where is the location of it?" Sean asked.

"For now, that is not for you to know. When the time comes and all is in ready, you will be given your final orders. Now your own detachment is somewhat depleted, so Major Nicholas has been instructed to give you as many men as you deem necessary. The island that the two are held on has a small garrison of troops, mostly local. They are there erecting a fortress, using slave labor, and the king's cousin is a doctor kept there treating the sick and injured soldiers and slaves. I cannot stress the importance of this mission enough. If we are to get the French to help us, you must succeed!"

"When do you want us to leave?' Sean asked.

"As soon as you and your men can get packed, you are to return to Philadelphia to gather what supplies you will need. You will then proceed to your brother's ship and set sail for the Caribbean immediately. The British may reinforce the island by summer, so we must act now! If there are no further questions, I must return to the city immediately, and I suggest you do so also." The man turned and walked away. He did not even reenter the headquarters, but mounted his horse and rode off.

Nicholas was watching from the window and came out. "Scary kind of fellow, isn't he?" he joked. "Sean, I know that you cannot tell me anything, and all I know is that you and your men are to leave right away. You will need more men to replace those that you lost, so I will give you enough to bring you up to a strength of thirty in all. That way, we'll get as many of you Marines away from the army as we can. Now go get your men ready while I go get your replacements from the other companies."

Sean walked back to their encampment, and after gathering the men, he told them of their good fortune. "Ah, it will be grand to feel the deck beneath me feet again!" exclaimed Lanigan. "Now, laddies, hurry and get ready, unless you want to lay about here the rest of your lives."

The men scattered, and noisily started to gather and pack their gear. They were all glad to be rid of this place and the army. They were glad to be going back to being marines again. "Angus, we'll let them get a good night's rest tonight, have a good meal in the morning and then head out. The major will have twelve men report to us as replacements later today. I'll want you to look after them and split them between Beckett and Calhoun," Sean advised his sergeant.

"Aye, sir, I'll look to them when they arrive. I'm sure that 'e'll send us proper Marines. They'll be replacing some very good ones! 'Tis a shame to have lost those lads, but ye done all that you could do to prevent it. There will always be those who don't make it back from the fray. Those were good lads, every one of 'em!" Angus mused.

That evening the twelve replacements, worn and tattered-looking, reported to Sean. They all came highly recommended, and he had no doubts that they would fit right in. Nicholas joined Sean at the fire in front of his "shack" later that night.

"I thought it would be appropriate to share a last drink before you set out tomorrow," he said as he poured rum into their tankards then sat on a log seat by the fire.

"This has been quite the experience, all this marching and winter warfare. I truly am surprised that we did not lose more men to the elements than we did," Sean said.

"Yes, it has been an experience, one that will give us many a tale to tell at our fishing club gatherings when this is all over. I cannot wait to get back to our favorite spots and bring in some fine fish on that new rod and tackle that I received just before I got involved in all of this," Sam replied.

"What are you going to do if Washington has his way and disbands the Marines as a separate body of troops?" Sean asked.

"I'm not sure. I suppose that I could take a commission in the army, or better yet, take over a Marine detachment on one of the Navy's ships, if any are still afloat when I get back to Philadelphia. They stayed bottled up in port all winter because of the British ranging all over the lower Delaware Bay," Nicholas answered.

"Well, good luck to you. I am eager to get back out to sea again. There is something fresh and invigorating about it that you do not experience on land," Sean replied.

"I know that feeling, and with luck will get out there with you again," Sam said.

The two friends talked over the fire until the rum was gone. They said their farewells, and Nicholas left to return to his quarters, while Sean stoked the fire a little higher before turning in for the night.

The next morning the marines had a big meal before they were to leave. Sean and Lanigan inspected the men in ranks when they were ready to leave so that they were assured that they had their packs set correctly on their backs, and that their shoes were in good enough repair to make the eighty-mile journey back to Philadelphia.

It was eight in the morning by the time they marched out the main road from the army's encampment. They had marched for a few miles beyond the camp when they came upon a group of sick soldiers going home. They were a bedraggled-looking lot; two men rode slumped over on the backs of two sway-backed horses, each pulling a travois with two sick men on each. The others limped along, using their muskets as crutches or being helped by their friends.

As the Marines came up from behind, one of the nags stumbled and fell, trapping its rider underneath its side and flipping the two men off the travois as it overturned. The others stopped and looked helplessly at their sick companions.

"Company halt!" Sean called out as he held up his hand. "You men come with me and let's help those men," he said as he turned to the first men in his column. They handed their muskets to the men behind them and dropped their packs.

The other sick men had stepped to the side and sat down while Sean directed his men in extracting them from the wreckage of the travois. When they had dragged them over to where the other men had sat down, they turned their attention to the man pinned under the horse. It took four of them to lift the horse enough for Sean and Lanigan to pull the man out from underneath the animal.

"Here, put the nag out of its misery while I tend to this man's leg," Sean said as he handed his pistol to Baum. Sean knelt down by the injured man as the pistol shot echoed across the surrounding field. He cut the cloth of the breeches up the leg to reveal a wicked-looking break. The leg bone protruded from the skin, and was bleeding. Sean tore the leg of the man's trousers further to get enough cloth to bandage the wound.

"Two of you come over here and hold this man down. Angus, break off a couple of sticks as long as his leg from that contraption so I can splint his leg," Sean ordered as he returned his attention to the man's leg. He had passed out, so the work would be easier. He pulled the leg out until the bone receded back into place and then tied the splints to the leg.

Sean stood up as the men wrapped the injured man in his blanket. "Sergeant, those appear to be wagons coming from the direction of the camp. They must be the supply wagons that showed up there yesterday and are returning to Philadelphia. We may be in luck." He turned and looked towards the sick men. "Where are you men headed?" he asked.

"Most of us live in Philadelphia or on farms just outside of town. How's my brother?" he asked.

"He should be all right. We'll have to keep him as comfortable as possible on the way back. My sergeant will get you men and us a ride in those wagons," Sean replied.

He looked down the road where the wagons had come to a halt where the end of Sean's company had stopped. Lanigan and the driver were engaged in a heated argument. He turned and looked at Calhoun.

"Get some men ready; those wagon masters may need your style of convincing." Sean directed.

"Aye, aye, sir!" Calhoun replied. He turned and went down the column, picking certain men and giving them instructions as Sean walked to the lead wagon and stood next to Lanigan.

"Sergeant Lanigan, is there a problem here?" he asked in a quizzical tone of voice.

"Aye, sir that there is. It seems that these 'gentlemen' are refusing to be gracious enough to give those sick men and us a ride back home. It seems that they were paid to haul goods to the army, but not to haul sick soldiers home with them." Lanigan said in an animated, and angry manner.

"Is this so? Will you not have the human decency to assist those men who are in need of a ride? They are sick and injured and may not make the long journey home without your help." Sean inquired. He stared hard at the man on the wagon. He was a greasy-looking man with wild hair and was bundled up in what appeared to be a bearskin coat.

"That's right, damn-it! We get paid for hauling loads for the army; we ain't no charity! We get paid for what we do, and no one rides these wagons if'n they don't pay us first!" He punctuated his statement with a long stream of tobacco juice that he spit over the side, and then he wiped the spittle from his bearded chin with his sleeve.

"Now that is not a very Christian-like attitude, would you say, Sergeant Lanigan? This man refuses to help those in need. What do you think we should do about that?" Sean asked with a smirk.

Without a word, Lanigan motioned to Julius Caesar Jones, who was standing on the other side of the wagon, and the two launched themselves up the side of the wagon and sat down on either side of the startled driver. Sean looked down the road at the other wagons and saw that Calhoun and his volunteers had repeated the action on the other wagons.

He looked up at the man on the wagon before him and tried not to laugh as Lanigan spoke. He had his left arm around the man as if he was his best friend. Jones just sat quietly, glaring at the man every time he turned his head to look up at the large, black marine next to him.

"Now, laddie, as I was saying before, those poor lads over there have been fighting hard all winter trying to make sure that the dirty Redcoats don't come to town and run you out of whatever little hovel you live in, take your horses and burn your wagons." He paused as he withdrew Sean's empty pistol from his belt, where he had stuck it after shooting the injured horse. He laid the pistol in the man's lap and pulled back the hammer.

"Now, as I was saying to you, what did you say your name was? Mister Blackwell, was it?" he asked as the man looked nervously to the pistol resting on his leg and nodded. "Good, then I'll be asking ye again, wouldn't you like to assist those poor lads and us marines get back to Philadelphia? Those poor lads may not make it back alive unless they have a ride, don't you see?" he smiled.

The driver looked at him, then turned his head and looked up into the fierce eyes of Jones next to him, who said nothing, but uttered a low, guttural, menacing growl. "Yes…yes, sure I would. The others would too," he stammered.

"Why, that's mighty charitable of ye, laddie! Good show! Now, you soldier boys, help your friends up and into this wagon. My lads will help you, if needs be." Lanigan called out to the soldiers who had gathered in closer to watch the drama unfold.

Sean directed his men and the soldiers until all the ones who could not walk were loaded in the back of the first wagon, and then the others were helped on board. He pointed his men to the other wagons, and within minutes the four wagons were loaded down with the two groups, and the remaining horse had been tied to the back of the first wagon.

Jones joined the others in the second wagon, and Sean took his place next to the driver, who had a pungent odor about him. The man was obviously so relieved that the big Marine was no longer menacing him, that he shook his reins and called out to his horses. The wagon jerked into motion. Sean and Lanigan looked at each other across the driver, who was slouched over as he drove, and winked at each other like conspirators who had pulled off a caper of sorts.

The procession moved on, stopping only along the way for the men to stretch their legs and refresh themselves. At each stop, Sean inspected the injured man and the sick men. The wound on the man's leg did not appear well at all by the time they stopped for the night. After the men made camp and prepared their meals, they made sure that the drivers were accompanied everywhere by two escorts and were not allowed to sleep off by themselves.

The next morning the man's wound looked worse. Sean cleansed the wound and changed the dressing. By the time they camped the second night, the wound had taken a turn for the worse. As soon as Sean unwrapped it, he smelled the smell that he feared-- that of gangrene.

"Angus, get some rum into that lad, and get the four biggest men to hold him down. I'm going to have to take that leg off or he'll be dead by dawn. He's burning up with fever now, and the infection has spread. As soon as you get him liquored up, Edward George and I will take the leg off at the knee," Sean said, somewhat unsteadily.

Lanigan turned to his tasks. As soon as they had the man sufficiently drunk, the four marines held him down while Sean and George turned their attention to the leg. Sean had the sharpest knives that he could find among the men and had held them in the fire for a moment to clean them. He had two men put the heads of their tomahawks in the fire to heat them for cauterizing the leg as soon as they were finished.

He tied a tourniquet around the leg and took a deep breath. He looked at George, who nodded, and together they proceeded to cut through the meat of the leg. The strap that was placed in his mouth stifled the man's screams.

They paused to tighten the tourniquet, then cut through the cartilage of the knee and pulled the bottom of the leg free. Sean called for the heated blades, and as soon as they were brought to him, he seared the flesh of the stump with them. The smell of the burning flesh was sickening; he could hear someone retching off to the side.

They wrapped the wound and stood up. The man's brother knelt by his side as soon as the marines who held him down stepped aside. Sean looked around and saw that Blackwell had been standing there watching him operate.

He walked past him and shoved his hands into his coat pocket to conceal their shaking as he brushed past the foul-smelling man. Angus stood there waiting for him, rum in hand. Sean took it and tossed his head back and drained the mug.

"Yer a hard man to figure," Blackwell said as he walked up next to Sean. "Them boys of yer's say that you fight like a bearcat, and yet you care enough fer strangers to do what you did back there and tend to the sick ones also. I figure I owe you boys an apology. You won't get any trouble out of me and the boys here on out. If'n they don't cooperate, I'll bust their heads meself!" He said as he held his hand out to Sean.

Sean shook the man's hand then turned and walked out into the night. He stopped when he had walked fifty feet from the wagons and looked to the sky. The moon was half full, and the sky was filled with stars. He stood staring at the stars as a shooting star went arching across his field of vision. He watched as the green-burning meteorite disappeared behind a stand of trees far to his left.

True to his word, Blackwell and his men were quite cordial the rest of the journey. The last morning of their trip, they awoke to find the injured man had succumbed to the infection that had spread throughout his body. Just miles away from home, he passed away.

The men gathered around the brother of the dead man and offered their condolences. Sean spoke a few words as they stood around the body. Since they were so close to the family farm, the brother requested that they take the body with them so that he could be buried with his family.

They reached the farm on the outskirts of town late in the afternoon. Five of the soldiers got off to stay with the family, and the rest continued until they reached town. Sean gave his men two days to visit their families, replace their clothing and meet at the Taggert wharf.

Blackwell deposited his passengers along the way, stopping at each one's home to let them off wherever they wanted to stop. Sean jumped off at his home after thanking him for his kindness. Angus handed his pack down to him and rode off to his home.

Sean stood in the street and looked up at the family house. It was good to be home after all that he had been through. It was good to be home, but he was eager to get back to the war at the same time. He shook his head trying to sort out his feelings, shouldered his pack and walked up the cobbled walk to his home.

9

The *Osprey* Reborn

Sean and Lanigan sat in the office with James, waiting for the men to arrive. They were to assemble at noon, and none had shown up yet at half-past eleven. "I'm concerned, Angus. How many do you think will come back? After what we all went through, I would not be at all surprised if they all decided to quit and stay home," Sean lamented.

"Don't you worry, sir. They'll be back; they will feel the need to come back, just as you did, just as I did. Once it's in your blood, it's there for life. The need for the challenge, for the fight, it grabs you like a wench and won't let go of you, no matter how hard you try to break free of her grasp. You'll see, they'll be here," Lanigan exclaimed.

Just then, Calhoun entered. "Good day to you, gentlemen. Some of the lads have arrived and are waiting," he said as he turned and went back out.

"Well, Angus, let's go see who we have," Sean said as he donned his hat and stood up. The two walked to the door, Sean not sure that he wanted to go out to see just how few had returned.
He opened the door and stepped out into the sunshine. There, just as Angus had predicted, stood the men of his company, standing in formation at attention.

"Sir, all Marines of the *Osprey*, present and accounted for!" called out Beckett, as he and Calhoun stood in front of the formation. Sean returned their salute, and the men let out a cheer. Sean turned to face Angus; somehow, he figured that he had set him up for this surprise.

"Welcome back, men. It's good to see you all again. We will be leaving as soon as you get your gear and the last of the supplies loaded onto those wagons. Yes, we get to ride again. The *Osprey* is still where we left her and should be ready for sea. All that I can tell you about our mission at this point is that it is of the utmost of importance to the war. Now, let's get loaded up and under way."

"All right, you 'eard the man, let's get moving!" Lanigan shouted out. The men broke formation and turned to the task of loading the last of the sacks and barrels onto the last two wagons. As they were doing that, Sean went back into the office and retrieved the packet of orders that had been sent over to him that morning from the Secret Committee. In it were their orders, maps and charts of the area where they were to go to for their mission.

He shook hands with his brother James and walked out the door. The men were finished loading the supplies and were climbing on board the three wagons in the front of the line. Sean climbed up beside the driver of the first wagon, who set his horses in motion the moment Sean sat down.

He glanced over his shoulder to look over the men in his wagon. They had managed to get replacement uniforms, which Sean had sent to their homes after they were delivered to the warehouse. The men looked far better than they had when they had reached town a few days back. That short time of good food and being with their families had done them all a world of good.

If all went well, they should reach the *Osprey* by nightfall tomorrow. They would have to ferry the men and supplies across the river to the hidden cove in the dark to avoid British patrols of the river. James had told him that he had reports of them coming way up into the bay, patrolling for rebels, and that many people would not venture that far down into the bay to avoid losing their ships.

The early March weather had turned cold again but remained clear of foul weather. Sean held the packet of orders close to his side in his pouch. He resisted the temptation of taking them out and reading them before he reached the ship. The packet was heavy, and he heard the jingle of gold coins in the packet. There appeared to be a lead bar in the packet also, to aid in sending it to the bottom of the sea if they were in danger of being captured.

They rode on, Sean making small talk with the driver and listening to the men behind him in the wagon swapping stories and bragging of their exploits and conquests. The question of their mission came up a few times during their talks, and Sean just smiled and told them they would be warmer where they were going and nothing more.

Their journey was uneventful until the next day. Late in the afternoon, they approached a small brook that the road passed through, as it was no more than hub-deep. As the lead horses stepped into the cold, clear water, a red-coated figure stepped from behind a tree along the bank, startled at their approach.

"Halt!" he stammered as he raised his musket. Sean pulled a pistol from his belt and fired. The powder in the flash pan ignited, but the charge in the pistol failed to discharge. The red-coated marine fired his musket, and the same happened to him. Before he could recharge his musket, Sean threw his tomahawk, which struck the man in the head with the blunt end.

"Load your weapons, men, and be prepared!" Sean called over his shoulder as he leapt to the ground. He retrieved his weapon from the ground, and as the hapless marine tried to get to his feet, Sean smashed him in the face and sent him reeling backwards, unconscious. He heard a shout from downstream and noticed several figures along the bank of the brook about a hundred paces away.

"Take the wagon across the stream. Men, fire as you see the targets downstream," Sean ordered. They had stumbled on what appeared to be a watering party filling casks with the fresh water of the brook. Sean could see a ship in the river beyond the trees that lined the riverbank, another hundred paces further. The first wagon lurched forward into the stream, and as the wagon got to midstream, nine muskets and rifles belched out a cloud of smoke.

Sean watched as the sailors and marines downstream ducked for cover behind their water kegs and boats. They returned fire, and their shots went wild, most falling short of where Sean stood. He climbed onto the back of the lead horse of the next wagon and rode him across. The men of that wagon and the next all fired on the water party, a few of which fell to the ground, hit by the shots of the few rifles in the last wagon.

Sean climbed off the horse on the other side of the brook and ran to catch up with his wagon. A cannon fired from the ship sent a ball sailing over their heads. It crashed into the trunk of a tall elm tree. The top half of the tree plummeted to the ground, snapping branches off trees next to it as it fell.

"That should be the last of them; we'll be under the cover of trees the rest of the way," Sean exclaimed as they traveled on. The presence of the ship bothered him. He had seen that it had been headed upriver; however, it was likely that they would need to watch for it coming back down past where the *Osprey* was hidden. The road paralleled the river at a distance, so it was unlikely that the ship or crew would be of any further threat to them as they traveled.

The rest of the trip was uneventful, and an hour after dark, the road took a sharp turn towards the river. It ran alongside it for a stretch of a mile then turned away from it again. Sean recognized where they were. The hidden cove was directly across the river.

"This is the place, sir, we have been unloading our cargoes here for your brother's men to row across to pick them up. Just go down to the bank and call out to them; there is always someone on guard over there. If you would, have your men unload us fast, for we want to get far away from here before we camp for the night," the driver explained to Sean.

"Thanks for your help. Sergeant Lanigan, get the men and supplies unloaded here and stage them over there in the trees by the river," Sean ordered. He shook the hand of the driver, then walked through the trees until he stood on the riverbank.

"Hallo! This is Sean Taggert. I need a boat!" Sean called out just loud enough for anyone on the other side of the river to hear. There was no reply and no lights that he could discern. He stood and listened. He could hear the rustling of leaves and then the slow dipping of oars in the water. He tried to focus his eyes in the dark, and could just make out the outline of the cutter coming across the river.

"Lieutenant Taggert, I thought I recognized that voice. It's me, James Cameron!" a voice called out softly as the boat ground to a halt in the mud at the water's edge. Cameron stepped off the bow of the cutter and strode over to Sean and shook his hand.

"It's good to see you again, James,. How is it with the crew and the ship?" Sean asked.

"Aye, it was a terrible hard time of repairing 'er but the old lady is fit and ready to get back to sea. The weather kept us from being able to work on 'er, for a few weeks, but we made up for lost time. We just have to load what is left of the supplies and the guns, and we're ready to go," Cameron appraised him.

"Good, I think my lads have had enough of playing soldier to last them the rest of their lives, and they are eager to get back to sea. We have a load of supplies and thirty of us to get across the river. We had a run-in with a watering party of a British ship, earlier so we must take care not to get caught in the open." Sean warned him.

"We've managed to stay hidden from their patrols all winter, so don't you worry, we'll have everyone and everything ferried over in no time. Now let's get you and some of the men loaded and across. We can bring the launch back across with us and get things moving faster."

Sean and several of the men climbed aboard the cutter and shot across the river. There they stowed their equipment in the woods and helped to bring the launch down to the water and row it back across to bring off the rest of the men and supplies between the two boats.

While they were doing that, Sean picked up his gear and followed the path through the trees to the cove. There, in the light of the stars, he could make out the outline of the *Osprey*. It was good to see her once again. He wound around the beach and came to a halt in front of the makeshift huts that the crew had lived in all winter.

The men all rushed out to greet him, and he tried to answer all the questions that they threw at him. He sought out his brother and embraced him when he walked over to him. "It's good to see you again Little Brother!" Thomas said as he looked at him. "You're a mite scrawnier than when you left here, but the rest of us are too. Now that you and your men are here, we should be able to get under way a lot quicker. We have to load everything back on her, and then it's off to sea! I suppose that you have our orders?"

"Yes I do. They told me that they had briefed you on the mission. I haven't opened these, as they instructed me not to open them until we are under way so that no one would know of their contents. We will have to be careful the next day or two, for we had trouble with the crew of a British ship upriver earlier today," Sean explained.

"Yes, we watched her go by. It's a frigate patrolling the river. There is one a week lately. I think that word may have gotten out about us, and they are trying to hunt us down, so the sooner that we get out of here, the better. We should be able to finish up tomorrow with the help of your men," Thomas exclaimed.

"Good, Then we will get started first thing in the morning. How are we fixed for powder? They could not spare us any when we left. All that we brought is in our powder horns and flasks," Sean replied.

"We have barely enough for one brief fight. Most of our powder got soaked. There are several barrels of it all dried out, but I don't think that it is any good," Thomas answered.

"Has the redoubt at Cape May been reinforced? If not, we can raid it on the way out of the bay," Sean suggested.

"No, I think that they have just a small detachment there to man the guns. That is a good idea, but we will have to make it a night raid," said Thomas.

"Then it is settled. We will get the provisions and guns back on her tomorrow and time our departure to reaching Cape May after nightfall. We can set my lads loose in the boats to attack them from behind, while you sail by and create a diversion with what little powder we have left. That should work. The lads are eager for a fight, and after what they've been through, they should do quite well," Sean offered.

Sean walked around the narrow beach at sunrise to get a good look at the ship as daylight grew. He admired her sleek lines, the crossed yards with their sails tightly tied, and the fresh paint all around. It looked like a new ship, not like the battered hulk that they had muscled into the cove so long ago.

He looked over at what remained of the *Daphne*. Her masts and yardarms were gone, having been put to use on the *Osprey*, or served as firewood for the crew as they braved the horrid winter weather. Great sections of decking and sideboards had been removed, and the ship looked worse than the *Osprey* had.

Sean spent the day with Thomas, overseeing the sailors and marines as they toiled all day getting the casks of provisions loaded below decks. The sacks of fresh food were stored with care. By late afternoon, they started conveying the cannons over to the ship. They were taken apart and reassembled once they were on deck. The work lasted until well after dark. The men were able to set up their berthing area on board the ship for the first time since they had put into the cove so long ago.

They were crowded below decks with the extra marines, but they were able to make due, as seamen generally did. Sean set up his possessions and equipment in his cabin once more. It felt like being home again after all this time. He took dinner in Thomas' cabin with Doctor Faircloth, who had spent the winter with the crew, tending to the usual injuries and sicknesses that always plagued the crew of a ship in inclement weather.

Thomas and Sean finally broke open the packet containing their orders and studied them after the doctor had been excused. The three-page document instructed them to proceed to an island just north of Anguilla, known as Scrub Island. The British were building a stone fortress there, which could harass ships headed for the other islands of the Lesser Antilles.

There the cousin of the French king and his daughter were held as "official guests." Doctor Maurice Dubois and his daughter Monique tended to the health of the people, garrison and slaves involved with the construction of the fortress. They were housed in a plantation mansion that the British officers used as their quarters.

The two were kept under guard at all times, even when tending to the sick slaves, many of whom were American prisoners of war. There was a small village on the island that served as a small harbor on the west side of the island. The eastern side of the island faced a smaller island, more a sand spit covered with vegetation. The smaller island formed a sheltered lagoon with an opening at either end, barely navigable at high tide.

Their orders instructed them to capture a small vessel, a schooner, or sloop and go to the island in disguise, spirit the two French nationals away, and if possible, blow up the fortress before it was completed.

"It says that the British force on the island is composed mostly of provincial troops overseen by a corps of regulars. There are at least two hundred troops present. The fortress was only half complete, with the walls facing the ocean finished and some of the long-range guns mounted. Sounds like a walk in the garden for my lads!" Sean said sarcastically.

"The real problem will be in staying clear of the British Navy," Thomas said. "We will be sailing through their territory and will need to be on the lookout day and night on the trip there and back. If there is a weak spot in all of this, getting around their ships is it," Thomas pointed out.

The two talked over their orders and the plans for obtaining powder from the redoubt at Cape May. They would have a busy day tomorrow, making last minute adjustments to the trim of the ship and the rigging. They would be leaving shortly before noon, which would put them at Cape May right about sundown.

The next morning, Sean went on deck as the sun was coming up. He looked up at the rigging, which was wet with the morning dew. The water in the cove was obscured by a layer of steam rising from it to a height of about two feet above the surface of the water.

He turned and saw the lookout up in the top of a stately oak tree by the river's edge. He was moving about, so Sean knew that he was awake. The ship seemed to come alive as the crewmen and marines started to come on deck to stretch their legs.

He looked over at the floating logs that they had chained together across the opening where the stream flowed into the river. There was quite a pile-up of river debris on this side of it, and they would have a difficult time clearing it out of the way for the *Osprey*.

Sean went below to eat his breakfast and discuss with Lanigan who would be assigned the task of clearing the entrance of the cove. Depending on the situation, they might have to blast the debris to clear the passage. If they would have to do that, it would deplete them of most of their powder.

"I'll take a look at that mess as soon as I get the lads going on their assignments. Calhoun and Beckett can watch over them then," Lanigan suggested to Sean.

As soon as the men were fed, they turned to the last remaining tasks for getting under way. The last of the provisions were brought on board, the lashings on the guns were completed, and the rigging was checked and rechecked. Thomas got in the cutter and had the men row him around the ship, fore and aft, so that he could inspect the trim of the ship.

He shouted a few orders to Cameron, who in turn relayed them to men waiting below to move some of the ballast and cargo to adjust the ship's trim. While this was taking place, Sean had joined Lanigan as he inspected the camouflaged entry to the cove.

"It looks like we'll have to blast 'er loose. There's just too much in there to shake loose; some of those logs are dragging bottom and won't float loose. I had the lads break the chains on shore, but nothing has moved. Let's go check the old powder kegs to see how much might yet be usable," Lanigan told Sean.

The two walked to the far end of the beach, where several casks of the unusable powder had been stacked. Carefully, Lanigan used a wooden mallet to knock the end off a few of the casks. The powder that had been inside had long ago gotten soaked and was now all a black, caked-up mass.

Lanigan broke off a chunk of the caked-up powder and turned it over in his hands. "There's only one way to find out if it is any good," he smiled. He broke off another chunk from a second cask and walked over to the nearest fire.

"Stand back," he cautioned Sean. Sean watched as Lanigan stood ten feet back from the fire and lobbed the black chunk onto the fire. It sat in the flames for a few seconds, then a large puff of white smoke flared up without a sound. He then tossed the second chunk in the fire, and it flared up sending a cloud of smoke billowing upwards.

"That second barrel still has a kick to it, so if there are a few like it we can add it to the good powder and get a bigger kick out of it without having to use all of the good powder," Lanigan surmised.

"Good. Take however many men you need to test the rest of it, and get it into place with a fuse. We will wait until it is time to go before setting off the charge, so that we can be under way before any guests show up. The British ship has still not come back downstream yet, so we may have to contend with that yet also," Sean instructed.

He assisted Lanigan and his work party rowing the kegs of powder to the raft and getting them put in place. Even with the gentle current of the stream pushing against it, it did not budge, being anchored to the bottom with so much of the debris that had piled up.

As he held the dinghy steady while the men worked on the raft, he turned to see the cutter glide by, the men in it pulling against the oars, hauling a cable from the ship to the shore of the stream. There they disembarked and secured it around the base of the largest oak on the bank.   They would have to pull the ship out from the cove to the confluence of the stream and river by the use of the capstan and anchor cable. There was not enough wind in the cove or push from the stream to move it out into the river.

The work was finished by midday, and after the men were fed, it was time to get under way. Sean and Thomas stood by the helmsman, both eager to get started. Most of the crew stood at the capstan bars, ready to start pushing against them to move the ship.

Others were at the ready to set the jib and topgallants as soon as they were clear of the cove.

Lanigan and Calhoun were in the *Daphne's* dinghy, ready to light the fuse to the powder that would clear their way. They were all standing, waiting for the lookout ashore to climb down from his perch in the tree and return to the ship.

Thomas gave the signal for the fuse to be lit. They watched as Lanigan leaned out over the edge of the boat and stuck his portfire in among the branches of the debris. A white plume of smoke rose as they pulled at their oars in eagerness to get away from the raft.

All eyes were upon the lookout as he started to descend. He stopped his descent suddenly and went back to the branch where he had stood his watch. "Deck below! I see the tops of masts moving through the trees up around the bend of the river! It's British!" he called out and then rapidly started his climb down.

The words sent the men into action. Sean raced to the bow of the ship, shouting orders for his men to man the starboard bow guns and the second squad to get to the fighting tops with rifles. The ship was at least two hundred yards upriver, and they would have to come out of the cove fighting.

Marines ran to their stations as Calhoun and Lanigan climbed up the side of the ship. They were followed by the lookout, who had raced across the beach and ran out through the cold water to get to the ship. The men at the capstan took in the slack and stood poised, ready to start the walk around the capstan and pull the ship from the cove.

The silence of the cove was shattered by a deafening blast. The entire mouth of the cove was shrouded in smoke and falling debris. The old powder had had the desired effect, and as the smoke rose from the surface of the water, they could see that the entrance had been cleared.

"Quickly men! Put your backs into it!" Thomas yelled. The men at the capstan all gave a collective grunt as they threw themselves against the capstan bars. The deck at their feet had been covered in sand so that their feet could gain traction.

Ever so slightly, the ship started moving out into the cove. The sound of the explosion echoed around the cove and out across the river. In the distance they could hear the staccato beat of a drum calling the enemy crew to quarters.

"Starboard guns manned and ready, sir!" shouted Beckett as he saluted Sean.

"Good! Remember, men, you will need to make every shot count. We do not have enough powder for a prolonged fight. Aim right at her bow, right at the water line," Sean ordered. The gun crews acknowledged his order.

The smoke of the explosion hung in the air at the entrance to the cove, and Sean turned to see the jib boom disappear into it as the ship neared the entrance. "The enemy is rounding the bend!" shouted the masthead lookout.

"Calhoun, get up there and tell the sharpshooters to mark down the gun crews as soon as they are in range," Sean ordered.

Calhoun acknowledged the order and scampered up the rigging to take charge of the men in top. "This could be a close one, sir." Lanigan said as they disappeared in the smoke. The ship seemed to take forever to pass through it, but finally the sunlight broke through and Sean could see upriver where the enemy ship was finishing its turn around the bend.

He turned when two sailors ran up from behind with boarding axes to cut the cable to the shore. The sound of the axes biting into the cable was replaced by the sound of two cannon shots from the enemy ship. The shots were hastily fired and went wide, one landing in mid river, the other crashing into the forest.

"Get ready, men. Fire as your guns bear," Sean instructed them as he stood behind the crew of the first gun. The gun captain had been kneeling behind his gun, aiming it as if it were a musket. He stood up, stepped aside, and touched his portfire to the touchhole of the gun.

The gun roared out, and crashed back against its tackle. Their view was obscured by smoke, and when it cleared, they could see a white plume just a few feet in front of the bow. The second crew fired, and they saw the ball skip across the water and slam into the bow of the ship right above the water line.

The enemy ship fired two more shots, this time landing closer together, short of the *Osprey*, which was gliding out into the middle of the river. The crew was busy aloft setting the jib and topgallants, trying to catch the small amount of breeze that was moving.

Sean's crews fired again. This time both shots struck the enemy ship, one at the water line and the other punched through the hull, a few feet higher just to the right of the prow. The ship seemed to stagger for a moment. Sean stood watching the ship as his gun crews reloaded. Slightly at first, then suddenly and violently, the foremast of the ship swayed against its backstays. It jerked to the left, and then fell to the right, crashing down, tearing up a great portion of deck, and entangling itself in the trees along the bank of the river.

The ship heeled over slightly, which put the shot holes under water. One more gun banged out across the water, sending up a waterspout twenty feet from the starboard side of the *Osprey*. Overhead, the rifles of the marines barked out at the scurrying figures on the deck of the other ship, which was just over a hundred yards away.

"Fire once more at them and put a couple of more holes in their side to hasten things along," Sean ordered. He stood to the side as the guns spoke out one more time. Both shots found their mark in the port side of the foundering ship. The crew hung on the rigging and stood along the railing, watching the ship as it filled with water as the stern started to swing around towards them, the bow having been affixed to the shore by the foremast.

The men let out several cheers and shouts at their adversaries, relieved that they had achieved such a quick victory over a ship that outmanned and outgunned them. Sean felt pride well up in him and found himself shouting along with them as he realized that they had just sunk a frigate of eighteen guns in such a short fight. *This was a good beginning to our mission,* he thought to himself.

The men aloft set the rest of the sails as the ship turned south in the middle of the river. Freed of the confines of the sheltered cove, the sails filled at once with the breeze blowing from upriver. Combined with the flow of the current, the *Osprey* took flight again for the first time in months.

"It feels good, having a deck moving under foot again doesn't it Sir?" Lanigan asked as he came up alongside Sean, who was leaning on the railing looking out in front of the bow.

"It sure does, Angus. All those weeks of marching in the cold, freezing weather with so little food, all of that just seems to have vanished as if it never happened as soon as the current took hold of her," Sean exclaimed.

They stood watch at the bow, enjoying the view as the ship made its way down the long river. The trees were showing the signs of new leaves starting to spring forth. Even the grasses, bushes and plants were starting to show forth a new life after such a harsh winter.

Sean turned to watch the men as they moved about the ship. There was a jaunty, new animation to them, fresh from such an easy victory. They were all ready to be rid of the land and for what lay ahead of them. There was a lot of speculation floating among them as to where and what their mission was, but none of them had guessed the true purpose of their journey.

Time seemed to melt away as they floated downriver. Sean looked at the empty boat tier as the ship's boats were being towed astern in readiness for their night action against the redoubt at Cape May. It was getting close to sunset, so the two went aft to have the men fall in with their weapons and equipment for inspection prior to them disembarking.

They would leave the ship and row ashore a mile upriver from the fort. The *Osprey* would continue on, after giving them enough time to march to the fort.

Then the ship would be sailed close enough to the fort to fire shots at it, to attract the attention of the defenders. That would allow the marines to get in close enough to attack them from behind and capture the badly needed store of gunpowder.

"Listen up now, men," Sean said after the inspection. "We will march overland about a mile and come up to the fort from behind. The *Osprey* will fire two broadsides at the fort to get their attention, then we will charge in on them. I will take the squad that will come straight in from behind, and Sergeant Lanigan will take the squad to come in from the right. We will press them forward and left out of the fort."

"Both patrols will be in two ranks, one rank fires, then the other advances and fires, and so on until we get close enough to rush them or they surrender. The half-moon will be overhead, so we should have enough light to see. Be loud, to make them think there are a hundred of us. The surprise of the bombardment, followed by the surprise of our attack, should scare the blackguards into surrendering. Once they see the glint of the moonlight on your bayonets, they'll lose the fight in them," Lanigan added.

"The artillerymen will not be armed, only the contingent of infantry there will have their weapons. If there are no questions, then get down into the boats; it's time to go ashore," Sean instructed them.

The men filed over the side into the two boats that were manned by sailors. "As soon as we recover the boats, we'll set sail to bombard the fort. As soon as we fire the second round, we'll turned seaward to get out of their range until you fire the signal rocket for us to come back," Thomas said to Sean at the side rail.

"We should be in place about thirty minutes after we get ashore. From what I recall of the terrain, it should be easy going to get to the redoubt. Just be sure that your lads don't over-fire the fort and hit us," Sean replied.

"I know that they haven't had the experience that your men have at the guns, but they learned well from your boys, so don't worry," Thomas reassured him.

Sean climbed down the side of the ship and stepped down into the rocking boat. His foot slipped, and he would have fallen headlong into the water if it hadn't been for several hands reaching out and grabbing his coat.

"Can't have me showing up wet for the party now, can we?" he sheepishly joked as he took his seat in the stern sheets. He heard several laughs and turned his attention to the outline of the shore.

Minutes later the cutter slid to a halt in the sand of the beach. The men quietly climbed over the side, and once they had their equipment, pushed the boats back out for the sailors to return to the ship. Once the men were formed into two files, he and Lanigan led off into the brush with Edward George out front scouting the way.

Sean had fished and hunted along here several years earlier, and the landscape had not changed much. They followed a game trail through the brush and trees that led to the point of Cape May. They had marched for about twenty minutes when George appeared on the trail in front of them.

"The fort is just through those trees. I stumbled over one of the sentries sleeping at his post at the head of the trail. He will not be bothering us tonight," he said as he ran his finger across his throat. "All is quiet in their camp. I only saw two other sentries, and they were looking out to sea."

"Good, you go with Angus and get his squad into position; I'll take my squad and get them lined up just inside the tree line. We should be hearing the cannons from the *Osprey* any minute now," Sean said. The two groups split up, and within a few minutes Sean's men were in two lines, just inside the trees and brush.

Sean flinched as he heard the broadside fired by the crew of the *Osprey*. Three of the shells exploded short of the redoubt and two just inside. The camp became a scene of pandemonium as men leapt out of their tents, weapons and clothing in hands, as the drummer beat out the call to arms. Soldiers ran to and fro as the second round of shots were fired. This time, two fell short, one exploded on the rampart, and one flew over their heads and exploded into the trees behind them.

"Damned glad they ain't goin' to fire anymore rounds like that one!" a voice said in the dark.

"All right, men, advance!" Sean said. They stepped into the clearing and stopped. The first rank stood and fired at Sean's command, and then the second rank stepped forward and fired as the first rank reloaded.

Sean looked to his right and could see Lanigan's men doing the same. "One more time now, lads, and yell at the top of your lungs!" The men started screaming as they fired. The second rank stepped forward and fired again. Sean looked to see the effect of their fire on the defenders. There were several bodies on the ground between them and the redoubt, and a few groups of men huddled together as they tried to load and return fire. The artillerymen were unable to get the guns loaded under the fire of the marines and hid behind their guns and the bombproof that housed the powder.

"Charge, men!" Sean yelled over the top of his men. They surged forward, bayonets leveled at the enemy. A few shots were fired at them, but they were fired too quickly and passed harmlessly overhead. He could hear Lanigan encouraging his men onward, "Wade into them, lads! Give them the cold steel!"

The marines, yelling at the tops of their lungs, lunged into the groups of startled defenders, who broke their formations and ran out the left side of the redoubt, throwing their weapons down and shouting for quarter. "Hold, men, they've had enough!" Sean cried out as he jumped in front of his men. It was difficult to stop them as their "blood was up." However, after he and Lanigan repeated their orders a few times, the men stopped, chests heaving from their exertions.

"Sergeant, set up your squad to watch the prisoners, while my squad rounds up the others," Sean said to Angus. He turned to face the frightened soldiers on their knees in the sand. "As long as you men stay put and do not give us any trouble, you will not be harmed. However, I am having my men load that twelve-pounder to be pointed at you while we are about our work. At this range, you know that there would be nothing left of you to identify if it is fired at you," he warned them.

His men got busy herding the wounded and the men found still hiding in their tents to the group of prisoners while two of his men turned the cannon nearest them and pointed it in their direction. One of them had brought forth a canister round from the bombproof and made a great show of loading it into the gun so that all could plainly see what he was doing.

Sean slipped off his shoes and walked down the wooded steps into the powder magazine. He felt his way around and realized they would have more than enough powder for the ship. He stopped at the top and put his shoes back on and gave Calhoun his orders.

"Get as many of the prisoners as are able, and start moving the powder down to the beach. Be very careful that none of them do anything to set it off, or we will not see the sun come up with all that they have in there. Once we have ours safely stowed on board ship, we will set a fuse to destroy the rest of it. I'm going to set off the signal rocket and get a few of the men busy spiking the guns."

He walked over to where he had laid the rocket and took it to the beach. He stuck the end into the sand of the beach. Baum came up behind him with a portfire glowing in the dark. He touched it to the fuse of the rocket and stepped back. They watched the fuse sputter and spark its way up into the body of the rocket. With the scream of a banshee, the rocket shot skyward.

He looked seaward, where he could barely make out the silhouette of the *Osprey*. He saw a lantern swung back and forth in acknowledgement. He walked along the parapet and stopped at the end overlooking the prisoners. Angus came up beside him.

"Ah, it was a fair night's work, sir. We only have two of the lads nicked in the arm from the shooting and one twisted ankle. Not a bad price to pay for a hold full of powder!"

"Not a bad price at all. How did the enemy fair?" Sean asked.

"They have sixteen dead, and twenty-seven wounded. We took them by complete surprise. There are at least one hundred-twenty artillerymen, and forty-eight infantry as guards. Things could have been much worse for us; however, most of these are local troops—Tories," Lanigan explained.

The two watched as the men got the prisoner work party busy moving the kegs of powder from storage to the beach. By the time the *Osprey* came as close inshore as she dared, the task was complete. The sailors came ashore and started to ferry the powder out to the ship, as all of the weapons of the soldiers were taken along also.

Sean turned and watched as his men spiked the guns of the redoubt and put a keg of powder under the carriage of each one. Once each had been prepared for destruction, Sean addressed the prisoners. "Get up, take your wounded with you, and head down the beach. Keep walking, because we are going to blow up what is left of the powder magazine and the guns. I thank you for your cooperation."

Suspiciously at first, and then as a group, the men got to their feet and marched slowly away from the fortification. The first faint traces of light were creeping upward in the sky as the last of the powder was taken off the beach. The boats returned for the marines, and as they were loading into the boats, Sean, Lanigan and Calhoun set the last of the fuses and set the torch to them.

They ran to the beach and jumped into the boats. "Row fast!" Sean shouted as he climbed on board. The men did not need any further encouragement to get away from the fort, knowing that it was about to explode.

The boats reached the side of the *Osprey* as the first of several explosions tore apart the silence of the morning. They all turned to watch the destruction and let out a cheer as the largest explosion, that of the powder magazine rent the air.

Once the men and the boats were hoisted on board, the *Osprey* was turned towards the open sea and pointed south. As the ship broke into the Atlantic swells for the first time in months, she came alive again. Sean could feel it as he stood by the fore rail, watching the bow wave. The ship was as good as new, and now with the weed gone from her hull, she was faster than before.

He looked back at the men at work; over the stern of the ship raised the plume of smoke, marking their morning's work. Victory felt good, and he could see in the eyes of his men; that they felt the same. Although he despised the killing, it felt good to win.

Taggert of the Marines by David Ekardt

10
The Rescue

The days seemed to fly by as the ship raced forward towards its destination. The weather was fair, and the further south they went the warmer the air became. The men were rejuvenated as they felt the warm sunshine on their backs after the harsh winter that they had been through.

Sean looked about the ship from his vantage point at the bow railing. The work that his brother and the crew had done during the winter months made the ship look new. The freshly tarred rigging and newly painted sides and fixtures covered the battle and storm damage that the ship had sustained.

They were three weeks into their journey south with very little to break the monotony of the voyage. There was the occasional sighting of strange sails on the horizon, yet they managed to steer a course to avoid meeting them. One of the new top men missed his footing while he was out on a yardarm and fell to his death on the deck below. That had been the only casualty except the usual rope burns, bruises and blisters that were common among the crew of a ship at sea.

The course they took kept them clear of the Bahamas and most of the British shipping. There were some tense moments one morning at sunrise when they saw a frigate only a couple of leagues off, but when they hoisted the Union Jack, the frigate acknowledged and veered off away from them. They would reach their goal in another two weeks if their luck held. Sean turned to look seaward; they still needed to capture a small trading vessel to carry out their plans.

The *Osprey* would stand off shore at the horizon while Sean, a few of the crew and his marines, dressed as common merchants, would go ashore ostensibly for provisions and trade goods. While in port, they would try to locate the two hostages and affect a night rescue of them.

The *Osprey* looked too much like a warship to try to disguise, especially with all the men on board. There was too great a risk to the mission to use it as the main rescue ship. It would remain offshore for assistance in case the landing party ran into trouble.

Sean, Thomas, Lanigan, Beckett and Calhoun had gone over the plans many times until they had decided on the course of action they would take. The main body of marines would be landed under the cover of darkness at the south end of the lagoon on the southern side of the island. They would go inshore and take up a position under cover by the trail that came across the narrow island from the port on the western side.

The captured vessel with Sean and a small party of men would enter the port by daybreak and set about obtaining provisions, all the while trying to discern the whereabouts of the hostages. Once they discovered them, they would attempt to capture the daughter of Doctor Dubois and get her back to the ship, which would then leave port and wait for the others off the mouth of the lagoon. The *Osprey* would move in closer under the cover of darkness to support them if needed.

Sean and his men would meet up with the landing party on the other side of the island and attempt to find the doctor among the prisoners at the fort. If possible they would destroy the fort as they rescued the doctor. It would make for a busy night, Sean thought as he mulled over the plans.

So much could go wrong with each variation of the plan that the five men had discussed, yet this had the better chance of succeeding. Even a small bit of bad luck could unravel their plans and cause the mission to fail. If their efforts would bring the French into the fight with the British, they would have to succeed.

A few days later a small sail was sighted on the horizon. "Let's give chase; that could be just the ship we are looking for," Thomas said to Sean.

"I agree. We don't want to get any closer to Anguilla, as any ship we get there will be too well known," Sean replied.

The British flag was hoisted, and the ship was brought around on an intercept course with the sloop. Sean had his men stay low as they loaded the guns on the starboard side, while the sharpshooters stayed below, right at the hatches, ready to race topside and take positions along the railing when they came alongside the unsuspecting craft.

It took an hour for them to come alongside the smaller craft. When they did, Thomas hailed them that he wanted to come on board to give them some information. As the captain of the other ship gave the orders to reduce sail, the crew of the *Osprey* did likewise; all the while, the helmsman edged ever so closer to the ship.

As soon as they were close enough, Sean shouted for his men. The five guns were run out and twenty marines lined the railing, muskets all pointing at the crew of the sloop. Six grapnels arched over the distance, grabbing the other ship, and the sailors pulled them together.

"Captain, I suggest that you and your men do exactly as you are told, and no one will get hurt here today," Sean called over to the bewildered man. As he did so, the Union Jack was hauled down and replaced with the Grand Union flag of the new nation. The captain then realized that they had been tricked.

Having no one armed, he gave up. Sean and several of his men jumped down onto the deck of the smaller ship and took charge of the crew. "You and your men will be treated fairly as long as you cooperate, and your ship will be returned to you as soon as we are finished with it," Sean instructed the captain.

The man just nodded and hung his head. The prisoners were sent on board the *Osprey*, put in irons and taken below. Sean and his men inspected the sloop. It was the *Dove* out of Charles Town. The captain, who was also the owner, was a Tory who had no love for the revolution, or its supporters. Work was started immediately as the two ships got under way. The marines had been transferred to the sloop along with six crewmen to work the ship. They painted out the old name and renamed the ship the *Hawk*.

They had been on the way to the islands for picking up spice, cloth, and other trade goods that they could sell to the people of Charles Town. So far on this voyage, according to the log in the captain's cabin, they had not gone as far as the Antilles. The ship was cramped, and the men had to make do in the quarters below decks, which had a lower ceiling than they were used to having.

The two ships were kept at a great enough distance away from each other so as not to give the impression that they were sailing together as they continued their voyage. They had no further incidents and within a week, they had come twenty miles off the coast of Scrub Island. They waited until nightfall before approaching the south side of the island where the main body of marines would be put ashore.

They brought the sloop in as far as they dared and prepared to disembark. "Angus, you keep the lads out of sight. If you get spotted, you may have to fight your way off the island. Get to the lagoon; there is a small fishing village and you may get some boats there to use for your escape. Edward George can take up a position to where he can watch the fort and determine where we are to find the doctor," Sean instructed Lanigan.

"Don't you worry about us. We'll be waitin' at the crossroads for you tomorrow night just as we planned. You have the more difficult task, going into the lion's den and bluffing your way in and out, so you take care," Angus replied.

"All right now, shove off. As soon as we get the boat back on deck, we will depart for the harbor," Sean said as he shook Lanigan's hand and bade farewell to the others. The boat with his men disappeared into the darkness. An hour later it reappeared, minus the marines. The crewmen hoisted the boat back onto the boat tier and set sail.

It was well after midnight when they sailed into port. They dropped anchor where the sentry boat directed them to, and stood by for an official inspection.

The men of the sentry boat came onboard and inspected the paperwork of the *"Hawk."* Sean had painstakingly altered the documents for just this eventuality. The corporal in charge was only partially able to read what he held in his hands, and with a gruff acknowledgement gave them the official approval to stay in port to do their business.

Sean escorted him to the side after allowing him to take a bottle of port from the wine rack in the captain's cabin. He turned and looked at his men in the lantern light and gave a sigh of relief at passing their first challenge of the mission.

"'Tis fortunate that he was already drinking when 'e came on board or we might not have been so lucky!" Calhoun whispered.

"I'm sure that we may still face a more stringent inspection by someone of greater rank tomorrow, so make sure that your uniforms and weapons stay stowed away. Make sure that you don't shave either; the rougher you look, the better. Now let's turn in. I'll take the first watch with Baum; Calhoun, you take the second watch with Jones. Now get below with you," he dismissed the men.

He watched them go below, dressed in the tattered clothing left behind by the original crew. They had been lucky so far. He walked the deck as he stood watch with Baum. He was too excited to turn in this early, which is why he took the first watch. He was sure that none of them would sleep too soundly this night, knowing that they were in the enemy's territory.

The night passed without incidence. The sentry boat hailed them after sun-up to take up a berth at the wharf. They raised anchor and warped the sloop to its mooring. No sooner had they tied off at the wharf, than they were besieged with vendors trying to sell their wares.

Sean left the haggling to Calhoun, along with a pouch of coin, and left to go to the tavern for breakfast and to listen to whatever he could find out. An older, nearly toothless woman greeted him as he sat down. She went away to fix his fish and fruit that he ordered after pouring him a mug of hot coffee.

He slowly sipped the hot brew as his eyes moved around the room looking at the other diners. He could have been in any seaport in the Caribbean from the appearances of the others in the tavern. They were a mixture of locals, soldiers and seafaring men of dubious backgrounds. Sean listened to the conversations as he ate the food brought to him.

He looked toward the door as it opened, and a shaft of sunlight fell across his table. Two soldiers entered, looked around and then approached the woman who had served him his meal. They were in an animated conversation, with her wagging her finger in the face of the tallest of the two Redcoats.

He kept eating as he noticed that all three were suddenly looking in his direction. The two soldiers walked over to him as the rest of the patrons turned to watch what was happening; glad that they were not attracting official attention.

"Excuse me, sir, are you the captain of the sloop *Hawk* that put in this morning?" asked the corporal as he grasped the hilt of his sword in its scabbard.

"Yes I am. What concern is it of yours? The harbor watch checked me in when we arrived this morning," Sean replied defiantly, still chewing his food.

"I apologize for the intrusion; however, new arrivals to this island are always required to report in to the commandant with ship's papers," the corporal stated apologetically.

"I was not informed of this by either the sentry boat last night or this morning when we were given a berth. I will report in as soon as I finish my meal," Sean snapped back.

"I am sorry, sir, but we will have to escort you to the commandant. You may finish your meal first though," stammered the Redcoat.

"Then step away from my table. I do not like having you staring at me while I eat," Sean ordered.

The two men retreated to the doorway and waited for Sean to finish. He took his time finishing his meal then tossed a few coins on the table. He brushed the front of his coat, borrowed from the sea chest of the *Dove's* captain. He walked to the door and stopped while he waited for the corporal to open it for him.

He fell into step behind them as they walked up the street and out of town. They reached a large house about a quarter of a mile outside town. At one time it had been a stately looking manor, however it seemed to have fallen into a state of disrepair.

They walked up the steps and past the columns and twin sentries at the door. They led him into what had been a sitting room, where he was given a chair facing a large desk. He sat waiting, trying to maintain his aloof attitude that he had taken with the two soldiers.

The door from the hallway was thrown open, and a major of infantry, immaculate in his uniform, stepped into the room and took his seat without acknowledging Sean. The major glanced at the paper on top of the pile in front of him, and then looked up from it to study Sean.

"So, you are the captain of the *Hawk*, John Armstrong?" he asked as he laid the paper down onto the stack.

"Yes I am, and you are major...?" Sean asked.

"I ask the questions here; however since you are new to our island, I will overlook your impertinence. I am Major Lewis of the 20th of Foot. I am in command here, and new arrivals interest me, what with the unpleasantness in the colonies," he smirked.

"I can assure you, Major, that I am a loyalist and owe my allegiance to the Crown, not to a lot of rabble," Sean responded.

"And what is your business here?" asked the major.

"We put in for provisions. We were chased by a rebel ship out from the Bahamas and decided to come further south for new goods to take back with us. We intended to get goods in Cuba and in the Bahamas; however, the Dons in Cuba and the others in the Bahamas have raised their prices too much for us to make a profit, so we are looking for new business partners," Sean explained.

"I understand that your papers were checked by the harbor patrol and were found to be in order. You obviously passed the inspection of your ship, so you will be allowed to get what you need today and then get under way. Be sure that you do not dawdle, and be gone by midnight tonight," ordered the major.

Sean was about to respond when they heard a commotion in the hallway through the open door. The sound of a woman's voice rattling off a stream of epitaphs in French could only mean one thing to Sean; he had found the Dubois woman.

Before they could rise to their feet to check on the disturbance, the young woman came charging into the sitting room. Sean got to his feet as he gazed at the beautiful young woman in her early twenties. Her long, black hair hung down in ringlets about her shoulders, and her tanned face was flushed with her anger.

"Major, I must protest! I cannot have these two soldiers following me everywhere. They are starting to be too bold in their intrusions into my privacy!" she demanded.

"Miss Dubois, may I introduce Captain John Armstrong of the ship *Hawk*? Captain Armstrong, this is Mademoiselle Monique Dubois, our official guest."

"Good day to you, sir," she said as she offered her hand. "I apologize for the intrusion. He would be more correct to say official prisoner!"

"I can understand wanting to protect one as lovely as yourself," Sean said to her as he bowed and kissed her hand.

"Miss Dubois, I must insist that you tolerate your, ah, escorts. They are there for your 'protection'," smiled the major. He looked at the two men and said firmly, "You two will respect the lady's privacy while attending to your duties, or I will have you flogged!" he admonished them.

"Thank you. Now I must go into town," she stammered.

"Major, if you are finished with me, I would be happy to escort Miss Dubois into town. Being at sea, I do not get to enjoy the company of a beautiful woman such as her very often," Sean said.

"I have no further need of your presence. Just remember what I have said, and you will deport yourself as a gentleman with the young lady!" snapped the major.

Sean offered his arm to her, which she took willingly, glad to depart the company of the officer. Together, they exited the house and walked slowly towards town. "Thank you for being such a gentleman, Monsieur Armstrong. I only wish these two dolts behind us would not walk so close to us!" she snapped as she turned and glared at her escorts.

"Maybe I can convince them," Sean said as he fished two gold coins from his pocket. He turned and flipped one to each of the soldiers and winked. They both stopped and let the couple walk further ahead of them before continuing.

"Now mademoiselle, please listen carefully to what I have to say," Sean whispered to her, drawing her closer as he spoke. "Do you and your father wish to leave this island?" he asked and waited for her to answer. She nodded and he continued.

"I am an American Marine here to rescue the two of you and escort you to safety in France. I will need for you to give me some information for us to be able to get you out of here. I need to know where your room is in the house, what time things quiet down at night, the number of guards, and where we can locate your father," He fired off in rapid succession.

She answered all his questions as best as she could. Both of them laughed during their talk to throw off any suspicions that their escorts could have. They walked slowly so that they could agree on a plan. By the time they reached the marketplace, they had decided on her being ready to leave the house at eleven p.m., just before the changing of the guard.

Sean and two of his men would get her on board the *Hawk*, in time for it to sail at the midnight deadline. They would then join the other marines on the other side of the island to collect her father and destroy the half-built fortress.

"I cannot thank you enough for what you are doing!" she whispered. Sean looked longingly into her eyes and kissed her hand.

"Until tonight, then," he said as he turned to go towards his ship. Once on board he informed the men of what they were to do that evening. Calhoun and Baum would accompany Sean to the house to collect the girl and bring her back to the ship. Once the ship got under way, the three would head inland to meet Lanigan and the others. He knew that they would have observed everything at the construction site of the fort and have their plan formulated by the time they got there.

It seemed that everything was going smoothly, but he knew that anything could happen and they might have to call the whole thing off. The men spent the rest of the day repairing sails and rigging, all the while keeping an eye on everything that happened in the small harbor.

Sean spotted one man hanging in the shadows between two buildings, watching their every move. He made sure that his men were all aware of his presence and went about their tasks as if nothing was happening. They would have to make sure that he was taken care of when it was time to get things in motion.

Vendors came with the produce, pigs and fowl that Calhoun had ordered in the morning. They loaded the stores on board and paid the vendors in gold. The cages with the animals were stacked on deck. Baum took one of the piglets, slaughtered it and cooked up the fresh ham for the crew.

The tide was due to go out at midnight, which was the reason for the major giving them until then as their deadline in port. The men grew restless as the day wore on into evening. After dark they started to prepare the ship for departure.

Sean sent Baum and Calhoun ashore to take care of the man spying on them. They returned in fifteen minutes with the body of the spy. "We couldn't leave 'im lying there in the alley, so we brung 'im back," Calhoun explained as they climbed back on board, carrying the lifeless body between them as if he were a drunken shipmate.

"Fine, get him below, and then we have to go. We don't have much time, so hurry," Sean ordered.

The two men came back on deck after depositing the body in one of the hammocks below. "We'll be back within the hour if all goes well. If not, get out of here and meet the others on the other side of the island as planned," Sean ordered the others.

Quietly the three left the ship and headed through town. There was noise coming from the tavern, but the rest of the houses were quiet as they passed by. They walked along the road until they came to the wall around the plantation where the girl was being held.

They watched for movement and could pick out only one of the guards standing at the corner of the house. The three men climbed over the stone wall and followed it until they were opposite the side of the house. There was a shaft of light across the lawn between them and the house from the candlelight inside the room on the first floor facing them.

They raced to the side of the house and crept up behind the guard. Calhoun hit the man over the head with a pouch full of shot. He dropped to the ground. Sean took a rum bottle from his sack, splashed some on the guard, and poured some in his mouth. "'E smells like a regular sot now!" whispered Calhoun.

Quietly they went around the backside of the house, searching for the second guard that Monique had told Sean about. They found him nestled between two bushes sleeping. He, too, was knocked unconscious and treated to the bath of rum. They left him leaned up against the side of the house, bottle in hand.

The men pressed up alongside the house when they heard the back door quietly open. A shadowy form stepped out onto the porch and down the steps. It was her! "Over here!" Sean whispered.

She rushed over to them, and Sean grabbed her to him when they heard a cough from inside. He could feel the shapeliness of her body against him and the racing of her heartbeat. "We have to hurry now. Don't worry, the hardest part is over now," He whispered in her ear. She squeezed his hand and smiled at him.

They ran back across the lawn to the wall and followed it back to where they had climbed over. They did not have much time before the guards would be changed and the hapless Redcoats would be discovered 'drunk' on duty. Sean hoped that they would not suspect foul play and inspect Monique's room, for that would cut down the amount of time that they had to get her to safety and meet the others.

Once they reached the road, they hurried back into town. They did not meet anyone along the way and got her on board. "You men get out of here as soon as we leave. If there is trouble that the *Osprey* cannot get us out of, you must proceed to take her to safety," Sean instructed the crewmen who would take the ship out of the harbor.

Sean, Calhoun and Baum quickly shed their civilian clothes and donned their uniforms. As they turned to go, Monique took Sean by the arm and said, "I cannot go without my father, so you must bring him back. Thank you for what you are doing for us!" She reached up and kissed him.

"Don't worry ma'am, we'll bring him back to you," Calhoun smiled. He spoke before Sean recovered from his surprise. He looked her in the eyes and squeezed her hands.

"I'll bring him back. Fear not, these men will protect you until then," he stammered.

The three men left the ship and snuck out of town. Sean turned to see that the sloop was under way before they turned down the road that led across the island.

As they were walking on the road leading across the island, Calhoun finally said to Baum, so that Sean could hear, "I seen the Lieutenant face down imminent death with a smile on 'is face, but I ain't never seen the look on 'is face that I seen tonight when that lassie kissed 'im."

"Aye, they make a right proper couple, they do indeed," Baum responded.

"All right, now that you two have had your fun, let's be quiet the rest of the way," Sean said in response to their kidding. The girl was enchanting he thought as they walked. They continued on in silence until they came to the crossroads. They stood off the side of the road and in a moment, they found themselves surrounded by Lanigan and the others.

"'Tis good to see you ,lads!" Lanigan announced. "We were hoping that you hadn't gotten lost out here in the dark. We have the fort under observation and know in which tent we will find the good doctor. Edward George is ready to go in as soon as you give the word," Lanigan told him.

"Fine. How about the soldiers and sentries?" Sean asked.

"The soldiers are encamped on the beach around the tip of the island from the fort. They get a better breeze there at night rather than being behind the fort wall. The prisoners are encamped there under a minimum of guards. Not many are needed, for where would they go? The doctor has 'is own tent by the infirmary tent. The prisoners are all sleeping on the open ground."

"How many are there?" Sean asked.

"There are about a hundred of them, the poor devils. Many of them have remnants of uniforms, so

they are military prisoners from General
Washington's army and ships, no doubt. Most of
them are in pretty bad shape, and the Redcoats are
quick to use the whip on them while they work,"
Lanigan explained.

"If you look up on the parapet, you'll see that
they have already mounted six thirty-two pounders;
that's enough to sink any ships that venture in close
enough. Right down there in the middle of the
courtyard, the large hill in the center, that is the
powder magazine. I seen a couple of men go in there
earlier today and since they removed their shoes and
put on felt slippers, I'd venture a guess that it is full
of powder," Lanigan pointed the magazine out to
Sean in the dark.

"We'll need to take out the guards and get the
prisoners to help us move the powder up against the
walls to destroy them. How long between the
changing of the guards?" Sean asked.

"Every two hours. It's about one now, so we
should have to wait until the next change, because an
hour would not give us enough time to do what we
came to do," Lanigan suggested.

"You're right. We'll get back under cover until we
see them change again. Have you secured the boats at
the lagoon?" Sean asked.

"Aye, there's a few fishing shacks there, and the
occupants came back with their boats earlier in the
evening, so we'll have the use of the boats when the
time comes. Sir, what of those poor lads there. We
can't just leave them behind," Angus asked.

"No, I suppose that we can't do that. I have been
thinking about them the whole time since we got this
mission. We'll take them with us; there should be

enough room on the sloop until we catch up to the
Osprey. Once we get started, the injured will have to
start down to the lagoon and wait for us to finish our
work."

"Aye, you're a good man, Sean Taggert; I knew
that as soon as I laid eyes on you. Now why don't we
catch a quick nap while we're waiting?"

"You go ahead, Angus, I know that I won't be able
to get any sleep. But an old veteran as yourself could
sleep during an artillery barrage if you needed to,
eh?" Sean smiled.

"I have done that at least once! So, if you'll excuse
me," he replied as he sat back against the side of the
hill. A few minutes later as Sean sat in the dark, he
could hear Angus snoring.

The men lounged as best they could until they
spotted the corporal of the guard and the next shift
making their rounds, replacing the men on watch.
Sean watched them as they completed the rounds and
headed back to the encampment, out of sight, over the
rise next to the fort.

They would wait another half-hour to let the new
watchmen get used to the night sounds and get sleepy
in the dark. He crouched down by a bush and tried to
see where George was in hiding. He spotted him in
between two bushes to his left front and crept over to
him.

"We will get started in a few minutes. You and I
will get the doctor while the men roust out the
prisoners. We'll get him headed to the beach with the
injured while the rest of us set the powder charges to
destroy the fort," Sean advised him.

He went back to the others and gave them their
instructions. Six men were sent out to dispatch the

guards while the others got in position to make their way through the prisoners to wake them up and enlist their aid.

They waited while the six went about their deadly duty. Sean could see the silhouettes against the night sky on the parapet as the dead sentries were unceremoniously dumped over the side of the wall.

"All right, lads, there's the signal; Angus, you take charge at the magazine. Beckett and Calhoun, you direct the setting of the charges against the walls. Don't forget to set one at each gun. We can't risk spiking the guns while we set the charges; the noise will surely be heard. If there are no questions, then move out," Sean ordered.

The men broke out into their groups and moved down to the courtyard of the backless fort. Sean and Edward George entered the tent of the doctor. He stood next to the cot that the doctor was on and shook him by the shoulder.

"Doctor Dubois, wake up," he whispered. The man in his fifties rolled over and sat up as George lit a candle. "We haven't much time, sir. I am Lieutenant Taggert of the United States Marines, and we are here to take you and your daughter back to France."

"Monique, is she safe?" he asked, half awake.

"Yes, sir, she is already out to sea, and now we must get you and the others out of here. We are setting charges to destroy this place and take everyone out to the ships by boat from the lagoon. You must hurry, and go ahead with the injured."

"Yes, yes, I will gather my things, and we go now," he said as he pulled on his clothes and piled his papers and instruments into two cloth bags.

"Edward, you go with him and the injured to the boats. Get them out to sea; the *Hawk*, and *Osprey* should be right off the mouth of the lagoon by now, if all went well," Sean directed him.

He watched as they headed off toward the lagoon with about fifteen injured men, all being assisted by others. Sean found Angus at the powder magazine, supervising two men bringing kegs of powder out and passing them on to the prisoners.

Sean's men, except for those standing watch, all pitched in with setting the powder kegs where Calhoun and Beckett instructed them. Sean moved away and looked at his watch by the light of the moon. They did not have much time, and the work was slow going, as the prisoners were weak and had a hard time moving the kegs of powder.

The men worked on in silence. Sean kept an eye on the time. It was nearing four, and almost time for the next changing of the guard. They may not make it in time. "Quickly men, stop what you are doing; we need to try to grab the guards when they come up. We still have too much to do before we can light the fuses. Prisoners, get back to your sleeping areas, we need everything to look normal. Angus, go get Beckett's squad, and get in the dark area along the wall over there. That is where they will come up and into the fort area. Knives and tomahawks only; I want no noise, no shots, understand?" Sean asked.

"Aye, sir, we'll take the buggers down, have no fear," Lanigan answered as he hastened off with Beckett's men.

"The rest of you, get in the shadows along here. If any of the enemy break loose, charge them with your bayonets. They all must be put down so they cannot raise the alarm!"

Calhoun and his men moved into their position and got down on the ground. Sean could hear the quiet clatter of bayonets being affixed to the ends of their muskets, and then silence. He walked around the area to encourage the prisoners to be still while the guard was attacked. Anything could go wrong at this point and turn the place into chaos.

Sean took up position behind a water barrel, close to where the guards would be marching. He could hear slight noises coming from the area of the enemy camp, which told him that they were on the way. They were not quiet as they approached, not being the least concerned about waking the prisoners. Sean tensed, his hand on his sword, ready to lunge forward if necessary.

The soldiers tromped up the path and right along the wall as before. When it came, the attack was swift and a total surprise. Except for a muffled scream and the clatter of a couple of muskets falling to the ground, there was no noise.

The marines came forward after checking the bodies for any signs of life. They had done their grisly work well. "All right men, let's get back at it. Baum, you watch the trail. Remember there, may be someone down there expecting to see the returning guards come into camp, and when that does not happen, an alarm may be raised. The rest of you, let's get finished up and get out of here," Sean exclaimed.

The men returned to work with the prisoners. They labored for another hour. It was getting near sunrise, and already a faint line of light was on the horizon.

"The charges are set, and the fuses are laid in, sir," Lanigan reported, the strain of the night's work noticeable in his voice.

"Fine. Let's get the prisoners moving to the lagoon so that we can light the fuses. I want our men to form up as a rear guard while we load the boats. The Redcoats are bound to come after us once the charges detonate," Sean instructed.

"We'll get them moving right away, although some of those poor devils are played out. They've been near-starved and beaten while they worked on building this place," Angus replied. He saluted and jogged over to the prisoners, who had sat down to rest once they had finished putting the powder kegs in place.

Sean motioned for his men to gather around in the pre-dawn light. He looked over at the haggard prisoners, whose faces were beginning to take shape in the increasing light. They were a wretched-looking lot, and he felt pity for them after what they had been through. He could not leave them behind, for surely they would be put to death for taking part in the destruction of the fort.

"Listen men, we need to get down to the lagoon quickly. The Redcoats will be falling out any minute now, so we have to destroy this place and get back on board the ships before they find us. You lads will go into the boats first, and my men and I will act as rear guard. There is no time to lose, so get on your feet and head down the road," Sean ordered them.

"The name's Hoskins, Sir; Captain of the Virginia Dragoons. I want to thank you for all of us for getting us out of here. We are all that's left of almost a thousand men who have been forced to work on this place. The others died of starvation, disease, or were beaten to death by those bloody bastards, and we, too, surely would die here if not for you," exclaimed a gaunt man, uniform in tatters, who stood and saluted Sean.

"Thanks, but we haven't gotten you out of here yet, so get the men moving," Sean said as he shook the man's hand.

"Redcoats coming!" called Baum from his perch on the partially completed wall facing the enemy encampment. Just then the sound of several muskets rent the still morning air.

"Get moving, men!" Sean shouted at the prisoners. "Marines with me!" he called as he ran to the far side of the courtyard. The others followed him as the prisoners hurried down the road leading to the lagoon.

"Form up here in two ranks!" Sean ordered as he looked down toward the enemy. There he saw a partially formed company of Redcoats, some not fully dressed, falling into attack formation. He ducked as their front rank fired a volley. They had misjudged the distance in the growing light and the shots went high.

"Front rank, fire!" he shouted. The air around him filled with smoke as his men fired their muskets. He could see several figures below had fallen to the ground. "Fall back and reload. Second rank, fire!" he ordered.

Once more he saw figures below fall to the marksmanship of his men. The enemy fired again, but the vicious fire from the fort rattled them, and their shots went wild. "Once more, men, then fall back to the road!" Sean shouted

The first rank fired and fell back. The second rank followed suit. Sean picked up a torch lying in the nearest fire and walked over to the fuses for that side of the fort. He touched the end of each trail of powder and watched long enough to see that they were well on their way to the charges. He turned to see Calhoun and Lanigan standing by the other fuses for the charges under the big guns and the seaward wall.

"Fire the fuses and get out of there!" he shouted. He threw his torch into the remains of the prisoner's tenting and raced over to the far end of the courtyard where the others waited at the road that led to the lagoon. The torch set the whole area into a conflagration as Calhoun and Lanigan reached them. They looked back as the first enemy troops arrived at the far end of the partial wall. They stopped and formed up to fire.

Sean ordered the marines to form up for firing. "We have to keep them out of the fort until the charges detonate; otherwise, they are likely to see the fuses and stop them," He called to his men as they fell into formation.

"Look, sir, one of 'em is going for the fuse over there!" shouted Beckett.

"Front row, shoot that man down!" Sean ordered. Thirteen muskets barked out, and they watched as the wall around the Redcoat was peppered with their shots, three of which hit him, knocking him to the ground.

"Fallback; second rank, fire!" he ordered as the first rank fell back and reloaded on the move. The second rank fired at the same time as the enemy, and two men went down, one clutching his shoulder, the other hit in the leg.

"Pick them up and fall back!" Sean had barely gotten the words out when the first of the charges closest to the enemy exploded. The shock knocked them to their feet. "Come on men, let's get out of here before the others explode!" he said as he picked himself up off the ground. The others needed no further encouragement, as debris and chunks of masonry started to rain down among them.

Sean looked back as the others passed him. The enemy troops took the brunt of the explosion, and all he could see of them were scattered remains and parts of them falling down from the sky into the blazing courtyard. He turned to follow his men; the second round of charges, ten in all, exploded.

As they hurried down the road along the side of the slight hill to landward, they could see the first of the boatloads of prisoners rowing out of the lagoon to their left. Suddenly, a chunk of masonry hit the man in front of him, knocking him to the ground. "Hauser, Betts, lend a hand here with Johnson," he called out. The two slung their muskets and picked up the dazed man between them and continued on.

They heard bugles and drums beating madly as they trotted down the road. In the distance they heard the sound of cannon fire. *The ships must have run into a British warship!* Sean thought. He looked back and saw the sky over the rise they had just gone over filled with smoke from the inferno that had been the fort. Just then movement along the side of the hill caught his eye. Redcoats! There was a small trail leading through the brush, over the top of the hill from the other side of the island where the enemy camp was. The men had missed seeing this in the dark.

"Men, hold up and form into firing ranks! Those with the wounded, continue on to the lagoon," Sean instructed. The men obeyed, and those not carrying the wounded fell into their ranks.

The enemy stopped when they reached the road to form up. "Separate yourselves into four ranks. I want a continuous fire as we fall back. As narrow as the road is, neither of us can put on a broad front," Sean ordered the men as the first volley of the enemy was fired. Two men spun around but remained on their feet, having sustained minor hits to their arms.

"Front rank, fire, fall back; second rank, fire, fall back; third rank, fire, fall back; forth rank, fire, fall back." Sean called out the orders as he walked alongside the men. Like a machine, the four ranks fired, reloaded as they fell back and were followed by the second rank, the third and the forth, by which time the first rank was in position to fire again.

They repeated this three times, taking a terrible toll on the enemy. The men finally reached the beach of the lagoon. There was a group of forty men still waiting to get onto boats, but they had not returned yet from the *Hawk* to gather them up.

The enemy sensed the situation and pushed forward again. Sean advanced his men to some rocks at the head of the road where it came down to the beach. "Fire as a target presents itself," he told the men as they settled into their positions.

They kept up the exchange of gunfire for fifteen minutes. Sean saw that the officer and sergeants of the enemy were having a difficult time trying to get their men to charge. Obviously provincial troops under professional officers, he thought.

The Redcoats withdrew over the rise. The smoke of the musketry drifted across the water. Sean had been watching for the boats to return, but none appeared. He could hear the men murmuring amongst themselves that they might not make it off the island as the sound of cannon fire increased. Suddenly, the British came rushing over the rise, shouting and firing as they came en masse. They had been reinforced and were determined to take the field.

The men resumed firing again. They stopped the onslaught short of their positions, and the enemy withdrew to form up and return fire. Just then they saw a boat coming through the lagoon. It was being rowed hard, and even with several muskets fired at them by the enemy, they kept at it until they reached the beach where the rest of the prisoners were still huddled.

The men on the beach rushed the boat, and in no time it was overloaded and backing out. The British held their position and continued to return fire. Sean watched as the British officer rallied his men to make another charge.

"Here they come again! Let them have it by volley again lads." Sean said as he watched the enemy. They formed up and marched at the marines with their muskets held at waist level, bayonets gleaming in the morning sun. A second company formed up behind them and started their approach.

"Sir, there's an awful lot of 'em this time, and we're almost out of powder," Said Potts.

"That just means that more of 'em than us are going to die here, laddie," assured Lanigan.

Sean looked at the men. They were tired from their night of work and the fighting this morning.

They were just about out of powder and shot, and might not be able to hold the enemy off long enough for the boats to get them. He saw how they looked to him, as if he could will their troubles away.

"Take heart, lads. Those boys over there haven't seen near as much fighting as you have, and they show signs of breaking. Take time to aim well, and we will take down as many as we can, and that should take the fight out of the rest." He hoped what he said would happen. He tried to look as confident as he could.

"Get ready, lads, and fire!" he shouted as the first Redcoats came into range. They faltered momentarily but came on again. The marines poured a heavy fire into the oncoming mass, and finally they broke.

The first company turned and ran, smashing into the company behind them. Sean saw two more boats approaching. "Now, lads, let's get down to the beach!" he stopped to help one of the wounded to his feet. They had sustained several more wounded in the fight.

The men reached the beach and gathered with the remaining prisoners. The two boats stopped before they hit the beach, and the men had to wade out to them. The marines followed, their backs to the boats, facing the road in case the enemy regrouped.

Sean looked behind him to see that the prisoners were all on board, and there was only room for his wounded. "Get the wounded on board," he directed.

"'Ere they come again!" someone shouted.

"Men, get out of the water and form up on the beach. Front rank, kneel and fire; back rank, stand and fire!" The men surged forth out of the knee-deep water and took their places. The two boats backed out into the lagoon.

The enemy troops charged across the beach at the waiting marines who stood their ground and fired on command. Each time, the firing rank fell back to let the other one fire. This time the enemy did not break and run. Instead they kept coming, although their numbers were greatly reduced.

"Bayonets!" shouted Sean. The men stood and leveled their weapons toward the oncoming enemy. "Charge!" he yelled as he sprang forth, sword waving above his head. His men slashed into the enemy, bayonets flashing, muskets being swirled about as clubs, all the while both groups of men yelling like banshees.

The sand made it hard to keep balance, and many combatants went tumbling to the ground, locked in mortal combat. Sean parried a bayonet and smashed the hilt of his sword into the face of the soldier who slashed at him. He fired his pistol into the belly of another who turned towards him, then flipped it around and used it as a club to knock senseless a Redcoat who was down on top of one of his men, choking him with his bare hands. The man rolled off, and Baum got back to his feet in time to push aside a musket and bury his knife in the chest of his attacker.

Lanigan had tangled with three men, knocking aside their bayonets with his spontoon and knocking two about with the blunt end of it. The third grabbed a bayonet on the ground and buried it into the thigh of Lanigan, who in turn ran the man through with the spear point of his spontoon.

Sean leaped across two men rolling about in the sand and warded off two who charged at his sergeant, who had fallen to the ground. Sean ran the first one through with his sword, which came free of his hand when the man fell back. The other soldier grabbed his musket by the barrel and swung it at Sean's head. He ducked, and as he came back up, he pulled his knife from the top of his boot and sunk it into the man's chest.

As he turned to help Angus up, a cannon fired from close by. The men in the melee, all paused to see from where it was fired. It was the *Hawk*! Cameron had braved the reef at the mouth of the lagoon and came in to rescue them.

The Redcoats threw their hands up in surrender as another cannon was fired. The shots had landed close to the remaining British troops on the road. "Let them go, lads," Sean said to his men. "Go on, get out of here!" he shouted at the British.

The marines staggered to their feet, gathered their weapons and helped those that who wounded to their feet. Four lay dead. "What about them, sir?" asked Calhoun as he looked down at Heinrich's lifeless body, the side of his head blown away by a pistol shot to the head.

"Bring them along too. I won't leave them to those butchers!" Sean said angrily. He bent down and helped Angus to his feet. He had pulled off his neck cloth and bandaged his leg.

"Guess I won't be dancing a jig anytime soon!" Angus laughed, trying to hide the pain. "I think that I may be getting too old for this foolishness," he said to Calhoun, who got under his other arm to hold him up on his feet.

The men waded out into the water while they watched the Redcoats stand their ground. Once the prisoners had climbed aboard the overcrowded sloop from the two boats, the men at the oars pulled back towards the beach to pick up the marines.

Sean and ten men stood, weapons at the ready as the wounded and dead were taken on board the boats. The rest of the men climbed aboard. As the rest of his men were climbing onto the boats, the Redcoat officer was seen walking toward them across the beach.

"Should I pick 'im off from 'ere, sir?" asked Sheldon as Sean climbed onto the cutter.

"No, let's hear what he has to say." Sean said as he stood in the stern sheets and brushed sand off his coat. He saw two tears in the sleeves, both lined in blood. He had been grazed by bullets and had not even noticed.

He looked at the British captain as he walked through the carnage on the beach. Several of the men lying on the beach were moving, rocking back and forth from the pain of their wounds, some crying out for their mothers or for help. Weapons, uniforms and equipment lay strewn about at the scene of their brief but bloody fight. The captain stopped at the water's edge.

"I salute you and your men, sir." he said as he raised his hand to his hat. "They put up a remarkable fight for so few men in the face of overwhelming odds. I admire bravery, and you and your men have shown my pitiful provincial troops how real troops fight. Might I know who you are, Lieutenant?" he asked.

Sean looked at his ragged men in the boats around him and smiled. "My name is Taggert, Taggert of the Marines!" The men shouted and waved their hats.

They all knew there was no higher compliment than that given by an enemy.

"I salute you then, Lieutenant Taggert, and all of you Marines. You have taken the day, and we will bother you no more." He saluted again and then walked back across the beach. The men rowed the boats out to the waiting sloop and climbed on board.

There was not enough room for everyone. They had already started pitching cargo over the other side to make room for everyone. "We heard the sound of musketry and I decided to risk the reef to get you and the lads off the island," exclaimed Cameron, who had met Sean at the side.

Sean shook his hand and asked, "What was the cannon fire that we heard a few minutes ago?'

"We need to get under way right away, sir. The *Osprey* had closed with us this morning and about the time the fort blew up, a ship rounded the island. It was a schooner, and the *Osprey* engaged it. They started a running battle, and the other ship struck its colors just before we entered the lagoon. There may be others nearby, so we must get under way."

The two made their way to the tiller, and Cameron shouted orders to the crew. They set sail amid the crush of humanity on the deck in their way, and slowly the sloop moved forward. "We'll go out the other end, since we do not have enough room to turn around without warping her. One of the fishermen that we had come across this morning indicated that there should be just enough clearance over the reef. I have a leadsman forward to be sure, though," Cameron informed Sean.

"What of the girl and her father?" Sean asked as he looked around the deck to see them.

"We met up with the *Osprey* early this morning and put her aboard. The doctor is below tending to the injured and wounded," Cameron replied.

Sean felt relief that she at least was out of danger. They still had to cross the reef at the far end of the lagoon. They could still run aground or be discovered by another British ship. He watched as their passengers continued to toss things overboard to make room and lighten the ship to clear the reef.

"Listen! Cannon fire! The *Osprey* must have been found by another patrolling ship," Sean said as he strained his ears to the sound. "There's no way the lookout can see anything with the two parts of the island in the way. Calhoun, Calhoun, get the guns loaded and run out!" he shouted over the heads of the others.

He watched as Calhoun waved back and gathered some of the men. Captain Hoskins and some of his men stepped forward and assisted in passing the powder and shot from below to the men at the guns. The crowd parted away from the cannons so that the men could load them.

"'Ere we g, sir. The leadsman is signaling, the reef is dead ahead," Cameron said as he tightened his grip on the tiller. The points of land from either side of the opening were so close that the palm trees on either shore would brush against the sides of the *Hawk* as she passed through the opening.

"Lower the mainsail!" Cameron shouted out in an effort to slow the ship down in case they struck the reef. Word had passed amongst the prisoners of what was happening, and as a group they all got to their feet as if that would help the ship to cross without grounding itself.

Sean stood by the side rail and watched the water in front of the bow. He could see the decidedly darker water that stretched cross the mouth of the lagoon, indicating the coral bottom was closer to the water's surface.

He tensed as he held onto the shrouds as the bow crossed into the darker water. They felt a bump and then heard the bottom of the sloop scrape the reef as she continued out into the emerald green water beyond.

"Well that took some of the weed off the keel!" Sean said with a smile of relief. The others cheered as they realized that they were in the clear. "Now let's get the sails back on her and go help the *Osprey*! Marines, pass out all the weapons to anyone who still has the strength to fight. We may need them!" he called out.

The men on the deck sprang into action. The sails were set and weapons were passed hand-over-head to those standing along the railings. The sloop moved faster once it cleared the end of the island and her sails caught the wind. Cameron put the tiller hard over to come around the spit of land that made up the seaward side of the lagoon. They were heading back toward the tip of the island where the fort was and where the *Osprey* was engaged in combat with the enemy.

Everyone on the vessel strained their neck as they tried to see what was happening. They were a few minutes from reaching the end of the island to where they should be able to see what danger lie ahead of them.

The sound of cannon fire ceased as the sloop rounded the end of the island and headed towards the two ships that were a mile distant from them. They could hear musketry and the sound of grenades exploding, as the two ships appeared to collide.

"They have grappled the *Osprey* and are attempting to board her. It looks like they have extra troops on board. There are way too many Redcoats from here to be the normal compliment of marines on board," Sean said, as he peered through his telescope while he hung onto the shroud with his arm locked around it as he stood on the rail.

"It's that damned *Charon!*" he swore as he made out the name behind the figurehead of the boatman of the underworld. He could see that the enemy was about to board the *Osprey* from the aft deck. The enemy had put its port side along the *Osprey's* starboard side.

They could hear the occasional report of a swivel gun being fired into the masses on the decks of the two ships. "Listen to me, men," Sean called out. "So far the enemy has not seen us, and we will use that to our advantage. Our cannons are of no use since the shots could hit our men over there also. We will come alongside the enemy, board her and attack across her deck and catch them between us and the men of the *Osprey.*"

"We ain't got enough weapons, sir," A voice called out.

"I know that, but they won't. If we hit them hard and fast enough, they won't have time to see that many of you only have knives or belaying pins. Make as much noise as you can, and when they see all of you coming at them wanting revenge for what they did to you, they will lose heart," Sean explained.

He counted on the prisoners to have hatred for the Redcoats boiling inside of them, which would sustain them in this battle for their lives. He watched as several of them started pulling the railings apart and breaking the pieces up into clubs. Others who had nothing broke up other fixtures below decks and passed the pieces up to the others. Within minutes, almost every man on board who could stand on his feet had some form of weapon in his hands.

"Marines, when we get closer, I want you to shoot their men out of the tops before they discover us. After that, reload and fire a concentrated volley once we get on board," Sean shouted out to his men. He could see Angus had made his way back to him through the press of men.

"Before you say it, sir, I cannot stay behind, wounded or no; my place is with you and the lads." He said, as Sean was about to order him below. He knew he could not make Angus stay behind.

"I know it is useless for me to tell you to stay back, so watch out for yourself over there, Angus," Sean said.

"Get ready Sir, we'll be alongside her in just a minute or so." Cameron said. He called out to his men to shorten sail. The sloop's two sails came down in an instant, just as the marines fired on the British marines on the fighting tops of the *Charon*. They fell from their perches as the two ships ground together.

Grappling hooks sailed through the air and caught hold of the other ship. The crew tied off their ends and picked up their weapons. All eyes were on Sean. He drew his sword; and, standing on the ratlines of the mainmast, waved it in the air, and shouted, "Boarders away!"

He leapt across the space between the hulls and slipped as he landed onto the other deck. He picked himself up in time to avoid being trampled by the charging mass of men coming up from the sloop and over the side of the *Charon*. His men paused long enough to fire a volley at the backs of the Redcoats who were firing onto the deck of the *Osprey*.

Their surprise was complete! The marines and prisoners charged across the deck, yelling at the tops of their lungs, stabbing and clubbing anyone who stood in their way. As they went, many of the men threw their clubs down and claimed the muskets and swords of their victims. After a brief fight, they had cleared the deck of the *Charon* and stood at the rail looking down onto the *Osprey*. The remains of the crew were huddled together at the foremast, fighting for all they were worth. Sean saw Thomas among the men and was relieved that he was still alive.

"Over the side, lads! One more push and the day is ours!" Sean yelled out above the din of the battle. He climbed over the rail and jumped down on the deck of the *Osprey*, grabbing a British marine who turned and saw him as he landed on the deck. Sean swung him around by the lapels of his coat and slammed him into the capstan.

The others followed suit, and in an instant the enemy found themselves being attacked from behind by a mob of disheveled, wild men interspersed with the green-coated marines. Sean and the others surged forward into the crowd of British sailors, marines and soldiers, slashing and clubbing away at anything in front of them.

Sean instinctively ducked when he saw an officer point a pistol at him. The shot grazed the side of his head; before he could strike out with his sword, he saw the man's arm severed by a boarding axe wielded by one of the freed prisoners. Sean parried the knife of one of the enemy sailors with his sword, then swung his arm backwards and knocked him senseless with the hand guard of his sword. The man collapsed to the deck and was trampled under foot by other combatants.

As the fighting continued up and down the deck, Sean looked around for Captain Jennings, the officer in command of the *Charon* and the killer of his father. He would have his vengeance today if he found him alive. He saw a man charge out of the crowd toward him brandishing a cutlass. Before the man reached him, Lanigan impaled him with his spontoon.

Sean saw Hoskins take a cutlass to his midsection and pull his attacker to him. Together they plunged over the side of the ship, where they were ground between the hulls, their screams muffled by the roar of the battle above.

Sean spun around as he heard another scream, that of a woman coming from aft. There he saw Jennings coming up from below, pulling the French woman up by her hair. He was surrounded by four of his men as they reached the deck.

Sean's hatred came welling up inside of him. He knocked two combatants aside as he forced his way aft. When he reached the capstan he bellowed out, "Jennings!" He was full of rage, and tried to calm himself down as he saw the officer throw the woman to the deck and pull his pistol.

Calhoun and Lanigan both heard Sean's voice and saw what was happening. "Quick, laddie, we have to fight our way back there before he gets himself killed!" Lanigan called out. They both tried to push their way aft as they watched Sean.

Sean drew his second pistol and pulled the hammer back. The two men fired at the same instant; Sean missed, while Jennings's bullet tore away his left shoulder board. "Kill that bastard!" he snarled at his men. The four charged at Sean, cutlasses raised. He sidestepped the first one, sending him sprawling on the deck past him.

He locked blades with the second one, who spun him around. He pushed the man back and realized that he was between him and the two others. The man in front of him charged again, cutlass at belly level. Again Sean parried the blade and hit him in the mouth, sending him backwards again. He turned in time to see the two behind him come straight at him.

The one in front lunged at him with his blade as Sean stumbled over a body. The blade was aimed straight at his heart when a blur passed in front of his eyes. Lanigan screamed out in pain as the blade sunk into his chest. He threw his attacker back and pinioned him to the deck with his spontoon.

The fourth man hesitated and never saw the axe that hit him in the head, thrown by Calhoun. Sean and Calhoun raced over to Lanigan and caught him as he fell to the deck, cutlass still sticking out of his chest.

"Why did you do that ,Angus?" Sean stammered looking at the pain in the older man's face.

"Don't worry about me, laddie, I've been stuck worse," he said as he coughed up blood. Sean pulled the cutlass out and Calhoun stripped his neck cloth off and shoved it into the wound. "Now you get a hold of that hatred in you and go get that bastard!" He grabbed a hold of Sean's collar and said again, "Get a hold on your anger, it will cloud your thinking!"

Sean looked up and saw Jennings standing by the wheel, sword in hand. Monique had crawled to the safety of one of the cannons and tried to hide behind it. Sean let Calhoun take Angus from him as he stood up. He picked up the cutlass that he had taken from Angus' wound and walked slowly to face his adversary. His body suddenly shuddered as he got his rage under control. His mind cleared, and he suddenly felt relaxed.

"You Scottish rebel trash, you will die today for what you have done. You'll die just like your father did!" Jennings spat on the deck as he snarled. He swung his blade back and forth through the air.

Sean said nothing; he just stared at the weasel-like eyes of the man before him as he moved around, placing himself between the woman and Jennings. He noticed perspiration break out on the man's forehead and a slight tremble in his facial muscles.

Sean stopped and slowly raised the tip of his blade and pointed it directly at his heart. He could sense that Jennings was fearful of his life. He waited unmoving, arm and blade outstretched.

Jennings lunged at Sean, knocking his blade aside. Sean let him come and stepped aside, tripping him as he charged past. Jennings crashed to the deck on the opposite side of the cannon that Monique clung to. He was back on his feet in an instant and charged Sean again.

He swung his sword madly trough the air, slashing back and forth like a madman. Sean found himself having to move quickly as he parried the blade of his opponent at every swing. He almost could not keep up and pulled his pistol out with his left hand to ward off blows with that as well as his sword.

The two men kept at it until Jennings started to wear down from his overexertions. Sean felt himself wearing down as well, and with a great effort, locked blades with Jennings and threw all his weight at him, sending him sprawling across the deck again.

His antagonist hit his head against the bulwark as he fell and did not move. Sean walked over and stood at his feet. The man rolled over to push himself up off the deck. "I suppose that you think you have won, Taggert?" he asked, face hidden. "Think again!" he shouted as he rolled back onto his back and pulled forth a small pistol from his coat and fired it at Sean.

The shot hit him in the upper left chest and threw him back. He tripped on a cutlass and fell to the deck. His own cutlass went clattering across the deck as he fell down. Jennings leapt to his feet and recovered his sword.

He swaggered over to where Sean laid bleeding. "Now I'll finish what I started!" He grasped the handle of his sword with both hands, point down, and raised it above his head to deliver the final blow. Sean looked to his right to where his cutlass lay just beyond his reach; he saw Monique looking at him. She jumped forward, scooping up the cutlass and put it in his hand.

As Jennings was about to bring his blade down, Sean pushed himself up with one hand and drove his blade up into Jennings's heart, lifting him from his feet. Sean twisted the blade with all of his might as his opponent dropped his sword. He stood there as Sean got to his feet, and stared at him in disbelief.

"Like my father said, 'Get off my ship!'" Sean shouted as he withdrew his cutlass. The man's blood flowed from the wound and onto the deck as Sean pushed him to the side and pushed him over the railing. He watched as the body of his father's killer sank beneath the red, frothy waves.

Sean felt lightheaded and fell back against the mizzenmast and slid to the deck. He saw Monique's face before his as she ripped his coat and shirt aside and proceeded to bandage his wound. "You have done a wonderful thing. You have rescued me twice. Now lie back while I fix your wounds," she said, all fear in her voice had vanished.

"I must have died and gone to heaven, for this is the face of an angel before me," he said with a smile. He cringed a bit as she stuffed his neck cloth into the hole in his chest. He watched her as she worked and noticed how she blushed when he said that.

Suddenly several faces loomed over him as he heard cheering from many voices. "Sean are you all right?" he heard Thomas ask. He looked up to see his brother's bloodied face looking down on him.

"I got him. I got the bastard that killed Father. What about Angus?" Sean responded.

"He's hurt pretty bad from what I have seen. Doctor Faircloth has already started working on him. You consider yourself bedridden with that wound; Calhoun can take over for you. I have to get us under way as soon as we get the remnants of the enemy put ashore," Thomas reassured him.

"Baum, you and George help him below to his cabin. Don't you worry about a thing, sir. We'll take care of everything." Calhoun said.

"How many did we lose, Corporal?" Sean asked as the others helped him to his feet.

"We lost a few; I don't know who all yet. You just worry about yourself. I'll report to you as soon as I get everything under control." Calhoun replied.

They walked him to the steps, and Monique followed as they took him to his cabin and helped him out of his clothes. She stepped in as he lay down and started barking out orders. "Get me some boiling water, my bag out of the captain's cabin and some brandy, or rum, whatever is available. Now you be still, I will have you sewn up in no time. My father, he is safe?" she asked as she looked at the other cuts and bruises that he had.

"Yes, he is safe on board the *Hawk*. He was eager to see that you were safe," Sean said, trying not to wince in pain as she inspected his wounds. He watched her face as she went about her work and knew that he was in good hands.

Shortly after she had stitched his wounds and bandaged them, he fell into a deep sleep. The rum that she had given him for the pain, along with the exertions of the past thirty-six hours, took its toll.

Above, the others went about the grisly task of cleaning the ship from the battle. The dead were unceremoniously dumped over the side, while the wounded were taken below decks where Faircloth, assisted by Dubois, attended to them. The enemy prisoners and wounded were sent ashore in the *Charon's* boats, while replacements for the dead and wounded crewmen were recruited from among the liberated prisoners, many of whom were sailors.

The remainder of the men were split between the *Hawk* and *Charon*, and within an hour of the battle,

497

the three ships were under way heading north. The men worked the rest of the day after getting under way on clearing away the remnants of the battle debris and scrubbing down the decks.

Thomas had placed Cameron in charge of the *Charon*, while Stark took over the *Hawk*. There were just enough experienced seamen among the prisoners and among the British who wished to change sides to man all three ships. The sloop that the *Osprey* had engaged earlier in the day had been scuttled due to too much damage from the *Osprey's* broadsides.

The damage to the *Charon* and *Osprey* were relatively light due to Jennings using mostly Landridge and grapeshot in an effort to damage the rigging and take out most of the crew so that he could capture the ship that had been such a torment to him.

There had been enough clothing captured in the *Charon* to clothe the prisoners, who were glad to part with their rags. They also were appreciative of having full meals to eat once more instead of the paltry fare they had been served while in captivity.

Thomas finally had the opportunity to go below and clean up late that afternoon, as he had been kept busy overseeing the many details of sending the vanquished enemy ashore, dividing the men into three crews, and seeing to the many details of the ship's repair and sailing orders.

After he had washed up and changed, he stopped at Sean's cabin to check on him. He had just awakened from his deep sleep and tried to sit up, much to the annoyance of his newfound nurse. "Has your brother always been so stubborn?" she asked lightheartedly as Thomas helped his brother sit up in bed.

"Aye, he's the worst of the lot, but he's family so we put up with him," Thomas joked. "You better do as she says Little Brother, you aren't looking so good," Thomas scolded his brother.

"He has lost a lot of blood, but his wounds were all clean so he should recover. His chest wound is the only troublesome one, as it was deep. I think with plenty of rest he should heal and be on his feet in a few weeks," Monique said with authority.

"I can't stay here for three weeks, I have a job to do." Sean protested.

"Now you don't worry about that. Calhoun has everything under control; you and Angus did a fine job training that one," Thomas interjected.

"Angus, that's right, how is Angus?' Sean said suddenly worried about the old man.

"He's in good hands. Doctor Dubois and Faircloth have been administering to all the wounded, and he has been their top priority. That old bugger is strong as an ox and should pull through," Thomas replied.

"I hope so; I owe him so much. He has been a pillar of strength and encouragement to all of us during all the long cold months fighting with the army. I really learned a lot from him and could not have done everything without him," Sean said as he thought back to all that had happened to them since they had joined up together. "How did we fare? What was the 'butcher's bill'?" Sean asked.

"Not too bad, all things considered. I lost eight dead, and a few more that will probably die from their wounds; eleven more wounded. As for your men, besides the four that died ashore, three more died and almost all of them were wounded, four seriously besides you and Angus. The prisoners, at least eighteen dead and twenty wounded. Considering how many we were up against, it could have been worse," Thomas lamented.

"Now you must go and let him rest. This is too much for him to bear," Monique protested.

"Yes, ma'am," Thomas said, "You do as she says Little Brother, and don't let her get away," He smiled as he left the cabin.

"Your brother is quite the joker, is he not?" she smiled, blushing at Thomas' last remark.

"He is that indeed, and I always listen to what my older brother tells me to do." Sean said as he took her hand in his and looked into her eyes. That was all he remembered as he drifted back to sleep from the loss of blood.

The next few days, Sean drifted in and out of consciousness as fever swept over him. Monique stayed by his side day and night ministering to his wounds and needs. One night she awoke in her chair to see him shivering as the fever racked his body with chills.

She locked the cabin door, dropped her dress and undergarments to the floor and climbed under the covers with him to use her body heat to warm him. She wrapped him around her and sometime during the night, the fever broke. She got up from the bed to get him some water for his parched throat.

She climbed back into bed with him and woke him up to drink. Sean came to and looked at her not knowing if he was dreaming. He drank the water when she put the cup to his mouth; the liquid quenched his dry throat and mouth. As he drank, he became aware of their nakedness.

"What are you doing here?" he whispered when he finished drinking.

"You were suffering from chills; I used the warmth of my body to warm you up. The fever has broken; you are healing," She said not moving away from him.

"Thank you for all you have done. I remember only seeing your face as I faded in and out. How long have I been like this?" he asked.

"You have been three days like this and we weren't sure you would pull through, but now you have," she said as she laid her head on his shoulder. They stayed like that for a few minutes before they moved. When they did, they fell into each other's arms and entwined themselves in their passion.

Sean fell unconscious again after they finished, and she stayed in bed with him until she heard the morning stirrings of the crew. She carefully slid out of bed, got dressed and left the cabin to see to her morning ritual of washing and preparing their meal.

The "flotilla" kept its northern course, steering clear of the other islands along the way to avoid the British Navy, which had stepped up patrols in the area. The two hardly spoke as they ate the breakfast she brought them. They could not keep from staring into each other's eyes as they ate.

When they had finished, she removed the dishes, and sat him up in the bed to bathe him. "Today, I think it would do you good to go on deck and walk around; I think you have gotten some strength back."

"After last night, I think you are right about that," he said, causing her to blush. She changed his bandages and helped him to dress. Then she led him to the stairs. "Do you think that you can manage?"

"As long as you are here, I will always manage," he said as he put his arm around her shoulders for support.

"You are a charmer, Sean Taggert, and I think that I would always like to be there with you," she said in a whisper as they walked up the steps to the main deck.

Sean held his arm up over his eyes as a shield from the bright morning sun. He had spent too much time in the semi-dark cabin and his eyes were not ready for the onslaught of the tropical sun.

They walked the deck slowly, stopping to talk to everyone they met along the way. Sean was glad to see the deck had been put back to rights after the carnage he had seen before going below the day of the battle. Several of the men on deck were sporting bandages on arms, legs, and heads, giving the deck the looks of a ship full of invalids.

They stopped at the stern and leaned up against the transom, looking out over the ocean behind them. "Good morning, you two," Thomas said as he came on deck and saw them there.

"It's good to see you up and around Little Brother; I told you that you were in good hands." He noticed the slight blush on both their faces as he said that but let it pass without saying anything.

"Here, look back at the *Charon*; the freed prisoners who are sailing her decided to change her name," Thomas said as he handed him his telescope.

Sean tried to hold it steady as he found the ship in the telescope. The figurehead had been removed, and in big white letters where the previous name had been, he read the name "*Liberty*." "The lads decided that they did not care for the previous name and, after having been thorough hell on that island, decided that was a more fitting name for that ship," Thomas explained.

"Good for them. I approve of their choice," Sean said as he turned to give the telescope back to his brother. He was surprised to see his men had gathered around to see him. They all congratulated him on his recovery and wished him well.

"It is good to see all of you well also, after we have lost so many of our number. They shall be missed, and yet they will not have died in vain, for the French will now join us in our war against the British," Sean said to them.

They all stood talking for a while until Sean felt dizzy and decided to go below again. Calhoun and Monique helped him down the stairs, but before he would return to his cabin, he insisted on seeing the wounded men.

"Only Sergeant Lanigan is still in sickbay," Calhoun protested. "He ain't been conscious for the past two days, and he may not make it, sir."

"All the more reason for me to see him now," Sean insisted. They led him down the corridor into the area that was crowded with wounded men still lying in bedding on the deck. Lanigan was in a makeshift cot against the hull, blanket pulled tight up against his chin.

Sean pulled away from his helpers and sat down on a chest next to Angus. He looked at his face, all pale and haggard-looking. Sean sat there for a few minutes and said a prayer in silence, crossed himself and stood up, bumping his head on the beam above.

Without protest he let them lead him back to his cabin and be put back to bed. He fell asleep as soon as they closed the door. The next few days, Sean extended his exercise and attended to some of the daily business with Calhoun. He appointed him as acting sergeant, and Baum as acting corporal until Angus' fate was determined. He was pleased with Calhoun's handling of the men in his absence and gave him a list of duties for the men to see to while he recovered.

He sat at the table in Thomas' cabin looking over the list of names of those they had lost. Betts, Schultz, Lee, they had been with them since the beginning. Johnson, Rogers, Thompson and Bell, they had been some of the replacements that Sam had sent with them from Morristown. They would all be sorely missed; they had given their all for the sake of freedom; and their fellow marines.

He had checked on Angus earlier and sat with him, listening to him as he rambled on about some of his earlier adventures as a British Marine. He spoke of the scoundrels that he had encountered as well as the men he had known who showed the utmost bravery under extreme conditions. He was most proud of all, though, of the marines of the *Osprey* whom he and Sean had developed into first-class marines.

He left his dying sergeant when he became too weak to talk anymore. Angus had good times and bad, as he seemed to waste away from his wound. Faircloth and Dubois both concurred that he would not last out the voyage.

Sean shuffled his papers back into his leather folder and looked out the open window at the *Hawk,* which followed behind. She and the *Liberty* would be parting company in a few days, as they would sail back to Philadelphia while the *Osprey* would turn east to France.

They were to take their important passengers on to their homeland to complete the mission. Sean hoped that their sacrifice would bring France into the war against England; it would help bring an early end to this long war.

He thought about Monique as he stared out the window. Her long curled raven hair that smelled so good when she was near. The curl of her lips and the sparkle in her eyes had enchanted him since they had met. He thought back to their first night of passion and how it made him feel complete, not like the trollops he had dallied with earlier.

He felt emptiness when she was not near him, and immense joy when she reappeared; she confessed to feeling the same way. They had managed to have a couple of more nights together before he was able to get around better on his own. She had taken a cabin next to him for propriety's sake, since his health was improved and he did not need around-the-clock attention. He was not sure what he would do once they reached France and she would stay while he had to return to the war.

"Daydreaming brother?" Thomas asked as he entered the cabin. "I'm sure I know what you are thinking about, and I cannot say I blame you; she is an incredible woman. If I were you, I would marry her as soon as we set foot in France."

"Don't think that I haven't considered that." He replied. "I just don't know if I could leave her behind to be a widow if something happened to me before the war is over."

"If you think like that, you may miss out on what could be the love of your life, and those do not come around twice in life Little Brother," Thomas admonished him.

"You're probably right," he said as he stood up and filed his folder in a slot over the chart table. "I'm going above for a walk; care to join me?"

"No, she's up there waiting for you. I came down to get you out of here for her," Thomas replied.

Sean smiled and left the cabin. He climbed the steps and stepped out onto the deck. He breathed in the warm, salty air and looked around. He saw her standing by the rail with her father. They were conversing in low tones while they watched a sea tortoise lumbering along a short distance from the ship.

Sean nodded to the helmsman and others nearby as they all watched to see what he was going to do. When he turned to walk over to their two passengers, they all averted their eyes, smiling at his discomfort.

"Good afternoon, sir, Monique. Fine-looking creature that tortoise, must weigh out at least nine hundred pounds," he observed to them.

"Ah, and good day to you, Lieutenant! I see that you are recovering nicely from your wounds. I will inspect them tomorrow myself to be sure they are healing properly. I have the utmost confidence in my daughter's medical abilities and always like to follow up on her work," Dubois offered. He eyed the two as they stood before him, trying to avoid his gaze. "You two think that you are so clever as to be able to keep a secret from me?" he smiled.

"What do you mean, Father?" she asked, surprised at his question.

"It is written all over your faces, you two are smitten with each other. Everyone on the ship knows this to be so. Before you say anything, let me finish. I approve of your match; you two have found what everyone seeks, so don't let it slip from your hands. We have a long voyage ahead, so get to know one another." Dubois kissed his daughter on the forehead and walked away leaving the two together.

"I suppose we have been rather obvious, but I don't care," Sean stammered.

"We have a lot to talk about before we reach France. I know that I will not be able to keep you from returning to the war; I see how concerned you are about your men and your cause. I will not stand between you and that, but you must promise to come back to me when it is finished," she said as she looked up into his eyes.

"Nothing will be able to prevent me from coming back to you," he whispered as she sank into his arms.

"They make a good couple, *oui*?" Dubois said to Faircloth and Thomas, standing off to the side.

"Aye, that they do," Thomas agreed envious of his brother.

"Thomas, I have some bad news for him, though. Lanigan has taken a turn for the worse. I think today will be his last. I hate to interrupt those two, but he has asked for Sean to come see him," Faircloth reported.

"Damn!" Thomas swore. "Sean, I need to have a word with you, please," he called to his brother.

Sean and Monique walked over and joined the others. "Sean, Angus is dying; he may not make it through the day and he wants to see you right away," Faircloth said apologetically.

507

"You go to him, quickly," Monique offered.

Sean did not waste time saying anything; he just hurried down the gangway and made his way to the sickbay. There, in the dim light of the lanterns, sat Calhoun, Jones, Baum and Beckett around the old man. They all stood up when Sean approached.

The strain on Angus' face was apparent even in the faint light. "Angus, old friend, how are you?" Sean said as he took his hand and sat on a cask next to him.

"I'm done for, sir. The doctor said there is no hope at this point; I'm not healing inside," he said as he coughed, spitting out blood on a rag next to him. "I want one thing before I pass on. I want to go topside one more time to have a pint with the lads. Will you see to that?"

"Sure, Angus, we'll do that, but you'll be back on your feet in a few more days, you'll see," Sean said, not believing his own words. "Calhoun, you, Beckett and Jones help him into his uniform and bring him topside while I gather the rest of the lads and pipe up spirits," Sean ordered.

He tore himself away to go above, hesitating on the steps long enough to compose himself. "Baum, call the men to gather at the mainmast with their mugs, and have a chair brought up from the captain's cabin."

"Aye, aye, sir," Baum replied as he hurried off through the lower deck. Sean returned to the others on the main deck and told them what they were going to do.

"It should not hurt to do this. He has no chance of recovery, so let him have his last request," Faircloth said dejectedly. Dubois nodded approval also.

508

A few minutes later, the marines gathered at the mainmast and waited for the others to bring up their sergeant. Calhoun, and Beckett came up first, followed by Jones. The big freedman carried the aging veteran up the steps and gently placed him in the chair by the railing.

Sean came forward and stood next to him and handed him his tankard that Baum had brought up from below. Beckett brought out the cask of rum and filled everyone's tankards. They stood, waiting for Lanigan to speak.

"Lads, a toast to the United States! Long may she prosper," he said as they all raised their mugs and took a drink. Lanigan looked out over the water and sighed.

"I know that you lads probably think that I don't like you the way I have had to yell at you and curse you." He paused while they all laughed. "Well, put that thought right out of your heads. I have served with many men in my career in His Majesty's Royal Marines and with you lads, The United States Marines, and I will say that I have never served with a finer group of men than those that are standing here before me today!" He rose his tankard and took another drink; they all followed suit.

"Now as to the names I called you and the mean things that I may have said, casting doubt on your parentage and the like, well, I meant every damned word!" his laugh was infectious as the others joined in the mirth.

"That is what has kept you lads alive throughout all of what we have been through together. You learned to listen, and to think for yourselves. You have conquered your own fears as well as your enemies. Determination and persistence is what will win this war, not weapons, uniforms or large armies. You have shown this in every challenge that has been thrown our way, and I am damned proud to have been a part of this endeavor!" They drank a toast again.

"Now, lads, you have some good men here in charge of you, and even Calhoun has turned into a fine sergeant, if he doesn't do a good job for you, I'll be back to haunt him!" he laughed as he watched Calhoun blush.

"Lads, my time to cross over has come, and I just want to say that you are a great group of people. We were called Bullocks in the Royal Marines, but I like the knickname they have given us better-- Leathernecks." He stopped while he struggled to get to his feet. Sean passed his mug to Calhoun as he helped him up.

"Lads," he said as he held his tankard high, "I salute you, Leathernecks. Give 'em hell, lads!" he immediately put his tankard to his lips and drained it. The others called out, "Here, here!" and downed their rum also.

Lanigan sat down hard and composed himself, straightening out his uniform that was loose- fitting, since he had not been able to eat much.

"Sergeant Lanigan, I just want to tell you," Calhoun stammered as he looked around at the faces before him, "I want to thank you for all that you have done for us. I know that I would have ended up dead in an alley somewhere if you and the Lieutenant had not come along. We all think of you as our father, and appreciate everything that you taught us. I salute you, Sergeant Lanigan." Calhoun straightened up and saluted stiffly.

"Thank you, laddie. I appreciate that, but if you remember only one thing that I ha' taught you, it's not to salute sergeants, we earn our pay!" He laughed and shook Calhoun's hand as the others joined in expressing their sentiments.

They enjoyed their time as Lanigan told them many stories of his adventures until, after about an hour, he nodded to Sean that he needed to go below; his strength had left him. They broke out of the group while Jones picked him up and carried him below, followed by Sean.

Jones sat him on the edge of the cot and started to unbutton his waistcoat. "No lad, leave it on, I want to be in this uniform today," Lanigan said as he lay back on the cot.

"Lieutenant Taggert, I want to say that you have been a fine officer and a leader, the finest that I have worked with. I'm going out now, and want to be in my uniform when the Grim Reaper comes for me. I want to be alone now to make my peace with my Maker. There's nothing more to say but thank you, laddie, you have been like a son to me." He offered his hand to Sean.

"It has been an honor, Sergeant Lanigan, and thank you for all that you have done. You will be missed by all," Sean said as he shook his hand. Tears welled up in his eyes as he turned to leave.
 Slowly he walked back to his cabin and shut himself inside.

That night, Lanigan passed away in his sleep. In the morning, the sail maker was summoned to prepare him for burial. He and his assistant sewed the sergeant in the remnants of an old sail, with two twelve-pound cannon balls in the bottom for extra weight.

Sean stood by the railing, looking out over the ocean at the departing ships. The ceremony this morning for Lanigan seemed to be an eternity ago. It had been brief as the Marines gathered around the plank set on the side with the flag-draped body on it. Thomas spoke the funeral service and Sean added his own sentiments at the end.

The men were formed up, and when the plank was up-ended, sending the body to the deep, they fired a salute with their muskets, which in turn was followed by each cannon on the three ships being fired in salute.

It was difficult to accept that he was gone. Angus had been the rock for all of them through thick and thin. Even when he thought he could not go on, during the winter campaign, Sean would see Angus there encouraging the men, giving them some of his rations, or talking them back onto their feet, always making the exhausted man feel that there was no pain, that he could go on a little further.

Now he was gone, and the *Liberty* and *Hawk* parted company to head back to Philadelphia to report the success of the mission, while the *Osprey* turned toward France. He straightened up as his wound started to ache. He was almost healed, yet it still pained him when he did too much.

The pitch of the ship in the waves had such a familiar feel to it after all those months on the march. It was good to be back on the open ocean. Things seemed so much brighter and clearer out over the open water.

So many strange twists of fate had brought them to this point, from the time that his father was killed by Jennings to the end of their fight off Scrub Island, where Sean got his revenge on his father's killer. He felt fulfilled yet empty at the same time.

His reverie was broken when Monique joined him at the railing. She put her arm through his and stood next to him. He knew not what lay in store for him with the war, but at least he knew that his future would include her.

Taggert of the Marines by David Ekardt

11
France

The weeks seemed to have flown by in the twinkling of an eye. Their passage across the Atlantic was blessed with fair weather and good winds. They had been challenged by a French corvette off the coast near Cherbourg and led into port once the identity of their passengers had been made known.

The warm May sun glared off the rooftops of the town as they approached the port. The smell of the land, all green and in full bloom, and of the town itself wafted across the water to them as they entered the harbor.

Sean had his men prepare the salute, and as they entered the harbor, the guns were fired by the marines as the crew wrestled with reducing sail and preparing to anchor. The harbormaster's boat led them to an anchorage near an aging three-decker that was being re-rigged.

As the anchors dropped into the calm water, dozens of small boats quickly swarmed around the *Osprey,* offering all manners of goods for sale, from fresh vegetables and chickens, to rum, wine and women.

The men, secured from their duties, lined the railings to see what the peddlers were offering and to see what they could of the colorful harbor town. The town had been built on the site of an ancient Roman army camp called Coriallum, as Dubois had explained to Sean and the others. It was now a bustling port for goods being shipped in from ports all over the world as well as goods being shipped out.

The harbor itself was crowded with all manner of craft, Sean observed. Several naval vessels were in various stages of repair, both at anchor and in berths. There were merchant vessels ranging in size from the largest overseas traders, to the local luggers and yawls, to fishing boats and the peddlers.

There were several water lighters plying back and forth between the vessels delivering fresh water to the ships preparing to go to sea. The corvette had anchored further into the harbor, and there was no mistaking the fact that they, as visitors, were under several guns of the naval vessels riding at anchor.

They were to remain at anchor until a boat was sent for the doctor and his daughter. Sean could imagine that a dispatch rider would be galloping hard towards Paris within minutes of the discovery of the Dubois' return.

The cooper and his work party were busy preparing the empty water casks for refilling and separating out those that were no longer in good enough repair to use. Those men not involved in that task were busy making minor repairs and cleaning up the main deck for the arrival of any official guests that might come on board.

"It is good to see my country again," Monique said as she walked with Sean. "Much of it is no different than the Pennsylvania countryside where you are from. We traveled through there a few years back on our way from Canada to the islands."

"I have been here once before and once to Le Havre many years ago, when I was young, and remember how beautiful the country is around here," Sean replied.

"Our home is in Versailles, not far from Paris, and some of my aunts and uncles still live there. It has been several years since we have seen them. I hope that you can visit there with us before you have to leave. How long do you think that you will have?" she asked.

"I do not know. That depends on what orders the American envoy has for us. We are to meet with Silas Deane as soon as we locate him," Sean replied. "Look, here comes a boat from the corvette. It looks like the captain is paying us a visit. You'll excuse me while I prepare the welcome."

Sean gathered his men to form the honor guard at the side while the rest of the crew fell into their places for the official welcome. The captain, resplendent in his best uniform and dress sword climbed up the side just as the last of the men fell into formation.

As the bosun piped the visitor on board, Thomas stepped forward to greet him. Sean watched as the two men shook hands. Thomas motioned for Sean to follow them as they quickly turned to go below to Thomas' cabin.

"Sergeant Calhoun, dismiss the men," Sean said to Calhoun. He returned his salute and then headed for the hatch. He removed his hat as he went down the steps into the gloom of the narrow hall leading to the captain's cabin.

"Captain Andre Mansart, this is Lieutenant Taggert of the *Osprey's* Marines." Thomas introduced the two men and then continued. "Sean, the Captain has instructions for us. It appears that they have been on patrol waiting for us for a few weeks."

"*Oui,* that we have. You must understand the delicateness of the situation that you have found yourselves in by agreeing to take part in your mission," Mansart interjected. "King Louis wishes very much to aid your people in their fight for independence; however, he and many of the ruling nobility is, shall we say, somewhat nervous about the word rebellion?" He paused a moment to accept the glass of wine offered to him by Plato Jones.

He continued after taking a small sip of the wine. "The King is most anxious to do anything that could gain all the territory lost to the British in the last war. What worries him though, like I have said, is the idea of a rebellion against the government of any country, especially one so close to our own."

"I can see that could pose a problem," Sean added. "If your troops go to America and help to win a rebellion, what is to keep them from coming home and possibly starting a rebellion of their own?"

"You are correct, my friend. Now that you understand the situation, I will inform you of what will become of you now. Doctor Dubois and his daughter are to stay on board until the express rider returns from Paris with orders. No one is to leave the ship here, because at this point it is not good for the King to be linked with your ship or your mission that you have accomplished for him." Mansart took the last of his wine and held out the glass for Jones to refill.

"You see, the British may find out and declare war on us now, when we are not prepared. Now that his family is out of danger, he can have the army and navy start their build-up of supplies and men to meet the threat."

"Do you think that your country will join us?" Thomas asked.

"Personally, I look forward to the chance to lay alongside British ships and let loose my broadside!" he stood up. "Now I must return to my ship. Be prepared to leave at a moment's notice. I have instructed the quartermaster ashore to see to your every need after your long journey."

The three returned to the main deck and parted company. "Better keep the deck watch on their toes while we're in port, Sean," Thomas cautioned his brother.

"It's already done. I have doubled the watch, and they are armed with cutlasses only. I'll be glad when we get out of this port; all of this intrigue is nonsense," Sean replied.

The rest of the day, the men took on fresh supplies of water and food. That night they had a dinner of the first fresh food they had in many weeks. The next day passed without any change in their circumstances.

Late that evening, Captain Mansart once again appeared at the side of the ship with a bundle under his arm. He was piped on board with the same fanfare as the previous day, and once more, he and Thomas headed for his cabin.

"Gentlemen, I give you this for tomorrow." He held out the paper-wrapped package. Thomas opened it to find a French flag folded neatly inside. "Tomorrow we leave at first light. You will need to fly this flag while we sail for Le Havre. The British are out patrolling in the Channel, and at times they come very close inshore," he instructed.

"Why are we going there?" Thomas asked.

"I received orders from Paris just moments ago. My ship and another is to escort you to Le Havre where the Dubois' will be whisked away to Versailles. Your ship will be given a refit, courtesy of the King, for your valiant service. Your men will be guests at our barracks there while the ship is refitted. You two are to accompany the Dubois' to Versailles. This will all be done as quietly as is possible."

"How long are we to be your guests?" Sean asked.

"The refit will take a couple of weeks. You will receive new sails, yardarms, cordage and cannons. What is more, you and your men will be fitted out with new uniforms, and your every need will be attended to while you are in France," Mansart stated proudly.

"I think that this is most generous of your King for what little we have done," said Thomas.

"Oh, Captain, you are too modest. I heard the story of what you two did from a trader who had arrived from the Caribbean a few days before you did. He was on the island when you rescued the Dubois' and all the prisoners and destroyed the fort. From what he described, you had quite a victory and brought back two ships also!!"

"We did have a busy day there, that is for certain," Thomas smiled.

"You must tell me all about it over some wine. I have had some of the best in town brought on board with me." He opened the door for his orderly to bring in a crate with twelve bottles of fine port. "Now, let us have a drink while the two of you tell me of your exploits against our enemy!" Mansart said as he poured out three glasses of wine.

The three sat in the cabin drinking and talking until two in the morning. They parted company and Sean returned to his cabin. His head felt like it was spinning as he lay back on his bed. He was not accustomed to drinking the quantity of wine that their guest was able to keep flowing.

The next morning before first light, the deck watch received a pilot on board who would remain on board until they reached Le Havre. When Sean saw him, he was at the wheel with Stark, discussing the perplexities of navigating the French coast in the Channel.

The man had the appearance of one who had been born and raised on the sea. He guessed his age to be in his late fifties. The man's face was pockmarked and weathered by the constant assault of the sea and weather. He noticed that the pilot was missing a few fingers on his hands, probably due to frostbite, working in the tops when he was younger.

As the sun climbed over the hillside, their escorts weighed anchor, and without any fanfare, the three ships left harbor. As they left the harbor, Sean had his men hoist the French flag instead of their own. The passage to Le Havre passed with only one incident. As they were sailing about a mile offshore, an English frigate approached them.

The *Osprey* held a position between the corvettes and the land. The British were eager to learn the identity of the three ships; when they tried to sail between the escorts and the *Osprey*, Captain Mansart tacked over at the last minute to prevent the other ship's intrusion, almost causing a collision.

The three ships entered the port of Le Havre late in the evening. The *Osprey* was given a berth along the wharf that had the appearance of a repair facility. As the crew secured from sea and headed below for their meal, the clatter of horses pulling an official carriage was heard coming to a halt alongside.

Two men came up the gangplank and presented themselves to Sean and Thomas. They were to escort the Dubois' to Versailles immediately. The two gathered their belongings and stopped at the entry port. "Sean, do come to stay with us in Versailles for a while if you can," Monique beseeched him as they were leaving.

"I'll get there as soon as I can. Mister Deane is to come on board tomorrow morning to give us our orders," Sean said as they embraced. He watched her as she disappeared into the carriage. The driver snapped his whip at the horses as soon as the footmen had climbed back on the rear of the carriage and they sped off into the night.

Sean was walking the deck with Calhoun the next morning after breakfast when another carriage approached their berth. This time a lone figure climbed out of the coach and came on board the ship.

The side guard announced him as Silas Deane. The immaculately dressed, middle-aged man approached Sean and presented himself. "I am the special envoy to King Louis' government, and I welcome you to France. May we speak in private?"

"Certainly, follow me." Sean escorted him to Thomas' cabin. Thomas welcomed him and offered him a seat and motioned for Plato Jones to bring a fresh pot of coffee for them.

"I'll get right to the point, gentlemen. I have heard of your heroic rescue of the Dubois' and might I add my congratulations on a splendid accomplishment! I

cannot tell you of the importance of your actions"
Deane said.

"What is the possibility of the King bringing
France in on our side?" Sean asked. "Captain Mansart
indicated that he may be hesitant even now, afraid of
revolution spreading to his country."

"That is the biggest stumbling block to France
entering the war. There are many in the government
and especially in the business interests that want to
join the war to win back all the territory conceded to
the British at the end of the French and Indian War.
What the King is now willing to do is to give safe
haven and supplies to any American warship entering
any French port. Your own ship will be refitted
starting tomorrow. You will have all repairs done,
new yardarms, sails, cannons; anything that you need
will be replaced. You and your men will be treated as
guests of France, and they will be catered to while
your ship is refitted," Deane explained.

"That is good news for our ships, and for us. The
men can stand a bit of a holiday after all that they
have been through this past year." Sean said.

"You two will be taken to Versailles and will have
the use of a villa outside of town. The King is
anxious to give you his thanks, but it will not be a
public ceremony. If you are ever linked to him and
what happened in the Caribbean, the English may
declare war before he is prepared for it." Deane
stopped to sip some of the coffee that Plato had
poured for him.

"He has instructed the heads of the army and navy
to start increasing their numbers and building up
supplies for the eventuality of war. He will also
increase the amount of supplies to our government

between now and the time he makes up his mind to enter the war. There will be quite a task for him to convince all within the government to go to war."

"What is to become of us once the ship is ready for sea?" Thomas inquired.

"Two transports here in the harbor are being loaded with supplies for Washington's army. Once they are loaded and your ship is prepared, you will escort them back to America. Once there, you will be part of the fleet again and will take your orders from the Navy Committee."

"How soon do you think the King will make up his mind?" Sean asked.

"I do not think that he will make any sort of announcement until the end of the year, if then. He is shrewd enough to want to be fully prepared for war before declaring it on the British. Besides, I'm sure that he will also try to convince the Spanish to join in the fray as well. Now, gentlemen, I must return to Versailles. The King has moved his court there for the spring, and I must be there for any chance I can get to bend his ear or that of his ministers." Deane shook hands with both of them and then departed.

The rest of the day, the crew spent preparing to turn the ship over to the shipyard crew for the refit. They removed themselves to a barracks used by the crews of ships in for repairs. Sean and Thomas, accompanied by Faircloth, were whisked away to a comfortable villa near Versailles.

The next three weeks were a whirlwind of activity. The day after their arrival in Versailles, Sean and Thomas were taken late at night to the palace. They were taken in through a service entrance and made to wait in a chamber off the side of the main court.

After an extended wait, the door was thrown open, and the king accompanied by the Dubois' and an admiral, entered the room. The two were presented with a medal of valor hung around their necks, and each received a dress sword and a beautifully carved box containing a brace of pistols from the King. As soon as the presentations were made, the King and the admiral left the room, and the others were quickly whisked out of the palace and to the villa.

Sean spent most of their time in Versailles with Monique and her family. They spent long afternoons riding horses through the countryside. A few days before they were to depart back to Le Havre to rejoin the ship, the two were married in the small stone church outside of town near the farms of Monique's uncles. After the ceremony, she had whispered in his ear that they were to be parents.

Monique and her father accompanied them back to Le Havre. Sean watched her disappear from the stern of the *Osprey* as they left harbor. He would be back for her when the war was over, and she and her father could return to America.

The two transports were ahead of the *Osprey,* and the two French corvettes again accompanied them until they were beyond the Channel and out of sight of land. They fired a salute as they tacked around to return to port. And the marines of the *Osprey* returned their salute with the new cannons that had been a gift of the French government.

After they secured the guns, Sean returned to the stern to watch the wake they left behind. "Well, Little Brother, you certainly have a wonderful wife in that one; you have done well. Did you two pick out names for the baby?" Thomas asked.

"Yes, if it is a girl, we will name her after her mother, Marie, and if it is a boy, we will name him Angus. Monique suggested that," Sean answered.

"Don't fret about leaving her behind during the war; she will be much safer there among her own family," Thomas reassured him.

"I know, but I still will worry about her," Sean replied.

"The shipyard crew did an excellent job refitting her. They even re-caulked the whole ship before repainting her!" Thomas exclaimed.

"Yes, the old girl looks brand new. The cannons that they gave us are of the highest quality, and the new uniforms that they had made for us are immaculate," Sean replied.

"Well, the breeze is freshening, and our two companions are keeping up with us, so we should make good time in our crossing. It is good to be under all new canvas again. Are you up for the journey ahead Little Brother?" Thomas asked.

"There is nothing that I want more than to be with my wife," Sean said, "so let's get back there as fast as we can and win this damned war."

.- .-. -.-

Afterword

The following list has sources of information on the Marines during the Revolutionary War.

1. Marines in the Revolution by Charles R. Smith
   History and Museums Division, Headquarters
   U.S. Marine Corps Washington DC 1975

2. The United States Marines by Edwin H. Simmons
   Viking Press New York 1976

3. The United States Marine History Center

4. The American Revolution from the American
   Heritage Magazine
   American Heritage Publishing New York 1958

5. Seafaring America by Alexander Laing from the
   American Heritage Magazine
   American Heritage Press New York   1974

6. The Book of the Continental Soldier by Harold
   Peterson
   The Stackpole Company Harrisburg Pennsylvania
   1968

7. Battle of the American Revolution 1775-1781
   by Henry Carrington 1877

8. Letter of Captain Samuel Nicholas

9. Diary of Captain of Marines, John Trevett

10. Journal of Lieutenant of Marines, William Jennison

11. Journal of Captain of Marines, Joseph Hardy

12. The Narrative of Thomas Philbrook

Taggert of the Marines by David Ekardt